Figure Instructor

T0380391

Figure Instructor

Lisa Bender

Copyright © 2011 by Lisa Bender.

ISBN: Softcover   978-1-4691-3451-2
               Ebook   978-1-4691-3452-9

All rights reserved. No part of this book may be reproduced or transmitted in any form or by any means, electronic or mechanical, including photocopying, recording, or by any information storage and retrieval system, without permission in writing from the copyright owner.

This book was printed in the United States of America.

To order additional copies of this book, contact:
Xlibris Corporation
1-888-795-4274
www.Xlibris.com
Orders@Xlibris.com
108906

This book is to all the skaters (beginners or professionals) who have the passion to skate for themselves instead of doing it to impress people, even their parents. And remember: look up, stand strong, hands at chest level, let your feet dance freely on the ice, and have fun!

Crunch . . .

Crunch . . .

Whoosh . . .

Scrape . . .

Scrape . . .

Whoosh . . .

Daniel Gray, if you wish to marry my daughter, this is what you need to do by approving the marriage:

You must learn how to figure skate

Chapter One

Daniel opened his eyes from a restless night in his twins size bed after hearing the stipulation again. He got tired of hearing it for the thousandth time. With the covers and blankets pushed off, he struggled to sit up in bed and his right hand was rubbing the nape of his neck. His agreement was stuck inside his mind for the past three days.

It continued to sting his heart after telling his fiancee's parents he wanted to marry his girlfriend of four years, Sally. He did not want to do figure skating just so he could marry the girl who stole his heart and love.

Sighing heavily, the idea of learning how to figure skate was not Daniel's only problem in life. Being a proper overall dog trainer was his other problem to deal with. He was happy on the job by only training the dogs, but he did not like or feel comfortable to show instructional advice for the dog's owners.

Danny lifted himself up from bed to begin his day.

It was Friday and the start of his three day weekend from the Pet store. His first employee evaluation as a Pet trainer happened the day before and he was grateful to take some time off. He needed to think what he should do about the figure skating stipulation. He got up from the bed to check on the weather from his bedroom window.

Outside of his apartment building in Santa Rosa, California, the sky was a bit cloudy. He needed to go out for a long walk.

After finishing a light breakfast of juice and toast in his kitchen, Daniel put on jeans, red t, his black athletic shoes, and navy blue synthetic coat on.

He opened the door of his apartment unit and went out for a walk. He thought back what happened three nights ago when he & Sally announced to her parents about their engagement.

Long blond hair Sally & short brown hair Daniel were sitting on a couch, looking at Hunts in awkward silence after telling them the lover's news.

Short blackish brown haired Paul & long red curly haired Joy were shocked. They hoped their sunshine daughter would wait a little longer and wishing their she would be with someone much better than Daniel Gray.

Sally's mother had a plan.

"Daniel Gray, if you wish to marry my daughter, this is what you need to do by approving the marriage: you must learn how to figure skate. Our family comes from a long line of well-known skaters and we don't want to lose that tradition. It doesn't matter where and who teaches you. As long as you understand the basic and advance skating terms, Sally will be yours forever." Joy strongly explained his stipulation.

The four of them; Paul, Joy, Sally, and Daniel were all sitting on the sofas in the big living room discussing young Gray's request to marry Sally, a figure skating champion.

"Okay. I can do that. Learn how to figure skate. Sounds interesting." Daniel pretended to say happily. He was uncomfortable about doing twirls and jumps on the ice like a perky ballerina.

He loved Sally for her as a woman, not a figure skating champion. He wished Sally's parents would not be so hard on him. Sally was especially harder on Daniel because she wanted to continue her family's ice skating talent. Sometimes he wondered if she really meant it or not.

Daniel's brown eyes looked at the ring he gave Sally. It was a slender silver band with three gems, clear diamonds on the ends and a light blue gem in middle. He was lucky to afford the ring to match his girl's gorgeous bluish gray eyes.

Sally loved her ring when Daniel proposed her.

"Well, Danny, we better leave and go for our date tonight." Sally sweetly said to her fiance, holding his right arm.

"Yes, we should go or you won't have any skating time tonight." Daniel quickly remarked.

The figure champion agilely ran upstairs to get her skates and bag.

The Pet trainer nervously waited in the living room with his future in-laws. He was hoping to win Sally's parents over without the task he must do to win their approval.

He thought back on all the dinners he had with Sally and her parents. They mostly talked about skating routines and tricks. No matter how much time he spent with Sally or her parents, he could never understand the names or how figures do any of the skating moves they did on ice. He always felt left out in ice rinks and visiting the mansion.

Sally gracefully pranced down the stairs to the living room with her light pink duffle bag strap on her shoulder. She sat next to Daniel.

Before the young lovers left the house, Paul, Sally's father, left the living room to go to his study room for something. Few minutes later, Paul came back into the living room and presented his daughter's fiance a check.

He strongly told the Pet trainer, "Use it wisely."

Danny held the check in his left hand. His eyes looked closely on how much Sally's father was giving him.

$10,000.00.

That was going to be more than he was expecting to be a good skater by impressing his fiancee's parents. His plan was to save up more money from his Pet training job. Relief filled his heart when Paul handed him the check. Daniel folded the paper check and put it in his black leather wallet.

He promised, "I will put it into good use."

They all stood up in the living room after Danny Gray agreed again with the task and use the money only for skating lessons and supplies he would need.

He and Sally left the mansion home to go to their ice rink date for the evening.

After spending a cold long hour at the rink, Daniel's ears heard Sally calling out his name from the bleachers. His head turned to his right and watched her sitting next to him. She looked tired from practicing her figure routines. Her trademark French braid with a headband was messed up.

They kissed. Her lips and face did feel very cold to Daniel. He did not mind that at all. He got used to it.

When their lips part, Sally asked, "You want to go somewhere else?"

She always knows when it's the right time for us to leave the cold rink. He thought in his head. He nodded at Sally and the two left the bleachers for the girl's locker room.

Twenty minutes later, Sally changed back into her street clothes and she & Daniel exited the skating rink for his car. He drove from the rink's parking lot to a public park's parking lot. A walk around the park did sound good to them. They got out of the car and walked on a large grassy field.

As they walked together hand-in-hand in the cold, dark night, Daniel pleaded, "Sally, teach me how to skate, please?"

Sally disappointedly told her best friend, "I can't."

He stopped in his track. His voice pleaded, "Why? Your mom wouldn't mind."

"Yes, she would." Sally stopped walking and stood next to Daniel. The female Senior champion sadly replied, "Daniel, it's competition season now. I'll be very busy."

His heart hated the idea of his fiancee being surrounded by the media and her parents around competition time. He was lucky to have some quiet time with her, especially when it was two weeks before her first competition performance.

The Pet trainer had an idea. "Are any of your friends competing?"

Sally scoffed, "They all quit after last year."

Daniel groaned.

"I don't know who would teach you. Danny, really, I want it to be me. I just wish you proposed after competition season." She did her best to cheer up the love of her life.

Daniel Gray understood how much of a bull Sally's mother could be during competition season. He wondered if Sally liked her to be so strict on her skating skills.

Her father on the other hand was not so strict with his daughter's skating skills, but he was very protective of her during competition time too. He would be like a hawk when he would see his daughter and Daniel leave or getting back from a date. Paul detested when saw them kiss or hug each other.

Sally smiled big and held her sweet loving man. Danny wrapped his arms around her tightly.

Their arms drifted apart for him to look into her eyes and confessed to Sally, "I asked you to marry me now because I don't want to lose you from being an ice skating Champion and find someone better than me."

His sad voice whimpered. "I Love You, Sally."

Sally's eyes were full of tears. "I Love You, Daniel."

Their lips meet for a long relaxing kiss. He sighed lovingly from their parted kiss.

Danny thought who would be able to teach him how to skate if all the local coaches and competitive skaters were going to be busy for the up coming skating shows and events.

Both their ears heard a ringing tone come on.

Daniel's left hand reached into his jeans pocket for his phone. It was 8 p.m. from his cell. Time to bring Sally home to her protective skating guards. They left the park for a long car ride back to the Sally's mansion home.

They kissed goodnight and Sally cheerfully said, "I know you'll figure out something to win over my parent's approval. My father wouldn't have given you the ten grand for nothing."

Danny grabbed and handed Sally her skating bag from the backseat. She gracefully exited the car to go back to her parent's home. He waited till his wonderful fiancee was inside the house safely. The car was turned on for a blissful ride to his apartment unit.

Daniel walked down the long stretched sidewalk for a half hour. He did feel his heart feel happy whenever he thought of Sally. It was one of the ways for the Pet trainer to be satisfied. The he thought of the only biggest flaw to fall for someone like Sally.

Her mother.

Joy never liked the idea of her sunshine daughter to date someone during her competitive years. Especially with someone who was not a figure male or part of the figure skating world.

He did not care about watching the skating tricks his love was doing. Spin rotations, fancy dance steps, freestyle glide stances, jumping from the blade or toe-pick, and strange looking ways to stop.

The Pet trainer never found the sport interesting or thrilling to enjoy. He also could not understand why skating fans find figure skating fun. He would rather enjoy baseball, football, basketball, or watch a good race from race cars.

His only reason to watch Sally practice figure skating was to see her smile and be free from her strict skating parents. She would smile as she danced, glided, and stretched her body by a being balanced, strong skater. Her arms floated around her body to match the moves she made with her boots. Perfecting complicated dance steps she learned from choreographed ballet training. Being artistic from head to toe. Maybe toe-pick instead of her toe.

When the two did date, Sally would not be so happy out in public. She would say short sentences, did not laugh, or had any real fun.

There were times when Danny wished Sally could be a normal girl by doing something other than figure skate on big solid, cold ice. It would be rare for the two of them to spend endless hours by doing something fun together.

During his long walk around downtown, he was having second thoughts about wanting to marry Sally. Except, if he gave her up, he may never find love again. He tried to cheer himself up by thinking more special moments he & his fiancee shared together.

How the lovers first met was a twist of fate.

Four years ago, as a Junior in High School, Daniel Gray was an average student. Good grades, ran track, worked hard at his part-time Stock Boy job for the Pet Store, had his own car, and friends he could hang out with at school, malls, concerts, parties, and movies.

On the night of his seventeenth birthday, Daniel's world turned upside-down. It was his day-off from work and he just finished up his homework for school. His friends gave him a buzz on his cell that they were coming over to take him out for a birthday celebration he would never forget.

Twenty minutes later, his homies came to the Gray's house to pick him up. They drove to the city's downtown for a grand birthday party. First they stopped at a pizza pallor for large pizzas and coke. Then the guys left the parlor for another ride in the car.

Inside the moving car, loud rap music was heard from the speakers and one of the guys, Nick, whooped out loud, "Stole some goods from my old man's secret fridge!"

He handed his friends cold cans of beer from his backpack. They all drank and the driver cranked up the tunes. The guys were chattering what else to do for Danny's B-Day. His buds secretly knew what to do. They wanted to play a trick on an old school bully.

The driver, Josh, pulled up and parked his car at an ice rink's parking lot. He yelled out, "We're here, guys!"

Daniel was puzzled. He asked Josh, "What are we doing here?"

The guys started to get out of the car. Daniel followed them toward the rink's building. They walked through the front doors. Inside showed lots of people in line paying for public skating admission or getting rental skates. The five teenage boys secretly sneaked in the building.

All the guys stood by a locker room door for the rink's minor league hockey team. The door was not locked.

Josh whispered, "Dan, tonight you will become a man by doing us a favor."

Daniel uncomfortably asked, "What kind of favor?"

Another boy, Kevin, explained, "We want you to pull a prank on the hockey team. Especially their captain, Walter."

Danny still remembered the pain Hefty Walter had given him and his friends a couple years ago when they were Freshmen and Walter was a Senior.

He decided to participate in his friend's prank.

"What do you want me to do?"

The five guys formed a circle and quietly discussed to each other their plan. Josh handed Daniel a sport bag full of destructive tools.

Four of the guys left the birthday boy behind.

Danny entered in the locker room. It was dark and his body could feel the cold air swirling around him from the ice rink. He took out a small black flashlight and started to vandalize the hockey team's equipment.

Twenty minutes till the hockey team's practice session. The locker room door opened and lights were turned on. What the team saw was the room all trashed up and their equipment were completely destroyed.

Their hockey sticks were smashed up or broken in half, jerseys and padded clothes torn-up and ripped to bits, pucks taped together with black tape, and all their hockey boots were covered in colorful paint and the blades were scratched and cut up into little pieces from strong rocks on the wet foamed floor.

Walter yelled out, "Goddamn, muther-fucker!"

Hiding in a locker box, Daniel was trying not to laugh out loud after seeing body builder, shaved head Walter be so pissed off through the little slim rectangular holes on the locker door.

"I'll find the little duchebag whose been messing with our shit!" He growled and promised to his teammates.

Both Walter's fist banged against the locker doors.

The guys all loudly agreed with their team leader.

But Danny did not keep quiet. He was laughing his hardest in the locker box.

All the hockey players heard laughter. None of them were laughing at their captain or the sight of the mess.

Walter opened his locker box and inside was Daniel laughing. The captain's face snarled and he demanded from the little dick, "Did you do this?"

Daniel stopped laughing when Walter grabbed him out of the locker box and threw him against one of the metal doors. He knew Hefty Walter was going to hurt him real bad. He tried to get up from the wet formed floor, but he could not move. His body and muscles were already feeling achy after being slammed against a metal door. His ears were ringing and his head was spinning in circles.

Then the metal door opened and in came four young girls. One of the girls asked, "What's going on here?"

"Get out, figures!" Walter shouted.

"Oh, Walter, Walter, Walter . . . ." Another girl teased at Hefty Walter. She swiftly walked behind him, her hands grabbed a hold the elastic band of his sweat pants, and was ready to pull them down.

She seductively whispered, "Have a taste of your own medicine, Captain."

Her fingers forcefully pulled down Walter's pants. Everyone in the room was laughing at the team Captain's undershorts. White with pink teddy bears on them.

"What the fuck, Walt?" His goalie asked.

Hefty Walter was immediately embarrassed in front of his teammates.

His face went red and left the locker room in a hurry. As he was making it to the men's room, he kept falling down. Everyone in the building were laughing and took pics of his little 'teddy bear' secret from their cells.

He screamed, "I didn't get them! My girl did! They're lucky to me!"

Finally, he made it to the men's bathroom and locked the door. He hid in there for hours.

Back in the locker room, the rest of the guys from the team and some of the girls were cleaning up the mess. One of the girls helped Daniel up to his feet and led him to a bench.

She soothed him. "It's okay. You're safe from the stick dopes."

Daniel took one good look at the girl who comforted him. She had blond hair and bluish gray eyes. For some odd reason, he was really liking this girl a lot not because she saved his life. He quickly leaned in to kiss her. Their lips touched and the girl shoved him away.

"Hey, what gives you the right to kiss me?"

Danny still felt sore from being thrown against a heavy metal door. He rasped, "You did save me. And it's my birthday."

The blond girl sweetly spoke, "Well, in that case, birthday boy, you may kiss me again."

They both leaned in and kissed and kissed some more.

The girl laughed from their kiss, "You know, that was pretty funny of you wanting to play a joke on the hockey team. Can't believe you were brave enough to do it alone. Walter would have beaten the crap out of you."

"Actually, my friends thought of that plan. They wanted me to do it." Achy Daniel explained to the pretty blond girl.

"Oh, where are your friends?" She curiously asked, looking around to see if she could find them.

Daniel slowly got up from the bench to find his friends. The pretty blonde girl followed the sore birthday boy.

In the rink's parking lot, Josh's car was gone.

Daniel was stranded. He found his cell and tried to get a hold on one of his friends three times. No one answered.

Achy and tired Danny sadly stated, "My homies ditched me."

"Awe, poor thing." The blond girl solemnly spoke. "And on your birthday. That's not right."

Her left hand took his right hand. "Come with me."

They walked toward her little blue convertible.

After a short drive to a cafe, Daniel and the pretty girl were sitting at a small table drinking toffee mochas and just talked. He was doing his best to ignore the pain his muscles were feeling by focusing at the pretty blond girl he was with.

Daniel wondered, "What's your name?"

"Sally."

"Sally . . . cute name."

Blushing Sally giggled and asked, "What's your name, birthday boy?"

His strained voice told her. "I'm Daniel."

"Daniel." Her voice breathed out. "Nice. I like it."

He took another sip of his hot drink. It was helping his muscles and heart feel better.

When the warm sip left his throat, he curiously questioned Sally, "So, what were you and your friends doing at an ice skating rink?"

Sally squirmed in her chair and felt chagrined on how to answer the birthday boy's question. She slowly put in, "My girlfriends and I normally hangout at the rink a lot."

She leaned in and whispered, "Daniel, can I trust you with a secret?"

He leaned in slowly and softly said, "Sure. You can tell me anything you want."

Sally's hands stroked back her flowing blond hair. She was nervous and told him in an inaudible voice, "My name is Sally Hunt."

Danny wondered why the cute blonde had to hide her name out in public. His brown eyes noticed lots of people were looking at her, especially guys. He felt jealous. His eyes focused back at Sally's pretty face.

"So, your name is Sally Hunt. What's wrong with that?" Daniel asked softly.

Sally was surprised that Daniel had not heard of her. She gulped, "I'm the current Junior Ladies figure Champ."

So that's why Walter called the girls 'Figures'. Daniel thought in his head. He offered Sally, "Would you like to go somewhere more private to talk?"

"Yes, please." She hurried herself out of her chair to get her car keys out of her left jeans pocket. "It doesn't feel right to be here."

The couple left the cafe and went to a deserted parking lot to talk in the car. They enjoyed talking and getting to know each other.

After Sally drove her car from the deserted parking lot to her parent's house, she and Danny kissed goodnight and they could not wait to talk and see each other again. The two teens exchanged numbers and email addresses. Daniel Gray started to head back to his folk's home on foot.

Back inside his apartment unit and heading for his comfy couch, Daniel was still hurt when his old friend ditched him on his 17th birthday. He took off his coat and shoes.

His heart was very happy after he & Sally Hunt first met. His grateful heart was glad he was not to be beaten down to a pulp if Sally and her friends had not rush into the locker room. He certainly gained a little bit of respect for figure skaters from his fiancee. He loved and adored her so much, he would protect her no matter what life had in store for them.

Sally was not the only important living being in his life. More thoughts came to mind from that b-day night when he closed his eyes and got relaxed on his couch.

The night on his 17th birthday was also the night when fate gave Danny a special surprise after his buds left him. A newer and more faithful friend.

Ten blocks from the Hunt's large home, bright shining headlights was heading toward Daniel Gray's way. His eyes saw the car and he immediately recognized it. It was Josh's car. The car passed by quickly and a gust of cold wind hit Danny through his coat.

He dug out his phone to call one of his buddy's cell.

Kevin answered his cell. Daniel heard on his cell's speaker, "Hey, Dan, we see ya. You need a lift?"

Danny knew it was not necessary to get a ride, but he did want to talk to his buds.

He answered, "Sure. I'll wait."

He hung up his cell and waited on the sidewalk for Josh's car to come back around. The car was put into park in the middle of the street and all his friends came out.

Surprised Josh exclaimed, "Danny! We're glad to see you all in once piece after dealing with Walter!"

Daniel was very pissed off.

"Where the hell were you?" He demanded.

Feeling not guilty, Kevin respond, "We had to split after we heard that Walter wanted to kick your ass. We all thought you were a goner."

"Well, I'm not, thanks to some brave figure skaters." Daniel unhappily said.

The guys laughed at what the birthday teen told them.

Josh chortled, "Figure skaters? A bunch of perky, ice dancers came in to your rescue from Hefty Walter?"

"Yes," Daniel strongly replied.

They continued to laugh.

Danny added, "What? You don't want to know what happened in the locker room?"

The guys stopped laughed and listened to his story.

Their eyes were wide-open at Walter's little underwear secret and people were taking photos of his teddy bear shorts. The guys understood why Daniel was not beaten down to a pulp or got all tired and bruised up.

Then he told the guys about Sally Hunt. His friends laughed even more and teased him by getting involved with a figure skater. Danny tried to explain she was a figure Champion and really famous. The teenage boys did not want to listen or seem to care for their friend's feelings for Sally.

Daniel was tired of his homies' excuses.

He yelled out, "Screw you!"

He was ready to walk home, but Josh stood in front him for a serious chat.

Josh solemnly said, "Danny, it was worth what you did to Walter. Remember our first day in high school?"

Daniel shivered. He thought about that first day. Hefty Walter sure was a bully to them during their Freshman year. They were very relieved they did not have to deal with the bully all their high school years.

"Yeah, I remember." He whispered.

Daniel abruptly yelled back, "But you dicks left me stranded at the rink!"

His friends did not seem remorse to leave him behind.

Danny made up his mind. He rather be with strong and truthful friends instead of stupid frauds. He spoke, "Sally was really nice to me tonight. I like her."

"Dude, can't you find some normal girl to hangout with?" Kevin asked.

"No," protested Daniel, "I want to date her."

"Whatever." Josh scoffed, "Let's leave twinkle-toe's lover boy."

They guys left the birthday boy behind again and got in the car. Loud music was blaring from the car's speaker as Josh sped his car down road and was gone in the dark night from Daniel's tired eyes.

His legs slowly kept walking and walking to his parent's house. His mind was thinking what happened when Hefty Walter threw him against the door, his muscles were in aches and pain, and thought he was going to be a goner before Sally and her friends saved him.

All of the sudden, Danny's eyes saw a tiny brownish-red and white puppy running for the left side of the road. His head turned just in time to see the little puppy leap into a leafy bush. The pup could not be seen from the inside of the bush.

Slowly moving forward to the bush, Daniel softly called out for the brownish-red and white puppy.

"Puppy. Here, puppy, puppy, puppy, puppy, puppy . . ."

He leaned his head over the leafy bush. His eyes found the little brown and white puppy, frightened and scared, from the tiny openings of the bush. The pup was lying in the dirty on its stomach and softly whimpering.

Daniel smiled sweetly at the little lost puppy. He did feel sorry for it. The birthday boy remembered feeling what the little pup was feeling earlier.

Lost and abandoned at the ice rink when his once called 'friends' ditched him.

His knees bent down to the ground and took the chance to see if he could get the scared puppy out from the strong rooted bush.

Daniel's hands were being poked by the green leaves and wooden twigs. He called out more to the sweet, cute puppy. "I'm not going to hurt you. Just want you safe and happy."

The puppy's head lifted up from the soil. Its huge sad eyes looked up to see who was talking to it.

Danny smiled even more. He wondered if the puppy was trusting him. His hands managed to feel the puppy's soft, soft fur. Soft as silk. His fingers gently petted the cute puppy until the pup felt content enough to be picked up.

After several seconds of petting the soft puppy, Danny could no one longer take the stabbing pain the bush's leaves and twigs were giving him on his hands and arms. He reached in deeper, his fingers and palms wrapped around the tiny, silky puppy-dog, and was able to pull the little pup out of the bush.

Daniel Gray kept the pup close to his coat. He noticed how the puppy seemed to enjoy being in his arms. He once had a dog before and old memories of his sweet golden retriever came to mind.

His voice whispered to the stray pup, "I'm going to take you to my folk's home and I'll see if we can find your owners tomorrow."

He hoped his parents would be okay by letting him watch over the pup. Thankfully, he did not have anything special or important to do the next day.

Danny's mind was startled back to the present when he heard a loud dog bark. His eyes saw a cute little beagle in his unit's living room wanting some love and attention. The good owner got up from the couch to give his cute little dog some food in the kitchen. Dry kibble and dog meat.

The famished beagle ate and drank lots of water.

Daniel Gray felt like a good dog owner for his sweet fury friend. He knew his dog wished to have a long walk.

When his sweet-loving dog finished eating, Danny slipped on his coat and shoes, got his dog's retractable leash, attached it his dog's collar, stuffed plastic bags in his right coat pocket, and gathered his keys.

Man and his dog left their home for a good morning walk. The human's mind remembered back the night when he took the stray pup to his parent's house.

17-year-old Danny Gray carefully made his way to his house with the blissful sleeping pup in his arms. The lights were not on in the house.

Outside the house, Daniel quietly made it for the front door. His right hand held the puppy while his left hand was digging for his metal house key in his front right jeans pocket.

His fingers found the golden key for the golden door knob and unlocked it. His left hand slowly turned the knob. He lowered his head to see how the sleeping puppy was doing in his arms. His ears heard little puppy snores coming from its tiny mouth.

Danny's heart smiled even more.

His free hand pushed the door and stepped softly inside. He silently closed and locked the door. He wanted to go to his room upstairs, but he decided to get some water for the tired and hungry puppy.

Daniel walked to the kitchen and placed the pup on the sofa not far from the kitchen's entrance. He turned on the lights, found his old dog's ceramic water bowl in a cabinet, and filled it with clean water from the sink.

Then he went to the living room where the stray pup was resting on the sofa. He sat the bowl of water next to his feet to wake up the puppy.

"Puppy. You need to wake up." He softly whispered in the pup's floppy ears.

The puppy's sad eyes opened. It stretched its body and let out a big yawn with a little yelp.

"Shhhh . . ." Danny shushed the puppy.

It was too late. His ears heard rapid foot steps coming from the wooden and carpeted staircase.

"Ah, man." He mumbled.

Who came down the steps were his brown haired mother and father all dressed for bed with disappointing looks in their eyes.

His mother covered her yawn with her left fist and tiredly asked, "Daniel, where have you been? It's one in the morning."

Danny stood up from the sofa to face his folks and uncomfortably said, "My friends played a trick on me and made my way home by foot."

The concerned parents felt sorry for Daniel.

His father questioned him, "Are you okay, son?"

"I'm fine, Dad." Danny yawned and covered his mouth with his left fist. His sleepy eyes blinked. "Just tired."

Mrs. Gray walked up to hug her boy.

"We were worried about you." She worriedly told him.

"I'm sorry, Mom." He apologized and hugged her too.

She let go of Daniel and her eyes saw something brown and odd looking on the white sofa.

Mrs. Gray asked, "Daniel, what is that?"

He stepped away from his mother and his legs walked to the sofa to pick up the little stray puppy. The pup's dark sad eyes touched his parent's hearts.

"Where did you find that puppy?" His father curiously wondered.

Sweet Daniel explained, "I found it running out in the streets. I felt sorry for the pup and brought it here to see if we can find its owners."

Mr. and Mrs. Gray knew their son had a soft heart for his old dog, and dogs in general. Daniel's mother told her son, "It's okay with us for you to watch over the pup."

"Thank you, Mom, Dad." His voice was filled with relief and gently held the puppy in his arms.

He slowly placed the pup next to the water bowl. The puppy's tongue was licking the cool, fresh water with it's small pink tongue.

Lap, lap, lap. The puppy's tongue made from drinking the water.

Before all the Grays went to bed, Danny and his parents sat on the sofas to talk about what happened to him that evening. Daniel explained about him and friends having a pizza dinner, playing a trick on an old school bully, and meeting Sally Hunt.

Mr. and Mrs. Gray were surprised of Danny wanting to date a girl, even with someone like Sally. They did feel happy for him.

His father did tell Daniel the pup was a tri-color, bastard beagle. They all laughed at Mr. Gray's discovery.

Mrs. Gray happily offered, "Would the tri-bastard like something to eat?"

The little beagle lifted up his head from the bowl and let out a tiny yelp for a 'yes'.

Laughter was heard when they all left the living room for the kitchen so the puppy could have some meat to eat.

The day after his 17th birthday, Danny woke up from his bed and saw the beagle pup laying next to him on a comfy purple blanket on top of his bed. His fingers slowly stroked the puppy's soft fur coat.

The pup's cute face turned to see Danny and his little pink tongue kissed his face. The tongue endlessly kissed his new friend like crazy.

Daniel laughed and giggled at the pup's loving affection. His heart was sad from knowing what he needed to do next for the puppy.

He quickly showered, dressed in clean clothes, and lead the pup outside for potty. While the pup went, Danny had some breakfast before going back to his room with the tiny beagle pup in his arms.

Danny found his small gray digital camera in one of the drawers of his computer desk. He turned it on and took some pictures of the beagle pup on his purple blanket. Then he turned on his desktop. The beagle leaped into his lap by surprise. Daniel contently petted the puppy.

He connected the camera's UBS cord to his desktops' hard drive and downloaded the pup's pictures from the computer's pic software program.

Danny picked one pic, copied it, and paste it to a blank page from his desktop sheet program. He typed: 'Found Stray Beagle Puppy' on the blank page. He also typed in his phone number, address, and email for contacting him. His heart did not want to give up the sweet pup. But he had to because the beagle may belong to someone else. All he wanted to do was do the right thing.

His printer printed 30 fliers of the stray pup.

A knock was heard on his bedroom door.

"Come in." He answered.

The door opened and in came his mother.

"Here." She handed him his old dog's brown leather collar and black leash. "You'll need these."

"Thanks, Mom." He took them and put the collar on the pup.

Her eyes saw the fliers coming out from the printer. She whispered, "I am proud of you, Danny, and you are doing the right thing."

That made him feel a little happier. "I hope so."

Smily Mrs. Gray left her son's room and closed the door behind her.

The beagle yelped again and again by looking out the window. He jumped out of Daniel's lap and on the bed to get a better view of the window.

Danny joined the beagle by laying next to the pup. What his eyes saw was the magic of nature. A pair of robins building a nest on a tree branch.

He told the pup, "Aw, be nice, puppy. It looks like they're having a family."

Thoughts came into his head after saying the word 'family.' Danny asked the beagle, "Do you have a family?"

Puppy turned his head and kissed him with his pink tongue. "Awe, thanks."

His thoughts were the pup wanted Danny and his parents to be his family.

Sun was still shining when Daniel Gray and the pup left the bedroom to walk around the neighborhood and posting up fliers of the beagle puppy. On strong trees, wooden telephone polls, windows of business places, and street light posts.

He asked neighbors, kids from school, or anyone about the pup. He even talked to people at animals shelters or vets. He did have the beagle be checked out at the vet to make sure the little pup was healthy, had his first round of core vaccine shots, and to see if he had a chip on him. The pup had no microchip on either of his shoulders. Danny also gave the beagle a nice warm bath in the tub with puppy shampoo later that night.

He waited a month to see if anyone would call and claim to be the beagle's owner. He secretly did not want anyone to come by to tell him the pup was theirs.

While he wait for the month to go by, Danny introduced the beagle to Sally. They bonded real well together and Sally enjoyed going out on walks with her boyfriend and his little beagle pup. He worked hard at his job, school assignments, and taking care of the puppy. He had crossed off the days on his wall paper calendar and counted how many more days till the month was over.

He was not done there.

The pup and Danny were busy being friends together by playing with toys, going on walks or to a dog park, worked on some basic obedient and good dog behavior training, and Daniel read some special books about beagles.

The month went by without someone claiming that the beagle puppy was theirs. One Saturday morning, Danny Gray was very ecstatic with the news. He knew what he wanted to do next.

He stepped up to his folks and asked permission to be the beagle bastard's new owner since he had no owner.

They happily answered, 'Yes.'

Mr. and Mrs. Gray noticed Danny being very happy with the little pup by his side. A spark would light up his eyes whenever he and the beagle would do something together as a team. Especially when it came to dog obedient training. They both figured their son would be smart enough to understand why he acted that way.

Daniel got legal claim on the beagle and a license tag.

The cute pup wore a nicer brown leather collar with a small silver metal octagon license and on his little gold bone-shaped metal tag was the name 'Butch.'

Danny and his faithful tri-bastard of four years, Butch, got back to their apartment unit from their walk. The beagle bastard went for his green ceramic water dish to have a long drink of water in the kitchen. The human had a little drink of water from his cold silver water bottle stored in the fridge.

He called up Sally to see how she was doing.

Sally told her fiance she had a good skating practice, she missed him, and could not wait to see him again the next day for dinner at her parent's house.

When night time came, Daniel and Butch had dinner, went on their second walk, and got settled in for the night. The caring human went to his bedroom for some shut eyes. He laid in his bed. His heart wished he was not alone in his skating quest.

It was a tough night for the dog trainer to sleep blissfully. He thought about the figure moves he would learn on the ice. Maybe he had to wear silly, colorful, and sparkling clothes or skating outfits, dance on his toes, doing jumps, spins, and freestyle positions in stupid, lame figure skates.

The worse part would be: everyone laughing at him by being a male figure skater who only wanted to impress his girl's strict figure skating parents.

Danny got over that fear by thinking on where to find a coach or befriend another figure skater. At an ice rink of course, but he might have to ask someone who worked at the rink for a coach if he did not make friends with a good skater.

He thought and thought about how good skaters start out to be wonderful figure skaters in the end. Reliable figure skates, coaches, and money.

He had money for lessons and skates, but all he really needed was an easy-going coach or skillful skater to teach him the basics and learn all the moves the pros do.

Then he remembered what Sally told him about her early skating years.

My parents put me through lots of private lessons with super dedicated coaches and made friends with other competitive skaters on and off the ice. It's still a wonderful pat of my life as a figure skater. I wasn't alone, I learned a lot, and my parents are very supportive of me.

Daniel knew what he had to do.

Go to the ice rink, skate during a public session, and see if he could befriend a really good local skater who was not participating in the same skating competitions as Sally Hunt.

Chapter Two

5:00 a.m.

Skates laced up.

Gloves on.

Clothes and tights fitted comfortably.

An MP3 player was blasting out the beating of the drum from an ice rink's speakers.

The cold building was not going to have a quiet morning. A figure skater wanted to have some alone time.

Sounds from an electric guitar strings were stringing.

The ice was smooth like glass.

The figure skater was stretching its body for an early morning practice session. Melody notes from a keyboard were being heard.

The rink's doors opened.

Light purple plastic guards were taken off from the figure's boot blades.

From anybody's point of view, an ice rink would be very cold. To a figure skater, the cold was comforting.

This skater loved the cold and ice skate when there was no one else around to spoil its fun.

It knew what time it was.

Fun time out on the ice.

The skater stepped on the ice and skated around the rink as fast as it could. Forward and backward. Crossovers, three turns, mohawk steps, and edges all over the ice.

After going around the rink three times, the skater glided forward on its left blade and jumped up high in the air to land backwards on its right blade for a waltz jump.

It skated backwards clockwise and prepped itself for a scratch-camel spin. The skater winded its body, left boot stepped into the circle and leaned forward with its back arched, right shoulder back, and lifted up its right boot to do a camel spin.

The figure skater loved that spin the most.

It could be strong, go fast paced, and practice it with other single spin positions or more positions for combination spins. This skater loved to be devoured in its spins and ice skating moves.

The skater ended the camel position by doing a normal scratch spin and checked with its right blade.

During the song, skater decided to do most of the dance steps and jumps it can do. Quick paced dance steps, arms flew around its body, and lips smiled big at the pretend audience by the steel bleachers.

Going clockwise backwards again, the skater stepped into its small traced circle with its left blade for a camel spin. After spinning six times, the figure's left blade pushed up from the spin and landed on its right blade with its back arched, left shoulder back and left boot up to spin in the opposite way.

The camel-jump-camel was ended with a back sit and back scratch spin combo. It checked the combo spin with a right back edge pull.

After the back edge pull, the figure turned forward and continued to skate around fast and gracefully.

The once smooth, glassy ice was covered with spin traces, edges, turns, small holes from the skater's toe-picks and excess of snow. Being surrounded in the cold ice rink did not feel cold for this competitive skater.

The lithe skater wanted to do a challenge that morning with edge jumps. Now was the time to work on a quadruple-quadruple edge jump combination.

First, it did a waltz jump take off, but in the air the figure did a back spin and landed backwards on its right boot and then both blades glided on the ice to lift up for a two rotated back spin jump. The figure landed its single axel and double loop jump combination smoothly.

Next up, a double loop and a triple loop.

Nailed strongly.

Still determined to get the quad-quad, the figure was feeling tired from all the spins, dance steps, and jump combinations it worked on so far. The skater could not give up on what it was meant to do on the ice.

The figure's theme song came on and started to dance, spin, and jump like a champion skater would to the judges and audience. The skater was very happy and more focused to nail a quad-quad jump.

Doubles and triples were feeling too easy.

Time for a little jump test.

The lithe figure did a triple axel-quadruple loop jump perfectly. When it came to doing a quad-quad jump, the figure skater did a quad first and tried to do another quad, but the skater did not succeed into the take off for the second jump. The skater fell on its right side.

Getting up quickly from the cold, cold patch of ice, the figure did a few forward power strokes, leaned forward to lift up its right boot as high as it can behind its back. Then it lowed the right boot to do a little waltz jump and landed it on the right boot to do a back spiral with the left boot up in the air.

It felt very happy after doing the spiral jump spiral.

The skater skated and skated for a full hour practicing rotation jumps from edges or toe-picks, accomplished many centered spins going forward, backward, or combinations with other spin positions, stretched its body for freestyle moves, and danced so much, its feet felt very tired.

Music stopped playing.

The figure skater was proud of itself to do a grand practice with an amazing, powerful tune to skate to. The only thing that could make it better was if the skater had a real audience to cheer for the skater. But truth of the matter was, the figure was not alone in the building.

A shadowy figure was keeping a close eye at the figure out on the ice.

It was nine in the morning when Daniel Gray woke up in his twin size bed. His dog, Butch, leaped up on the messy bed. He slowly walked toward his owner's face for a 'good morning' kiss.

"Hey, fuzzy-butt," said happy Danny.

His right hand petted and scratched his tri-bastard's soft fur coat. The sweet beagle was very happy to get some love and affection from his master.

After stretching and getting up from his bed, Danny gave himself and his sweet dog something to eat. The two chowed down their meals in the kitchen like two pals at the bar.

It was Saturday and he knew his fiancee's regular rink's schedule. There was a public session that afternoon. He had to go.

Daniel dressed for the fair weather outside, stuffed some baggies in his back jeans pocket, and the gray retractable leash in his hand. He clipped the leash to Butch's collar.

They left the unit and went on another long walk in the city's downtown. What the dog trainer thought during the walk was a very nerve wreaking moment in his life. The first time of meeting Sally Hunt's parents.

It had not been two weeks since Danny & Sally first meet and both decided to introduce themselves to each other's parents. He was very nervous of the idea.

Paul & Joy Hunt were exceptional figure skaters as singles before they met and fell in love.

Sally came to Daniel's house.

She was dressed in a cute yellow long sleeved and skirt dress. Her feet wore gold color low heeled shoes. Her blond hair was all curly without a hair tie or clip to pull it back.

Danny was dressed in tan pants and a really nice white dress shirt. His feet had on brown laced up dress shoes.

He introduced her to his parents. They had a half hour chat and Mr. & Mrs. Gray really liked Sally Hunt a lot.

Danny was glad his parents were happy for him to be involved with a gold medalist Junior figure champion.

Then it was time to face the music.

Sally & Danny left the Gray's house and drove to the Hunt's mansion in Sally's car.

Daniel Gray was so nervous, he was unable to keep still in his seat or put on a smile. He wished his heart would calm down enough to talk clearly and not faint in front of Paul & Joy Hunt.

Sally's car was parked in the driveway behind her parent's gold SUV. Before the two young lovers left the car, Sally noticed Matt's look was frightened and scared as hell just to meet her folks.

Her right hand took his left hand. Her fingers wrapped it tight for comfort.

Daniel saw his girl's hand giving him some strength. He softly whispered, "I can't do this, Sally-babe."

She leaned in for his left cheek. Her smooth pink lips kissed it.

Her voice spoke inaudibly, "They promised to be nice and I'll be there with you, Danny. If you do get too nervous or scared, close your eyes, take deep breaths, and clearly say what's in your heart."

Daniel nodded and his fingers twisted in Sally's right hand to squeeze it for reassurance. He leaned in so his lips could kiss her lips.

Her lips kissed back.

The two left the car together and hand-in-hand went forth for the Hunt's mansion. Daniel calmed his heart. He had Sally for support.

The blonde figure champ unlocked the front door.

She called out, "Mommy? Daddy?"

"In the living room, Sally dear," her mom, Joy Hunt, respond.

Danny & Sally bravely walked front the front door entrance toward the living room where Joy & Paul sat in separate comfy chairs.

The young lovers sat on a huge white couch together.

Paul was dressed in black pants and a light blue color long sleeved shirt. Joy was dressed in navy blue sweat pants and a long sleeved creamy gold shirt.

Sally happily told her parents, "This is Daniel Gray."

Both her parents were not impressed of Danny.

The young man with dark brown hair and brown eyes was not an ice skater nor did not seem the type of guy who would be good enough for their talented daughter.

Joy & Paul thought Daniel only wanted to use Sally for fame and have access to her money. They thought their daughter was going to ruin her life to be with someone like Danny.

Stuck-up Joy Hunt asked the teenage boy, "So, Daniel, do you have a job?"

"I do." He started out slowly.

He was not sure how to answer to Mrs. Hunt's question with high expectations. He looked at his lovely blond Sally for support. Her hand squeezed his.

Danny figured out what to say.

He spoke, "I work at a Pet Store as a Stock Boy."

That was said. He & Sally waited for the parent's response.

Paul & Joy thoughts were different from each other.

Mr. Hunt said, "Well, it's a good start, Daniel."

"Huh! Is that what you want to do for you life, Daniel?" Joy sternly wondered.

"I don't know, Mrs. Hunt."

Is she always this stubborn? Danny thought in his head.

Mrs. Hunt strictly stated, "You know my Sally is busy with her skating career for the next five to ten years, do you still want to be with her and be able to support both of you when that's all over?"

"I'll have to figure out a plan." Daniel candid to the Hunts.

He lifted up his left arm and placed it on Sally's shoulders. He strongly said, "There's no rush. Sally & I are still young and have lots of time to plan out the future."

The teen lovers turned their heads for a sweet kiss.

Joy spoke rudely, "Don't do that in front of us."

Sally broke from the kiss and replied, "Mommy!"

"Sally Hunt, don't you understand what boys really want girls!" Joy yelled and stood up from her chair. "Sex! It's what all teenage boys want from famous, attractive girls with money!"

Paul got on his feet to protest against his wife. "Stop it, Joy!"

"Don't you bark at me, Paul!" Joy shouted.

Danny & Sally were feeling very uncomfortable to see that happen. They wondered what was going to happen next.

"Can't you give the kids a break?" Paul pleaded. "Daniel seems like a nice young man."

Sally and her boyfriend were happy to have Mr. Hunt on their side.

"Yeah, on the surface!" Joy argued back. "I will not have our champion daughter get involved with a crazed, hormonal high school boy!"

That drew the line.

Sally started to cry. She let go of Danny's hand, abruptly left the couch, and hastily went upstairs for her bedroom.

Danny knew what to tell Joy Hunt.

He lifted off the couch and without fear, he spoke strongly, "Mrs. Hunt, I don't have any sexual urges or lustful feelings for Sally. I like her a lot and want to be friends with her from the inside out. Please, give me a chance?"

Joy was surprised.

Not only Daniel was standing up against her, but her husband was fighting for the teenager's relationship as well.

"Joy, I really don't think Danny wants to use Sally for money or sex. Be a good mom by respecting the kid's wishes?" Paul kindly asked.

Mrs. Hunt was shocked at her husband. She thought he was going to be on her side when it came to Sally and boys. What changed his mind?

She angrily stuttered, "Well, I—this isn't—Sally's in no-"

Paul and Danny stood side-by-side in front of Joy with stern looks on their faces. They were not going to let her win this debate.

Mrs. Hunt gave up.

"If you do anything bad or break my daughter's heart, I'll have not only your head, but the other thing men hold near and dear to them." She threatened the young man.

Danny gulped.

His broken voice said, "Yes, ma'am. I promise you no funny stuff will happen between Sally & I."

Joy told her husband and her daughter's new boyfriend, "Now, I have to tend to my daughter for the night."

She left the living room for Sally's bedroom.

Paul sighed, "I think that went well."

To the Stock Boy's point of view, having to fight and protest against someone like Sally's mother was too much for him. He wanted to get the hell out of the house.

Before he could, Paul Hunt requested from the young man, "Daniel, do you really promise to treat my little girl with love and respect, or were you just saying it to get my wife to say, 'Yes?'"

The teenage boy remembered what Sally told him in the car. *Say what's in your heart.*

He knew what was in his heart.

His heart felt good love and he wanted to be a faithful friend for Sally instead of a fraud like his once called friends did when they left him stranded at the ice rink on his seventeenth birthday. After Joy gave him that warning, Danny knew he had to be good to date & love Sally Hunt.

"I really do promise, Mr. Hunt." Daniel honestly respond. "I enjoy dating, getting to know, and spending time with Sally in every good way."

They walked toward the front door.

What made Mr. Hunt changed his mind about Sally having a boyfriend was Danny had a job and he seemed to make his daughter happy by being friends with her off the ice. That could be a good thing for her when she was not skating or competing.

Paul said, "I like you, Danny. The thing is keep your distance from Sally and do not get too heavy in love before marriage. My daughter is a special girl and skater and you do not want to make my wife more mad if something you did something bad to Sally."

Now that kind of promise he could be happy with.

The Stock Boy's head nodded in agreement and the two men shook hands.

When the flashback ended, Daniel Gray's heart was very, very satisfied whenever he would take his cute dog out for a long walk. Then he felt his legs being tired after walking around downtown for more than forty minutes. His eyes saw a park bench not far from a public park.

In the nice sun shine, Danny sat down and his cute beagle dog laid on its stomach next to his owner's feet. The Pet trainer was glad Paul Hunt would be friendly toward him when the two were in the same room. He was surprised he gained Mr. Hunt's trust after respecting Sally and her curfews during skating seasons.

He always hoped Joy Hunt would the be same as her husband, but she never changed or really wanted to be nice to Daniel. She always had the same stuck-up attitude for him ever since he & Sally told their folks they were an item.

The human could hear Joy Hunt's voice with the figure skating stipulation again. Dealing with someone as complicated as Joy was not his only fight. He wished he could get over his fear by talking to the dog's owners in the Pet store's training booth.

Suddenly, both boys noticed a struggling female dog walker with ten dogs coming down on the sidewalk. Danny's canine stood up on all four and felt the need to growl at the girl walker and the dogs.

As a dog trainer, Daniel knew how to control his dog.

He took hold of the gray retractable leash connected to his dog, made the string shorter, and strongly and clearly spoke, "Stay."

After hearing that command, his dog comfortably sat on the sidewalk and waited for the dog walker to pass by without him snarling, growling, or move from his stay stance.

The brown and white dog's owner calmly reached into his right jeans pocket for a little treat for his well-behaved dog. Little pieces of a doggie biscuit were in his hand.

His voice spoke, "Good boy."

The dog turned his head to his master and jumped up onto his lap for his treat. The dog loved his blueberry flavored biscuit snack.

Daniel petted and scratched his dog's fur.

He was very happy to have his 'man's best friend' in his life when he & Sally could not be together. His legs felt the loving dog wiggle over on his back for a nice belly rub.

The young dog trainer let out a big laugh and his hands rubbed and rubbed his dog's happy tummy. He wished he could be like that all the time at his job. But he remembered what his boss told him what an 'overall' dog trainer should be from his Pet training evaluation day.

The Pet trainer thought back what happened at the Pet Store a couple days ago.

It was the first Thursday of October.

Seven in the morning.

Daniel Gray got himself ready for work. He put on his green work shirt, clipped on his name tag, wore his tan work pants, and his dark brown slip-resistant dress shoes. His heart felt sad and scared.

He was going to hear the results of his first employee Pet trainer evaluation. He hoped his scores were not affected of him not showing or teaching the dog's owners obedient training.

Daniel's legs moved from the third floor down to the parking garage for his car.

The car ride lasted twenty minutes from the apartment building. He put the car in park, took some deep breathes, and got out of his little two door, light blue car.

Even though he was still very nervous and scared, Daniel slowly made his way to the back way behind the Pet Store building and opened the back door with a key.

After opening and locking the door, he turned to his right and walked down a long hallway for the manager's office door. Next to the office door were some metal padded chairs placed by the wall.

Daniel Gray unzipped and slipped off his coat. He took his time by sitting on the chair closet to the office door and his mind was thinking what his boss, Jack Randell, wanted to tell him what his scores were.

The office door opened.

Jack's voice called out, "Daniel Gray."

With his dark blue coat in his hands, Danny stood up from the chair he sat in to head inside Jack's office room. The room was average sized for a small office and a medium size sliding windows at the other side of the room.

The floor had bluish-gray carpet, the walls were bright white, against the walls were two large black bookshelves on the left and right side of the room filled with file folders and hardback and paperback books. In the center was a large dark brown computer desk with a black leather chair behind it.

There was an updated flat screen desktop on the computer desk with a wireless keyboard and mouse next to the screen, a gray cord phone set on the opposite side of the desktop, and two small black padded chairs in front.

Daniel noticed a cream color file folder on the desk. The folder's tab had his name printed on it from a black ink pen. His heart pounded hard from knowing his evaluation scores were in that folder.

Jack Randell was sitting in his leather chair. He was an average man in his mid-fifties wearing his dark green work shirt, black slacks and dress shoes. His light brown hair had been getting some more grays, new wrinkles were forming from his furrow, and his gray eyes remained the same ever since Danny first met him when he was 16 years old and looking for a pet related job.

Young Daniel sat on the left small padded chair. His brown eyes looked at his boss with a wary heart.

The Pet Store owner happily told Danny, "Well, now . . . let's look over your evaluation scores, shall we?"

Jack opened the file folder on his desk.

Daniel silently gulped.

His heart was beating faster and faster. His palms were getting sweaty. He closed his eyes to breath in deeply. Then he opened his eyes to diligently look at Jack reading over the scores.

His boss' eyes looked up from the folder to Daniel. The store manager spoke, "From what I've seen of you training the dogs, showing up for work, and completing your tasks for the day over the past five years, you're a real dedicated worker, Daniel Gray."

Danny sighed a little from hearing something positive from Jack. Any worker would feel the same way from their progress report meeting with their superior.

Then Mr. Randell continued on. "On the downside, you don't do your job by teaching the dog's owners what they should do with their dogs outside the training booth."

Silently, Danny felt his heart sunk down to his feet. His only work problem he had to face in the Pet store. Not to be afraid to teach the dog owners obedient training.

"I understand, Sir." He softly responded.

He thought his boss was going to look beyond that little problem. He was wrong. He did wonder what the store owner had planned to do by improving his pet instructing skills.

Jack closed the file folder. He was not sure what to do about Daniel's people problem.

The Pet trainer calmly sat in the padded chair while his boss folded his hands on the office desk. Their eyes eyed at each other as their thoughts ran through their heads like the student was stumping its teacher.

Minutes ticked by until Jack Randell told Danny, "Try harder, Daniel. Customers think you do a great job to train the dogs. Except, to be an overall dog trainer, you need to interact with the owners. You need to show them the ropes and tools for them to bond and experience the joy on having a dog."

The young dog trainer was feeling a bit better from his boss' wise words.

He agreed.

"Yes, Sir."

Both men shook hands to seal the deal for Danny to work better at his job.

Before the Pet trainer got up from the padded chair, his boss warned him, "Your next evaluation is in three months. If you have not improved your training skills with the dog owners, I'm going to have to let you go as a dog trainer and you're back to your old job as a stock boy."

"Thank you, Jack," Danny relieved, "I won't let you down."

The Pet store owner believed in Daniel's promise. He let the young dog trainer get out of his office room and went to the employee room to store away his stuff in a locker box. Then he was off for the training booth.

The dog trainer had fun-filled day by training puppies about potty training with newspapers and meaty treats without talking to the owners.

It had been an hour and a half since Daniel and Butch went out for their walk and his second flashback came to an end. The dog trainer was having second thoughts about wanting to continue his job position.

No pressure or stress to show the dog's owners training techniques. But his heart belonged in the training booth. He could not let go of doing something he really enjoyed of doing.

The boys headed back to their unit home.

There was one other thing Danny could do without getting more stressed out. Him not marrying Sally and not having Joy as his mother-in-law. Except, if he did not marry the blonde Champ, he may never find love again.

Inside the unit home, Danny rested on the couch and his sweet beagle dog went for his pillow to sleep on. It was a good walk for the two to share together.

Danny was relaxed ten minutes later.

He showered, put on jeans, long sleeved black shirt, and his heavy gray seater. He was dressed ready to ice skate.

The Pet trainer said to Butch, "See you later, Butchie-Wutchie."

He went the stairs for his car and drove to the ice skating rink. Parked his car, lifted himself off his seat, and went forth of the rink's chilly building.

Inside the building were a couple of long tables being set-up for a child's birthday party. Danny purchased a public session skating time and rental skates. Three and a half hours of trying to skate for the first time was going to be hard.

He walked to the rental skating counter and got a pair of used up brown skates. His hands carried the skates and sat on an empty bench. He reached down to take his tennis shoes off and slipped on one of the skate boots.

The toe-pick felt very small and not very supportive for Danny. He had a feeling he was going to fall down a lot throughout the whole session.

Lacing up the skates were very difficult for him to figure out on his own. He was too embarrassed to ask for help. Then he noticed some parents helping their children lace up their rental skate.

Start from the bottom. Lace them not too tight or too loose. Take the laces in each hand and crossover all the hooks till its reached to the top and the laces should be crossover downward or wrapped around the boot with a tied up bow.

Daniel stood up after lacing both skates on his feet. It felt very weird to him. He started to walk slowly to the coin lockers to safely put away his keys, wallet, and phone. He paid it in quarters and kept the locker key with him in his right jeans pocket.

His feet and ankles felt very uncomfortable of wearing the rental skates. He thought back when Sally had to break in a new pair of figure skates. She told him her feet would hurt but it would worth it in the end.

That must be what his feet were feeling by wearing a strange boot with a toe-picked blade attached to the boot. He was going to have to get use to.

From the big screen window, Danny saw the Zamboni gone and a worker was on the ice pushing off the extra snow and watery ice from the rink with a big shovel and a long sticked rubber scrapper into a drain.

The first time skater was very nervous to skate all by himself. His heart longed for Sally. But she and her mom were busy drawing and deciding her new ice skating outfits for her routine competitions.

The big gate door closed.

Lots of little children and some adults were skating on the ice.

Daniel mumbled to himself, "Gotta do what I have to do for Sally."

From opening the lobby door to the ice rink, he did his best to walk comfortably toward the rink.

Loud music was playing, people were chattering and skating around the rink, and the rink was very, very cold to the Pet trainer. He did not see any good skaters like Sally or someone who seemed to be a coach.

He sadly stepped and slowly walked on the ice.

Danny felt very unsure how to work his uncoordinated feet in these weird looking ice skates. He constantly looked down at his brown rental skates, every part of his body wiggled a lot, and he was not standing up straight.

Twenty feet from the open gate door, the struggling and cautious Pet trainer slowly lifted up his worn out right boot and blade.

Before he knew it, he misused his right toe-pick on the ice and fell down. He felt silly being on the wet patch of ice. He was glad Sally or her parent's were not there to see him fall.

He had to get up fast. People were skating around him fast and the cold ice was making his clothes wet. He was glad to wear his heavy gray sweater.

When no one was around Daniel, his knees moved for the rink's board and climbed back on his feet. He knew he could not skate around the rink without support.His hands holding on to the rink's short walls to support himself to skate. He continued to look down at his feet walk to make sure he would not trip and fall on someone.

He watched other people ice skate. Some were so good they did not need to hold on to the short height wall or look down at their feet. He felt jealous from those skaters' skills. But he was not alone in his situation.

There were other skaters who would fall down, hold on to the wall, or hold hands with other good skaters.

As he stepped slowly around the rink holding to the wall, Danny wondered what the big deal was with people loving to skate where it was super cold, having their feet and legs work hard with a heavy boot and blades, and understanding what figure skaters really do on the ice. He detested figure skating so much, he would not pay attention to Sally's skating skills, other people's skating tricks, or listen on what others had to say about the sport.

Daniel also wondered why his feet were feeling very tired and uncomfortable of wearing rental skates while others were not having a terrible time trying to ice skate. Probably because this was his first time and other people had skated longer or had more experience than he did.

After spending a long boring and achy hour at the cold ice rink, upset Danny was sitting on a bench in the lobby area while the ice was being resurfaced. He fell at least thirty more times after the first fall. His heart felt silly by wanting to learn how to figure skate from the start.

He decided to check on his cell from the coin locker box. He wanted to see if Sally called him. There were no missed calls from her. He paid again for the locker box with three quarters and went back to the bench.

The Pet trainer noticed his rental skates were a bit loose on his feet. He leaned down, undid both skate's laces, and made the boots tighter.

He thought, *Maybe that's why I couldn't skate. I didn't lace them up right or tight enough.*

He hoped it would work this time. Then it was time to skate again.

Danny slowly got up from the bench and his uncomfortable wobbly boots walked toward the ice rink. Making the brown boots tighter did not do the trick. He wished he knew someone who could help him be a good skater.

At the ice, his eyes saw a young girl with brunette hair and dressed in long black stretch pants, a light blue t-shirt. Her feet were wearing white figure skates.

The figure girl skated around the rink strongly and gracefully. Forward and backward without falling down, holding on the to the wall, or was afraid to ice skate.

The Pet trainer thought that skater was skating just like Sally or another competitive skater. His heart felt happy to come to the rink after all. He had to talk to the figure skater. He made his way for the rink.

Slowly stepping onto the smooth ice, Daniel Gray made his way to get the outstanding figure skater's attention. His hands held on the wall and skated wobbly.

"Um, excuse me!" He yelled out.

The figure skating girl did a right inside mohawk turn to face the person who was calling out for her. She saw the stranger. It was just another novice holding on to the wall with all his might and the skater knew the stranger's feet were not feeling well from the brown rental skates he was wearing.

And to think she thought she could be left alone that skating session so she could work on her figure skating stuff.

The unhappy figure skater asked, "Yes?"

Daniel pushed away from the wall.

He stood in front of the figure female skater and spoke tiredly, "Hi."

The brunette girl looked impatient. She sternly wondered, "Can I help you?"

Danny panted out, "I need help."

"Help with what?" The figure skater was puzzled on what the novice would want from her.

He put in, "Ice skate."

The girl scoffed, "I don't have time to deal with this kind of idiocy."

She had a bad feeling that the first timer wanted more than just 'ice skating lessons' from her. The figure girl turned away from the novice by skating backwards fast.

Danny was losing his balance from wearing the worn-out rental skates. His legs wobbled and he fell on the ice by landing his back hard.

The girl saw him fall down and laughed her hardest.

She yelled out, "I can see you need a lot of lessons to be a good skater!"

The dog trainer tried to push himself up with his arms and legs, but failed and was down on the ice.

He moaned, "Ow."

The figure skater skated close to Daniel and annoyingly suggested, "Please don't push up backwards."

She kneeled on the ice to show idiotic first timer, "You get on your hands and knees and push up."

The girl slowly pushed herself up from a crawling position and managed easily to get back on her blade quickly.

Danny did what the skater showed him to do. He slowly pushed up and was back on his blades too.

He huffed, "Well, that was easy."

"Now, I would like to skate." The strong figure smug.

Daniel Gray knew he did not want this skater to get away from him. He needed her to help him skate.

"Teach me how to skate." He requested loudly.

The skater turned around to look at Danny. She scolded, "What? And why would I do that?"

"Because your the best skater I've seen here today and I need to be taught how to skate." He begged. "Please? I'll pay you big bucks?"

The girl slyly smiled and thought of an idea.

She skated up toward Danny and declared, "Tell you what: since ice skating is my passion and no one can put a price on someone's passion, I would be happy to teach you how to skate for free."

Danny exclaimed, "When do we start?"

The smily figure skater purposely pushed the first time skater on the ice with both of her hands at his chest.

Young Gray was on his back and trying to get up from the cold icy rink surface again.

The brunette hair girl proudly stood over to tell him, "We've already begun."

Chapter Three

This time, first time novice skater remembered not to push up backwards. He got on his hands and knees and slowly lifted himself up off the ice.

He was back on the blades.

He introduced himself to the skillful figure skater, "I'm Danny."

"Hi, Danny. I'm Allison." She greeted back.

The figure skater skated around the novice and announced, "Well, the first thing you need to do is wear a pair of blue rental skates."

Danny looked down at the brown rentals he was wearing.

He asked, "What's wrong with the one's I have?"

She pointed out, "Your ankles are tilting inward. That's why you can't skate. People need to wear skates where their ankles aren't tilting inward or outward."

Daniel's eyes noticed other skater's skating skills.

Their ankles were not bent out of shape and they were skating grandly. No wonder he was having a bad time trying to ice skate.

"Skating is like walking?" He wondered.

The figure skater pushed herself around by going backwards counterclockwise. "In a way yes. Skating boots should be comfortable on your feet and your ankles are to be aligned when you skate, or as you put it 'walk'."

She continued on, "The brown rental skates are for people with strong ankles and it looks like you have weak ankles. That's where the blue rental skates come in. When you put those on, you will feel like a whole new skater."

"Does it cost extra?" Danny worriedly asked.

"Nope." The figure girl assured him. "Just take them off, hand them to the rental counter table, and they'll give you a free exchange."

The two got off the ice.

Daniel walked into the lobby first.

Allison last since she needed to put on her light purple color plastic guards on her skate's blade to protect them off ice.

She saw Danny on a bench and took off the worn out brown skates. He carried the brown boots to the counter for a pair of dark blue rental skates.

The figure skater adjusted her figure skates with her laces while the Pet trainer put on blue rental skates. He mimic her way to lace up the skates.

Danny stood up.

His ankle had no discomfort from wearing the blue skates. He exclaimed, "Wow! What a difference!"

The girl laughed and said, "A lot of first timers always have that problem. Anyone can skate, they just need the right kind of boot to help them skate."

"Let's go!" He triumphed.

Onward for the rink.

Daniel and Allison made their way to the center. His feet did feel a lot better in the strong blue boots instead of the worn out brown boots.

Allison told her student a helpful skating tip, "Another thing to remember to be a good skater is proper stance."

He listened to her figure advice carefully.

"Stand up straight, head up, relax your shoulders, arms at your side, let your legs and feet glide smoothly on the ice, and when you are doing certain skating tricks or skills always keep your hands at chest-level." She explained.

Allison skated forward with her figure stance.

She stood up, only her legs and boots helped her glide on the ice, shoulders were down, and looked really relaxed when she skated forward. The figure girl smiled big too.

Daniel understood what his Figure Instructor meant.

He decided to try it himself. Stood up, head up, his shoulders were relaxed, and skated better than he did. He felt like a good beginner. He started to smile and was not struggling as he was with the pervious rental skates. His feet moved little by little without falling down.

After going around four times, Danny watched the good brunette figure skater skate. She was backwards at first with both skates on the ice then both her feet jumped up in the air with a little spin and landed backwards on her right foot.

He thought, *Must be a skating trick I have to learn.*

The figure skater glided up to Danny.

She happily asked him, "How do your feet feel now?"

He looked down at the blue rentals skates. His feet cringed inside the boots.

He delightfully spoke, "They feel really good."

"Great!" The figure squealed, "Let's go to the center of the rink and practice some basic skills."

Danny and his Figure Instructor stood in the middle of the rink.

Allison skated gracefully around the red marked circle on the ice forward and backward. She was very happy to be that good of a skater.

Daniel had to admit.

This figure female was a pretty good and natural skater on the ice.

She explained, "To be this good, you need to practice a lot on and off ice."

"Off ice?" He wondered confusingly.

"Yes. Sometimes I work on my balance off ice by walking on straight lines or uprising narrow cement in parking lots or sidewalks." Allison explained. "To be good at something, practice all the little things in your everyday life so you won't forget what to do and it will make you stronger."

Danny thought more what Allison was going to teach him off ice. He had to trust her judgment when it came to figure skating.

Allison showed him how to skate without falling and how to prevent from falling down.

She showed her student, "If you do feel yourself falling down, slowly bend your knees and keep gliding until you don't feel like falling."

She did a little prevention demonstration. Her skates pretended to be out of whack, glided, bent her knees, and waited till she did not have the need to fall on the ice.

Danny understood the technique.

He asked, "Do you still fall down by getting so good in figure skating?"

"Yes." Allison admitted.

Daniel was surprised. *How is it possible for skaters to fall down after all the years of lessons, practice, and competitions they had done?*

"Why?" He wondered.

Allison did not answer his question. She quickly skated forward. Her left foot was on the ice but her right boot swung in front of her and back to tap the pick on the ice. Her left boot did an outside three turn, then paused, her right boot had its toe-pick on the ice and Allison popped up into the air while spinning around twice from her right boot and landed backward on her right boot.

Danny was amazed at Allison's figure skating skills.

She skated back to him and cursed, "Damn. I thought I was going to mess up my double flip."

"What's a double flip?" Daniel wondered.

The figure teacher relieved out, "We'll have to start from scratch, don't we?"

The nervous novice student agreed.

"All skaters, no matter how good they are, figure skaters, hockey players, or speed skaters, they still fall down." Allison replied.

She added, "It happens whether they are tired from working on their moves for endless hours or working on something new to show-off."

Danny figured out what Allison meant why good, skilled skaters fall down too. He wondered, "So, what I am going to learning today?"

"Nothing extreme." The Figure Instructor explained. "I'm letting you practice skating around the rink without falling for a little while."

That made her student's day. At first.

She asked Danny, "How long were you planning on how to learn figure skating?"

He answered, "As long it takes to be good in basic and I guess some advance levels."

Allison insisted, "If you want to be that good, you'll need your own skates."

"That doesn't seem that hard to me." Daniel said.

"Having your own skates isn't as easy as it sounds." His instructor strictly told him. "Like a new pair of boots, you have to break them in and that takes a few weeks for your feet to be comfortable in them."

He slowly asked, "Are my feet-going to hurt?"

"Oh yea." Allison snickered. "Sometimes people would get bruises, blisters, or sores on their feet by breaking in new skating boots."

Daniel thought if this was a good idea or not. But he could not give up on Sally. He loved her too much to worry so much about breaking in a pair of figure skates and foot pain.

He answered, "Let's go for it."

"Come with me." Allison skated for the rink's doors.

They left the cold rink for the arena's skating store.

In the rink's skating store, the store was big and full of lots of skating equipment from hockey to figure skating. Mostly hockey since puck chasers need more essentials than toe jumpers.

From the left side was a check-out desk, a little sitting area to try on skates, and a shelf full of hockey skates and other hockey essentials. The middle part of the store had a two level circular rack full of ice skating dresses and other figure outfits. There was a special rectangular rack full of strong wooden hockey sticks behind the figure outfit rack. The right side of the store had a shelf of figure boots and two more shelves of other hockey equipment too.

Allison and Danny saw a worker helping out another customer with an ice skating dress at the back part of the store.

They walked to the back and Allison spoke to the worker, "Hi, Jessica."

Jessica, a Caucasian girl with strawberry thick hair and wearing her light blue and hot pink employee skating jacket.

She turned away from young girl for a skating dress and greeted warmly, "Hi, Allison. What can I do for you?"

Allison said, "Well, this newbie figure needs to look at some male figure skates."

The employee nodded and asked her other customer if she was going to be all right for a few minutes. She said she wanted to look at some other dresses and would wait.

"What's your shoe size?" She asked Daniel.

"A ten." He answered.

Jessica left the store to go into the storage room for some male figure skates.

Allison sat on a chair. Danny joined with her by sitting in a chair next to his Figure Instructor's chair.

He wondered, "How many skates have you went through?"

"Ooohhhh . . . ." Allison laughed. "Seven."

"Damn, that's a lot." Daniel spoke surprisingly.

She put in, "I'm sure other skaters had much more than me. As a child grows into figure skating, their feet would get bigger and stronger. Then they'll need better skating boots and blades."

"That's true."

"I've had my current skates for three years now." She proudly stated. Her feet flexed and showed off her white figure skates.

"I love them." She whispered.

Jessica came back into the store with four boxes of male skates. She sat in another chair and said, "Skates off, please."

Danny took his blue rental skates off and straightened his thick shoes. He was feeling scared for his feet.

The store worker took out a real strong pair of black figure skates. She unlaced them from the boot to make a big hole for his left foot.

He lifted his foot into the boot's hole. The leather boot was on a tilted shoe table. It did not feel right for Danny's toes when Jessica was lacing them up.

He winced, "Um, not these. My toes hurt."

"Ok, we'll have you try something else." The store employee politely told him. She put the skate back and went for another box.

Allison did say, "You know they're going to hurt your feet for the first few times."

Her student admit, "I didn't get a good feeling about those skates."

The Figure Instructor's head teasingly turned away and decided to follow along her student's point-of-view.

Jessica fixed up another pair of beautiful black skates for Daniel to try on. His right foot tried on the skate. His toes tried out the blade's toe-pick by stabbing them on the tilted table. The pick felt very small to him.

"Not these." He huffed. "I don't like the toe-pick."

Allison and Jessica were puzzled.

Danny explained to the girls, "I like the big toe-picks Sally Hunt has for her skates."

Jessica laughed, "Are you a fan of Sally?"

"No." He strongly stated, "I'm her fiance, Danny."

The store worker gasped, "Really?"

Danny breathed out, "Yes. That's why I need to get some skates. The Hunt's will allow me to marry her if I learn how to figure skate."

Allison relieved a little from that news. Danny was not looking for sex from her. But her new figure student was Daniel Gray. Hunt's precious Danny.

Secretly, Allison was very angry to be teaching him how to figure skate.

"Wow." Jessica gasped, "I didn't think Joy & Paul Hunt were going to be that hard on Sally's lover."

Instead of going for another pair from the boxes she brought out, the rink employee declared, "I do have a special pair of skates in the back that would be wonderful for you to use."

Then she smug, "And to impress the Hunts."

Jessica stood up and carried all four boxes in her hand. She headed back into the storage room.

Allison tried nicely to tell Daniel, "Don't worry. Jessica is good when it comes to finding a good pair of skates."

He sighed unhappily and waited.

A minute later, smily Jessica came out of the room and back to her customers. She sat in her chair to present Danny, "Here we go. Male Platinum Classic. Something Paul Hunt loves."

The black skates Danny saw was a huge shock to him.

The brand new, shining, platinum blades had big toe-picks and looked fun to use on the ice. The outside of boot was black with suede material while the inside had lots of white color padded material.

"These skates are prefect." He breathlessly spoke.

Jessica carefully unlaced the skates and the boot had a big enough hole for Daniel to try on the skates. His right foot felt very comfortable in these skates.

Then both of his feet had on the skates. He strutted around the store like he would with his regular athletic shoes. His ankles were not tilted or bent out of shape in the male figure boots. He was looking forward to use those skates.

Secretly, Jessica and Allison giggled to each other, "Who would've thought a normal guy would be so happy to wear a pair of figure skates?", "You know he's only doing it to win the Hunt's approval."

Danny came back to the girls and announced proudly, "I'll take them!"

He sat down in the chair he was sitting in and slowly took off the Platinum skates and putted on the blue rental skates. His feet wished to wear his new skates.

Allison was very glad to make Daniel happy with his new skates. She was looking forward to help him be a good skater for Sally Hunt. Maybe better than her.

The three went to the light blue countertop so Daniel could purchase his new skates.

Jessica asked, "Do you think he would need care-take essentials for his skate's blades?"

"What care-take blade essentials?" Danny confusingly asked.

"Like guards and blade covers to protect the skate's blades off ice or storing them when they're not being used." Allison explained.

"That would be a good idea." He gave in to the girls' suggestion. "Show the Hunts I can be a good skater by protecting my skates on and off ice."

The Figure Instructor remarked, "It is an important thing to remember."

Daniel paid $825 dollars for his new skates, a pair of closed-sided red plastic guards, small black gloves, black cloth blade covers, and a small red and black sport bag.

The suede material boots were to be specially polished and the Platinum blades would be sharpened and cleaned in the shop.

He wanted to take his skates, but Jessica stated, "Your skates will be ready the day after tomorrow."

Danny's heart was hurt. He wanted to skate in his new skates now.

"Why?" He disappointedly asked.

She replied, "The polishing wouldn't completely be dried overnight and there are other skaters waiting for their skates to be sharpened."

Jessica handed him his receipt and an orange proof of purchase card when he would pick up his skates. She took the new purchased figure skates to the shop and handed them to Tony, the sharpener.

Danny walked out of the skating store feeling very sad. He saw his new skates being on a shelf with other figure skates, mostly girls.

Allison tried to cheer up her new student. "Look at it this way: with a little practice now, you'll be ready for your new skates when they're done."

He knew his Figure Instructor was right. He tried to say cheerfully, "Let's practice skating without falling down."

They went for the rink and skated and talked together, even though Danny fell down a few times, for the rest of the afternoon session.

Allison did show him how to skate smoothly in all her figure tricks. She glided naturally and took her time by doing all her moves.

The two new skating friends sat on a bench feeling tired and achy from skating together for two long hours. Both took off their skates to put on their street shoes. Daniel brought his blue rental skates to the rental countertop.

Before Danny and Allison departed from the rink, she requested, "Why don't we look over our schedules and see when would be a good time for your next lesson?"

They talked and debated for five minutes until the two decided to meet again next Friday night during public session. Danny was happy with that idea. He would be wearing his new figure skates by then.

Allison also reminded him not to wear jeans for their future ice lessons. She thought about the type of clothes he should wear at the rink.

"What would you recommend?" He nervously asked the Figure Instructor.

Danny was afraid she was going to say tights and a colorful spandex bodysuit. That would be worse than seeing or remembering Hefty Walter's white and pink teddy bear undershorts again.

Allison noticed Danny's discomfort look in his eyes.

She happily told him, "I would say for you: comfortable sweat pants, a t shirt, light cotton or dress socks, and a smaller sized sweater or sweat shirt so you won't get too warm or tired from working hard on the ice."

The Pet trainer was content with those suggestions. He was also shocked to hear 'getting too warm on the ice.'

How was that possible? He wondered.

He questioned his Figure Instructor, "Do you get sweaty from skating around the rink?"

"Yes." She answered. "People who work hard by skating in an ice rink do make their bodies feel warm and they do sweat like they're doing a workout on weight training machines or going for a run."

That made Danny thought about his high school track years. He was unsure if he could run for a long time again. He agreed to his instructor's clothing ideas.

The dog trainer lifted himself up from the bench, packed up his things from the coin locker box, put his things in his new skating bag, and he decided to drive over for the Hunt's mansion for dinner that evening.

Danny looked at his cell. No missing calls or texts from Sally.

Just when he was leaving the arena's building, the Pet trainer noticed a beautiful shiny black truck rolling in the rink's parking lot. He did feel a little ping of jealousy from seeing the hot-looking truck. The beautiful black truck parked in the lot.

Driver's door opened. Out came a big muscular guy in jeans, a black soft shell jacket, and cool N+ white, black, and turquoise color running shoes. He pulled out a big black hockey bag from the backseats. His strong right arm lifted the bag and carried it by his side. The truck's lights lit up to know the owner the alarm was on.

Seeing that guy made Danny remember seeing Hefty Walter four years ago. But the truck's owner did not look like his old school bully.

The black truck's driver had short light brown hair, hazel eyes, nice looking appearance for girls to ogle at, and he did not give the novice skater the impression he wanted to beat him up just because he played hockey or thinking he was the tough one.

A thought came to Danny's mind after he scrutinized closely at the brown haired and hazel eyed hockey guy. The black truck's owner did look very familiar to the dog trainer for a certain sports team.

Which hockey team is that dude part of? The figure student wondered.

The Pet trainer watched the beefy hockey dude go in the building and headed toward the big rink's lobby room without paying for admission. None of the employees seemed to care of the hockey dude wanting to skate without paying.

Danny wondered why the dude got special treatment and he did not. He was engaged to Sally Hunt after all. Maybe that hockey guy was more famous or got better skating treatment than a gold medalist, sunshine figure skater. The dog trainer wanted to know about the hockey dude's skating business.

Daniel noticed the light brown haired guy stepped into the men's locker room. The novice choose to hide in the men's bathroom until the special hockey guy comes out of the locker room.

After checking the lobby area by opening the door for the fifth time, the hockey dude was walking in the lobby room in his hockey skates, jeans, and a black jersey shirt. The front part of the guy's shirt only had the design of orange, red, and yellow color flames. The back side had no name or numbers to determine if the jersey shirt was part of a particular professional hockey team.

The light brown haired hockey guy carried two strong wooden sticks in his left hand. One was solid black and the other was silver with turquoise and black colors.

Danny walked out of the men's room and saw the big rink being empty, except for the hockey dude and his Figure Instructor, Allison. They were talking and skating around the rink.

That made the Pet trainer wonder. *What would a figure skater and a hockey player be doing on the ice together? Maybe they're friends, or does Allison teach hockey as well as figure skating?*

One of the rink's employees had a net set up on the ice close to the lobby area. Then Allison glided off the ice and picked up a large plastic blue bucket by an open gate door. She lifted up the bucket, tilt the bucket down, and lots of black pucks were dumped on the ice.

The hockey dude grabbed his black stick from another open gate door. He started to swing his hockey stick side to side smoothly with one of the pucks on the ice.

Danny watched the hockey dude prep himself to shoot the pucks in the net. He also noticed Allison skating at the other half of the rink doing her figure tricks. Spins, jumps, dance steps, and occasionally talking to the hockey dude.

It looked from his brown eyes that his Figure Instructor was giving the hockey guy some pointers with his shooting and skating techniques with the silver, black, and turquoise hockey stick.

The hockey dude seemed happy to see Allison again rather than listening to her advice. He practiced more on his hockey moves and sure enough, he did get better in his skating and shooting skills ten minutes later.

Danny had his doubts for the hockey dude's need for teaching skills from a figure skater. The novice figure needed to ask his Figure Instructor about her knowledge in hockey and who was her hockey student.

Before he wanted to go out of the lobby, Danny checked on his cell from his jeans left pocket. Time to go to the Hunt's mansion home for dinner and see his fiancee. He would ask Allison his questions during his next skating lesson with his new suede figure boots.

Danny hoped she would not get mad at him by questioning her teachings in hockey as well as figure skating.

The Pet trainer turned around from the large screen window and walked out of the arena's building. He made it to his car with new skating bag. The car was started up and drove away.

Standing in front of the mansion's front door, Sally Hunt greeted Daniel Gray with a big hug and kiss.

She exclaimed, "Danny! You feel cold! Are you ok?"

"I feel tired." He relieved.

They walked into the house.

Joy & Paul were in the kitchen fixing up dinner. They were fixing up grilled chicken, beets, and side salad.

The Hunts saw their daughter and future son-in-law in the room.

Surprised Paul announced, "Well, if I didn't know better, I'd say you just came back from a figure skating session, Danny. You look tired and your cheeks are pink."

"Really?" Danny wondered.

Sally sweetly awed at her lover. "Awe, Danny. Are you doing figure skating lessons?"

To impress his future in-laws, Daniel Gray proudly spoke, "Yes, I am doing private skating lessons with a skater named Allison. She's pretty good. As good as Sally."

When Joy Hunt heard this, she sternly replied, "That's a good start, Daniel. Did you use the money my husband gave you?"

"I bought a pair of figure skates." He showed the Hunt's his proof purchase card to them from his wallet.

"What kind?" Paul Hunt huffed.

With his left hand wrapped around Sally's right hand, Danny said, "Male Platinum Classic."

Mr. Hunt was surprised at Sally's fiance. How could he have known his favorite type of skates? His eyes looked closely at the young Pet trainer.

"Did Sally tell you that secret of mine?" He asked.

"No." Daniel truthfully said. "I went to the rink's store and the employee who fitted me the skates told me about your type of skates."

Paul seemed to like Danny a lot more than he already did before.

The four went to the dining room for dinner.

They talked about ice skating stuff and a few times Daniel would jump into the conversation with a thing or two from Allison's figure teachings.

He asked sunshine Sally, "How's the costume project coming along?"

"It's coming along well, Danny." Sally cheerfully said. "Mommy and I were doing some newer and flashier designs for this season."

His heart hurt when he heard Sally say, 'flashier designs.' He hoped she wasn't going to show off a lot of skin.

Danny wished to have one special date with her before she did her first competition routine. He wondered, "Would it be all right if Sally & I had the day to ourselves tomorrow?"

Mrs. Hunt did not like that idea.

"No, Daniel, she can't." Joy strictly said. "Sally, has a special physical exam tomorrow for the Senior Ladies' Regional competition on Sunday, the twenty-third."

"Oh . . ." He sighed sadly. "Never mind."

Dinner time with the Hunts was over and Daniel headed back for his unit to take care of Butch. The two happy boys walked to the dog park after Butch had a tasty dinner. Butch played with other dogs. Danny played with his beagle and all the different types of dogs that were at the park.

The fun-loving dog trainer thought more of his future skating lessons with Allison. He hoped she was going to be fair with him when it came to learning all the different skating terms and skills that figures do on the ice.

His mind thought more of Allison's surprised teachings with a hockey player. He could detail out more of his Figure Instructor with the beefy guy. He had wondered why the figure skater was not scared to be around that muscular dude.

Like he thought before, *maybe the two were old skating friends or something.*

But it seemed to the Pet trainer that the puck chaser was no first timer in hockey skates or think what hockey was like as a six year old boy.

When the sky was getting cloudy, Daniel and his faithful fury friend left the park for the apartment building. The boys made their way home carefully in the dark of night.

As Danny and his dog were having a peaceful evening walk, alone and out on the big ice rink with soft music playing from the rink's speakers, his Figure Instructor, Allison, was struggling of the fact that Sally Hunt's fiance, Daniel Gray, asked her to help him figure skate.

She knew Sally's mom, Joy, was going to keep her sunshine daughter away from Danny during competition season. That must be Danny's reason on why he had to ask some other skater to show him how to figure skate instead of one of the Hunts.

Allison kept herself busy and get rid of her frustration by doing a lots of hard-to-do figure combo jumps, centered spin positions, and fast-paced dance steps.

She did feel happy to practice more on the ice.

Her heart was happier to help out Danny and the mysterious hockey dude in their skating skills earlier that day. Her novice figure student was going to take her a while make him be a good skater. The puck chaser on the other hand was in good hands for his evening's game after a few helpful tips.

The Figure Instructor worked on some dance steps.

While her blades made turns and steps, Allison wished she knew from her new figure student was when Hunt's wedding date was so she would know how long she had to suffer by showing figure skating to her competitor's lover boy and what kind of level schedule she needed to create for Danny.

She finished the steps when an idea came to mind.

Maybe teaching Danny how to figure skate could be useful for Allison. If she started out slow with her student's figure skating lessons and move him up fast after he breaks in his skates, then his future mother-in-law would see what a passionate figure skater Allison really was by teaching a normal guy how to be a wonderful figure male in a matter of months.

Back at the apartment building, Danny unlocked his unit's door and slumped inside. He unleashed his dog, put away his coat, and went for the bathroom.

Butchie-Wutchie reached his water dish and drank all the water in his green ceramic bowl. Then he slowly went toward the bedroom. He found his pillow and laid on it.

A minute later, Daniel exit the bathroom for the bedroom. He tipped toed in so he would not wake up his sweet dog's sleeping slumber. He silently changed his clothes for something to wear for bed.

The dog trainer's eyes were tired and his heart was getting more and more scared by becoming something that he, or any other normal guy, would really detest on doing. Being a perky, graceful male figure skater and spinning, jumping from the toe-picks, and dancing around the ice like crazy.

Daniel could not ignore the stipulation he agreed with Joy, Paul, and Sally Hunt. He loved Sally so much, he was willing to go the distance in the world of figure skating to have his girl's heart permanently.

"Oh, Butch . . ." He whispered to his sleeping beagle dog, "What have I gotten myself into?"

Chapter Four

The morning fog was rolling in when Danny woke up from Butch kissing his face with his pink tongue. He laughed and told his beagle dog to stop. Butch got down from his master's bed for the front door. He sat there patiently so his owner could take him to the park.

First Danny showered, put on clean jeans, green t, and his tennis shoes. He also wore his synthetic coat. Then had a little breakfast. Warm coffee and a bagel with cream cheese.

The faithful beagle remained sitting by the door. Daniel attached Butch to his retractable leash. The door open and closed before Butch hurriedly ran out of the building to do his doggie business and to the dog park.

Daniel did his best to stop worrying so much about Sally and her special physical checkup that day. He kept reminding himself, *There's nothing wrong with Sally. It's only a normal exam procedure for her to ice skate competitively. Her mother & father know what's best when it's skating season.*

Butch and Danny came back to the unit feeling tired.

The happy beagle went to his water bowel for a long drink of water and headed over to his soft pillow for a long, soothing nap.

What Danny did throughout the rest of his Sunday was rest his achy body on his couch from yesterday's skating time at the rink and thought on his two promises that reflected his future. His professional promise to Jack Randell by interacting more with the dog's owners. And his skating promise to Allison with his figure skating lessons.

Daniel only had a short amount of time to excel both his stipulations. He did not know which one was most important. Losing his pet training job, or losing Sally?

His heart was very satisfied with what he already have, but to stay on top of his game he needed to prove himself worthy by getting over his fears. His fear to talk to the dog's owners and his fear to learn a new sport that was not fun or cool to him or any normal guy.

So much he needed to do in his life, Daniel Gray was not sure where he should start to solve each problem.

His mind had one question.

Do I have what it takes to fulfill both promises at the same time?

His heart hoped he did.

Monday and Tuesday work days were the same as always for Danny. Get up, take Butch for a walk, go to work, come back to his unit after training time, had dinner, went on another happy walk with Butch, and he could only talk to Sally for no more than fifteen minutes. They told each other they loved and missed each other very, very much. He was also looking forward for his new skates and lessons with Allison.

Wednesday was his toughest work day to go through.

Nine a.m. he walked through the back door, stored his stuff away in his locker, fixed up his uniform and was ready for his dog training day.

Eleven a.m. he was having the time of his life by pet training the dogs until an unexpected middle-age lady with short dark brown hair and brown eyes who was dressed in a purple t shirt, white pants, and slip on black shoes came to the training booth with a little white fluffy dog and brown purse in her arms.

The lady asked, "Excuse me!"

Daniel used his clicker to click three times and the dogs were quiet. They all sat down and did not bark or move from their 'stay' position. He turned around to face the woman who was calling out for him. He answered, "Yes, ma'am?"

"Is this the pet obedient training booth?" She wondered. Her little white fluffy dog was struggling and barking out loud.

"It is. I see your cute Samoyed dog doesn't like to be held." He sweetly observed. "May I?"

The lady handed her dog to the pet trainer.

"Oh, you're so cute!" Danny happily exclaimed to the unhappy dog. "You look like a cute fluffy toy!"

He held the soft dog tightly. He did reach in his left pants pocket to give the little Samoyed a biscuit treat. She excitedly ate the biscuit.

The lady requested, "Can you train her to behave when it comes to meeting new people and being held?"

Daniel professionally told her, "Absolutely! Let me try something with her."

He turned away from the lady and put her dog down on the floor.

The white dog's owner was confused. She asked, "Aren't you going to show me what to do?"

Daniel Gray gulped.

I wish I can say, 'no,' but Jack told me to try to show the dog's owners what kind of training they should do. He thought in his head.

He turned his body around and said nervously, "Okay. Let's try something."

He let the lady in the booth.

The Samoyed's owner was shocked to see all the dogs were sitting and not making any noises when people were in the booth. Something else came to her mind too.

"Where are the dog's owners?" She wondered.

Danny explained, "They usually dropped their dogs off and let me train them myself."

The lady stated, "That doesn't seem fair for the owners. A pet trainer who doesn't show the dog's owners what to do to train their own dogs."

His heart was hurt. He never thought he would see the day when a customer would be mad at his dog training technique.

"Ma'am, I was never one to show people what I can do when it comes to pet training." He sadly admitted.

"You must have for your pet training test." The upset lady protested.

Danny still remembered his pet training test. It was the only time he did show the dog's owners what to do to obedient train their dogs.

He sighed, "Yes, I did. But I'm not comfortable to do it again."

"So, it's only you in the booth with the dogs?" She strictly asked.

"Pretty much." Candid Daniel spoke.

The lady lost her trust with the Pet Store's dog trainer to pet train her Samoyed dog.

She picked up her dog and had some words to the young trainer. "You listen to me, young man. I signed up to be taught how to train my dog. If the employees don't follow what's been said in the sign in sheet, I feel you're not being a good dog trainer."

When that was said and done, the lady and her dog up and left the booth.

Danny was worried. He knew his boss, Jack, was going to find out about this soon. He calmed his heart and went back to work with the dogs. His eyes noticed the lady talking to Jack Randell.

An arrow stung the dog trainer's heart.

The two were arguing about her getting her money back and Daniel heard, "I demand you find a better pet trainer than your lazy freeloader!"

Upset Jack went to a cash register and gave back the lady her refund from the pet training. She and her dog strictly left the pet store.

The pet store owner went to see Danny.

"Daniel." He ordered him. "A word please?"

He clicked the clicker again and all the dogs sat down with their muzzles closed.

His boss complained, "Ah, Danny. Why did you let that happen?"

The dog trainer nervously said, "I can't show people how to train their dogs."

"Do you want to lose your position?" His boss disappointedly asked.

Weak Daniel shook his head.

Jack Randell eyed at the dogs. They were all still and continued to stay quiet.

He blew out a big sigh and warned him, "One last chance. Please, interact more with the dog's owners. If this happens again before your next employee evaluation, you're a stock boy."

Danny tried to say strongly, "Yes, sir."

He turned around and trained the dogs with the clicker and treats.

When four p.m. came, his heart felt relief. He could go back to his unit and enjoy on being with his dog.

Daniel made it for his unit and Butch was waiting by the door. He lowered to his sweet beagle for a long hug.

The two boys went on a long walk.

As they made it inside their unit home, Butch went for the bedroom and was happily sleeping on his pillow.

Danny changed out of his street clothes and into his normal night clothes. Just before going to bed, he was surprised that Sally called him.

They told each other they missed each other and Daniel did tell Sally about his tough day at work.

She felt sorry for her fiancé's work day. Their voices said their 'I Love You's and 'sweet dreams'.

Danny closed his eyes and drifted off to sleep.

Thursday and Friday work days went normally for Daniel and he did not receive another complaining customer or stern chat with his boss.

After taking Butch for a walk on Friday night, Danny changed his clothes into a white t shirt, black loose sweat pants, black light weight cotton socks, and his small blue sweater. He also got his orange card proof of purchase and his skating bag with his skating supplies. Including a rag he rarely used.

Butch noticed his master gathering a black and red bag. His black eyes looked sad and he started to yelp at his master. He wished he could go where his owner was going to.

Daniel was feeling scared and nervous again. He thought about Allison and her skating skills. His heart was feeling better after figuring out his teacher was as much as a pro like Sally Hunt. But his mind remembered seeing his Figure Instructor talking and helping out a hockey player. Now he was unsure if he really wanted to learn skating from someone who knew figure and hockey.

He happily told his sweet beagle dog with his skating bag in hand, "Well, Butchie-Wutchie, wish me luck."

Butch stood up on all fours and yelped once.

Danny laughed at his wonderful friend and left his unit for a car ride to the skating rink. He made it to the rink in good time. He exit his car with his new skating bag in hand.

Inside the rink, Daniel paid for admission and asked for his Male Platinum Classics. A female worker behind the counter went to the workshop. She came back and presented Daniel his bran new figure skates.

His skates looked beautiful to him. The suede material were very black and the blades were shiny and sharp too.

The female worker did tell him, "Make sure you don't cut yourself with these blades."

Danny listened to the worker's advice and got his bright red plastic guards from the skating bag to place them on the sharpened blades. He safely carried his new skates upside down in his right hand.

There were empty benches to sit at so the Pet trainer decided to put on his new skates. He sat on a bench and his fingers nervously unlaced his tennis shoes.

He fixed his socks and lifted up his right boot to slipped it on his foot. His right foot flexed to make sure the boot was properly aligning his foot and ankle. The new boot and inside padding felt comfy to him.

The boot raised up and the back part of the plastic guard stood there for the beginner skater to lace up his skates.

Danny leaned over so his fingers could start lacing the boot from the bottom and work his way to the top. The laces were very new and silky to his touch.

Not too tight or too loose. He kept reminding himself in his head. Lacing up the new boots were making his feet snugged in the boot. He knew in time the boots would break in nicely and would not feel discomfort from the figure boots.

After lacing up both skates, Daniel slowly push up off from the bench in his new figure skating boots. His knees bent forward and raised both boots to see if he laced them right. He walked around the room a few times and felt ready to go out on the ice.

He gathered his things and his feet were carefully moving toward the public quarter lockers and stored away his things. Then he turned to the rink for his first skating lesson with Allison.

Daniel walked toward an open gate door, took off his guards, and stepped on the ice. His eyes saw Allison out on the ice, skating her heart out.

Her eyes saw Danny and glided up to him by.

"Hi, Danny!" Allison spoke cheerfully.

"Good evening, Allison." Danny replied.

He was starting to feel cold out on the ice.

The Figure Instructor suggested, "For tonight, you are just going to skate around the rink without worrying about learning certain tricks and such. You need to break in your skates before practicing figure skills."

"Sounds good to me." He sighed happily.

As Danny and Allison started to skate around the whole rink, he questioned her, "Allison, forgive me for asking you this but why were you teaching that big beefy dude hockey last Saturday afternoon?"

The Figure Instructor was stunned. She stopped herself from gliding and stood by the wall next to them. Her face looked upset to her student's eyes.

Daniel held on the wall to make himself stop skating.

He solemnly spoke, "I'm sorry. I can see that was none of my business."

Allison strictly replied, "It is none of you business, Danny. Just concentrate on your skating skills and don't worry about me teaching others about skating."

She skated away from the wall to let go of the frustration her student gave her. Her legs and feet made her skate fast forward and backwards.

At the center part of the rink, Daniel watched Allison do a wonderful centered figure spin with her leg behind her and the upper part of her body leaning forward. She ended the spin by standing up, her right boot crossed over her left boot, and pushed out of the spin with her right blade on the ice.

He was surprised to see the brunette figure girl gliding back to the wall he was standing at.

Her tired voice said, "I feel better. Let's skate."

And the two figures started to skate around the crowded ice rink for most of the whole public session.

The Pet trainer did fall down a few times. He was glad his Figure Instructor was there to give him some more helpful pointers on how to skate without falling down so much.

Danny did get a little better during the last half hour of the session from his first try in his new figure boots. They were starting to hurt his feet.

Before their session ended that night, the Figure Instructor suggested to meet the next morning for a special off ice training. They would meet in front of the arena seven a.m.

Daniel liked that idea.

Allison told him, "First wear street clothes and bring some comfy workout clothes in your skating bag, a hand towel, and a water bottle filled with cold water."

He mentally penciled on what to bring.

After his first time on using the new skates, Danny moaned and groaned. His achy and sweaty feet were killing him from wearing a new pair of figure skating boots.

The Figure Instructor advised him, "Rest your feet by stretching them and wiggle them carefully. Also, when you have 'nothing' to do, walk around in the skates for a little while to break them in more."

Allison's tips sounded good for him.

He stretched and slowly moved his tired feet around in circles in front of him. His breathing went back to his normal rate and his feet were still hurting him. His legs and butt were getting sore as well.

The two figure friends both cleaned their blades with rags and stored the skates in their own bags.

Allison had some presents for Daniel. She said, "Danny, here are some books for you to read about figure skating and the skills."

His eyes saw a couple of big sized paperback books and one small white book with a black spring on the edge. He took them and put them in his skating bag.

"Thank you." He tiredly replied, "I'll take a look at them."

She smiled and asked, "Did you have fun?"

Daniel insightfully answered, "Besides falling down on my ass a lot and getting my feet very sore, it wasn't that bad."

"Good."

Then Allison was curious about Danny & Sally's wedding plans. "So, when's the big day?"

"Of me & Sally's wedding day?"

"Yes." Ally said.

Danny shrugged. "I don't know now. Sally and Joy are doing the planning."

Ally was disappointed. She wanted to know how long must she suffer with Hunt's Danny for skating lessons.

"Would you tell me when you do know?" She asked.

"Why?" Danny wondered.

"That way I can create a schedule for your skating lessons and get good before the wedding." Ally explained.

The Pet trainer spoke, "I'll ask."

"Thank you." The Figure Instructor happily said. "Rest up tonight and I'll see you tomorrow."

"Looking forward to it." The Pet trainer cheerfully spoke.

He grabbed his skating bag and left the ice rink for his unit home and Butchie-Wutchie. He got settled into bed with his cell in hand.

He called up Sally and told her all about skating in his new skates.

Danny groaned, "Ohhh, my feet are really in pain, Sally-babe!"

His eyes saw his feet turning pink and feeling very stiff. His legs were achy too.

"Well, that happens to all skaters with new boots, Danny." Sally sweetly said.

"I miss you and I Love You." His heart felt sad by not being with his girl.

"Awe . . . I Love You too and miss you like crazy." Sally's honey voice spoke. Her lips kissed over the speaker.

Daniel did the same too.

His fiancee asked, "Was Allison good to you tonight?"

"She's a wonderful instructor." He admitted.

Sally did tell Danny, "This coming Sunday morning, Mommy said it's okay for you come over for a special breakfast and plan a little for the wedding."

"I'll be there." He promised. "Have you set a date?"

"Valentine's Day!" She squealed.

Daniel thought that was a cliche date. But it made his girl happy and he spoke, "Sounds good to me, babe."

They whispered their 'I Love You' s and good-nights.

He hung up and set up a six a.m. alarm on his cell.

What he concentrated most was not his off ice training with Allison. It was the troubled work hour with the lady and her Samoyed dog. Even his boss, Jack, was pissed off because Danny was not trying to show dog obedient training to pet owners.

He thought during his last skating hour, *Allison never had a tough time teaching me or others how to skate. She's a strong knows what to show people certain skating techniques.*

An idea popped. He made a mental note to remember to ask Allison what her secret was when it came to teaching others how to figure skate.

The dog trainer's heart was a little relieved and closed his eyes for a goodnight's rest.

Daniel Gray's ears heard a ringing tone coming from his cell phone.

Must be six a.m.

He rolled out of bed and whistled, "Butch. Time to get up for a walk."

The sweet beagle got up from his pillow waited patiently by the front door.

Danny dressed himself for their morning walk. He sadly said to Butch who was being a very good dog, "Sorry this morning walk is so early this morning, Butchie. Allison and I have a special off rink training."

Butch did not mind. All he wanted his walk.

It was a fair morning. He and Butch walked around the neighborhood for half an hour and went back to their unit home.

Daniel opened and closed the door.

Butch immediately went for his green water dish for a long drink of water.

Then the human showered, put on his street clothes, gathered his skating bag with the essentials his Figure Instructor wanted him to bring, and left his unit for his car. The drive was soothing in the dawn of day. He made it to the rink in good timing.

Allison was already there with her car. A very shiny white convertible. The top was down and she was standing next to the convertible wearing a light purple t-shirt, comfy black sweat pants, and purple and white N+ running shoes.

Daniel parked his car and got out.

He spoke out, "Nice Horundi!"

Allison was proud of her German Horundi convertible. She smug, "Thank you!"

The Pet trainer walked toward his Figure Instructor. He asked, "So, what's the plan?"

"I'm taking you for a drive to the gym I normally go to and have you do some workouts with me." She happily explained.

She unlocked her car's doors.

They both got in the Horundi and the car drove off from the rink's parking lot.

During the drive, Ally and Danny talked a little. The novice figure student did tell his teacher when the blonde champ wished to get married on.

Allison was surprised that Sally & Danny's wedding date was on Valentine's Day. She needed to do some serious skating teachings for Daniel to accomplish in four months.

The drive lasted for forty minutes.

Allison's car was parked in front of a huge gym building. It looked bran-new. A three-story high, light tan, rectangular stone building with some see-through glass windows and silver windowed metal doors for the front doors.

Allison advised Danny, "Just stick close to me."

His nodded 'yes' for her idea.

The two got out of the Horundi convertible.

Daniel grabbed a hold of his skating bag's strap in his left hand while his figure instructor carried her nice navy blue gym bag in her right hand. He followed his Figure Instructor for the gym building.

Inside the cool-looking gym building from his eyes was a huge open area for black and dark gray colored cardio work-out equipments, another big area for new white and black weight training machines, a special corner filled with lots of mats and tables for stretching and such.

He noticed the smell of chlorine from his nose. His eyes saw another see-through glass doors that showed an enormous swimming pool, hot tub, and a small wooden box for a steam room. And opposite from the swimming room were a staircase to the second floor and a huge tan wooden door with and silver door handle and no windows on that door.

Pumped up music was playing from the building's speakers and there were ten massive flat screen TVs around the cardio area that are connected to the ceiling with strong metal poles and wires.

Danny did feel happy to be in that kind of gym.

The Figure Instructor went for the check-in counter by the front doors. She said, "Hey, Becky."

Daniel waited for Allison.

The African American employee staff behind the counter was dressed in a yellow work shirt and black pants greeted Allison, "Hey, Allison! How are you?"

The figure quietly respond back, "Good, thanks. Me and this gentleman would like to use the track and an empty studio room this morning."

She dug inside her gym bag for her member card. Her fingers found the card and handed it to Becky.

Becky did see a cute guy a few feet behind Allison.

Danny's legs were getting stiff. He walked around the front door to make them not stiff.

"Ooohhh, are you and he hooked up?" Becky softly snickered.

She took Allison's card to scan it on the scan gun. It made a little chirping noise that indicated she was checked in properly.

Allison rolled her eyes and unimpressively whispered to the lady employee, "No, nothing like that."

"Ah." Becky sadly spoke and handed back Ally her member card and a key for one of the studio rooms. She leaned in closer and asked, "Figure student?"

"Yes." Allison unhappily admitted.

She really did not want to teach Sally's fiance how to skate, but if she did maybe Danny could help her out with her secret mission in figure skating against the Hunts.

Daniel Gray continued to wait patiently for his Figure Instructor. He was not listening or paying attention what the girls were telling amongst themselves.

The Figure Instructor needed a huge favor from the gym. Her mind thought on how long would it take for her figure student to be good on ice with some workout training.

Allison whispered, "You wouldn't mind giving Danny three free months by coming to the gym with me, would you?"

Becky thought and thought of the figure's request.

She professionally stated, "You know we can't."

The figure pleaded again, "Just add it to my bill. I have to do it."

The dark-skinned lady staff seriously wondered, "Why? If you two aren't together, why do you have to be nice for him?"

The Figure Instructor turned her head to see Daniel. He was standing by the front doors with his skating bag in hand and being extra patient with Allison.

Her head twisted back to face Becky and explained to her, "Danny is Sally Hunt's fiance. If he does not learn how to be a good figure skater, he can't marry Sally."

Becky was shocked.

"Oh . . ." she softly gasped, "never thought Sally Hunt's parents would force someone she liked to do something like that."

Daniel was getting the feeling that coming to the gym was a huge waste of time. He turned his attention at his instructor. He was upset because she was still talking to the staff member behind the counter.

He thought, *What the fuck are they up to?*

He sighed unhappily and moved from the front doors to check on his Figure Instructor.

Becky lowered her head to a computer screen and began typing rapidly on the keyboard.

Danny asked, "Is everything all right?"

Allison assured her student, "I think so."

Becky announced to the two figures, "Okay. An extra month is added for your next three member bills, Allison. And Danny-"

He had the lady staff's full attention.

"You are allowed to come here only if Allison is here with you."
Becky strictly told them.

Daniel firmly spoke, "I understand."

He and Allison left the check in counter. He asked, "What took so long?"

She huffed, "I had to think of a way for you to come into the gym without getting you in trouble."

"Don't they have guest passes?" Daniel wondered.

"Yes, but it doesn't last for more than a month." Allison put in.

Danny thought she did a really nice thing for him.

She showed him where the men's locker room was. Before he walked through the open door, Allison said, "Here, you'll need this."

She gave him a lock. It was silver with a blue dial.

She also whispered in his right ear what the lock's combination was.

He took it and went inside the room.

It locker room was huge, clean, and some half-naked guys were showering, dressing, or cleaning from a worked out morning. His mind thought of the lock's combination.

Daniel found an empty locker.

He put the bag on a bench behind him. The bag was unzipped and Danny took off his tennis shoes and jeans to exchange the jeans for his sweat pants. His cell, car key, wallet, and jeans were zipped up and stored in the locked up locker.

He grabbed his cold silver water bottle and a light green hand towel. His legs strutted himself out of the room.

Danny's eyes saw his Figure Instructor standing by a wall in a different outfit too. Her t-shirt and shoes were the same, but the only thing she changed was her sweat pants. She was now wearing tight black shorts to show off her leaned toned legs and ass. Her brown hair was styled in a long braid with a black hair tie at the bottom.

Even Danny admit that Allison was one hot-looking babe, but his heart longed for Sally more than his Figure Instructor.

She saw her student and encouraged him, "Are you ready for a good workout this morning?"

He proudly answered, "Lead the way."

Allison and Danny went for the staircase. She had her mp3 phone in her left hand and touching it with her right hand.

While the two walked, guys in the gym were whooping and wowing at the figure skater's workout outfit and killer bod. Daniel was surprised that Allison was unimpressed of guys whooping at her.

He concernedly wondered, "Aren't you bugged about those guys howling at you?"

"Nope." She stated.

The two started to walk up the metal staircase.

"Then why don't you date one of them to get them to shut the hell up?" He curiously questioned his steamy looking instructor.

Allison softly groaned. She detested the idea about going out or being involved with a guy.

"First off, no guy had actually asked me out for a date, and secondly, I still think men are selfish, arrogant, horny pigs." She strictly explained.

"O-kay." He hurtfully said as a guy whose heart had been crushed.

Daniel accepted Allison's honesty when it came to guys. "I can understand why you feel that way."

She calmly said, "Thank you, Danny."

The staircase ended and they made it to the second floor. His eyes noticed that the second floor was only an indoor black carpeted track. He was going to enjoy working out with Allison if there was track or running involved. The only thing that could make it better was if Allison was Sally.

His figure instructor instructed him, "Let's do a little warm up before doing actual workouts."

Allison went for an mp3 player dock that was on a table and connected her phone to the dock. The dock was connected to speakers around the second floor indoor track. She grabbed the dock's small rectangular remote.

Danny placed his water bottle and towel on the dock's table.

"You ready?" She breathed in deeply.

"I'm ready." Daniel excitedly answered.

She raised her right hand and used the remote to turn on her phone's music 'Pump' playlist. The remote was slipped in a tiny pocket of her black shorts.

Danny and Allison started to run around to the song 'Delusional Madness'.

Allison loved to run with that kick-ass song.

She ran strongly, but her student carefully listened to the music's beats and kept up with his instructor. She was impressed that Daniel was keeping with her to her favorite running song.

She pointed out, "You've ran before, haven't you?"

Danny breathed and confessed, "When I was in high school, I'd done track."

"That's a good advantage, Danny." Allison steadily spoke out loud. "Keeping yourself active on the ice would impress Joy & Paul Hunt a lot."

Daniel was grateful to learn that little helpful clue to win over Sally's parents. He was more curious on what other hints Allison knew about the Hunt's knowledge in ice skating.

The two figures kept their running pace, breathed in comfortably, and just listened to the tunes from the speakers.

The Pet trainer was breathing more heavily than Allison. She was not so tired since she trained herself to go on longer runs. But that did not make him stop running around the carpet track. Their warm up jog lasted for ten minutes.

When it was ten minutes into their jog, she grabbed the remote and turned off her phone's music player.

They stopped by the speaker's table.

Daniel leaned forward and was breathing and coughing.

He gasped, "Shit. Hadn't done that—in a long—time."

Allison happily laughed at her figure novice's defeat.

Danny's body felt warm. He went for his water bottle and sipped three long cold drinks. His free hand got his towel to wipe off the newly formed sweat from his brow.

The Figure Instructor took her phone off the speaker's dock and headed for the staircase. Danny followed her.

He did feel very tired after that jog. Maybe he should get back into running if this was part of his off ice training.

Allison and her student slowly made their way down the stairs and he wondered what was next for their workout. His heart hoped that he was going to have the chance to get his muscles work with weight training machines.

When Daniel made it to the first floor, he breathed out, "So, where are we going now?"

The Figure Instructor described their workout plan, "To a studio room to do some special strength training."

His heart fell down to his feet. He wanted to pump up with machines, not do fancy dance routines or stretches.

The Figure Instructor and her student went inside an empty studio room. Allison closed and locked the door with a key in case her figure student wanted to escape for the weight training machines.

She went over to a shelf. She picked up two small, smooth blue balls.

The Pet trainer placed his water bottle and towel on a table next to the studio's door.

He was puzzled. "What am I going to do with that?"

He so wanted to work out on weight training skills.

Allison explained, "We're not here to build up bigger muscles, Danny. The body of a figure skater is lean, toned, and flexible. I'm going to teach you how to do Pilates."

"Is that like Yoga?" Daniel confusedly asked.

She shook her head 'no'.

She told her figure student, "Yoga is a body stretching, meditation exercise that makes a person be one with their feelings and cleanses their heart, mind, and soul from anger, jealousy, envy, and hatred. Pilates is similar to weight training more than Yoga. Instead of your muscles working against a heavy, clunky machine, you're working against your own muscles and doing smoother strength training so your body would have a healthier, toner look."

Allison also said, "Pilates will even help you gain better balance."

"How?" Daniel wondered.

She stretched out her arms with both her hands holding out the small blue ball. Her body leaned forward and slowly lifted up her right foot off the hardwood floor as high as she could behind her. She kept her head up and not looking down at the smooth wood floor.

From Danny's point of view, he could have sworn his Figure Instructor was doing a banana split spiral. She did not lose her balance or get wobbly from her spiral stance.

Allison stood still for a full minute.

She lowered her right leg down to the floor and was back to her normal standing position. She took some deep breaths. Her left arm curled around her ball by her left side.

Daniel curiously asked, "How'd you learn to do that?"

"I used to take Pilate classes. When I got bored of the classes, I decided to work on my own and add in some skating exercises too." She answered.

Her right hand got out her phone and docked in the studio's speaker. She picked out her 'Pilate' playlist. A ballad metal song was playing.

She suggested to her figure student, "Let's do some abdomen workouts."

Allison and Danny did some standing crunches with the ball in both hands and close to them before working on floor crunches with mats underneath them.

For an hour, the figures did four different stomach strength training, five Pilate leg maneuver with or without bungie cords, three butt workouts, arms, shoulder and chest presses, and did lots of relaxing stretches in the end.

Lying on his mat and taking in some deep breathes, Daniel had to admit, after doing that ten minute jog he would not feel strong enough to do some weight training. Doing Pilate workouts was much more comfortable and easier to do.

After a five minute rest, Allison suggested, "Do you want to go for another run?"

Her voice did sound tired from doing their Pilate workout. Her student did not mind another run around the carpet track again.

"Absolutely!" Exhausted Danny exclaimed happily.

His sore body got up from the mat. His tired legs moved toward the table by the studio door for some cold water. He continued to remember what he wanted to ask her when it came to teaching someone on how to do something.

Allison put back the mats, blue balls, and bungie cords in the shelves and turned off her phone's music player. She and Daniel exited the studio room. Up they went for the indoor carpet track to do another ten minute run. During the second run, Danny was feeling more stronger in his running.

Their gym workouts came to an end.

Daniel went to the men's locker room. He found the locker with the silver lock and blue dial. He remembered the combination and it unlocked. The door opened and Danny changed out of his sweaty clothes for his clean street clothes. His left hand carried his skating bag while he grabbed the lock in his other hand.

Outside the locker room was Allison dressed in jeans, a white t-shirt, and her N+ running shoes. Her hair was fixed up in a downward ponytail.

She asked, "How do feel?"

Achy Danny replied, "Tired. But it's a good tired."

"Good." She spoke. "So, let's go for a skating lesson tonight that way you'll rest up from your first Pilate workout and runs on the track."

"Sounds like a plan." He happily said.

He wanted to hand back her lock, but her voice did say, "It's okay for you to keep the lock. I don't need it anymore."

So Daniel put the silver lock with the blue dial in his skating bag and the two ice skaters left the gym for a ride back to the skating rink.

Then he remembered what he wanted to ask her from the night before. The Figure Instructor's teaching secret.

Five minutes after leaving the gym parking lot, Danny wondered, "Allison, what's your secret by teaching someone how to ice skating?"

She was shocked from hearing that question. She slowly answered, "That's something I'll show you at the ice rink tonight."

Daniel did feel hurt of the instructor's response.

But she did tell out a little secret: "The big idea of teaching someone your passion is to show people what you do from the little things in life when you learned about so-and-so. For me and ice skating, or even something else I can do well at, I always have fun and make sure the person I'm teaching to are happy too. That's a reason why I ask you 'what do you want to learn?' You are my teacher too."

He surprisedly wondered, "How can a student be a teacher?"

The Figure Instructor giggled, "Daniel, everyone has a way of learning things differently from others. So for each person to be good at something, the teacher learns from their student's point of view of doing stuff and let the teacher figure out a way to do special teachings for certain students."

He listened closely to Allison's advice.

"For example, if a little kid wanted to learn how to do the 'twirly-wirily,' I would take one of their hands above their head and twirl them around for fun. But if an adult or teenager wanted to learn how to spin, I show them how to pump themselves around with their blades in an invisible circle and some of them would spin around pretty well from that helpful trick."

The figure student imagined in his head about her skating examples. He could picture himself doing a spin with her fun figure instructions. Their conversation from that topic was dropped.

At the rink's parking lot, Daniel told Allison, "Thanks for the workout."

His Figure Instructor spoke, "My pleasure, Danny. See you tonight."

He left her Horundi car for his car. He did feel achy after two-ten minute runs and a special Pilate workouts for an hour. His fingers went for his car key in the skating bag. The car was unlocked and he slipped inside on the cotton padded driver's seat.

Before starting his car, Danny sipped some more water from his bottle. He closed his eyes and leaned down in his seat for a few minutes.

When he opened his eyes, the white convertible was no longer in the lot. Daniel lifted up his tired self to sit up straight and drive back to his apartment unit. He hoped Butch was okay.

Inside the unit, Butch was happily playing with his Bong toy in the living room. His paws kept on pushing the toy around and his nose was digging inside the hole to get the rest of his biscuit treat.

His cute dark eyes were wide open when he saw his owner home. The beagle's tan and white tip tail wagged and his mouth was panting with a big smile on his face.

Danny tiredly said, "Hey, Butch. How you doing, pal?"

He went to his bedroom to put away his stinky workout clothes out from his skating bag and into his plastic dark blue clothes bin. Then he slumped over on his bed and rested. Butch joined with his master on his bed. He laid on top of his master's lap.

He knew he should have a long nap before his evening skating lesson. But Danny got his cell and called up Sally to see how she was doing.

A minute after he called her, he said, "I miss you a lot, Sally-babe."

"I long for you, Daniel Gray." She lovingly told her fiance. "I Love You."

"I Love You too." He groaned on his bed after feeling a muscle pinch from the back of his right leg. His free hand was rubbing out the pain.

Sally asked, "Are you okay?"

He spoke tiredly, "I'm a little achy. Allison took me to a gym to do some running and a Pilate workout. It wasn't that bad. Nothing like Yoga or something."

"Oh." Sally wondered. "Is she doing off ice work for your lessons?"

"Yup." Danny said while he was petting his sweet beagle with his right hand. He stroked the dog's soft fur and floppy ears.

"Allison told me what a skater's body is like and thought it would help impress your parents more if I did it." He explained.

"I am happy you're doing this for me, Danny." Sally happily sighed and her heart was filled with glee.

His love and passion for Sally grew more and more inside of him. "So, brunch and wedding plans tomorrow?"

Sally excitedly said, "That's the idea! Can't wait to see you again!"

"Me too, babe."

The two ended their conversation before Danny's tired eyes were fully shut and closed. His right hand kept on gently brushing Butch's soft fur.

Daniel instantly fell asleep as he did his best to continue petting the pooch.

Chapter Five

It was three-thirty in the afternoon when Daniel Gray woke up from his nap. His ears heard Butch whimper for attention. Danny slowly stretched out his achy, tired body in bed. He gently rolled over and saw Butch standing by his doorway. Butch lifted his head to howl a little.

The beagle owner knew he really had to get up and give his pooch what he needed. Potty break.

After he carefully took a warm shower to sooth his tightened muscle, ate a little chili lunch and soda, and put on clean street clothes, Danny found some baggies and the gray retractable leash.

Butch was leashed. Danny opened the unit door. His loving dog walked out first. He waited for his owner to close and lock the door. Off they went for their walk around downtown for the next hour.

It was five p.m. and the sky was cloudy when Daniel and Butch came back to the unit. The two boys drank some cold water. Danny's body did feel better by going on a good walk with his sweet beagle dog. He knew the off ice training was not going to be over until his future in-laws approved his skating skills. So he was going to experience more muscle pain than what he currently felt.

Then the human went for his closet to change into some sweat pants and long thin socks. He packed up his skates, wallet, and rag in his bag. His cell was in his left pant's pocket and keys in his right hand.

Daniel told Butch, "I'll see you later tonight, pal."

His dog did not seem to mind of his master leaving the unit without him. The playful beagle got on the couch for a long puppy nap.

The dog trainer closed and locked up the unit's door. His legs were still tired from the gym workout. He did not care or wanted to moan and groan from it. He remembered feeling that kind of pain before during his track years. He just had to get use to it again.

He made it to the rink a little before seven.

Admission was paid, skates were laced up, gloves were on, and he stored away his valuables in a quarter pay locker. Key was in his pant's right pocket.

Before walking out of the lobby, his eyes saw his Figure Instructor at the center of the rink talking to a small crowd of people who wanted to learn a skating move. She pushed her skates around to do a spin. The other first timers tried it. Some did good, others wobbled and fell on the ice.

Danny remember what Allison told him in her car about teaching people how to do spins or the 'twirly-wirily.' She did look happy and the people she was talking were happy too.

He felt ready to skate that night. He walked out of the building's lobby in his figure skates to skate around the rink.

Through the door metal glass doors, he felt the cold wind blow around him and his ears heard loud music playing from the rink's speakers. He walked slowly to the rink's swing door.

His red plastic guards were off and his blades touched the ice. Daniel skated slowly around the crowd of skaters. He noticed Allison was still in the center and teaching people how to do a spin. He decided not to bother her now.

What he did was glide around the rink five times before going over to his Figure Instructor for his lessons of the night. He did fall down on his ass, sometimes he held on to the wall, and his ankles did not feel comfortable in his skates.

Danny said, "Hey, Allison."

She turned around and respond, "Good evening, Danny."

He eagerly asked, "So, have you figured out an answer for my teaching problem?"

The Figure Instructor's head was tilted upward to the side and listened closely to the next song that was playing.

"Not now." She announced. "It's time for me to have some fun on the ice!"

She skated away fast from her student to rapidly glide around the rink with another kick-ass song was heard from the speaker.

During the song, Daniel stood at the center and watched Ally do high jumps, lots of graceful spin combinations, and fun dance steps to the beats of the song. He wondered why she needed to do that.

The song ended and Allison went for the center. She did feel tired, but was filled with determination to teach Sally's Danny how to figure skate. "Now we can get to work."

Daniel questioned his figure instructor, "How come you do that?"

"Because all teachers need to have some alone time with their passion!" She smug.

He understood what she meant by that.

Then Allison asked, "Well, Daniel, what do you want to know about teaching?"

He took a deep breath and sort out his unpleasant, job-related thoughts.

Daniel gulped, "I think I'm going to lose my job soon."

Still standing at the center of the rink, the figure teacher knew this was not the place to talk about his professional problem.

She suggested, "Let's get off the ice."

He agreed to her idea and the two figures glided off the ice. Their guards were on their blades. They walked in the lobby and sat on an empty bench.

After sitting there for a minute of silence, Allison wondered, "What do you do for a living, Danny?"

She did feel sorry for her figure student's statement.

Why is he losing his job? She thought in her head.

He told her, "I'm a dog trainer."

"Awe . . . That must be a fun job." Allison sweetly spoke.

"Thank you." Danny sighed disappointedly.

"What is wrong with your dog training job?" She questioned him. "Dog's aren't behaving or something?"

Daniel shook his head 'no.' "I can't . . . I . . . don't . . ."

He angrily groaned and felt chagrin how to tell Allison about his job problem. In his heart were full of strong, painful emotions that could not be let out all at once. He got up from the bench and made his way to the ice rink. Took of his guards to skate off his embarrassed feeling inside of him.

The figure student made it around the cold rink a few times. He did feel pleased that Allison did not skate with him or wanted to talk more. All he wanted was to have a clear head before explaining his profession problem.

Allison was on the ice herself, but she was practiced some advance dance steps to another song she liked from the rink's speakers. Her boots, entire body, and arms moved gracefully like a ballerina. She smiled big and looked very proud to be a wonderful lithe figure skater.

When the song ended, Daniel's mind did feel much better. No pressure or the uncomfortable feel to tell Allison his on-the-job problem. He glided over toward the figure at the center of the rink. She gave him a friendly smile when he reached her.

"Do you feel better?" She slyly wondered.

Danny breathed out, "Yea, I do."

They both started to skate around the center to talk and figure out a way to overcome his stage fright.

Then he asked Allison, "How do you do it? How do you understand figure skating from the inside out?"

"Danny, I've done this for years and ice skating never gets old for me." She started out.

She turned around to skate backwards.

Her voice spoke out loud, "I learned a lot from watching other people skate, the kind of training or warm-ups they do off ice, read many ice skating books, and always asked questions to my coach and other good skaters how do they improve their skills and their way of learning something new."

She also put in, "And I never get tired of learning more in this sport. I still continue to work on the basics before I do advance skating skills."

Learning how to teach others about something was getting easier for Danny to comprehend.

Finally, he admitted his work problem to his Figure Instructor. "I'm afraid of teaching the dog's owners how to obedient train their dogs."

Allison was shocked and stopped skating backwards.

Why is he afraid of being an instructor for the dog's owners? She thought in her head. *If I did not love figure skating so much, that would be a very fun job for me to do.*

She insightfully replied, "I kinda understand why you feel that way."

"I don't know why I can't teach in front of people with their dogs." Danny fearfully said. "Being around dogs makes me more happy and comfortable to teach them good dog behavior."

After spilling out his secret, the novice skater quickly left the center to skate around the whole rink a few more times. He did feel wobbly in his figure skates and fell down a few more times.

His Figure Instructor watched her student glided on the ice. Her eyes noticed his figure boots and blade more. They were not moving smoothly and gracefully. She needed to teach him fast.

When she felt ready, Allison bravely skated next to Danny. She turned around in front of him to face him. He saw her in front of him. They skated forward for most of the session.

Ten minutes before public session ended, she questioned her student, "Have you told Sally about your Pet training job problem?"

Again his head shook 'no.' He nervously respond, "I'm too embarrassed to tell my fiancee and future in-laws that I might lose my job position soon."

"Why? Did something bad happen?" Allison concernedly asked.

"Last Wednesday, a lady with a cute Samoyed dog came to the training booth for a little training time. I was about to teach the lady and her dog some obedient skills when she noticed the dog's owners were not there." Daniel replied. "Now, she doesn't trust me with her dog and she thinks I'm a lazy pet trainer. She complained about the problem to my boss, Jack. Jack did warn me before to interact more with the dog's owners, and yet, I still don't do it."

Allison carefully imagined in her head of Daniel Gray's dog training problem. She was understanding the picture.

He continued to say, "My next employee evaluation is in three months and if I don't talk to the dog's owners about dog training, I'm going to lose my position and have my old job as a stock boy. That's why I need some teaching assistance. I do not want to give up my passion to obedient train dogs and puppies."

Now that she knew the whole story, the figure confidently promised, "I won't tell Sally or her parents your secret."

It was 9:59 p.m. when an idea came into his mind.

"Allison, besides ice skating and gym workouts, could you somehow teach me by being an overall pet instructor with dog owners?" Daniel requested.

The lady announcer's voice was heard from the rink's speakers, "You're attention please. This concludes this evening skating session. Everyone off the ice, please. Thank you."

The newly figure friends skated off the cut up ice.

At an empty bench with their skating bags and shoes by their side, Allison answered Danny's previous question on the ice, "Sure. I would be happy to help. What is it that you want me to do?"

Daniel and his instructor were whipping off the extra ice, snow, and water off their blades with their rags. He thought and thought about a plan. Another idea lit up his eyes, but he stopped himself before he explained his plan.

"Um, I did think of a way for you to help me, but I realize it has to be done in secret or Joy & Paul would think I'm cheating on Sally." Danny sighed.

His Figure Instructor thought carefully with that statement. *Don't want to get Joy Hunt mad because her daughter's lover might be getting close to another female figure.*

Daniel and Allison's skates were cleaned and dried. They put away their figure skating inside their own bags.

"Well, what is your idea?" She curiously wondered.

He breathed out, "I have a dog. He's a sweet beagle named Butch and has good behavior for a dog. Maybe you can take him over at your place for a night, have you pretend to be his owner, and you ask for my dog training advice at a dog park or at the pet store I work at."

Allison figured that was a good idea. It was a good thing she had a big loft and nothing breakable for his beagle to destroy.

"That's a good plan, Danny." She softly agreed. "Do you know when you want to do this?"

He leaned in close and whispered, "Let's wait a while. For the meantime, I have to act like I'm involved with some of Sally's wedding plans with her parents."

Allison assured him, "It's okay. We'll talk about it during our next skating lesson tomorrow afternoon."

Danny had a good feeling to be good friends with Allison on and off ice.

It was 10:30 p.m. when they finally got up from the bench with their skating gears and went their separate ways for the night.

The next morning for Daniel was brunch time with Sally and her parents. He dressed himself in a nice dark green dress shirt, tan slacks, and dark brown dress shoes. His sweet beagle, Butch, was tired from his morning walk and had a full tummy from his snack earlier that morning. He was sleeping happily on his comfy pillow.

Dressed in a warm coat for the cloudy weather, Danny exited his apartment unit for a car ride to his fiancee parent's home. He arrived there at eight o' clock.

Sally Hunt greeted him warmly with a big hug and kiss in the front door's doorway. She was dressed in a long flowing, cream color, long sleeved dress with white low heeled shoes and a black thread embroidered flower on each shoe. Her blond hair was all curly around her sunshine face.

Daniel thought his fiance looked very gorgeous that morning. They walked together in the mansion hand-in-hand.

Brunch was wonderful in the Hunt's comforting dining room. Eggs, waffle, fruits, hash-brown, sausages, bacon, coffee, and the topic they talked about was figure skating.

The figure novice took the chance of asking Sally about some of the terms. She was happy to explain some to her fiance.

Paul was glad of seeing his daughter & Daniel Gray together. Mr. & Mrs. Hunt was surprised at young couple using ice skating terms as the theme of their exchange use of words. It did remind the married Hunts of themselves when they were younger.

Danny became very happy after he & Sally's ice skating conversation lasted for more than a minute. But he knew he had a long way to go to win over his future in-laws' approval by marrying Sally Hunt.

Then brunch time was over.

All four cleaned up the table and stored away the dirty dishes in the sink. Paul and Daniel went back for the dining room table while Sally and Joy went upstairs to get something.

A minute later, Joy and her daughter, with big smiles on their faces, came back to the dining room with huge white folders in their arms. They put on the table four three ring binders.

"What's in the folders?" Daniel curiously wondered.

"My wedding plans, Danny." Sally happily spoke. Her right hand flipped open her decor folder. There were lots of pictures and hand written ideas on pieces of lined paper.

They all talked, debated, and discussed the locations of the ceremony and reception. Joy strongly suggested to have the ceremony at the ice rink and the reception at a nice hotel restaurant.

Paul and Sally seemed to like the idea.

Daniel did not. His heart fell to the floor. Doing figure skating lessons was bad enough, but getting married on ice was more than he could handle. He did not have a say in it since it was the bride's special day, not the groom's day.

Maybe Allison could help him get through an ideal wedding ceremony on ice.

Daniel was noticing Sally being very interested in the flowers rather than the rest of the wedding decors. He wondered if his fiancee had a secret passion that he did not know about.

The wedding plans ended as Joy spoke, "That's good enough for now. Next step is just for 'us' girls, Sally."

Mother and Daughter hugged each other tightly.

Their arms let go from a ten-second hug.

Sally got up from her chair and went for the backyard.

Danny lifted himself up and walked to the back doors in the kitchen. He stood by the doors. His eyes saw Sally kneeling on the grass and her fingers were playing with some Lilies, Carnations, Stephanotis, and Laelias in a small patch of dirt. She pulled some of them out to make a very pretty bouquet. Her eyes were lit up and her lips created a very big smile after the floral bouquet was fixed up perfectly.

The Pet trainer observed his loving girl be more happy just by fixing up a lovely grouping of flowers than out on the ice, performing or competing for ice skating events.

Sally put her cute little bouquet on a little brick wall by the back doors. She got up on her feet and smiled sweetly at Daniel, still standing by the back doors. He opened the doors for her to come in. She stepped in and their lips touched softly.

When the kiss ended, Sally moved to her right and washed her hands at the kitchen sink. Her hands were dried from a light green cloth towel on a rack by her left side connected to a cabinet box.

Daniel Gray & Sally Hunt walked from the kitchen to the living room, hand-in-hand. They sat on a sofa and talked for a little while longer. The sunshine champ brought up a special request.

"Danny, Mommy & Daddy said it's ok if we can go out tomorrow night."

"I like that."

Joy kept a close eye at the young engaged couple. She detested to see Sally lying next to Daniel on the sofa and their arms wrapped each other tightly.

"Joy, leave them be." Paul Hunt firmly whispered behind his wife.

She softly spoke, "I need to go."

Mrs. Hunt immediately left the mansion from the backdoors in the kitchen. Her eyes spotted something on the small brick wall. It was a bouquet of flowers made from the dirt patch. She knew who fixed the grouping.

"Sally . . ." Joy sighed unhappily.

She picked up the floral bouquet and professionally walked to the trash can. She angrily tossed them in there and closed the lid.

Then she made it to her ruby red SUV in the drive way. Joy turned on the car and drove off.

Danny & Sally said their 'byes and I Love Yous' twenty minutes after Joy left the mansion.

The dog trainer drove back to his apartment unit. He was greeted by his cute beagle at the front door. Both boys head over for the bedroom and Danny dressed out of the clothes he wore and into sweat pants and a dark green t-shirt.

After that was lunch in the kitchen. A yummy deli ham sandwich for the human and savory rice & lamb meat stew for the beagle.

It took the dog trainer a half hour to finish his lunch and get himself ready for his next ice skating lesson with Allison. He dressed himself in navy blue sweat pants and a light gray t-shirt with a blue sweat shirt. His feet had on thin black socks and his tennis shoes. The black and red skating bag was all set for Danny. The Pet trainer left the unit, went down the stairs for his car, and drove off to the skating rink.

At the rink, he paid for admission and immediately went for the lobby area. Before he sat on a bench, his eyes saw Allison and the same hockey dude from a week ago on the small ice rink.

Daniel went toward the small arena for a better look.

Both Allison and the puck chaser were skating in unison even though they were wearing different kind of skates. The two did figure dance steps, played with five black hockey pucks, and they seemed to have fun by being on the ice.

Just when he wanted to talk to Allison, he remembered what his Figure Instructor told him about her teaching other skaters.

It's none of my business.

The dog trainer headed to a bench and put on his suede figure boots. His boots were a bit uncomfortable on his feet after they were laced up. His feet wiggled to make room and break in the boots more.

Danny's brown eyes saw the Zamboni truck leaving the big ice rink. It was almost time for his skating lesson.

The driver parked the truck in the Zamboni box. He also pushed off the extra snow and water off the ice. The box's gate door was rolling down.

Kids and adults stepped out on the ice.

Daniel walked through the lobby's rink door. He felt the cold air blowing on him. His ears heard loud music player from the rink's speakers. Everyone on the ice were happy to ice skate.

Danny stood by an open gate door, leaned down, took off his guards, and his blades were on the glassy patch of ice.

The Pet trainer slowly glide around the rink in his suede figure boots. His feet struggled to glide smoothly like his sunshine fiancee and the brunette Figure Instructor.

After going around the ice a third time, Danny saw Allison and the hockey guy walking in the big rink lobby area together. They both looked tired from skating on the small rink. The hockey dude went to the men's locker room while Allison travelled to the door for the big rink.

Daniel Gray wondered if his Figure Instructor was not exhausted to go through his skating lesson. He decided to go easy on his teacher by not asking about the hockey dude or talk much during his lesson.

He skated and tired Allison caught up with him.

She greeted him, "Hi, Danny."

"Hi, Allison."

His lesson that day: skate around the rink to break more into his suede figure boots.

The Figure Instructor and her novice discussed when they want to meet for instructional training. The first Saturday of November and let Ally have Butch at her place on Friday night, then go to a dog park with a 'misbehaved' Butchie-Wutchie.

Later that night in Daniel Gray's twin-size bed, he called up Sally and they talked for a good half hour. She offered to take him out for dinner the next night. He accepted her offer. They ended their phone conversation.

There was one special thing Danny wanted to do before going to bed. Try to do some reading from the figure books Allison gave him. One of the oversized books talked about the history of ice skating, type of skating people can do, skates, blade styles, costumes, moves, fitness, and special training for competitors.

Danny could not understand what the moves are and what the skaters do to work on certain type of skating tricks. He closed the oversized book to read the little white book with the spring on the end. The book was a figure skating handbook.

In the little white book were what different levels are for beginners and advance skaters, what each level should the skater should master before moving up, and diagrams of traces for specific skills. Three turns, brackets, mohawks, rocker, counter, choctaw, and dance steps for freestyle, figure, pair, or couple, and dancers.

The Pet trainer could not understand what each skating term meant. He tried to reread both books again. His mind was feeling a headache coming on.

He tried to imagine how the skaters do their tricks from reading skating books. He can vividly see the skating tricks from Allison and Sally, but not know what type of tricks they were doing.

It was Danny's goal for his next skating lesson with Allison that coming Friday night. Her help him read skating terms.

Monday went well for Daniel Gray.

After his shift and arrived back at his unit, he took Butch out on a soothing walk for forty minutes. They returned to the apartment unit so Danny could shower, change his clothes, and get down to the building's front doors and wait for Sally's convertible to arrive.

Her car pulled up.

Danny rushed out from the building's front door for his girl's car. He got in and sat in the passenger seat. They kissed before Sally drove off.

They went to an authentic Japanese restaurant where the cooks would cook in front of them. The food was wonderful and very tasty. After that was movie time at a theater. And lastly, a long walk around a park.

It was ten p.m. when they reached Sally's car. Time for them to head home. The drive lasted for twenty-five minutes from the park to Danny's apartment building.

Inside Sally's car, Daniel requested, "May I take you out tomorrow night?"

Sally breathed out, "Not tomorrow night or the rest of the week."

His heart was crushed hard in his chest.

"Mommy and I are going to look at some wedding gowns most of the day on Tuesday. Then she and I are going to be busy on the ice for Regionals." She explained.

Danny understood. He leaned over and deeply kissed his blonde bride-to-be.

Below chest-level, both of the lover's hands held tightly. Their kiss parted slowly and their eyes looked into each other's hearts.

"I Love You, Sally-babe . . ."

"Love You too, Danny . . ."

The date ended as Daniel opened the passenger door and exit his fiancee's car. He pushed the passenger door back in its hole. Sally's convertible drove off into the night.

Danny did feel small and lonely without his beloved Sally Hunt by his side. He lumbered from outside the apartment building and into his unit home for a nice greeting from Butchie-Wutchie. Then the two best friends went to bed.

Work day for Tuesday was the same as Monday, but no date night with Sally in the end. He still did not instruct the dog's owners for obedient training. What the owners did was drop of their dog and leave the store or just hang around when the training time was over. Sometimes they would watch Danny instruct all the dogs together as if he was a teacher for young children and the kids were well-behaved.

He & Sally did talk on their cells after the Pet trainer took his beagle pal out for a walk and had some dinner. She did tell him she was very sleepy from going to five different stores and trying on over fifty gowns.

After their phone conversation, Danny was thinking of an idea what he should do for the rest of the night. A skating goal came to mind. Except, he more troubled by asking himself why was he so scared and afraid to talk to the owners on what kind of training techniques they needed for their dogs. His mind remembered back when he and Butch were doing some dog training together.

He read lots of dog training books, took little Butchie-Wutchie for obedient training, and worked what they learned as a team. But during those days, Danny did them by himself mostly. He did a little showing off in the obedient classes and felt no fear from being in front of people.

What changed? He needed to do something else that night.

Since Daniel Gray had 'nothing' to do, he decided to take up Ally's advice by breaking in his skates. His clothes were changed from his work uniform to his normal casual wear and went for his skates in the little black and red bag.

He unzipped the bag and his hands carefully took out his cool-looking figure skates. He never thought he would see the day to admire something his fiancee and her parents enjoy doing in the ice skating world.

Danny took off the black blade covers to put on the bright red guards on the blades. He sat on his bed, fixed his socks and the boot's laces, and slipped on his skates. Slowly getting up from his twins size bed, he walked into the sitting area where Butch was barking at his figure skates.

"Shhh . . . Butch." He shushed his beagle dog.

Butch stopped barking at Danny and went for his pillow.

Daniel found his unit's keys. His idea: to break in his skates would be to walk around the building until his feet are very tired and achy. He exited the unit and locked the door. His heart did feel chagrin by doing this little experiment. He had to get over his fear what other people think of him. This was one of the right ways for his feet to get used to the boots.

The Pet trainer walked around the hallways on his unit's floor. Thankfully no one was there to see him walk in his figure skates. His feet were starting to feel sore after walking around for ten minutes. He stopped in his tracks.

Without thinking on what he should do about his achy feet, Danny tried to wiggle his feet in his boots. The pain was getting to be less noticeable after he did that. He started walking around the floor until he felt as if his feet had enough for the day. Off he went for his unit.

Butch was by the door when his owner came back inside the room. He sat on the floor and wagged his tail as if he knew what time it was.

Daniel's stiff feet made it to the bedroom. He sat on his bed to unlace his skates, took the guards off the blades and put the blade cover on, and stored the skates in the red and black skating bag. His sore feet were giving him the same amount of pain he felt a couple nights ago during his skating lessons with Allison. He wondered if his feet were ever going to get used to the new figure boots.

He had enough energy to put on his tennis shoes, donned his coat, and got Butch's retractable leash for a comfortable, long walk. The two happy boys left the room for long walk around the city's downtown.

Two hours later, Danny and Butch returned to the unit and rested. Butch was on the couch next to his human friend as the human tried again to read the figure skating books he had. His mind continued to be confused with the how to steps for the tricks or moves.

Even his old dog training books were not that difficult for Daniel to read and understand. He did remember doing his old training years with Butch and a made up special game.

Four years ago . . .

While Sally Hunt was doing her ice skating off-season training, Danny Gray was working with five month old Butch on obedient training. The teenager really enjoyed reading dog training books. He tried them on pup Butch. Sometimes it worked, other times it would not work on the beagle pup.

Danny and Butch would normally be located in the backyard of the Gray's house and Danny would tell Butch what to do for sit, stay, lie down, roll over, come, how to go potty the right way, and paw shakes.

A few times Butch did forget to go outside for his bathroom time. Danny would always clean up after Butch's messes. His parents appreciated him for cleaning up after the puppy.

During his school days, Butch would be in the house with Mrs. Gray. But if she needed to go out and do errands on a warm sunny day, Danny's pup would be in the backyard and in a puppy octagon pen with toys, few treats, some food and water, and a special space for him to go potty in another enclosed pen fence next to the octagon pen.

Mr. Gray was kind enough to fix up two doggie doors for Butch and put plastic tube covers over all the electrical wires in the house in case Butch want to chew on the wires.

Daniel would always be happy and good to Butch. Worked on simple training with treats and the clicker. They did their best to have fun training in the backyard or somewhere else that's a little distracting to Butch.

Butch loved Danny being his owner. The two best friends had one very special game together. Hide-and-Treat.

Why Daniel decided to do that training game was because he admitted training the hyper beagle was harder than training his old golden retriever dog when he was a puppy. The sweet twi-bastard wished to hunt or discover new things more than do obedient training with his master.

Danny first realized he did have a different breed of dog and Butch was very energetic and curious about exploring bushes, trees, grass, different smells, and holes.

Then he remembered something he read from his good dog training book. It was in the 'Positive Punishment' section. A paragraph from the section had said, 'The reason for doing Positive Punishment is to do anything positive that was added to decrease punished behavior.'

Butch going on a hunt or scavenging in the yard during training time was a 'Negative Behavior' to Danny. The kind of attitude Butch should have for his obedient training time would be paying attention to his owner, not looking for something or someone to track down.

It was the kind of good dog training Danny needed to do for his loving beagle pup. Decrease the pup's attention to hunt stuff when he should be doing training.

For their first summer together, Daniel was thinking on what kind of game training would be good for Butch to learn from. Like a hunting game.

Early one July morning, Danny got up from his bed and he could not find Butch anywhere.

He left his bedroom and sweetly called out, "Butch! Here, Butchie-Wutchie!"

Down he went to the first floor, his ears heard a yelp close by. Butch was not on the couch, in the coat closet, behind the entertainment shelf, under the coffee table or the dining room table, or by the front or back door.

"Butch!" Danny worriedly spoke. "Where are you?"

His ears heard four yelps. It was coming from the kitchen. He got on his knees and the first thing he thought of doing was checking the doggie food cabinet. His fingers slowly opened the handle on his right.

His voice softly asked, "Butch?"

Arf!

The door was opened wide and inside was Butch with a little bone-shaped biscuit in his mouth. He was on all fours and his tail was wagging.

Daniel laughed at his cute beagle pup for being so sneaky.

"How did you get in there?" He chortled.

His hands picked up Butch. He felt his pup's mouth chewing and eating the biscuit. The dog food cabinet door was closed when Danny and Butch left the kitchen for the living room.

After seeing Butch in the cabinet gave his owner an idea for his training game. Have him hide the treats in his hands when it was time to work on obedient training and see if Butch could find the treat in which hand.

He and Butch worked on that training game and it worked. Daniel Gray could not believe he could get Butch's attention by playing that game. He was so proud, he showed his parents about the game. They were very impressed of their son's good dog training technique.

For more advance Hide-and-Treat training, Danny would secretly put treats or small toys around the house or out in the yard for Butch to find since he was a beagle longing to hunt and sniff out for doggie adventures.

The beagle pup did go through two puppy training classes for his first year. He also got the rest of his puppy core vaccines.

Daniel did not stop there for Butch's training.

The fun-loving beagle went through two more training classes until he reached three years old. He was very proud and satisfied that his little pup could be obedient when it came to good dog training time.

After graduating from high school and moving in to his current apartment unit, Daniel did train Butch how to be good when he and Butch were alone in the unit. The little red Bong toy with a treat inside helped and him having a little potty grass in the bathroom made things better for Butch and Danny by living together.

Danny's mind was back in the present and went to sleep with a confused mind from reading figure skating books.

What the dog trainer did throughout Wednesday and Thursday after his work shift and giving Butch his afternoon walk was listen to Allison's advice about breaking in his skates. He got into the habit of wearing his skates in the living room, kitchen, bathroom, going down the stairs for the laundry room, and around the floors if there was 'nothing' for him to do.

His feet were starting to get more comfortable in them when he took them off Thursday night.

Before going to bed, Daniel would read the figure books again. He still could not comprehend what the skating terms means from the skating books. He constantly wondered what his skating lesson would be like on the ice Friday night.

Chapter Six

The rink was really crowded Friday night.

Daniel Gray made it through the large crowd of people surrounding the rink and the admission desk. He paid for public session and was told to go to the small rink. Through a narrow hallway by the front doors would be the smaller rink.

The Pet trainer decided to put on his skates. He could not find an empty bench to sit on. He headed for the men's room. Inside, he found a metal fold up chair. He sat on it and slowly laced up his suede figure boots.

Danny was ready to skate that night.

Out from the restroom, he was not sure where to find Allison in this packed and noisy ice rink. He figured the rink was very crowded because Regionals was happening and lots of people wanted to see some of the good skaters skate.

Danny found an empty locker box to store and lock up his valuables. Kept the key close by in his sweat pants pocket. He slipped his small gloves on his hands.

Carefully, he did his best to walk through the throng of skating fans without kicking them with his new skates or shoving them out from his way.

What his ears heard from the crowd was an unusual cheer. "Ally-Loop! Ally-Loop! Ally-Loop!"

He knew where Allison was at. His eyes looked at the rink and his Figure Instructor was out at the rink all by herself, skating to a killer metal song, and was having fun by doing really high jumps, fancy dance steps, incredible fast paced spins, and unbelievably cool freestyle moves.

The crowd cheered for Ally's routine.

When the song ended, she bowed four times around the rink with a big smile on her face.

A male announcer spoke in the mic, "Wonderful job, Ally-Loop, and good luck this Sunday night at Regionals for Senior Ladies!"

Daniel's heart sunk.

Ally's competing too? Maybe she shouldn't be my Figure Instructor if she's doing the same competitions as Sally. His thoughts were heard in his ears.

He walked through the narrow hallway and stood by the small rink. Before stepping onto the ice, he took off his guards just how Ally would to her skates. The guards were placed next to a big swing door connected to the rink.

Danny breathed in the cold air deeply and lifted his right blade on the ice without looking down. Then his left blade was on the ice too. His eyes saw lots of other skaters, beginners or intermediates, crowding around Ally by the one of the small rink's gate door, talking and begging her to show them a thing or two.

Now would be a good time to skate around the rink. He thought to himself.

He slowly skated in his Platinum Classic skates around the rink once without falling down or holding on to the walls. He did exactly what Ally told him to do last Sunday.

Skating is like walking.

That was all he did after skating around the rink three times. His feet comfortably moved slowly and smoothly in his bran-new boots like he would with his tennis shoes. The boots still felt weird, but Daniel Gray knew it would all be worth it in the end.

By surprise, his right shoulder felt a finger tapping him. He stopped his moving skates by holding on to the wall. He turned around to see Ally standing next to him.

She loudly said, "Looking good, Danny!"

"Really?" He nervously asked, twisting his left boot.

"You really do." Ally proudly stated.

He speechlessly replied, "Thank you."

His eyes saw Ally's skating fans still standing at the center. He pointed out, "Looks like your fans are upset that you're with me instead of them."

"Oh, they'll live." Allison smug. "We have work to do."

She started to skate to the middle backwards and went as fast as she could. Then did a little wind up for a one foot centered spin.

Daniel knew Ally was going to beat Sally tomorrow for being that good on the ice. Her fans cheered and applauded at her spin.

She glided to Danny and spoke, "Now would be a good time to start with the basics."

"You mean getting up after a fall?"

"Nope."

Danny wondered what she meant by the basics.

Allison strongly explained, "Listen, you are doing a lot to impress the Hunts in four months so we need to work quickly. Basic skaters know how to do more than getting up after a fall and skate without falling or holding on to the walls. They know how to skate properly with the sides of their blades, skate forward and backward by doing little hip turns, and most importantly . . ."

She teased, "How to stop."

"Yeah, that would be very useful for me." Daniel admitted and hoped to learn how to stop that night.

Ally giggled and asked her figure pupil, "Well, what would you like to learn tonight?"

He breathed out, "Stopping would be nice."

The strong Figure Instructor went forth for a wall.

Danny was confused at Ally's skating action. He followed her.

From the loud, crowded rink's center, Ally and Daniel stood by the wall. She told him, "To learn how to stop, you need start by getting your foot to understand what a stop should feel like."

His ears heard scraping noise from Ally's blades. He lowered his head and noticed her left blade was making little a snow pile away from the wall. He confusedly asked, "Is that all?"

"Stopping while you're moving is harder than practicing against the wall." She strongly warned.

Allison skated away from Danny to show him how to do a stop while skating. She skated fast around the rink forward and just before she reached him, she stood straight up and her right boot was turned to the side and stopped next to him without falling down or feeling out of balance.

"See?" She huffed. "Your feet need to be ready when it's time to stop."

Daniel looked around the rink and watched beginners or first timers having a hard time doing a stop by falling down, holding on to the wall, or using their toe pick to help them. He understood what Ally meant. His left gloved hand held on the wall as his right foot began to scrape snow away from the wall. His new blade created a little pile of snow from his pushing.

Allison complimented, "Very good, Danny."

She joined with him.

At first she held on to the wall, then her right hand was moving away from the wall until she was no longer holding on to the wall while her left foot was still pushing away from her.

Danny wanted to try that.

He stood up straight, let his right foot continue to scrape snow, and the fingers of left hand were slowly not gripping the wall. His legs felt a little wobbly and lost his balance after his palm let got of the wall.

Ally knew that was going to happen.

Daniel stood back on his blades and asked her, "Why did that happen?"

She explained, "Because you're still new in figure skating, your boots and blades are new too, and you have not built up your own strength in both."

"My own strength in figure skating and my skates?" He curiously questioned his teacher.

Allison told him, "When I said, 'anyone can skate' it means everybody can skate, but every body have their own strength and weaknesses in anything. Strength is also known what they are good at or what their special talents are."

"What are your strengths?" Danny responded.

His right foot started to practice scraping again.

Allison thought and thought. "Well, let's see, skate without falling, forward and backward."

In front of him she stroked forward and did a little mohawk turn to skate backwards.

Then she yelled out, "Doing scratch spins."

His right boot stopped doing slow plows to watch what the figure was going to do.

She did a little wind up from her right boot while her left boot stepped in and did a centered forward scratch spin. The spin was ended with a smooth right foot back edge.

The Figure Instructor smug, "And doing loop jumps!"

Ally skated away from Daniel backward, did a few back crossovers, and with both feet she jump up, did two spin rotations, and landed on her right boot backwards.

The figure pupil's hands clapped at his teacher's amazing skills.

She skated back to her novice skater. "Does that answer your questions?"

"Yes, it does." He breathlessly answered.

The figure student wondered, "Is that why you're called 'Ally-Loop'? Because of your loop jumps?"

Allison laughed hard. "Yup. I love my loops!"

Danny's right foot went back to work on scraping snow from the wall.

Ally gave him a little tip. "When your right foot feels comfortable from doing all that practice scraping, hold on to the wall while skating forward and try to stop by doing snow plows."

That would be his skating goal for the week, if he could nail it correctly. He nodded at Allison in agreement.

She sweetly asked, "Anything else you want to work on?"

His voice excitedly spoke, "Skate without falling down and how to go backwards."

Ally's wise words insisted, "Let's not do backwards until skating forward is comfortable for you. We can work on forward strokes and crossovers."

She pointed out how beginning strokes were different from advance strokes. Beginners work with their toes like they're walking. Advance skaters would slightly push their blades to the side to skate faster than first timers.

Danny was also taught how to do forward counterclockwise crossovers that night. Little side pushes from the blade and crossing his right leg over his left leg. His feet were getting uncomfortable wearing his new skates. He fell on the ice quite a few times from doing crossovers and working on snow plows. Ally always cheered for her figure student by falling on the ice.

Daniel hated falling down. It made him feel like a failure. He complained out loud, "Why are you cheering after I fall down?"

She laughed loudly and spoke, "Because you are skating like a beginner! Beginners always fall down for their first few tries with something new! If they don't, they're not being a good skater or trying hard enough! The more you practice, the lesser times you will fall down!"

Ally's treating figure skating the opposite way from doing any other sport for the first time. He thought.

The time was 10 p.m.

Public session was over.

Daniel and Ally went inside the small rink's lobby to discuss their next meet. Tomorrow morning at the building for the gym and night for skating.

Saturday was a good day for Daniel and Butch.

They woke up early, had a good breakfast, went out for their morning walk, and made it back to the unit before six-thirty a.m. Danny gathered his skating bag and put on his skating clothes. He drove to the skating rink in his car.

Allison was already at the rink's parking lot. He got in her car and they went to her gym to struggle through 2 ten minute runs and an hour long pilate workout.

When they finished, Ally drove back to the rink's parking lot. Danny tiredly made it to his car and rested in the driver's seat for ten minutes. Then he was ready to go back to his apartment unit and Butch.

Before the time was six p.m., Daniel went inside his unit from his drive from the rink's lot, had a long drink of cold water, took a three hour nap, ate some lunch, went out shopping for human food and dog food, cleaned his unit, took his cute beagle out for a long walk, and rested on his couch with Butchie-Wutchie.

He did have a light dinner as he got himself ready for his skating session with Ally. His skating bag was packed up and ready to go. Danny said his, 'good-night' to Butch. Butch was sitting a few feet away from the unit's front door and he watched his owner leave the unit with the door closed and locked up.

Just like the night before, Saturday night at the big ice rink was very busy. Daniel paid public admission and went to the small rink. At the lobby, Ally was there talking to some skating fans. Danny sat on a bench not far from Allison and put on and laced up his skates.

The Figure Instructor noticed Daniel putting on his skates. She excused herself from the group of fans to talk to him before they hit the ice.

"Good evening, Danny." She happily greeted.

"Good evening to you too, Ally." He greeted back.

They took off their guards and skated around the rink together for the first and second hour. Ally had him work on stops, strokes, and crossovers. Danny would fall down a few times. His Figure Instructor would tell him constantly that he had been getting better from their last lesson.

When it was the third hour, he asked Ally, "Allison, I have been reading the figure skating books, but I am troubled by understanding each skating term and trick. Could you show me what they all mean?"

"I will, Danny." She promised. "But not tonight. In time you will comprehend all the terms and skills in no time. I want you to start out slow, and you will learn the new terms until you are ready."

His heart was disappointed with the news. He had to face the facts that his instructor was right when it came to figure skating. Learning a new sport and trying to do it all the skills in one day was not a good idea.

They skated around the rink for half hour more. The figure student's feet were too tired to continue on. The Figure Instructor agreed and let him go to rest up for their next lesson on Friday night.

Danny took off his skating boots. He cleaned the blades and put the covers on them. He was noticing some blisters were forming on his feet. On the sides and bottoms.

Now was a good time to rest up from wearing the boots for the day.

"So, I'll see you Friday night?" Ally asked.

A strange idea came to Danny's mind after hearing that question.

"Actually, I'll be here tomorrow for Sally's routine."

"Yeah? That would be nice for Sally." Allison softly spoke.

Her heart felt discomfort when she imagined Danny being at Regionals for Sally Hunt. She was jealous of Hunt to have someone special in her life. In the public's eye, all the Loop had was her skating coach. That did not count much as a friend for her. From private eyes, she did have a few selection of friends, but she could not see them whenever she wanted to.

Danny's skates and supplies were in his skating bag. He left the rink for his car. He drove home carefully with his blistered sore feet in his tennis shoes.

He safely made it to his unit and slumped on his bed. Before sleep took over his body, he called up Sally and asked her how she was doing.

Sally replied, "A little nervous for tomorrow night."

"Lots of fans were there for Ally."

"Good."

He warned Sally, "You know she's competing tomorrow."

"I know." Sally did not sound so scared after hearing his warning.

"I Love You." Daniel breathed, "Do your best, Sally."

"I Love You too." The figure champion told her man, "You know I will."

The two lovers said their good nights and went to sleep.

What Danny thought mostly the next day was Sally Hunt and Ally-Loop competing against each other. He never went to any of Sally's competitions ever since they met. This time, he really want to.

His gave Butch a walk.

Their walk lasted for an hour.

They went back to the unit so Danny could dress up and get to Sally's home before her and her parents go to the skating rink's building.

Daniel got to Hunt's house at four p.m. on the dot. Sally and her parents were getting inside of a beautiful ruby red SUV. He got out of his car and ran for the SUV.

Paul surprisingly asked, "Daniel?"

Danny got up to the vehicle and requested to the Hunts, "Hey, mind if I come?"

Joy, Paul, and Sally were very shocked of Daniel's request. They all thought what made him want to go to an ice skating competition?

Then Joy figured out why and gave in. "Of course you can. You'll learn a lot more from watching from the pros than just from your teacher."

"Thank you." Danny hastily replied and got into the car with Sally in the back seats.

Paul and his wife got in the front seats.

The SUV moved from the mansion to the same ice rink Danny went to the night before.

Daniel & Sally talked and talked about her routine for the night. Joy & Paul surreptitiously kept an eye on the two young lovers in the back seats. The young lovers held each other and whispered comforting words in their ears.

A thought came to his mind. Daniel wondered where Sally's skating bag and costume were at. They were not in the SUV vehicle. Seemed like an odd thing for the Hunts to do. Not bringing Sally's skating stuff for a figure skating competition event.

The SUV drove for thirty minutes was parked in a special V.I.P. spot in front of the rink's building. Before everyone got out of the car, Joy sternly spoke, "Sally, you need to go to the back entrance."

Sally whispered sadly, "Yes, Mommy."

"Why the back entrance?" Daniel suspiciously wondered.

"Because, Danny, it's to keep me safe from all the wild and crazy skating fans." Sally assured her fiance.

She left the SUV with her mother close by.

Daniel diligently kept watch at Joy and her daughter walking to the back entrance door and passing through the open door. He heard fear coming from Sally for some odd reason. Like she was tired of skating or competing against Ally-Loop or some other talented competitive skater.

Paul and Danny walked through the cold rink's, crowded front entrance. Paul whispered to his daughter's love, "Act like a pro and no one would think you don't belong here."

The Pet Trainer's throat gulped. He took some deep breaths and thought about all skating stuff Ally showed him the night before and he imagined that he could do those skating tricks too.

While both men walked through the throng of competitive skaters carrying their CDs or tape cassettes at the music/ check-in table, Danny asked his future father-in-law, "What do you think about when you come here?"

Chortled Paul answered, "Oh, sometimes I thought of the first time I nailed a double axel. I was nine at the time and man, my coach would be as sharp as a tack with my skating skills, but he was fair."

"Oh . . ." Daniel sighed.

Mr. Hunt and young Mr. Gray made it through the exclusive sitting area to watch the Senior Lady competitors practice their moves.

Danny was very shocked to see Sally out on the ice wearing her skating essentials. She was wearing a sunny yellow long sleeved and long tan sleeved skating dress. Her hair was also fixed up in a French braid with a headband on top of her head. His heart felt very happy to see his fiancee wear her engagement ring.

Paul yelled out, "Nicely done, Sally!"

He stood up to whoop and clap his hands.

Danny missed what his fiancee had done. He asked Paul, "What did Sally do?"

Paul sat back in his seat. He turned his head and whispered to Daniel, "Double axel jump."

Danny's eyes looked at the ice just in time to watch Sally leap up in the air from her left skating boot, did two spin rotations, and landed on her right skating boot.

"Yea!" Her father shouted again. "That's my girl!"

Her fiance felt jealous of Paul cheering Sally as 'his girl.' Sally was Danny's girl. Surely, she was not going to be Daddy's little girl in a few months.

Daniel saw Ally-Loop wearing a comfy long sleeved, plain, dark green skating dress and skated around the rink too. Some fans were cheering for her and Sally.

His eyes also saw Joy Hunt in a navy blue business suit with a white blouse and wore her special coach badge around her neck. She did not look so happy.

Joy's face was very strict and professional like with her arms crossed over her chest and her long curly red hair was pulled back in a ponytail by a small plastic hair clip. Then she reached in her left coat pocket for her phone. A few seconds later, she looked very angry from talking to the person who called her on her cell.

Daniel felt very unsure by being at in a cold building to watch his fiance do an ice skating competition event.

His ears did hear a loud whistle in front of him.

It was Ally-Loop standing by the wall.

Danny got up from his seat and went down the walkway to talk to his figure instructor.

She tiredly asked, "How you doing?"

"I feel silly by showing up here." He whispered and his body cringed.

"Any normal guy would feel the same way." Ally whispered back. Then she teased, "Maybe next time you should try hockey skates."

Danny shuddered at that thought. It reminded him of Walter and his 17th B-Day.

"Uh, I think figure skating is the way to the Hunt's marriage approval for their daughter." He spoke fearfully.

"Suit yourself." Ally reluctantly said.

She turned her head and noticed that her coach wanted to talk to her by waving her right hand. "Have to see what my Figure Instructor needs."

As Ally was heading over toward her coach, Sally forcefully pushed Ally on the ice with both hands and yelled out, "Do not put moves at my man, Ally-Loop!"

The audience gasped at Sally's illegal action.

Allison quickly got up and protested back, "Hey, I was not making moves on him! I only wanted to see how he was doing!"

Sally strongly scolded, "Don't get too close to him."

"Ladies, no rough housing." A male announcer spoke in his mic. "Do it again, you both will be kicked out."

They sadly spoke at the same time, "Yes, Gerry."

The angry rival skaters skated at opposite ends of the ice rink.

Daniel saw Joy was yelling at Sally by not being professional on the ice. Sally's eyes were full of tears and fear.

What he saw from Ally and her coach were of them talking and hugging each other after that hurtful push and misunderstanding. Ally felt better a few minutes later and went back to work on her routine. She did dance steps, worked on hard-to-do spins and really high jumps with double or triple spins in the air.

Danny was surprised that skating was all it took to make Ally-Loop feel better. He was sure getting lessons from Allison was better than from Joy Hunt.

Ten after five p.m.

From the walkway, Sally & Danny told each other their 'I Love Yous' and she went to the locker room to change into her costume. Daniel had not idea what Sally or Ally were going to wear for their routines.

Paul and Danny sat and waited twenty minutes for the evening competition to start. The lights dimmed and the rink was lit up.

A lady announcer spoke, "Good evening skating fans and welcome to Central Pacific's Senior Ladies' Regional figure skating event. We sure have a good group of talented ladies for the evening. First up is our own Sally Hunt."

People in the audience applauded and cheered.

One of the white spotlights was shown on Sally at the gates. She skated out to the lower part from the center of the rink in a light blue silky bodysuit and skirt with tan long sleeves and her polished white figure skates. Her hairstyle and headband were still the same.

Her stance was her arms wrapped around herself and her boots were crossed over. A second later, pretty classical music was playing and she started out by doing lots of turns on her right blade around the rink. She skated like a champion on ice by doing complicated spins, really high jumps with multiple spins, fast paced dance steps, and artistic freestyle moves.

Her routine lasted for two and a half minutes.

The audience, including Paul and Daniel, stood up to cheer for Sally's performance. Flowers and stuff toys were thrown on the ice.

She did her bows to the audience and immediately left the rink to follow her mother. Danny thought they were going to come back to the stands so he could hug and kiss Sally after doing a good job on the ice.

The Hunt girls did not go to the stands.

His eyes saw them going straight to the locker room. He wondered why they would go there first.

Daniel questioned Paul, "Why are Sally and Joy going in the locker room?"

Paul strictly replied, "Danny, forgive for saying this but that's none of your business. My wife knows what's best for Sally."

Sheesh. Danny thought. *Sally's not going to be your little girl any longer. She's going to be my wife when this competition season is over.*

Ally did not have her turn till four more skaters did their routine. She was dressed up in a hot pink, sleeveless, flashy skating dress and her hair was in a messed up bun with a hot pink hair tie. Her skates were covered up with her tights.

"Why are Ally's tights connected to her skates?" Daniel asked Paul.

Mr. Hunt explained to Allison's figure student, "There are tights long enough to cover the boot and a hook to keep the tights under the boot."

Paul sighed sadly, "Oh, no."

"What's wrong?" Danny wondered.

"I wished I brought my ear plugs." Mr. Hunt groaned.

The sound of high screeching keyboards and loud pounding drums were playing. Danny recognized that song. It was 'Vault!'

He understood why Ally would love to skate with that song. She started out by doing a fancy back spin with her left toe pick on the ice and her right blade was being spun around. She pushed out of the back fancy spin to do three big turns around the rink and did her first double loop jump.

Ally looked like she was having a lot of fun by doing loops and other jumps for the 'Vault!' choruses. Her smile was big and felt very proud to perform for the figure skating fans.

During the end of the instrumental part of the song, Ally leaned her body forward to do a freestyle stance with her left boot on the ice and her right boot was raised high up behind her. Then she stood up straight with her left foot on the ice, did a waltz jump, and landed on her right boot to do another freestyle stance on the opposite blade.

She kept doing her jumps after 'Vault!' was sung.

The 'Vault!' song ended.

Ally did her trademark lunge ending and the audience cheered and clapped for her routine.

Paul Hunt happily told Daniel, "Glad that's over."

Danny stood up and clapped for Ally. Paul was not keen of the idea that his future son-in-law was applauding for his Figure Instructor.

Six more lady figures skated after Ally and the evening's competition was over.

Daniel still did not see Joy or Sally after Sally's routine. He hoped his fiancee was doing all right.

Mr. Hunt said, "Now it's time to check out the scores."

He and Danny left their seats and saw what Sally's scores were. She was placed first. And Ally was placed second.

Danny saw Ally getting her silver medal and had her picture taken in front of a professional picture background with some bouquets of flowers from fans in her arms. She saw her student standing next to Paul whispering something.

Young Gray whispered to the man next to him, "I need to talk to Ally."

Paul warned him, "Don't take too long."

He left Danny and the skating rink's building to join his wife and daughter in the SUV.

Daniel waited a minute till Ally's picture time was up.

She tiredly walked up to him to say, "I'm really sorry about what happened earlier."

"It's cool, Ally." Danny spoke. "You did a good job."

"Yea, second place for the short program." Ally unhappily replied.

Her fingers played with her new silver medal.

"Just have to wait to see what tomorrow's going to be like." She sadly huffed.

"Tomorrow?" Daniel curiously wondered.

The Figure Instructor explained, "Danny, in the world of real competitive figure skating, we all have to do a short and a long program. Tonight was the short and tomorrow is the long version."

He responded, "I see."

Danny sadly asked, "Would you have time to teach me to skate?"

"Of course!" Ally cheerfully answered. "It will end on tomorrow night and I'll be back on the ice for Friday evening's public session at the small rink."

He did feel better after Ally told him her plan.

A new thought came to mind. "If you are going to be competing, aren't you going to too tired from your lessons and teachings with me? I don't want you to strain yourself or something."

Ally put down her flowers on a table and strongly instructed to her student, "Do not worry so much about my well being. I have done this for years and I am not backing out my teachings with you. It would be nice to have someone watch me practice my routines for fun and see what I am doing wrong so I could get better in my skills. Okay?"

"Yes, Figure Ally-Loop." Danny teased.

They both laughed.

When their laughter stopped, the Pet trainer insightfully spoke, "I take it this isn't the first time that you've done this."

"It isn't." Ally admitted. "Five years ago, a first timer wanted me to show it how to skate and after a few months of on and off ice training, the novice mastered all the basic skills strongly and gracefully while I was training for the up-coming skating competition season. We both helped each other and it was nice to have friends on and off ice."

She added sadly, "But that friendship could not last after the skater went off to do bigger and better things than sticking around here. People normally come and go in my life. I don't think I'm not meant to have someone long and lasting in my life."

Danny felt sorry that Ally was not able to have a close friend she could rely on when she could not ice skate or be away from the rink. Maybe he could be friends with her and make her not be so dwelled into figure skating all the time.

Then his mind thought over the hockey player Ally was teaching after the Pet trainer's first time out on the ice. He suspiciously wondered if that guy was her first student.

"So, Friday?" He wondered.

Ally nodded her head in agreement. She went over to the girl's locker room to change her clothes.

Daniel turned his back and left the rink to go to the Hunt's SUV.

The red car was still there. He was glad not to be stranded at the parking lot again. Danny opened the back side door and got in. He saw Sally and her parents happily talking.

She spoke happily, "Danny."

She leaned forward to kiss him and hug him tight.

From their kiss, her fiance whispered, "Good job."

"Thank you." Sally squealed and showed Matt her gold medal.

His eyes saw it. The gold color medallion was very pretty.

Paul drove the SUV from the parking lot back to the mansion house. The four left the vehicle and decided to sit, relax and talk in the living room.

Joy asked, "Daniel, did you enjoy this evening's Regional competition?"

He took Sally's left hand that contained her engagement ring. He strongly spoke, "Ice skating is a fun sport to watch. Especially with Sally out there skating."

"Good." Paul stated. "We're glad you feel that way."

Danny had another request. "Can I join with you guys tomorrow?"

Joy thought it over and decided, "You may come. But please don't talk to Ally during competition time. We don't want both girls to be disqualified because you wish to talk to Allison."

"I understand, ma'am." Daniel firmly agreed. "It won't happen again."

"Well, it's been a long night for us. Danny, it's best of you to leave so Sally can get a good night rest." Paul suggested.

Danny saw Sally yawned a big yawn and her eyes were getting tired. He lowered his head to kiss her sweetly.

He softly said, "I Love You . . ."

"Mmmm . . . I Love You too." Sally replied.

He let go of his love and got up from the couch for his car. He drove back to his unit.

Inside, he was greeted by his pal.

Daniel tiredly responded, "Hey, Butchie-Wutchie."

He leaned down to hug his beagle dog.

Danny let go of his dog and put on his coat to take Butch out on a walk around the cold dark neighborhood. He did break in his skates more in his unit later that night.

Chapter Seven

After Daniel Gray's Monday work shift, his cell phone was ringing. It was Sally.

"Hi." He answered happily.

"Good afternoon, Danny!" A cheerful honey voice said. "Would you like a ride to the rink today?"

"What time are you going to be here?" He wondered.

"Seven p.m." She put in.

His eyes noticed the time being ten after five. He told her, "I'll be ready by then. I Love You."

Under the cloudy sky, Danny hastily got into his car and started up his car. His ear heard Sally say, "I Love You too."

They hung up their cells before the Pet trainer drove out of the parking lot. The time was five-forty when Daniel made it to his apartment unit.

He whistled to Butch, "Butch, come!"

Butch got up from his comfy pillow and followed his sweet master for the kitchen. They had a quick dinner so Danny could shower, change his clothes, and get ready for Butch's afternoon walk.

The sweet beagle was leashed and the two left the unit for a short walk.

It was six-forty p.m. when Danny and his beagle dog made it back to their home. Butch drank some water and Danny drank cold soda.

He cleaned himself, put on some nicer clothes, and dashed out of his apartment home for the front door. He waited a few minutes till he saw the Hunt's ruby red SUV driving up.

Danny walked out of the building and got in the SUV.

In the car, Sally looked very happy to see him again. They hugged and kissed.

Paul made it to the rink in good timing.

Sally and her mother went through the back entrance without her skating equipment again. Paul and Daniel walked through the front doors. Danny saw Allison walking through the front doors too with her navy blue roller suitcase. He thought back what Sally told him why she needed to use the back entrance.

To keep me safe from all the wild and crazy fans. He could hear Sally's voice again.

Something did not feel right to him.

Then he heard Ally's voice calling for him.

"Hey, Danny!" She spoke loudly.

He responded, "Hi, Ally."

"How are you today?" She asked as she handed in her single purple cd cover case to the check-in table.

Daniel candid to his figure instructor, "My feet are a little sore from last night."

Ally got her lanyard badge and slipped it around her neck. She concernedly wondered, "Oh. Were you wearing your skates?"

"Yup." He admitted proudly. "I walked around in my skates."

He and Ally stepped away from the check-in table for the girl's locker room.

"That's good, Danny." She proudly stated. "The more you wear them, the lesser pain you will feel later on."

In front of the locker room, Daniel leaned toward Ally's right ear to ask her, "Do you know why Sally and her mom only use the back entrance?"

Ally eyed and strongly told her novice figure, "I do not know."

He sighed sadly thinking Ally-Loop would know why Sally was given more special treatments than Allison.

She left Danny behind after opening and walking through the girl's locker room to change her clothes.

Young Gray went to find Paul Hunt sitting on a seat at the stands. Mr. Hunt demanded, "Talking to Ally again?"

"Yes, sir." Danny truthfully said.

"Daniel, it's not a good idea to talk to other girls if you want to marry Sally." Paul strictly told his daughter's fiance.

Danny sighed, "I do not want to get involved with Allison. I was only wondering why Sally and Joy need to go through the back entrance. Ally and other skaters don't have to. I'm worried about my love, Mr. Hunt."

"Just do what I do." Mr. Hunt gave the young man a little tip about his overly protective wife. "Sally's a really good skater and my wife is trained to handle her special needs before, during, and after skating competitions."

Daniel Gray got even more curious about Sally's special skating needs. If her father or mother was not going to tell him, he was going to have to ask Sally to tell him her special figure skating needs.

The lights dimmed. Spotlights were on and a male announcer welcomed the fans and Sally was up first to skate.

Why is Sally always up first? Danny wondered.

Sally was dressed in a beautiful creamy white body suit and skirt with tan long sleeves on her dress. Her hair was in a French braid with a headband to match her blond hair color.

Her performance lasted for four minutes.

Danny hoped Sally was not going to be too tired from her long routine. Her turn ended and hurriedly went for her mother. The Hunt girls went straight for the locker room again.

Five skaters later, it was Allison's turn to skate. She was dressed in a ruby red, sparkly, short sleeved, skating dress and her hair was done in a bun with a ruby red hair tie.

Daniel had to admit, Ally-Loop's skating program was more entertaining and thrilling than his fiancee's skating routines. He wondered what kind of teaching techniques Ally was going to give him by letting her 'pretend' she was Butch's owner.

Six more female skaters skated after Ally's turn. The competition was over and the scores were read. Sally Hunt won first place. Allison Rigden won second place. Both girls were qualified to compete in Sectionals next month.

Paul Hunt and Daniel Gray went to the SUV for Sally and Joy. Sally was napping in the backseat and wearing her gold medal on her neck while Joy was softly talking on her cell.

Daniel wrapped sleeping Sally in his arms.

The car moved from the skating rink's parking lot to the Hunt's driveway.

Joy softly asked Danny, "Could you carry Sally into the living room?"

He delightfully answered, "Sure."

Danny slowly pushed Sally away from him. She laid back comfortably on the backseat. Her fiance unbuckled her seatbelt, his hands and arms lifted her out of the SUV, and gently carried her into the Hunt's mansion.

Paul and Joy were happy that Daniel came with them after all. The young pet trainer walked into the house for the living room and slowly lowered Sally on a couch so she could continue her nap.

He lowered his head and kissed her lips twice before leaving the house with Paul. He gave Danny a lift back to his apartment building.

Danny gratefully told Sally's father, "Thanks, Mr. Hunt."

Paul remarked, "I guess you really don't have other feelings for other girls, do you?"

Daniel Gray shock his head and stated firmly, "No, Sir, I do not."

He left the vehicle.

Paul drove off.

Danny knew what he needed to do next after he went inside the apartment building. A relaxing walk with Butch and strutted around the floors in his skates.

Tuesday at the Pet store was a normal dog training day for Daniel. He was happy that none of the dog's owners were there to mess him up or complaining his teaching skills. He still felt hurt after that rude lady and her misbehaved Samoyed dog came into the Pet store. At least she was not there that day.

He kept his concentrations with the dogs in the training booth.

Allison's Tuesday was very disappointing to her.

She knew if Danny wanted her to help him with his pet training teachings, she needed to watch him in action with the dogs and get an idea how a dog trainer is like to improve her figure student's dog training technique. So she tried to locate the Pet store Daniel worked at.

When Wednesday arrived, she received a call from her coach that there would not be a practice session that day.

"Good . . ." Ally breathed out after putting away her phone. "I'll be able to find Danny's pet store today."

She went for her laptop. She created a new list of Pet stores in the area. She saved the directions in her phone's GPS program. Allison left her loft for her Horundi convertible. She dressed herself in jeans, white sweater, and her N+ running shoes with her hair in a ponytail.

Ally drove around for an hour.

She made it to the fourth Pet store in her list. Her Horundi was parked in the lot and her eyes saw Danny's little blue car in the lot too.

"Finally . . ." She sighed proudly.

After exiting out of her convertible and went inside the wood-chip smell building, Ally casually wandered around the store. It was not long till she found the training booth. She secretly watched Daniel obedient train seven dogs in the booth.

He was really a good dog trainer with all those dogs.

It reminded Ally of her coach teaching little kids how to ice skate.

A silly idea came to mind.

I wonder what it would be like if Daniel was a skating teacher for young children instead of a dog trainer for dogs and puppies. Ally wondered in her head.

She was impressed of her figure student being a happy trainer for the Pet store. Except, she noticed more closely at the booth that the dog's owners were not in the booth. Allison was starting to get an idea on how to fix Daniel's teaching problem with the owners.

First thing she thought of doing was asking Danny if he had any books about dog training to understand dog training better. That way Ally would comprehend what an overall dog trainer should be with the dogs and how to properly interact with the dog's owners.

Allison Rigden left the Pet store without Danny noticing her there in the first place.

When his shift ended on Wednesday, Danny had dinner with Butch, went on a walk with him and called Sally to see how she was doing.

She told her loving fiance she was tired and was in need of a good long break from being on the ice. She also explained she & he could not see each other for a week.

That did not seem right for Daniel. He deserved to see Sally whenever he wanted to. She kindly answered it was best of her not to leave her parent's house for the next seven days. The only thing they could do was talk on the phone.

Danny knew her mother was on this. Joy Hunt hated him to take skating lessons from Allison. That was why he & Sally could not be together. But he was doing what he was told to do to win the Hunt's approval for marrying Sally. Him learning how to figure skate was the main thing to remember. It should not matter to Joy who was teaching him how to skate.

Daniel gave in to his fiancee's request. He pleaded when they could see each other again.

She told him, "The first day of November is when we can have a date."

"Thank you." Danny sighed happily.

Before ending their conversation, their 'I Love Yous' and 'good-nights' were spoken.

He needed to think of an idea for their date.

Something fun, special, and not ice skating related. His mind thought back on brunch time with the Hunts last Sunday. Sally and her unexpected love for flowers and creating beautiful bouquets. He had a net search to do.

He looked and looked until he spotted a Fall Floral Show that was happening in town. And in perfect timing too. He purchased two tickets, printed them and directions to the show, and decided to surprise Sally with them for their next date night.

Daniel continued to do his special off ice training by breaking in his suede material figure boots and rereading the figure books Thursday night.

He found his skating spiral bound handbook in the living room and did a little bit of reading in the basic level section. He studied for twenty minutes straight.

Two-foot and one-foot glides, swizzles and wiggles, stroking forward, crossovers counter-clock and clock wise, and snowplow stops. What he wished he could do was skate backwards.

Daniel was understanding the idea how to do backward strokes and crossovers too for both clock ways. He decided to try something new. How to step backwards.

"Left over right." He mumbled to himself.

Butch was looking strangely at his owner in the living room. Going backwards and doing weird foot steps.

The Pet trainer thought he was doing a good job trying to go backwards off ice first and then try it on ice in a few days.

He changed his circle direction by going, "Right over left."

Seemed to be working for him.

He did the figure pose while practicing backward crossovers. Head up, shoulders relaxed, hands at chest-lever, smile, head behind the shoulder, and let the feet and legs do the work.

"Maybe that's what Ally-Loop meant about practicing off ice." He spoke to himself.

Danny was glad to understand some of the basic skating terms. He did try to read about 3 turns, mohawks, and edges. Once again, he was stump of those terms. He was going to have to wait for Allison to show him some other time.

For the mean time, when he had 'nothing' to do, he would practice going backwards in his skates. Left over right. Right over left. Or just work on walking backwards in his figure skates and looking behind his shoulders. He hoped not to run into anything or Butch during those practice times.

Daniel went to bed that night with happiness and satisfaction from reading the skating handbook and trying out new skating moves. He even had a good idea for Ally. He should let her borrow his positive obedient dog training book so she could read it before their instructional time.

On Friday afternoon, Daniel Gray went for his unit, took Butch for a long walk in the sunny weather, went back home, ate some dinner, and was dressed for his skating lesson that night with Ally-Loop.

Skating was fun for at the smaller ice rink. He and Ally skated together with the basics. Skate without falling down. He was getting better at skating forward. Danny was looking forward on how to skate backwards.

Ally said, 'no' that night to teach her student that skating maneuver.

The Pet trainer was surprised at Allison's teaching way. If they needed to work quickly, he should learn to go backwards soon. But then, maybe Ally had figured out a skating level schedule for him.

He gave up from asking again and slowly worked on stops while moving. He was getting better at it. The dog trainer did fall down a few more times, but he would get back up and kept on trying.

Danny and Ally held on to the wall, worked a little stopping while moving and without holding on to the wall, and making his right foot understand how to stop as he glided.

Allison did show her figure student how to improve his crossovers around the center circle and the whole ice rink.

Daniel liked working on crossovers and just skate for fun. His boots were getting more comfortable for his feet. Maybe ice skating was worth doing after all.

The two talked about were his improved skating skills and how his skates were not hurting his feet anymore. Ally knew her figure student was doing a good job so far, but the breaking in part was not completed for him.

He wondered why.

His figure instructor explained, "Danny, for you or any other skater who really want to break in their own skates, it's not done when you're trying advance skating techniques."

"How is that possible?" He asked.

"As a skater works on something new, their feet and skates need to get use to the new moves. And since you're still a beginner looking forward to newer and complicated skating tricks, your skates will give your feet more pain." She continued, "From learning how to go backwards, doing little hip turns, edges, using the toe-picks for jumps, practicing spins, dance steps, and freestyle moves."

Daniel thought his boot breaking days were over. It wasn't. He had to trust Ally's teaching skills.

Ally was happy of Daniel Gray's skating improvements in only two weeks. She did secretly admit to herself that she was a good skating teacher. Even for men.

Without thinking, Daniel's right blade was pushed out to the side strongly and before running into Allison. He managed to do his first real snowplow.

The Figure Instructor announced, "That went well."

Daniel was surprised he was able to do a snow plow stop just like Ally. He exclaimed happily, "I want to do that again!"

He pushed his blade to skate around the rink once and with no trouble at all, Danny did another wonderful snow plow stop in his suede figure skates.

Allison's hands applauded for her student's accomplishment for the night. "Good job!"

She skated up to him and raised up her right hand. Danny raised up his left hand and their hands clapped for a high five.

He eagerly asked again, "Am I ready to go backwards?"

Sadly, Ally said, "Sorry. Not now."

"Can I learn something new?" He wondered.

The Figure Instructor decided to show her student something new to do on the ice. Forward crossovers clockwise.

Danny had a difficult time to go around the center the other way for crossovers. Doing left over right instead of right over left. It was a skating skill he had to work on.

Saturday morning went great for Daniel and Butch.

They had a tasty breakfast in their kitchen and a good morning walk around the city's neighborhood. The sweet beagle was happy to be on his comfy pillow after their walk.

Danny also got himself ready for a gym workout with Ally-Loop. He was getting better at running and doing Pilates for an hour long.

Skating was wonderful that night. The Pet trainer's skating moves had gotten better than the night before. Ally was impressed of him and her teaching skills.

Later that night in his unit, Daniel Gray called up Sally and talked for a little while before bed time.

She told him, "I am feeling much better than I did last week, Danny. Mommy took me to a soothing SPA all day for the past three days."

"That's good." He replied. "I glad you're feeling better."

They exchanged their 'I Love Yous' and ended their phone call.

The next morning, Sunday, was getting sunny and bright. Daniel was woken up from the sun's rays from the windows touching is face. He moaned and groaned as he lifted his body off his bed with his eyes closed.

Butch was getting up from his pillow too. His paw's nails were making tapping sounds on the hardwood floor to the kitchen for some breakfast. Danny got up and followed his fun-loving beagle.

He told Butch, "Looks like it'll be nice today."

The pet trainer feed his dog some dry kibbles and mixed in some canned beef together. Butch really enjoyed his meal. Danny fixed himself hot coffee and warm toast.

After finishing their morning meal, Danny dressed himself for the rain with his synthetic coat, hooked Butch's collar to his leash, and put some plastic bags in his coat pocket.

Out they went for a half hour walk in the warm, sunny weather.

When two got back, they were tired from their walk. The beagle's owner took his coat and hung it in his hallway closet.

The Pet trainer did want to try something first before going to the rink. He was determined to see if he could skate on the ice backwards. Maybe Ally-Loop would be impress that her student learned how to skate backwards without her help.

Danny went for his skating bag.

His hands grabbed his suede material figure skates, putted on the red guards for the blades, and sat on his bed to slip and lace up his skates.

His feet gave him a very odd feeling in his heart. They were very happy to wear the skates again. An ironic chuckle came out from his throat.

He walked out of the bedroom and made it for the living room. The handbook was on the coffee table. Danny looked inside the book for the backward crossover section. He found the instructional part to reread it carefully.

Daniel's booted feet practiced backward steps and crossovers. He did not forget the figure pose that was needed in most figure moves. Head up and looking behind his shoulders, arms at chest-lever, and letting his legs and feet do the work. He literally felt like he was really gliding backwards around the ice. Now if only Ally could show him or let him try the skill on ice. Maybe he could the next night.

"Try it slow first, Danny." He reminded himself.

It was a wonderful advice to remember from Ally-Loop.

Daniel Gray's figure boots worked on backward crossovers both clock ways for a half hour. His feet and toes were getting tired from his off ice practice. He hoped he would get use to it on the ice soon.

He went off to his car with more satisfaction than what he felt from Saturday night's skating session.

Daniel changed into his skating clothes, dark green t-shirt and black sweat pants, and carried his skating bag with his skates, guards, gloves, cleaning rag, and the small skating handbook. He even remembered to take with him his old dog training book for Ally to read. The time was six-thirty when he left the unit and saying, 'bye' to Butchie-Wutchie.

The dog trainer arrived at the rink's building a little after twelve. Parked the car, walked into the building, paid for the evening's session, and put on his suede material and guarded blade skates.

Just when he wanted to put away his skating bag in a public coin locker, Danny was stopped by Ally-Loop.

She greeted him, "Good afternoon, Daniel."

He responded back cheerfully, "Hi, Ally."

Ally had a surprise for Danny.

"Today and the for the rest of your skating time, you don't have to use or pay public lockers." She stated. "I made special arrangements for you to have a temp locker in the men's locker room."

They stepped over for the men's locker doors. Daniel was feeling content not having to pay for usage of the public lockers anymore.

Before he walked through the locker room's doors, Ally presented Danny a light blue piece of paper. On the paper had black handwriting on it. A locker number and the locker's lock combination.

Daniel Gray went inside the locker room alone.

The room looked like a normal locker room for athletes. Lockers, a long matted table, long open cubby boxes, and a nice men's room too. There was no one else in the room.

Danny found his locker number and practiced on the combination for the lock. The lock was unlocked. He put in his skating bag inside the box. He took his skating handbook. His locker was closed and locked up. Better than using the public locker. He decided to give Allison the dog training book when the session was over.

His hands wore his gloves when he exited the men's locker room. In his left hand was the skating handbook. The figure student was ready to skate. Especially his first time skating backwards on the ice.

Danny made his way to the cold ice rink with more excitement forming in his heart. His eyes saw Ally-Loop skating around the center of the rink doing advance combination spins. He was surprised he did not see the big beefy hockey dude again. That made the Pet trainer feel better to be on the ice with his Figure Instructor.

Standing by the gates, Daniel placed his handbook on a small metal table connected to the gates. He took off his guard one at a time so the blade touched the ice instead of the foamed floor. He started to stroke forward around the ice a few times counter clockwise. His feet were gliding gracefully and smoothly from the side of his blades instead of skating from the toe-picks.

Danny had to admit. He was skating faster than he did the night before. Much better than his first on the ice.

Fifteen minutes later, the dog trainer felt ready to do some backward skating skills. He skated for the center. Ally glided for the center too.

She commented, "You're really getting good, Danny."

He told her, "Thank you, Ally. You must be a great skating teacher if you can make someone like me into a good skater."

His Figure Instructor smug, "Well, I can be at times. What do you want to work on?"

That was the question he had been waiting for since this morning. He knew what he wanted to do.

Daniel nervously requested, "How to go backwards?"

Allison made a crooked right side smile after hearing that question again.

She strongly asked him, "Are you sure you're ready to go backwards?"

He nodded his head strongly. His heart felt more excited and happy to try out a new skating move.

Ally acted like a pro by instructing her student, "Try to do small crossover side steps."

She showed him right over left cross steps without gliding forward or backwards. Just little side steps on a painted line on the ice. She did not wobble or lose her steps from her figure pose.

Ally's always been a strong, well-balanced, bold figure skater.

Daniel started to imitate his instructor's form for side steps. Both arms out to the side, shoulders down and relaxed, head up, and slowly lifted up his left boot and blade to do left over right. He carefully followed her lead.

The Figure Instructor was impressed with Danny's skills. She wondered, "Have you been practicing this maneuver off ice?"

Then they did side steps the other way so they would not get into other skater's way.

"Yes, I did." Daniel admitted. "Without and with my skates on."

"Awesome job, Danny. That's a big plus for you." Ally-Loop happily spoke.

She and her student kept on doing side steps four more times both ways. They stopped doing steps in middle of the ice rink.

Allison had thought of a challenge for Danny. "Okay. Let's see you do some backward wiggles."

His mind remembered what wiggles were in the skating handbook. All he had to do was move his hips and skates in little twists.

Daniel made his left hip turn and then his right hip turn. He stopped there. He knew what could really help him move backwards. The gate walls. He headed for the nearest wall.

Allison was confused and baffled. She followed after her figure student.

Danny reached the wall and did a snowplow stop before his body touched the wall. He was standing backward. His left gloved hand held on the top of the three-and-half feet tall wall. Then his left hand pushed his body backwards.

He began to twist both side of his hips and skates. His figure pose was not up to par. Body not straight up, head looking down at his skates a little, and not keeping his arms up for balance.

The Figure Instructor watched Danny and figured out his backward trick. She giggle softly from his idea.

"Have the wall as a helper." She mumbled to herself. "That's clever."

Her eyes kept close of her student's movement from his hips and skates. She joined with him by going backwards herself with wiggles.

Danny saw Ally gliding backwards next to him.

"Hey, I'm doing it!" He excitedly exclaimed.

She also reminded him, "Just keep those twists moving and stand up straight!"

Danny stood up properly while moving his hips and skating boots. He was having trouble on how to keep on moving backwards as he stood up straight.

Figure student and instructor continued to skate backwards. They also talked about Danny's instructional time that coming Saturday. And if possible, her coming to the Pet store with Butch.

Ally explained to Danny, "If you want me at the Pet store, it should happen after Sectionals."

He understood the situation and would talk about it some other time.

Now was resurfacing time.

Ally and Danny skated off the rink forward. Their guards were on their blades before walking off ice and into the lobby. Allison sat on an empty bench while Danny grabbed his skating handbook off the metal table. He headed for the bench Ally sat on.

The two figure friends read more in the handbook about skating terms in the basic section. Daniel wanted to wait to learn the different fancy twist and turns that figures do on ice later in his skating journey. He was very satisfied he could move backwards well for his first time.

Danny went back to the men's locker room and stored away his handbook in his locker box. Ever since he started to skate on the ice, his locker's lock combination was the first thing that came to mind.

When the Zamboni was long gone and extra snow and ice went down the drain, Danny and Allison were immediately back out on the ice. They stood at the center.

Ally-Loop had a new challenge for the dog trainer to do. She suggested, "Daniel, don't you try to skate backwards without the wall?"

Danny knew then he had to step away from the wall as his helper and see if he could help himself glide around backwards on the ice. He started to wiggle is hips and boots strongly. Without thinking, he managed to move backwards without his helpful tool.

The Figure Instructor skated backwards with her student. She watched closely at Danny's skating pose and movement. He was standing tall with arms out, wiggling with his hips and boots, and looked over his shoulders so he would not run in or bump against walls or other skaters.

He kept on wiggling stronger and stronger. Sure enough, he was no longer at the center of the rink. He was heading for a corner.

"Daniel," Ally instructed her figure student, "now do left over right steps to avoid the corner."

Danny lifted up his arms, his head turned over his right shoulder, and his left boot stepped over his right boot. Just like how he did it in his apartment unit's living room. He did not bang his back against the corner wall and kept on moving backwards.

I'm impressed. Thought Ally-Loop. *Not many skaters could avoid that mistake.*

She was proud of Daniel by not running into the wall. She was even more glad of him to continue wiggling and not lose his figure pose too.

Danny did skate backwards around the whole rink once while doing the left over right crossovers. His feet were feeling tired and really achy after that challenge.

Ally kept up with him.

His tired voice requested, "Can we-work on-something-else?"

"Of course." She stated. "You did an awesome job this afternoon."

"Thank you," Danny breathed out, "I need to-give my-feet-a little rest now . . ."

His sore feet glided off for the gate doors. He got his guards and put them on the blades before stepping on the foam floor. Then Daniel made his way for the big rink's lobby area.

He lowered his achy body on a bench. He sat down and leaned forward slowly to unlace his figure boots. The boots were off his sore and sweaty feet.

Danny stretched out his legs and very carefully his feet were circling around. He flexed them gently, up and down.

Ally was right. Her figure student was not done from breaking in his boots. He definitely needed to listen and follow her advice in figure skating.

Daniel fixed up his socks and slipped on his skates.

Boots were laced up comfortably for Daniel's feet. He rose up from the bench and headed for the cold-air, ice rink for more figure lessons.

Allison was still skating around the rink and did a real good figure spin jump.

Danny took off the guards from his blades before he skated around the whole rink.

The Figure Instructor saw Danny back on the ice and gliding around pretty well. Much better than he did the first time they met two and a half weeks ago and literally begging her to teach him how to figure skate just to impress the Hunts. He looked ready for some more skating time.

Ally let him skate around the entire rink a few times.

Daniel's eyes spotted his Figure Instructor and skated toward her. She asked him, "How do you feel?"

He insightfully replied, "My feet a still a little sore from skating backward. Maybe I should stick to going forward for the rest of the session."

Allison let her student skate forward till public session was over. Their next skating lesson would be Friday night.

Yes . . .

Tuesday night was date night with his girl. He could not wait to see his love again. He wondered if Sally would like his surprise.

Daniel went to the men's locker room and remembered the lock's combination. His right hand turned the lock's dial. It unlocked when it reached the third number. He got his skating bag and valuables out from his locker box.

He sat on a cushioned chair. His fingers unlaced both boot's laces. The blades were unguarded, dried from the cleaning them with the rag, and the cloth black blade covers were on the blades. Danny's skates and supplies were in his skating bag. His feet wore his tennis shoes.

After leaving the locker room, the Pet trainer located his Figure Instructor, who was sitting on a bench and cleaning her figure blades. His left hand got out his dog training book from his bag.

He sat on the bench with Ally and said, "I brought you something to help me."

She looked up and saw a dog obedient training book in his left hand. Her right hand took it.

"Thank you, Danny." She sighed happily. "I wanted to ask you if you had any books I should read about dog training."

Allison stored the dog training book in her roller suitcase. The figure friends parted their ways and went on home.

Daniel made it to his unit quarter before five. Butch greeted him warmly in their bedroom. The loving human knelt on the hardwood floor to pet his pooch, who was happily napping on his pillow while his owner was out skating.

Both boys felt happy to be back together.

Twenty minutes later, after having dinner and exiting their unit home, Danny and Butch went out for an evening walk. The dog trainer knew his dog was going to have a good night's rest from a long walk and a full belly. They saw some dogs during the walk. Butch did not misbehave by barking or wanting to play rough with other dogs.

Butch's evening walk lasted for an hour. Both owner and his dog rested in the bedroom together. Danny in his bed and his sweet beagle plopped on his comfy pillow.

The Pet trainer called up Sally Hunt to tell her the exciting news that afternoon and the night before. She was proud of her fiance to practice backward strokes and crossovers on and off ice.

Their 'I Love Yous' were spoking meaningfully and said their 'good-nights.'

Chapter Eight

It was clock-out time for Daniel Gray from his Monday work day. He gathered his belongings inside his work locker and walked out of the Pet store building. He drove not to his unit first. He brought the Floral show's direction sheet to see where it was going to located at. It was easy for him to find the tent and headed back to his apartment unit.

Butch waited patiently for his human friend by the front door. His human friend unlocked and opened the door. Daniel smiled happily at his sweet beagle.

"Hey, Butch," he said.

The unit's front door was closed and locked up. He got down on his knees.

Butch scampered over for a big hug and friendly pet and scratching from his best human friend.

Daniel's hands and fingers rubbed, pet, scratched, and stroked the cute beagle's soft, short fur. He was happy to be home with his dog. He got up from the hardwood floor and changed out of his work clothes and into street clothes. Then it was time for the boy's walk. They walked around the neighborhood for an hour.

Butch was very happy by being a good dog for his pal during their walk. Danny felt the same way as his beagle did in his heart.

The boys arrived back for the unit a little before five-thirty p.m. For the rest of the night, Daniel wore his figure skates to work more on crossover steps and stroking smoothly.

Work the next day went the same always for Daniel Gray. He only taught the dogs how to do obedient training and letting their owners drop off their dogs. His heart was glad after his shift ended that day.

He needed to get super ready for his date night with Sally-babe at the town's Fall Floral show.

First things first, he went to his apartment unit to change into his street clothes, had a small bowl of pasta and soda to drink, and took Butch out for a long walk.

Secondly, the boys came back to their home. Daniel showered, put on nice outing clothes, dark gray slacks, normal green color dress shirt, and dark brown dress shoes, and grabbed the Floral show tickets.

Third, he said, 'bye' to Butch and left the unit. The Pet trainer went to the building's parking garage for his car and drove off for the Hunt's mansion. He made it at six p.m.

The Floral show tickets were locked up in the glove compartment.

Daniel Gray drew in some deep breathes. He got enough strength to go up for the house and take Sally out for her special surprise date. He exit the car and locked the doors. His legs walked on the front lawn and onward to the front door.

He stood nervously in front of the door. His right index finger pushed the door bell.

Danny waited a few long seconds before the front door opened. He smiled big until his eyes saw Joy Hunt behind the door. She was dressed in a pretty turquoise shirt and black slacks with her red hair pulled back in a bright brown hair clip.

"Oh, Daniel . . ." She snarled softly. "You look all dressed up. What are you doing here?"

He stated firmly, "Sally & I have a date tonight."

"Well, now, aren't you sweet?" Mrs. Hunt pretended to say nicely.

Danny blushed a little from that comment.

But Joy changed her attitude.

"I think it's wonderful that my future son-in-law wishes to take out my loving daughter out of her comfortable home and into the cruel, hateful world of shitty black darkness!"

"What?" He confusedly asked.

"I know why you really want from Sally, Daniel Gray, and you are not going to sex up my child tonight!" Joy scolded.

A harsh deep voice let out, "Joy! Back away from the door!"

"Not tonight, Paul!" She turned herself to see her husband in the living room.

"Can't you be nice to Daniel?" Paul requested. "Please?"

Joy protested loudly, "Then why would he come here unexpectedly and-"

"He didn't."

A sweet honey voice called out.

Sally was walking down the stairs in a light pink shirt and a white knee-length skirt. Her feet were wearing low heel strapped shoes. Her gray purse was hanging on her left arm. She wore her engagement ring too.

Danny's heart was happy to see his love wear her ring.

She explained to her Mommy, "Danny & I already made plans to go out tonight."

Paul spoke, "Be careful."

"I will, Daddy." She promised to both her parents.

Danny took Sally's right and they left the mansion together. The young happy couple went forth for Daniel's car.

Inside his car, Danny leaned over to give Sally a 'Miss You' kiss. She kissed him back.

Their lips softly parted.

Sally sweetly asked her fiance, "So, where are we going tonight?"

Danny teased, "It is a surprise."

His blond fiance sighed unhappily and waited for her surprise during their drive.

The drive lasted for fifteen minutes. Car was parked in the lit-up tent's parking lot.

Daniel told Sally, "Open the glove compartment."

She was baffled on why he would ask her to do that. Her left hand reached for the box's handle and pulled it toward her. What she saw in the compartment box shocked her heart.

She gasped, "Tickets for the Fall Floral show?"

"Yup. My treat to you, Sally." He said kindly.

Her right hand reached in the box and pulled out the printed out tickets. She surprisingly lurched into Danny's arms. Sally gave her man a big tight hug and loving kiss.

From their kiss, the blonde girl happily told her fiance, "This is a special surprise worth waiting for. I Love You, Daniel Gray."

"And I Love You too, Sally Hunt."

Their lips kissed again.

Danny then declared, "Let's go to the Floral show."

What a catch Sally Hunt had in her life. Not even her parents could be that nice and spontaneous for her.

She squealed and they both left the car for a relaxing evening of admiring and checking out flowers from all over the world just in a lit-up white tent.

Wednesday and Thursday work days went by quickly for Daniel Gray. He had a lot of puppies to work with in the training booth for both days. They were in need of some good ol' fashion obedient training. He even took the time to play with them too.

He did practice more of his skating moves off ice and continued to reread the skating terms in the skating books for the rest of the week.

Allison had her own reading for Daniel's dog training problem. She was enjoying reading about good positive dog obedient training. Her practice sessions with her coach were getting more intense because Sectionals was in the middle of that month. The Loop's coach was impressed with her figure student's skills and talent.

At two different skating rinks, Ally kept on working her quad-quad combo jump challenge. Day or night. Her coach, Barbra, knew Ally could do it. What her student needed to work on the heights of both jumps and the extra spin.

Daniel Gray's Figure Instructor had a goal for November. To nail at least one perfect quad-quad jump before Sectionals. But one of her big goals was to do a quad-quad jump combo for her long program in Nationals.

She did have one other secret goal for Nationals. To see if her student could trust her enough that his fiancee was not all she seemed to be when she was on the ice practicing her moves or competing in skating events.

It was the first Friday in November when Allison completed reading the positive obedient dog training book. She had learned and thought of the similarities between teaching kids how to figure skating and dogs with obedient training. More instructional ideas came to her for Danny's teaching problem at the Pet Store.

After work Friday, Danny's heart was much happier after he went inside his unit for Butchie-Wutchie. They greeted each other at the door before Daniel changed out of his work clothes and into a light blue t and jeans.

Time for some dinner.

Danny fixed himself a hamburger on the stove and pan. Butch wanted a share, but his human friend gave him some dry kibble and a doggie meaty meal instead of greasy human food. Simmered beef entree meat and lamb and brown rice flavor kibbles.

The hungry beagle ate his dinner happily.

An hour later, it was ten till six that night.

Daniel had gathered all of Butch's things for his overnight stay with Allison Rigden. His Bong toy with treats, a medium size plastic bowl full of dry kibble with a lid on top of the bowl, Butch's green ceramic bowls, a few play toys, brush, short leash, his pillow, and most importantly, his potty grass.

Inside the skating rink, Ally waited in the main lobby area as the Zamboni truck was resurfacing the ice for the night session. She was dressed in a hot pink cotton t-shirt, long black pants, and her feet wore her white figure boots. Her brunette hair was pulled back in a long braid and a hot pink hair tie at the bottom. No gloves were on her hands.

The time was five minutes before seven.

Ally-Loop walked out of the lobby and through the doors toward the glass-looking ice. She felt the cold-air touching her. She did not mind the temp at an ice rink.

In fact, she loved it.

A first timer or a beginner would consider an ice rink the last place on earth to go for some fun.

Zamboni's gate doors were closed.

Lots of kids and adults came rushing out from the gate's doors and began to skate around the smooth ice.

Ally stepped on the ice.

Her blades were being pushed strongly and smoothly. She skated around the rink once forward then did a right inside mohawk turn to go backwards.

What she worked on were crossovers but with different edges from each crossover step. She started to go left over right twice to the avoid the corner wall. Her edge changed after that last left over right step for a right over left crossover. Ally practiced her edge changes around the whole rink twice.

During the Figure Instructor's practice time, Daniel Gray got himself ready to skate and stored away his skating bag and personal belongings in his temporary locker. He quickly left the men's locker room.

The rink sure was loud and noisy that night with music playing from the speakers and kids and adults chattering loudly. Danny did feel a bit chilly from being surrounded by the rink's cold air temp. He slipped the plastic guards off his blades and began to skate forward for the center of the ice. He decided to work on forward crossovers around the center's painted circle.

Going backwards, Allison noticed Danny practicing his forward counter clockwise crossovers around a painted circle in the middle of the rink. Her head lowered down and inspected the way he used his blades. The figure student was doing his best to push smoothly from the steps. With a lot more practice and slowing things down, Daniel Gray would be a good male figure skater.

She stopped herself from moving backwards by doing a right push back snowplow stop. It was lesson time for the Pet trainer. Ally-Loop glided for the center.

Danny's brown eyes saw Ally skating for the middle of the rink and stopped doing his crossovers.

"Hi." He spoke.

"Hi." She spoke back.

His lesson that night was how to glide more smoothly in figure skating. Pushing out slowly instead of doing it with so much force. Daniel thought it would be a very hard thing to do as a guy. Guys always seem to do everything with quickness and strength, not slowly and smoothly like women typically do.

Ally always knew that both men and women had a soft side to do things smoothly and gracefully. All they needed were time, lots of time, and keep practicing it in their everyday lives.

The dog trainer listened carefully and applied his instructor's advice into his skating ability. He began to improve better with Ally's skating knowledge later that night.

Before the evening session ended, Danny teased, "Ready to have Butch over at your place tonight?"

Ally giggled and said, "Yes, I am."

"How about you follow me to my unit's building and we'll take Butchie-Wutchie out for a walk around the neighborhood?" He suggested.

"Sounds good." She agreed to his plan.

"I'll lend you some of the supplies he would need for an overnight stay and you can bring them back at the dog park?" He finished.

Ally was happy of the idea. "I'll do that."

Daniel stepped of the ice and went up to the front counter for scrap paper and a pen. He wrote on the piece of paper his apartment building's address, his cell phone number, and the dog park he wanted to go to.

Then the session was over.

The dog trainer had a good skating night. He did not fall a lot, his feet were feeling more comfortable in his figure skates, and was happier to be on the ice without any embarrassments.

Allison walked into the lobby area.

Daniel headed toward Ally and handed her the written piece of paper. She held the scrap piece of paper. She also gave back his dog training book.

Her reply for the book was, "It's a good instructional book, Daniel. I enjoyed reading it."

He nodded his head and went for the men's locker room. Inside the locker room, Danny unlocked the lock, sat on a chair to unlace his figure boots, and got out his skating bag from the locker box. His fingers found his cleaning rag and wiped off extra snow, ice, and water from his blades.

The box's door was closed and locked up.

Daniel moved from the locker room to his car and drove home.

Danny was in his synthetic coat and carried all of his pup's stuff down to the building's front door. He and his cute beagle pal waited by the front door for Ally's Horundi car.

A familiar white convertible pulled up and was parked out front. Ally exited her car. She was dressed in a maroon sweater, jeans, and black snow boots that covered the lower part of her jeans.

Daniel opened the door. Butch was attached to his gray retractable leash and his owner held the leash's hand in his firm left hand.

Allison said, "Hi there! And this must be Butchie-Wutchie!"

Her brown eyes saw the sweet beagle standing on the building's front steps. The dog cutely yelped at Ally.

Daniel explained, "Butch's stuff are inside the lobby."

Ally went inside the building and carried all of Butch's overnight stuff. She already opened the trunk of her car to put the doggie stuff inside her car. The cute beagle's things were stored and locked up.

She led them to her car for a ride of her loft building.

Under the building was a high-tech parking garage. Her car drove in the garage and parked her car in her special spot. She, Danny, and

Butchie-Wutchie left the convertible. All of the beagle's things were carried up to her loft.

They all rode in an elevator box.

Danny kept his loving dog close to him.

After the elevator ride, Allison Rigden invited her figure student and his sweet dog into her large loft.

Danny was very impressed of his Figure Instructor's home. He and Butch waited by the front door.

While they waited, Allison quickly put away Butch's things in her loft unit. Food and both his bowls in the kitchen, play toys were in the living room, his pillow in her bedroom, and potty grass in her bathroom.

She was done with that chore. Her brown eyes spotted both boys standing next to the loft's front door.

She offered, "Would you like a tour?"

"Sure." Danny answered.

First the kitchen, then the living room with a huge flat screen t.v., a dvd shelf, and a large glass cabinet containing her past skating awards from ribbons, medals, and trophies, and special photos of her with famous skaters.

Next up was her bedroom.

A Queen size bed with hot pink and black bedsheets, comforter, and pillow cases. A huge computer desk with a very cool laptop, all-in-one printer, and a comfy dark brown leather chair. There figure skating posters on the wall of famous skaters, a walk-in closet filled with her workout clothes, street clothes, past skating costumes, skates, athletic or ballet shoes, and a special hanger for her tights. There were more pictures of her practicing or competing on a nightstand and a special chested drawer.

The last room she showed was her favorite room.

Her beautiful ballet room.

In the ballet room were three wooden ballet bars connected to a wall, huge glass mirrors on one side of the room, big screen windows, a speaker for her mp3 phone, and a real surprise to Danny, an enormous trampoline. He knew that was a sign of trouble from Butch.

The dog was struggling in his leash to play on the trampoline. Daniel kept hold of the handle and commanded his dog, "Stay."

Butch stopped his erratic behavior and sat down calmly with his mouth closed.

The concerned dog trainer asked Ally, "Um, what's with the trampoline?"

She told her figure student, "Its to help me with my jumps off ice. I jump up high in the air and do my best to work on my 'in the air spins.' It does work better and feels more comfortably than being hooked up to strong cable wires and harnesses."

After hearing the words 'being hooked up to strong cables' made the Pet trainer's heart shuddered.

"Cool idea." Daniel commented calmly.

Allison was very surprised Butch had not moved or wiggled out of his stay position. She could use a little help from that trick.

"I am ready for our walk." She stated.

The figure friends and the cute beagle left the loft for a long walk. During their walk, Ally questioned Daniel something important about Butchie-Wutchie.

"Is there something that would make Butch misbehave?"

That question caught Danny off-guard. His pal rarely misbehaved since his puppy years.

Holding to the retractable's plastic handle, he admitted, "There is only thing that would make my beagle very unhappy. Not giving him his normal morning walk."

His Figure Instructor concernedly wondered, "You would not mind if I did that, would you?"

Daniel softly warned her, "Just be careful with him until it's time for the dog park."

He also did not want to tell Ally about Butch's favorite game. Hide-&Treat. That was the only thing that would make Butch happy and be well-behaved.

Allison nodded her head in agreement. Her voice spoke, "What time did you want to meet at the dog park?"

Danny thought in his head and responded, "10 a.m. would be good for me. And Butch too."

"Okay." Ally replied. "10 a.m. it is."

The walk lasted for an hour and a half. For the last half hour, Danny gave the handle to Ally and let her take control of Butch. His sweet beagle looked happy and comfortable with Allison so having his dog over at her loft would not be a huge separation anxiety problem for Butchie-Wutchie.

It was time to head back to Ally's loft.

The three friends had a real good time together.

In front of her loft door, Ally held Butch's retractable leash handle in her right hand and Daniel got down on his knees to wish Butch a blissful evening without him.

He let his hands smoothly pet and caressed his dog's short length fur. His voice softly spoke to his furry friend, "Hey, pal. I know we were never apart since I first I met you, but just for tonight-tonight, you'll be spending the night in Ally's loft."

Butch looked sad in Daniel's eyes. The good human knew his loving beagle was understanding what he was trying to tell him. The cute dog howled softly.

"Ah, Butchie-Wutchie . . ."

Ally felt sad for her figure student to let his precious dog stay at a friend's place for one long lonely night.

Danny hugged his pal tightly and promised him, "I will see you in the morning at the dog park."

His arms dropped from his dog's body. He also told Butch, "Be good and treat Ally nicely. She's a nice lady and will take very good care of you for the night."

His dark brown eyes eyed Butch strongly, "Can you do that?"

The behaved beagle raised his left paw and he and Danny shook hands.

Butch's owner stood up and told Ally, "If there's any problems, call me."

The Figure Instructor agreed. "I will. Butch and I won't have any trouble tonight."

Her figure student nodded his head.

He turned around for a ride down the elevator and exited the loft building.

Ally-Loop escorted the fun-loving beagle into her home.

Walking into his apartment unit all by himself made Danny feel lonely. Butch was not by his side or was there to make him happy.

Sitting on his couch, Daniel did do some figure term reading from the handbook and the oversized skating book. His mind was not feeling any pressure or discomfort on what some of the basic terms mean.

To keep himself busy for the night, Danny practiced some off ice stuff in the living room. Doing strokes, snowplows, forward and backward crossovers, and remembering doing his figure pose from each of the skating moves. He also did his best to let his feet glide smoothly from the skills he worked on.

But no matter how hard he tried, the Pet trainer's heart was still bothered of the fact that his dog was not home with him. His sad eyes looked around the unit.

No doggie bowls.

No lying around dry kibble or meaty dog food on the kitchen's countertops.

No play toys.

No fake grass in the bathroom.

No comfy pillow in the bedroom for his dog to lie on and sleep.

Daniel Gray's unit felt incomplete without his sweet loving beagle. He remembered the day he and Butch first spent the night in their new home. They slept on his twin size bed all night long. The bond between a man and his dog were stronger than ever.

The dog trainer got into his empty bed and laid down. Covers were over him and pillows were under his head. He silently whispered to himself, "Hope you're okay, Butchie-Wutchie . . ."

He flipped over on his right side and sadly spoke softly, "I miss you, pal."

He closed his tired brown eyes and his body and mind were relaxed enough to drift him off to sleep.

It was mid morning the next day.

Daniel unhappily went to the dog park by himself.

Ten minutes after arriving at the park, he saw Allison with Butch walking into the park. He hoped his plan of making his sweet beagle misbehave in the park and with other dogs would work.

The Pet trainer was pleased that Ally-Loop was not scared or nervous to be out in public as a famous figure skater. She held a struggling, barking Butch in her arms. He wanted to get out of her arms pretty badly. She put down the cute beagle on the dirt, gravel ground. Butch charged after other dogs roughly. He was very hyper and not playing nicely.

Ally called out to misbehave beagle to calm down.

Butch did not listen or would play friendly with other dogs.

Danny knew his idea was working. His beagle did not look happy that morning. The Pet trainer waited a little longer to see what was going to happen next.

The Figure Instructor was stressed out and frustrated that 'her' dog was not having positive behavior out in public. She wish someone could help her.

Daniel Gray knew that was his cue to walk up and ask the beagle's 'owner' for some obedient tips.

He casually asked her, "Hi there. Need some help with your dog?"

Allison tiredly huffed, "Yes, please. I can't seem to control his 'negative' attitude."

The Pet trainer stated, "Looks like 'your' beagle would rather hunt than pay attention or listen to your commands."

She wondered, "What should I do?"

He chuckled at Ally and the misbehaved beagle because he knew how to control Butch's bad behavior with only one little trick in his jeans pocket.

Daniel reached into his right pocket for his clicker.

Click!

Butch heard the click from his floppy brown ears. He immediately stopped being actively rough toward other dogs and his short little white legs ran for Danny and Ally. He stood in front of his human friends on all fours.

"What's your dog's name?" Daniel asked Allison.

He kept brown his eyes at the cute beagle and got down on his knees.

"Butch." Ally sweetly spoke.

The Pet trainer kindly told the beagle, "Hey, Butch. Can you sit?"

Butch, who was once not acting nicely toward other dogs or willing to listen to his 'owner,' had the Pet trainer's full attention and his floppy pink tongue was sticking out.

The beagle sat down on the sandy ground and closed his muzzle mouth after hearing Daniel's command. His cute alert face was raised up. He waited patiently for his treat or his special game.

Danny explained to Allison, "There is a special game I made up that can help 'your' dog's negative behavior."

Behind his back were his hands and one of his hands held a small piece of blueberry flavor biscuit. He stuck out both his fists in front of Butch.

Ally watched with anticipation.

Daniel cheerfully questioned the sit-still beagle, "Okay, Butch, which hand?"

The beagle looked closely at the Pet trainer's fists. He raised his left paw to tag Danny's right hand.

The human asked the dog, "Are you sure?"

Butch yelped out once loudly.

Ally and Danny looked at each other after hearing Butch's cute response.

The Pet trainer opened his right fist and there it was. The small piece of blueberry biscuit on his palm. He gave the sweet beagle his biscuit treat. Butch happily ate yummy treat and he was still sitting on the sandy ground.

Danny used his clicker again twice. That was the boy's code for 'play-time.'

Butch ran off from the figure friends to find a play-mate. He grabbed a piece of play rope and then another dog, a basset hound, grabbed the other end of the play rope. They decided to play a friendly game to tug-a-war.

Allison surprisingly asked, "How did you do that?"

Her right hand gave her figure student Butch's short black leash.

Daniel stuffed the leash in his jacket pocket and happily replied, "Practice, and it's me and Butch's special bonding time."

"I think I'm understanding on why you're uncomfortable to teach humans 'dog training.'" Ally insightfully said.

They started to walk around the sandy, gravel ground dog park.

She continued on, "You did your learning and training only with dogs, not much with people. You didn't want to lose your comfort zone and focus from the canines if you had to interact with the dog owners too."

Daniel knew then what Ally was trying to say. He also figured out why the Samoyed's owner told Jack that his Pet trainer was being a 'freeloader.'

That doesn't seem fair for the owners. A Pet trainer who doesn't show the dog's owners what to do to train their own dogs. Her voice echoed inside his head.

Jack and the Lady were right. Daniel thought. *I was not being fair or acting like a good overall dog trainer with the dogs and their owners.*

He did feel disappointment in his heart for failing his boss's orders and not honoring his Pet training career.

Danny and Ally stopped walking in the park to sit on a wooden bench.

A curious question came to Allison's mind.

"Danny, why did you want to be a Pet trainer?"

He breathed out a long breath from hearing that question. "Wow . . . Now that was an experience at the Pet store I'll never forget."

"Experience?" She asked him unsurely.

Daniel looked around the park for Butch. He was playing happily with a small group of big and little dogs.

Then he brought his attention back to Allison and began his story.

One year ago . . .

Daniel Gray was happy by being a Stock Boy for Jack. And yet he wondered uncomfortably about Sally's mother not liking his job by stocking up animal food and supply essentials for the rest of his life.

Sometimes he would feel jealous by coming into the Pet store and see the current Pet trainer. A very bitchy, rude blonde named Amanda. She was not being a good dog trainer at all. She also never worked with the dog's owners too.

Even though the booth looked good and proper on the outside, Daniel knew what was really happening within Amanda's dog training sessions. Her training techniques was much harsher and strict than what good Pet trainers should do.

At times, Danny would secretly follow Amanda and a 'stupid canine' to an empty room. He would stand behind the door and what his ears heard killed his heart.

The dog would sadly howl or yelp out for help and their claws would scratch on the door or the concrete floor.

Amanda would yell and scream at the lazy canine from being so stupid and not up to par by not doing what it was told to do during their training sessions.

The bitchy trainer would beat the dog up with her fists and feet. For more harsher punishments, she would use a strong leather belt and strike it on the canine.

Daniel hated Amanda for doing that to the dogs. It was always 'Per-fect this, or Ex-actly like that!'

His ears did over hear customers complain to employees about their dogs becoming so violent and aggressive from being in the training booth with Amanda.

He wondered why Jack was not told about it.

Then he realized something.

Jack's doing manager errands now. Amanda always do the beatings when he's not the store.

Maybe Daniel should tell his boss about Amanda punishing the dogs. He wished he could do something to help out the dogs.

Then one day had changed everything.

It was a normal day for Danny and the Pet store at first, but when an out-of-control three year old black lab mix came rushing into the store, trouble lay ahead.

The lab mix dog ran around the store like crazy, was destroying the store's merchandises, made the concrete floor messy with pee and poop, and began growling, snarling, and barking angrily at people and other animals too.

Customers left the store in a hurry.

Daniel's boss, Jack, called up Animal Control in his office to see if someone could safely take the rambunctious black lab out of the building. Then he called in all his employees to his office room.

Most of the employees were very mad and upset at Amanda for making the lab mix act so misbehaved.

Jack requested, "Can anyone control the dog?"

No one did at first. Danny knew what to do in that kind of situation from all the practice and patience he did with his Butchie-Wutchie.

He volunteered. "I'll try, Jack."

"You sure, Daniel?" His boss concernedly asked.

The Stock Boy nodded his head firmly. "I do need some supplies."

"What do you need?" Jack wondered.

Danny thought carefully and spoke, "A chunky play rope, some dog biscuits, and a short strong leash."

Good thing he secretly remembered to bring his clicker.

Everyone in the room were baffled of the stuff Daniel needed to get the black lab to calm down.

Jack and Danny left the office room for the back storage room. The Pet store's manager handed young Gray a bran new orange, yellow, and black colored chunky play rope, some bacon strips, and a short purple color strong leash.

The store's manager told Danny, "Good luck."

Danny told him, "Thank you, Sir."

The Stock Boy left the storage room alone, walked through some aisles of dry dog food, and his voice called out for the aggressive black lab.

His eyes saw the lab coming for him.

The dog's angry eyes stared at Danny. It snarled and loudly barked at the person twenty feet in front of it. Then the black dog started to charge toward the young man quickly.

The brave Stock Boy was not scared of the vicious black lab. He looked calmly at the wild mutt.

The running lab was five feet away from Danny when he threw the play rope in front of the black canine. The dog went for the rope and it began to play with the play rope with its mouth and paws.

As the lab was playing with the rope, Jack and the rest of his employees were watching Danny and the black lab from the employee's hallway in the store. They wondered what was going to happen next.

The Stock Boy sat on the floor with the lab mutt and grabbed part of the rope to play tug-a-war with the dog. The dog playfully growled and tugged and tugged with Danny.

He laughed and kindly talked to the black mutt.

Few minutes later, he let go of the play rope and stood up on his feet to let the dog have a little alone time with the rope. The dog wanted to tear up the rope by pulling it one way with its strong teeth and holding down the toy with its paws and claws.

Danny reached into his right pant's pocket for his clicker. He clicked it once.

After the black lab heard the click, it stopped trying to tear with the play rope and looked up at the Stock Boy with her brown eyes and the rope in hanging out from its mouth.

"Come!" Daniel's clear voice spoke out loud.

To his and the Pet store employee's surprise, the black lab dog calmly walked toward the human and dropped the rope out of its mouth. The dog stood on all fours in front of the brave Stock Boy.

Jack and his staff members wondered if the lab was going to attack his young employee.

Daniel commanded to the lab, "Sit!"

The black lab sat down.

He presented the behaved dog a small piece of bacon. It ate its treat happily.

Danny told the dog, "Lie down!"

The once out-of-control black mutt slowly laid down on the tile floor comfortably.

Jack's brave Stock Boy sat next to the black lab and handed it some more of the bacon pieces he had in his left pocket. The lab contently ate more of its treat.

Daniel petted and stroked its black and white patched furry body. The dog was tired and fell on its side for a little doggie nap.

Danny noticed the dog was female and she probably had all she could have handled from Amanda's doggie 'boot camp training.'

Jack and his employees were amazed at his Stock Boy's dog training skills. The manager was very proud of Danny's knowledge on how to deal with wild, rambunctious dogs.

The employee's brown eyes saw an orange-yellowish color truck from the front door's windows. The truck had cages on the flat bed and it parked in to store's parking lot.

Two men came out from the truck. One of them carried a long metal pole rope chocker in his right hand. They both walked importantly toward the Pet store building.

Inside, they asked for the manager and the troubled dog. Jack walked over to the front doors and explained to the Animal Control workers one of his employees managed to calm down the dog he called in and did not need their services anymore. He showed the guys Danny and the happy black lab.

Calm Daniel spoke, "She's all right. Looks like the Pet trainer pushed this loving lab a bit too far."

Then everyone looked at Amanda with disappointing eyes. She scolded at them by her unconcerned facial expression.

Danny quickly put attached the purple leash to the lab's collar. He stood up and held on to the leash. The black mutt stood up with him.

The worker without carrying the pole chocker said to Daniel Gray, "Kid, you did good work."

Jack happily announced, "Fine work, I would say."

Danny wondered where the black lab's owner was.

His boss exit the building to find the lab's master. Jack and a middle aged man who had dark brown hair and golden brown eyes were talking and went inside the store.

The Animal Control workers left the Pet store and drove off in the work truck.

Jack and the lab's owner went over to Danny and he handed the man the purple leash.

The Stock Boy recommended, "I think she needs to be in a safer and less distracting environment to rest before she could be social to other dogs and people again."

"Thank you for helping my Jackie-girl be happy again." The owner solemnly replied.

Then he sadly asked Jack, "Do I need to pay back the damages my dog did?"

The Pet store's manager thought on how to solve that problem. An idea came to his mind.

"No, you don't, Sir." Jack strongly stated.

He turned his attention to blonde Amanda who was standing against a wall and not listening to her dog teaching problem.

"But you do, Amanda."

The curly blonde with green eyes complained, "What? I was only doing my job, Jack!"

"By being violent, strict, and using punishable training to the dogs?" The Pet store's manager stroke back at his unfair dog trainer.

"Ha! Those imperfect pooches deserved to be punished if they don't follow my commands!" The bitchy trainer protested. "That's how I got so good!"

Most of the employees went to Jack's office room and Jackie and her owner left the Pet store together happily.

Danny stood in his place.

Jack argued, "You have not done your dog training job properly, Amanda! All you did was creating confusion and a big mess for the dogs' behavior!"

The blonde girl hated being told on what she was doing wrong, especially at her job. She got tired of working in the store and made up her mind.

"You know, I have enough of this shit! I quit!"

Danny's heart was very excited to hear the news. But what he did not know was his boss had a trick up his sleeve for his troubled dog trainer.

"You can't quit. You have some pay backs that are due right now," announced Jack.

He stepped over to Danny to tell him something.

They left the main part of the store for the cleaning room. Both guys were carrying mops, black trash bags, buckets, and floor cleaning bottles.

They handed them to the shocked Pet trainer blond.

Danny's boss commanded, "You can start by cleaning up after the black lab's mess."

Amanda moaned unhappily. She grumbled angrily and took the cleaning tools to start clean up the huge mess.

Jack and Daniel went back to his office room.

He told his reliable Pet store crew, "No one helps her."

Then he went for his office phone. He called up Amanda's cell and pressed the speaker on.

The Pet store employees snickered softly. They knew what was going to happen next.

"What do you want now, Jack?" The upset blond yelled from the speaker.

"Well, Amanda," Jack started out, "I thought we all should know . . ."

Here it comes.

"You will not get any more paychecks until your pay backs are all paid up. After that, you're fired." The store manager professionally said.

Amanda started to curse out angry shitty words from that statement.

All the employees in the room, even Jack, laughed at the blonde bitch's random cussing words.

She hung up her cell and Jack turned off the speaker of his phone's base. He decided to close the store early that day.

The employees cheered and left the room to pack up their things.

Jack requested, "Daniel, stay here and close the door."

The boss sat in his chair while Danny closed the door and sat in a chair in front of his boss' office desk. He wondered what Jack wanted to chat about.

His boss looked happy to his Stock Boy.

"Danny, let me start by saying you did a fantastic job for dealing with the chaotic, wild Jackie-dog." Jack extended his right hand out so Danny's left hand could shake it.

They dropped their hands and the Pet store's manager continued on with his speech.

"Also, since Amanda is going to be let go here, I would very much like to have you as my new dog trainer. Are you interested?"

What Danny heard from his boss was a huge surprise to him. He really like that idea a lot. Maybe it would impress Joy Hunt that he was going to be something better than stocking up animal food and supply essentials.

The Stock Boy strongly told Jack, "Yes, Sir. I'm very interested in becoming a Pet trainer."

"Excellent!" Jack exclaimed.

A thought came to his mind.

"How did you know what to do?"

Danny explained, "After training my beagle since he was a puppy, I learned a lot from doing good dog training techniques instead of doing abusive stuff from boot camps and such."

Jack felt very pleased of trading his awful Pet trainer for someone better. He did give Danny a very helpful career change. "What I recommend you to do to be a dog trainer is take a dog trainer class to be a proper instructor."

"I can do that." Daniel agreed to his boss' plan.

The two men talked a little more about the steps for Danny's job change and what he needed to do in more professional position in a Pet store than being a Stock Boy.

Sure enough, it was time for Danny to leave the store. He went to the employee locker room for his belongings and made it back to his apartment unit to tell Butchie-Wutchie all about his crazy day at the Pet store and new career change.

Chapter Nine

Allison was really surprised of Daniel and that story.

She asked him, "So how did you and Butchie-Wutchie first meet each other?"

He started off, "I found him wandering around alone four years ago when he was a stray pup. Took him in to my folks' house, posted up flyers to see if anyone was looking for, took care of him for a month without anyone claiming him as their pup, and claimed him as my own."

Danny turned his head and saw Butch and some other dogs continue to play cute with each other. They ran around, chased, and became instant friends. There was sand dust shrouding around the dogs.

She did question his Pet training experience with long time beagle pal.

His head went back around to face Ally. He went on with his Pet tale. "I did teach Butch obedient training and we had gone to some puppy classes and more training class until he was three. He's got pretty good behavior, except when it comes to him not getting his morning walk."

"Why would he be so fussy over that?" Fascinated Allison asked.

"Ever since Butch was a puppy, I would normally take him outside in the morning for his potty break. I guess he likes that routine so much he would not be happy if he didn't get his way in the morning." Danny chortled.

Ally could understand and relate to Butch's morning routine. She would not be her normal happy self if she had to stay away from skating or the ice for an entire day.

She requested from the Pet trainer, "Maybe you should teach me a thing or two about dog training and I can help you more with your instructional teachings."

He answered, "I would be delighted to show you the ropes in dog obedient training.

"That's another wonderful idea." Ally agreed.

Daniel looked around the park for Butchie-Wutchie. He was playing nicely with other dogs at a dirt hill.

Then he asked his skating teacher, "Was Butch any trouble to you last night?"

The Figure Instructor sighed and explained, "Daniel, Butch is a sweet, kind, fun-loving beagle. I fed and play with him until he was ready to pass out for the whole night on his pillow. He did use his fake grass for his business time. But overall, he's a well-behaved beagle. I'm very impressed with the work you did with Butch."

If only Sally or Joy Hunt could have Ally's characteristics, Daniel Gray would be much happier in the Hunt's family. He contently told Allison, "Thank you, Ally-Loop."

The figure friends stayed in the dog park until noon struck. Allison handed back Butch's doggie stuff from her Horundi's trunk. Daniel put his dog's things in his car's trunk.

Ally suggested of doing a skating lesson that night.

Danny told her he would be there.

In the Figure Instructor's mind, she had an important question to ask him at the rink.

Both cars drove off in separate directions.

Danny was very glad to have his sweet beagle by his side again. One night without his pal was a huge challenge for the two best friends to go through. But it worked out well in the end.

The Pet trainer's car arrived in the apartment building's garage. Danny and Butch went inside their unit home first and then the human decided to bring Butch's stuff after a quick bite to eat. Butch had some meaty roasted turkey flavor dog food for his lunch.

Daniel walked back to the car and brought his pal's essentials in their home. Bowls and doggie food in the kitchen, play toys in the living room, fake grass stored in the bathroom, and his comfy pillow placed by his owner's twin-size bed.

Young Gray's heart and his apartment unit were satisfied and completed with his fun-loving beagle be right where he belonged. Together as a team.

Four hours later . . .

Daniel had a nap and took Butch out for an afternoon walk. He was glad to have his old afternoon routine again.

It was dinner time for the boys. Butch had some dry kibbles and dog meaty chicken stew flavor while Daniel had some warm soup and crackers.

Then Danny got himself ready for a skating session. He showered, changed his clothes, and gathered his skating supplies in his bag.

Butch gave his master a little 'good-bye' by sitting on his hind legs and his left paw raised up high.

Daniel raised his right hand and waved at Butchie-Wutchie before he left his unit home.

At the ice rink, Allison was already skating around the rink. She continued to work hard on all her jumps, spins, few dance steps, and freestyle moves.

She did spot Daniel skating around the rink himself.

First forward and then, with the wall's help, he turned around to skate backwards.

Ally knew she needed to teach Daniel Gray how to change from forward to backward and backward to forward. Maybe she could that night. Then again, maybe some other night would be better for him to learn the turns.

The two figure friends met up at the center of the rink.

Both of their hearts were glad from their time at the dog park. Ally giving Danny a few teaching pointers while he taught her about certain things when it came to dog training.

She did not forget the important thing she wanted to ask Daniel at the dog park. She questioned Danny, "Is it possible for you to ask Sally if you can watch some of her old skating routines on dvd?"

He answered slowly, "I'm not sure. Maybe. Why do you ask?"

"Because watching other people skate is another good way to understand skating terms better than just from reading it in books." Ally explained.

Daniel remembered Joy Hunt telling him that same thing after being invited to go with the Hunts for Sally's first day at Regionals. He spoke, "I'll ask Sally."

The figures worked on skating forward and backwards throughout the night session. Danny was really getting good at doing crossovers or skating around the rink. But with more practice and patience, he would surely go much faster and smoother without having his feet be so sore and tired from all those strokes and crossovers around the rink.

Before the session came to an end, Ally had a special present for her figure student to watch. She handed him a red plastic dvd case. Danny took the plastic case in his left hand.

He asked his Figure Instructor, "What's this?"

His eyes carefully examined inside the case on what the disc could be.

Allison smug, "Its some of my past skating routines and practice sessions with my coach. Just in case you wanted a break from watching Sally's skating moves."

Daniel put the red case into his skating bag.

"Did would you like a skating lesson this Wednesday at the small rink seven p.m.?" Offered the Figure Instructor.

"Sounds good, Ally. Have a good night."

She nodded at him and went inside the girl's locker room. Her moving up novice student left the skating rink's building for a nice soothing drive back to his apartment unit.

When Danny woke up Sunday morning from his dog park time and skating lesson the previous Saturday night, he had some breakfast, put on some street clothes, took his sweet pooch out for his morning walk, showered, new clothes were on him, and decided to pay an unexpected visit to his fiancee's mansion home.

He arrived there in a half hour. He calmed his heart when he reached for the mansion's front door. His right hand knocked on the wooden door.

The door opened.

Behind the door was Paul Hunt. He was wearing a nice light blue dress shirt, black slacks, and black dressed up shoes.

He surprisingly asked, "Daniel. What brings you here today?"

"May I come in?" Danny requested.

"Sure." Mr. Hunt stepped aside from the doorway and let his future son-in-law inside the house.

The house owner announced loudly, "Sally! Danny's here!"

He closed the front door.

Sure enough, Daniel's ears heard rapid foot steps coming from the second floor and down the staircase.

Sally.

Her lithe form reached the first floor. She was dressed in a light gray long sleeved shirt, comfy jeans, and athletic tennis shoes. The blond figure champ rushed into Daniel's loving arms. Both their arms held each other tight.

Paul Hunt left them alone to go into his study room by the kitchen.

"Danny." Sally gasped. "What made you decide to come here?"

The young lovers part from their embrace and gave each other loving kisses on their lips. Their kisses ended and Danny requested from his love, "I'm here because I was wondering if I can watch your old skating routines. Ally suggests I should watch the moves that ice skaters do on ice instead of reading it from books all the time."

Sally Hunt softly replied, "Of course you can."

She stepped out of her love's arms to head over for the entertainment system's dvd shelf. Her bluish-gray eyes found her special dvd case. The fingers on her left hand pulled out a dark blue dvd case. She gave it to Daniel.

Sally did warn him, "Please take good care of it, Danny. Don't want Mommy to get upset if something bad happened to the disc."

Daniel Gray assured his fiancee, "I promise."

They sealed the deal with a long kiss.

Joy was surprised to see her daughter and Daniel in the living room kissing. She demanded, "What's he doing here, Sally?"

Their kiss was rudely interrupted from her Mommy once again.

Sally spoke, "Danny came by to get my old skating routine disc for learning purposes."

Mrs. Hunt huffed, "I see."

She was dressed in a white blouse, dark blue slacks, and navy blue heel shoes. She sure did not look happy to see her future son-in-law in her home that day.

Daniel took Sally's left hand for moral support. "If you won't mind me watching it?"

His permission felt odd to Joy. "Why?"

"Ally thinks it would be best if I did watch other good skaters skate, I can understand skating terms and moves better rather than just reading it from books only." Daniel explained.

Joy strictly answered to Sally's fiance, "Make sure only you watch it."

"Yes, ma'am." He nervously told Joy Hunt.

"Okay then. Daniel, would you like to join us for some lunch?" Joy offered.

The shocked Pet trainer happily said, "Sure."

"Let's go then." Mrs. Hunt declared. "Paul! We need to go!"

He called out from his study room, "Be right there!"

Daniel curiously asked Sally, "Where are we going?"

She whispered, "Mommy made special arrangements to have a special lunch with some of her old skating friends. Daddy's too.

"Ohh . . ." Danny sighed. "Sounds like fun."

He put the dark blue disc case on the coffee table.

Paul Hunt exited his study room and the four figures left the Hunt's mansion to go to a really nice hotel restaurant. Paul & Joy saw some old familiar faces. They ate good food and shared past skating stories from lessons, coaches, practice sessions, competitions, special events, and ceremony times.

Danny jumped into some of the conversations too. He was really glad to see Sally there with a big smile on her face, hearing her talk openly, and laugh at humorous stories.

The special lunch came to an end.

Joy hugged some of her old skating friends. Paul shook hands with the guests. Sally & Daniel walked out of the hotel and stood by the red SUV.

Joy & Paul stepped out of the hotel's building with their long time friends. They all went to their own cars in the parking lot. The SUV was unlocked from Paul's key chain. Danny and the Hunts got inside the car and rode back to the mansion home.

During the ride, Joy thought about how much Daniel Gray had talked and learned about figure skating terms with more experienced figure skaters. To be fair with him & Sally, she stated, "Daniel, thank you for coming with us and being very generous with your knowledge of figure skating."

The Pet trainer was surprised. Joy Hunt had never been that complimented to him before.

He breathed out, "It's my pleasure, Mrs. Hunt."

"How would you like to come with us to Salt Lake City for Sectionals?" She offered.

Sally gasped, "Mommy! Are you serious?"

"Yes." Joy replied. "It would be good for Danny to watch more experienced ice skaters at a major skating event."

Young Gray was scared. It sounded as if the trip was in need of him to take some time off from the Pet store if there was a plane ride involved. He answered nervously, "I need to ask my boss first."

"Please be quick about it. We have to leave on the morning of the 17th." Joy strictly said.

"Yes, Ma'am." Danny promised. "I'll ask him tomorrow."

It was late in the afternoon when Daniel arrived back at his apartment unit with Sally's dark blue dvd case in his jacket pocket. His dog Butch greeted him in the kitchen. The sweet beagle was waiting patiently for his meal.

The kind human took of his jacket, hung it on the hook behind the unit's front door, and went for the kitchen. He gave his sweet beagle pal something yummy to eat. Dog meaty beef stew flavor and chicken and brown rice kibbles.

Butch was very pleased to have something to eat and drinking fresh cold water for his tummy. His owner had a turkey sandwich and passion fruit tangerine juice to drink.

The Pet trainer placed Sally Hunt and Allison Rigden's dvd cases on his computer desk to watch later. He noticed from his cell that the time was six-thirty p.m.

Time to take Butchie-Wutchie out for a walk. Man and his dog left the unit for their evening walk around the city's neighborhood. The young dog trainer was feeling a bit more confident just by thinking of going to the Pet store that coming week and more.

The confidence did come from the satisfaction of talking to a dog 'owner,' even thought Ally did not have a dog, it still felt good of Daniel Gray to help someone out with a misbehaved dog who was in need of some obedient training.

"Maybe I should really try it tomorrow." He mumbled to himself.

The boy's walk lasted for a full hour. Butch was very content to have his walk and three potty breaks during the walk. Danny and his loving pooch went inside their unit home to rest. He walked into his bedroom.

Finally, it was the right time to watch one of the girl's dvds. He turned on his desktop's hard drive and computer screen. His mind decided to watch Sally's disc first.

Daniel opened the dark blue case, carefully pulled out the disc, and slipped it in the hard drive's disc box.

What the computer screen showed was fourteen-year-old Sally Hunt ready to do her skating performance. Even though she looked six years younger, his heart was still stolen from the young blond figure champ.

He did notice that Sally's appearance on ice remained the same as today. A French braid with a jeweled headband.

Danny also saw something very strange with Sally's skating outfits. It was the same style, but with different colors. Long sleeved, turtleneck, and full coverage bodysuits.

From her entire skating dvd disc, Sally Hunt would be up first and never stayed long in the building when her routine was done. Her mysterious disappearances did not make the judges or fans wonder suspiciously why she and her Mommy had to do that.

The dvd player stopped at ten-thirty that night. Time for bed.

Danny slowly got up from his computer chair for the bathroom. He brushed his teeth and combed his tangled short brown hair with a small blue comb.

He moved into his bedroom to change into his night clothes, hopped into bed, and hoped to have much better work days at the Pet store for now on.

A very unusual dream woke Daniel Gray up.

The dream was of him and Sally skating around the ice rink in traditional wedding clothes. Him in a nice black tuxedo and her in a white gown with a veil and they were both wearing their figure skates. But Sally was attached to lots of flexible cable wires all over her body. He did see Joy Hunt sitting at the stands and a laptop was on her lap. It looked to Danny that Joy was controlling her daughter's every move on the ice.

He immediately opened his eyes and gasped out loud in horror. His mind began to get some theories about what could the weird dream mean. Maybe Sally's mom was controlling all her daughter's skating moves on ice, or was his loving fiancee a figure puppet so Joy Hunt could feel like she was winning the gold herself. The Pet trainer could not wait to marry Sally and take her away from her strict skating Mommy.

Daniel lifted himself off from bed and got ready for a much good work day in the Pet store's training booth.

After changing into street clothes, ate a tasty breakfast, taking Butch out for his morning walk, a quick shower, and remembering the instructional tips Allison told him at the dog park, Danny left his apartment unit and went to the Pet store.

He walked through the back door of the store's building. Then off for the employee room to put away his belongings in his locker.

His heart was beating very fast and heard. He even felt lightheaded. His head was lifted up and took some very deep breathes and carefully thought over what to tell Jack Randell about getting some time off to go to Sectionals.

Danny stood alone in the room for ten minutes. Then he did feel ready to face his boss. The brown haired dog trainer slowly walked out of the employee locker room and made it to the manager's office room. He lifted his right fist to knock on the wooden door.

His ears heard, "Come in."

He turned the silver door knob and walked in the quiet office room. Jack was sitting comfortably in his leather chair. He was surprised to see Daniel in his office.

"Danny." He spoke, "What made you decide to come here?"

The young Pet trainer sat in a chair in front of the huge office desk. He folded his hands and sighed deeply.

Jack knew his employer needed to ask him something really important.

"Sir." Danny started out. "I know I have not been a good, overall Pet trainer for you and it's probably not the best time to ask you this but-" his left hand stroked back his soft brown hair and continued on with his requested, "May I have four days off to go with Sally Hunt and her parents for her Sectional skating competition in Salt Lake City, Utah?"

There. He did it. All Danny did was wait for Jack's answer.

His boss opened his mouth and wondered, "Huh. I never thought you were interested in figure skating. How did that happen?"

Danny gulped.

He slowly explained, "I popped the question to Sally a month ago and in order for me to get the Hunt's blessings, I have to learn how to ice skate and understand figure terms. Lately, I've been taking ice skating lessons from Ally-Loop because Sally's busy with her skating lessons with her Mother."

"Sheesh, Daniel. You're willing to do figure skating for your girl's hand in marriage?" Jack surprisingly asked.

"I Love her." Danny confessed, "I can't imagine loving another girl."

His boss reached down for a drawer handle. Jack got out a spiral folder with a dark blue cover. His calendar folder.

The store owner's fingers flipped through the pages until it reached November. He got a black pen in hand and asked, "From when to when?"

Daniel thought back of the date Joy Hunt told him when they were going to leave. "Joy said they need to leave on the 17th. I'll probably be back on the 20th."

Mr. Randell wrote in his folder Daniel's requested days off. He told his Pet trainer, "Good luck and hopefully learning how to figure skate would help your Pet training job."

The young trainer snickered in his head, *You have no idea what a good instructor Ally-Loop is.*

He said out loud, "Thank you, Sir."

Daniel got up from the chair he sat in and left the office room with satisfaction in his hear. His work uniform, all cleaned and fixed up, was ready to be taken on with dirty dog prints and slob. What he needed to do that day was break out of his shy shell. He started out by focusing his heart and mind on his dog obedient training technique for the dogs. And most importantly, the dog's owners too.

The dog trainer went forth for his booth. He had plenty of dog treats, cleaning supplies, and his clicker was in his right pants pocket. Even the training booth was clean and shiny.

It was ten a.m. The Pet Store's front doors opened. Daniel Gray was busy sweeping around the aisles. His left hand reached into his left pants pocket for his cell. He had an hour of free time to do other chores before the dogs would come to the training booth for class time.

When eleven o'clock arrived, the young Pet trainer putted on a happy face. He knew who was coming to the booth first the morning. Besides his loving, faithful friend, Butchie-Wutchie, Danny's heart had a soft spot for another sweet dog named Smokey.

Smokey was a cute pug that's lots of fun to play with and to Daniel's surprise, easy to obedient train. He and his owner, Bob, were good friends.

Danny's brown eyes noticed the little pug running for the training booth with Bob by his side. The dog trainer smiled at Smokey.

He yelled out, "Hey, Smokey!"

Bob was a Caucasian, Squid retiree in his late 60s and loved coming into the Pet store so Smokey could be happy. That morning, Bob was dressed in a blue and white checkered dress shirt and tan pants with dark brown shoes, and he did not look happy.

Danny wondered why Bob was not smiling today.

Bald headed Bob walked up to the training booth and said in his elderly voice, "Hey, Daniel. I'm sorry to say this but Smokey won't be coming to the booth for anymore training sessions."

The Pet trainer's heart was crushed hard.

"Why?" He asked sadly.

Smokey was barking loudly. He was on his hind legs and front legs on the training door, wanting to get inside the booth. His claws were scratching on the wooden door.

"Smokey! Down!" Bob commanded to his misbehaved pug.

His dog did not stand down or stopped barking.

Daniel's right hand slipped inside his right pants pocket for his clicker. He clicked it three times.

Click, click, click!

Smokey stopped barking and sat down on the cement floor with his mouth closed. He gray head looked up at Danny.

"Good boy, Smokey." The Pet trainer kindly spoke. "Now, Bob, what made you change your mind for Smokey to do obedient training sessions here?"

The elderly man explained strongly, "A few days ago, I was looking on the internet for some special diet food for Smokey's old age from the Pet store's website. I stumbled across a post review from a lady customer who did not get fair treatment in your dog training technique."

Danny's heart crushed more than before.

Bob continued on. "I think she made a point of you being along in the booth and not showing the dog's owners what kind of obedient training their dogs need in their homes. I wish you can show me how to keep Smokey quiet when it's necessary for me. But since you only want to be around the pups, I can't trust your training knowledge."

Damn it. Daniel thought. *That Samoyed owner needs a taste of her own medicine. I cannot lose my job over this.*

Just when Bob and Smokey were ready to leave the store, the young Pet trainer pleaded, "Please, Bob. I don't want to lose this position."

This was it. He was going to do what he showed Allison at the dog park last Saturday to Bob.

Daniel Gray offered, "I will show you how to keep Smokey quiet."

Bob seemed curious and very intrigued with the employee's suggestion. "Really?"

"Yes." Danny Gray professionally stated. "I need to start out slow though."

"Well, then," Bob chuckled, "let's get started."

Danny opened the booth's small swing door and Bob and Smokey came inside the training booth.

Instead of the Pet trainer taking Smokey's short leash, he let Bob hold the leash and instructed to the elderly man, "Stay calm. Make sure he has your complete attention before doing a trick or giving him a treat. Use short words only or he would hear blah, blah, blah in the end of the command."

Bob lowered his head and his eyes looked at Smokey. His dog was standing on all fours.

The dog trainer handed Bob an extra clicker.

He explained to the pug's owner, "I've trained Smokey and other dogs with a certain amount of clicks for a specific reason. One click to get their attention. Two clicks for 'play-time'. And three clicks for a 'sit-stay'."

Bob wondered, "How did you do it in the first place?"

Daniel replied, "I trained all the dogs simple first and then do more advance stuff later on. When the dog do what was commanded, I would give them a treat or click for saying, 'good job' after doing what they were told to do."

Bob had the clicker in his right hand and Smokey's short leash in his left hand. He clicked it three times.

Smokey looked up at his owner and sat down calmly.

The Pet trainer teased, "If you click it three more times, Smokey would lie down."

Bob clicked the clicker three more times and Smokey laid down. No noise, distraction, or anything annoying could make Smokey get up from his 'lie down' position.

The elderly man was impressed.

He and Daniel worked on some more simple dog training maneuvers together. Bob was understanding the techniques Danny was doing the in the booth with his dog and other dogs too.

All of the sudden, both men heard, "Can we join?"

Their eyes saw a small group of people standing by the training booth with their dogs.

Daniel exclaimed, "Come on in!"

He opened the swing door and the group came inside the booth. What he did was work with each dog and its owner one at a time. He was glad to interact more with the owners instead of just talking or befriending with only dogs. He hoped Jack, his boss, was watching him the training booth that day.

That Monday work day was a real good start for Danny's Pet training improvement, and yet, he still needed Allison's advice to be really comfortable of being an overall dog trainer. He also wanted Ally to come to the Pet store and have her bring in Butch to the training booth to help out more.

Danny's best thing about dealing with that work day was he knew what to expect and learn from the experiences. And he always kept reminding himself, "Start off slow and simple, and then progress to something complicated and fast paced."

He went back to his apartment unit and told Butchie-Wutchie he was starting to break out of his shy shell. The boys had a snack and went out for their evening walk.

After their afternoon walk ended, Daniel went into his bedroom to call up Sally.

Sally answered her cell on the second ring, "Hi, Danny!"

"Hi, Sally-babe. I talked to Jack and he granted me four days off so I can go with you for Sectionals." He declared.

"Ohhh! Thank you, thank you, thank you, thank you!" The figure champ squealed. "It's good that it'll be four days because Mommy wanted us to leave Sunday afternoon."

"Perfect." Danny sighed happily.

"I'll tell her and she will tell you what the plan will be next week." Sally spoke.

Danny replied, "I Love You."

Sally told her love, "I Love You too."

"Well, good night, babe." He wished her.

"Night-night."

They hung up their cells.

Daniel walked over for his computer desk and decided to watch Allison's past skating routines disc. Her disc was much fancier than Sally's dvd disc. It was double sided. One side was labeled as her past skating routines. The other was practice session. He decided to watch the routine side first.

It showed Ally at fourteen years old and she was the total opposite of what Sally and Joy would do during skating events.

He had to admit. Ally-Loop's figure skills were more fun to watch than his love's moves. From her costume styles to the cool tunes that fit well with her and her down-to-earth attitude on and off ice, his Figure Instructor was one passionate figure skater.

The time was a little after eleven p.m. that evening when Ally's routine disc was done. Daniel's eyes were getting tired and knew it was time for bed. He turned off his desktop computer, changed his clothes, said, 'good-night' to Butch, and fell asleep in his comfy twin-size bed.

Tuesday's work day went pretty well for Daniel, the dogs, and their owners. Instead of having owners drop-off their dogs in the training booth, they would come in and Danny would show them some hands-on training.

The once quiet booth was noisy with dogs barking or yelping happily and people just chattering away. Another reminder came to the Pet trainer's mind. Danny should look up what the Samoyed's owner had posted online about him and his lazy dog training technique.

Danny & Sally's date later that night went wonderful.

They went to a cute little cafe. The engaged couple enjoyed a little caffeine and talked about what he had been doing to improve his dog training technique while Sally chatted more about her skating time with Joy and the wedding plans.

Sally suggested their next date would be Saturday night. Danny loved his fiancee's idea.

After their date, the Pet trainer went inside his unit and Butch greeted him in the living room. The human's body felt tired. He needed to turn himself in for bed. Before he went to bed, he sat on his computer chair decided to search the web for the Pet store's web site.

He looked at the store's reviews post board and sure enough, the Samoyed's owner had typed up exactly what she told him and Jack in the Pet store. That really motivated the dog trainer to be a better Pet trainer for his boss, the Hunts, and his Figure Instructor.

The dog trainer slowly lifted up from his chair, changed his clothes, and went to sleep on his bed.

Daniel's Wednesday work day went much better than his other work days. He smiled at the dogs and owners, felt more comfortable by talking and worked with them one-by-one, and made sure everyone was behaving properly. His shift ended and went back to his unit.

Butch and his human friend had a fun walk. After their walk, the figure novice remembered that later that night was another skating lesson with Allison. He was eager to go and learn more about figure skating.

Danny had a quick shower, had some dinner with his loving beagle pal, and what felt like forever to the beagle's owner, the Pet trainer got himself ready for the ice rink. He just wanted to skate and skate as much as he can from breaking out from his shy shell. Especially skating backwards.

He made it to the rink in good time. He paid for admission and laced up his skates in the men's locker room. The brown hair and eyes novice quickly made his way for the small rink's glassy ice. His lungs were filled with the cold temp's air.

Danny was beginning to understand why the temperature in an ice rink was comforting. He was getting really used to coming to the rink a lot, he was starting to like it. And to think a month ago he would not set foot, or blade, on an ice rink and enjoy it.

Allison found him on the ice and skated up to Daniel. She asked him surprisingly, "How's the dog training going?"

Danny happily exclaimed, "Fantastic! I'm opening myself up and the dog's owners are doing hands-on training in the booth!"

"That's great, Danny!" She proudly said. "I am glad you are talking and instructing the owners as well as the dogs too!"

"It feels great!" He yelled loudly.

His feet moved his blades and boots and skated around the rink fast forward. Then he wanted to go backwards.

Allison watched her figure student fall on the ice without knowing how to go forward to backwards. She glided up to him.

Danny got up quickly from his fall on the cold ice. He stood up and he embarrassedly asked, "Um, how do you go forward to backwards?"

Ally just giggled and showed him, "This is called an inside mohawk turn."

First she glided forward on her right blade and her left blade did not touch the ice. As slowly as she could, Ally-Loop's left blade stepped on the ice close to her right blade and her right blade was lifted up from the ice while she did a little hip turn from the blade switch. Now she was gliding on her left blade and moving backwards.

Not only Daniel learned basic figure turns on ice and his skating handbook, he was taught about edges and how to tell the difference from an inside edge to an outside edge.

If the free foot, the blade not touching the ice, is inside the curve, it is an inside edge. If the free foot is outside the curve, it is an outside edge. That was pretty easy for Daniel Gray to remember.

Three turns were like a mohawk turn but the skater stays on the same blade for the little hip turn. Mohawks and three turns were new skills he was going to have to practice, on and off ice. He was really moving up in figure skating. Maybe he was wrong of hating this kind of sport in the first place.

Basic mohawk and three turns were what Daniel and Allison worked on till the evening session was over.

The figure friends planned on not having a skating lesson Friday night and go to the gym early in the morning and then skate the afternoon session. Seven a.m. in front of Danny's apartment building Saturday morning was their scheduled time.

Work day at the Pet store the next day was a good one for the Pet trainer and the dog training participants. He still worked with one owner and dog one at a time. He could not wait to do a whole group without being scared. Daniel wondered if his boss was keeping a closer eye at the busy, crowded training booth.

After getting back to the unit from work, Danny and Butch had some dinner, went on a walk, and came back inside the unit for a little r&r. The Pet trainer also knew it was time for him to watch Ally's skating practice session on the other side of her dvd disc. He slipped the disc in the hard drive's disc slot and the dvd player opened. His mouse clicked on the disc's icon.

What he saw first was Ally introducing herself and why she wanted to record some of her practices on ice. "To watch myself work on skating moves and see if I did them right or not."

After the Figure Instructor's introduction, she explained and did the moves she spoke of doing from spins, jumps, dance steps, freestyle positions, and certain combinations from jumps and spins.

The dog trainer was really comprehending what all skating terms means. An idea came to his mind. He wanted to watch Sally and Ally's routine discs and see if Danny would memorize all the moves each girl did from their routines without reading his notes or the skating books.

When the time reached quarter to eleven, Daniel's eyes were tired and knew it was bed time. He turned off his computer, put on night clothes, and settled himself into bed. Butchie-Wutchie was happily sleeping on his pillow by his master's twin size bed.

Chapter Ten

It was late Friday afternoon when Danny arrived back in his apartment unit from a wonderful teaching day at the Pet store. His heart felt very satisfied that he was really able to show the dog's owners good obedient training. He did what Ally would do to him when they would have his lessons. Ask owners what their misbehaved dog's problems were and how to do special training for their needs.

Butch's happy face showed Danny he was ready to stretch out his legs for a long walk. They walked and walked until both boys were tired and hungry.

They had their dinner together in the kitchen and then Daniel went for his desktop to do start out his skating term challenge. Desktop screen and hard drive were on, the disc was still in the dvd disc slot, and ejected the disc to flip it over for Ally's skating routine side.

He mumbled to himself what moves Ally was doing from each skating skill. He did the same when he watched Sally Hunt's disc too. He sure missed his fiancee a lot.

When his computer screen said 9:00 p.m., Danny knew it was time for bed. He found his cell and fixed up an alarm time for six a.m. to give Butch his morning walk. He also gathered his workout and skating clothes in his bag along with his skates and supplies. His fridge had his water bottle filled with cold water.

Daniel hopped into bed and closed his eyes.

Chirp-chirp . . .
Chirp-chirp . . .
Chirp-chirp . . .
Danny Gray rolled over in his bed for his nightstand to turn off his bleeping cell alarm. He sat up and stretched his still sleepy body.

His voice moaned, "Butchie-Wutchie!"

Butch woke up from his pillow and sat next to his master's bed on the hardwood floor.

Daniel yawned at his pooch, "Time for a walk."

The cute beagle yelped happily.

They both left the bedroom for some breakfast in the kitchen. Danny did spoil Butch a little with some yummy sausages that morning. The beagle's owner put on some jeans, a dark green t, and tennis shoes before he and his sweet dog left the unit for an early walk.

Their walk lasted for forty minutes.

Sleepy Daniel Gray made it to his unit for his skating bag. He tiredly said to Butch, "I'll be back later this afternoon."

He fixed up Butch's Bong toy with a biscuit inside so the behaved twi-bastard would not get bored by being inside most of the day. The plastic toy was on the floor. Butch did not want to play with it now. He went for the couch and laid down.

Danny left his home for the building's front door.

Ally's white Horundi arrived a few minutes after Danny exit his unit. He carried his skating bag and stepped out of the warm building. The car's passenger door was open when Daniel opened the passenger door. He sat down on the leather seat with his bag on his lap.

Allison greeted him. "Morning."

"Morning." His sleepy voice spoke.

The Figure Instructor knew Sally's fiance was not fully awake yet so she did not say another word and drove off from the apartment building for the gym.

Surprise, surprise to Daniel Gray's eyes. He was fully awake when Ally's car made it to the gym's parking lot and walked out of the car for an easy workout that morning. They did their runs and pilate workouts. The dog trainer was glad he did not feel so tired and exhausted from being on the carpet track and studio room.

It was quarter after nine that morning. Ally and Daniel left the gym building. She drove her car from the parking lot to the ice rink. The figure novice had a challenge of his own. Have Ally-Loop skate around the rink and let him name out the skating moves she was doing. That would show he had been reading and paying attention to Allison and Sally's skating dvd discs.

The inside of the rink's building was a little cold and very empty to Daniel's point of view.

Ally smug, "I got the rink to ourselves for a couple hours before public session. And you don't have to pay admission today."

"Wow." Danny said shockingly. "Thanks, Ally."

"Let's go." She smiled brightly.

They both went to their sex gender locker rooms to change clothes and lace up their boots. Daniel wondered what their skating session would be like. He rushed out of the room and saw Ally skating out on the ice all by herself. She smiled proudly. He stepped out of the lobby area and walked through the doors.

The rink had loud music playing and the temp was not cold to Danny. His body was still warm from the pilate workouts and running he and his Figure Instructor did earlier. He stood on the ice and skated around the rink forward once, then he tried to do a mohawk turn from his left foot. He fell down on the cold patch of ice when he let his left blade stepped in front of the right boot instead of the boot's side.

Allison skated up to her figure student after turning her phone off from a remote that went for her special speaker.

Danny got up from the cold ice and asked his Figure Instructor, "I guess I need some help on figure turns."

"That's why we're here, Daniel." Allison spoke strongly. "To practice and have fun out on the ice."

The two figures skated to the center and slowly and carefully practiced on mohawks for both feet, forward and backwards. They also worked on three turns for both feet, forward only. Ally would show Daniel backward three turns some other skating time.

Step-turn-step-glide was the key ingredient on doing mohawk or other figure change foot turns. Glide-turn-glide was for the three turns and for other figure same foot turns.

Danny and Allison worked and worked some more with the turns until the novice's hips and feet were tired.

"Ally," he breathed out. "I need a break."

"Okay." She kindly said.

Her figure student gliding off the rink and slipped on his blade's guards. His tired legs and feet climbed-up the short stairway for the rink's lobby.

Daniel slumped on a bench, leaned forward, and unlaced his figure boots to air out his tired, sweaty feet. His legs stuck out in front of him. His back was leaning against the bench's wooden back support. He lifted up his head and stared up at the ceiling.

Good thing the lobby and the ice rink was quiet. His mind did feel a bit of a headache from his changed work routine at the Pet store, learning all new figure terms, and a little fear of getting married to Joy Hunt's daughter. He was ready for Sally, but was not ready to have Joy bickering him after the wedding. He hoped his future mother-in-law would not continue to act that way in their lives together.

Daniel rested for ten minutes and headed back on the ice. After he fixed his socks, he slipped on and laced up his figure boots. He slowly lifted himself up from the bench to skate some more.

While the dog trainer had his break, Allison had her music player on and danced around the empty rink with jumps, spins, fancy freestyle steps, forward to backward glides, and just having fun of being a good figure skater. Her brown eyes noticed Daniel getting up from one of the benches and walking back to the rink. She let him stroke around the patch of ice for a little while.

The Figure Instructor found her remote in her left pocket. She lifted up the remote and her right index finger pressed the play button. The song that was playing was a soft metal song called 'Wish You Knew Better.'

Ally stroked forward around the whole rink with really smooth and graceful moves. After going around twice, she did an inside right mohawk turn and skated around backwards three times with crossover edge changes.

Danny watched the brunette passionate skater move like a lithe ballerina. She did her jumps beautifully. Her single or combination spins were centered. She even managed to do almost all the freestyle moves figure skaters do on the ice.

The figure novice thought to himself the maneuvers she performed to the song that was playing. He thought the most important thing about watching his teacher was Ally never lost her figure position in all the moves she did. From spin jumps, spins on ice, dance steps, and stylish moving positions. Her head was up. Her arms and hands always at chest level. She had her shoulders relaxed. Her legs and feet smoothly danced. She was a lot more passionate and happy than when he watched Sally Hunt or any other figure skater ice skate.

Ally found her remote in her left pant's pocket when the song ended. She paused it and skated up to Danny at the center of the rink.

Her student told her, "You haven't changed after watching your skating routine disc. Your figure skating is more entertaining than Sally's."

"Really?" Ally breathed out speechlessly.

"Yeah." Daniel admit. "Your skating routines are one of a kind. Sally's are good, but not enjoyable. Hard to believe for saying this but 'another figure skater is better than my sunshine fiancee.'"

The figure friends knew to keep that a secret. Ally also knew that Danny was trusting her more and more with figure skating than either of the Hunts.

The Figure Instructor pushed off from her right blade and skated around the middle painted circle. She stated loudly, "It's about time someone says I'm better than your fiancee!"

Ally stopped skating and seriously told her figure friend, "All Sally and Joy want to is win rather skate for fun of it. Winning is not everything, Daniel. The loving feel of passion is."

Daniel wondered, "'The loving feel of passion?' Could you tell me what that means?"

Ally sighed sadly, "That's a typical response. Not a lot of people seem to remember life's little passions."

She started to stroke forward and Daniel joined with her. They skated around the rink while Ally told him what's passion really about. "Passion is my key word in life. Love and passion are about the same, but love can be either true love or a fling of lust while passion is a much more powerful feeling than love or lust. Passion is the uncontrollable feeling you feel for something or someone no matter what happens in life. In good or bad times, it's always there."

Daniel's ears heard what was been said.

That's how I feel for Sally. He thought.

Ally went on, "People these days always want to be on top, have a big bank account, try out fancy cool skills, wear hot clothes, get into exclusive places, meet famous people, own the latest cars, electronic toys, and work little to gain a lot of money and credentials. Why do you think the typical American likes to have that, Danny?"

His mind thought and wandered of the answer and came up with nothing. "I guess I don't know."

The Figure Instructor did a snowplow stop.

Daniel stopped too. He wondered if Ally was mad at him for not knowing the answer to her question.

She stood in front of him and spoke, "It's called 'the flinging passion of success.'"

This term made Danny curious.

Allison told him, "That means you got success, but it doesn't last. People are always trying to find ways to keep that success, or 'fling passion,' to last on because they got their goal and want to do more with their success. Except when people do lose that success, they don't know why or how they lost it and don't take the time to remember what they did to get it in the first place. First timers or one time successors would waste money and time to get something that doesn't belong to them."

Daniel understood that really well. He did wonder what that had to do with Sally.

Ally happily said, "Figure skating is my passion."

He agreed with her, "I can see."

Then he remembered something odd from Sally's skating routines. He stated, "You know Sally has no true passion for figure skating."

"Uh!" Allison huffed, "I've known that for years! How would you know that?"

"It was easy to figure out from watching her skating dvd. I don't see passion or true happiness when she skates." He replied.

"It's true that Sally has no passion to be a figure skater, but all Joy Hunt wants is the gold. Let me tell you something very important about your fiancee's competitive career. What would happen when Sally's skating years are over? What is next for Joy Hunt?"

Daniel figured in his head, "She would have to let go of Sally and the thrill of winning the gold."

"Couldn't have said it better myself." Ally smug.

She was proud of her figure student to think of that strong answer.

Danny had a curious question to Allison. Something she asked him at the dog park on why he wanted to be a Pet trainer.

"What inspired you to ice skate, Allison?"

Ally stopped skating after doing a one foot snowplow stop with her right blade. Not many people had asked her that particular question.

Daniel stopped skating to stand next to the passionate figure skater.

"When I was ten years old, I used to read this one book for the school's library that told the bio of a little girl's skating life. What the photos showed and what the girl told in the story inspired me to go for skating and I loved it ever since." The Figure Instructor expressed happily.

Danny noticed a big difference from Allison and Sally's passion in skating. Ally wanted to skate because she wanted to do it for her while Sally was forced to skate and do nothing else to enjoy in life. He needed to show Sally's parents she had no passion in figure skating at all.

Ally continued on, "Ice skating made me better person from the inside out."

Her ears heard a song that she really loved and found the remote to turn the music up. She skated forward. Then backward while her body danced to the beat of the song's tune.

She sung out loud and smiled from ear to ear.

When the song ended, Ally turned down the volume for the next few songs with the speaker's remote. She skated up Daniel and told him more about her first skating year.

"As a kid, I was not smart in school, I had a speech problem, and I never knew what I liked for me. But when I found that figure skating book, I found my special love in life. I literally begged my dad to let me have ice skating lessons and he gave in." She giggled.

Danny listened more of her skating story.

Ally told her student, "I started in group lessons for six months and completed all the basic levels and moved up into the freestyle levels. I was a natural and I did not want to stop doing figure skating because I was doing well in school. I even found a way to beat my speech problem all on my own just by singing and learning the lyrics from my favorite songs. For lunch time in middle school and high school, I would always be in the gym to dance or practice my skating moves."

"Have anyone seen you work off ice?" Daniel wondered.

"I didn't pay attention." Ally curt.

The figure student left it at that. For now.

"My mind was blown-away after doing spins and jumps so well, I wanted to compete badly. My current coach has been there for me since I was thirteen and she taught me a great deal of on ice and off ice practice. I did my own skating learning and explored more of my figure passions. One of my favorite things to do for skating is being out there first when the ice is freshly cut. I could just glide smoothly like I'm flying in a 318 Jet Air bus high up in the air. My point of view of saying, 'the ice is freshly cut' means 'the ice is smooth or resurfaced.'" The Figure Instructor replied.

"Now that's a clever name for a smooth patch of ice." Danny chuckled.

Both skaters then did a mohawk turn slowly to glide backwards. Daniel struggled a little with his mohawk but he turned without falling down on his ass again.

"After graduating from high school, this became my job. Being a competitive skater trying to get to the top." Ally stated. "Lots of Pros want to be on top for many reasons. Fame, fortune, travel, supporting the sport, or because they have what it takes to be part of a good team. It's funny how we athletes have an inner animal to be good in certain sports. We have the passion to do incredible skills or go to the next level to be good. That's our hunger. We crave to be active and show people new things from a particular sport. But there's a down side to get good."

"And what's that?" Danny wondered.

Ally sighed with hurt, "Being told 'no, you're not made for this sport' or 'you have no exceptional talent to be a champion.' But sometimes the feel of defeat or rejections can be a good thing for the wanna-be athletes. Either the coach or team players are right, or the person just need to keep fighting until they can't go on anymore."

His mind thought, *I think Ally's been through a lot of hurts and unfair judgments in figure skating too.*

"Even though not everyone can be incredible in professional sports, they can have fun by pretending to be a wonderful athlete. To me, one of the saddest things of being an athlete is learning about those who are good at sports and don't take the time to practice the basics first and then do the complicated skills last."

Daniel remembered her saying those similar words during his first few skating lessons. *Start out slow and then move to more advance stuff.*

It was working for him at the Pet store for Pet training time in the booth.

Ally added, "Those athletes usually end up with a bad injury or they simply can't work well with others in a team. There is one other big disappointment in my opinion. A once wonderful athlete was forced out or step down because someone better came along and the wonderful athlete still have a lot of passion left in them to continue on."

Daniel did remember what happened to hefty Walter after his teddy bear underwear secret. He quit hockey and was never heard from again. The Pet trainer felt bad because if Sally and her friends had not came in to the team's locker room to save Danny, Walter would still play hockey and Daniel would not be in good shape after beaten down to a pulp by a bunch hockey players.

He said, "I can imagine that feeling."

"It kills my heart that lots of people would waste their special talent for possessions or have their fifteen minutes of fame for nothing. I never forget my passion over money, being well-known, or live the lap of luxury. My passion is what makes me happy and I don't take that for granted if I feel sad, tired, or bored by not getting what I want out of figure skating." Ally explained sadly and strongly.

Danny had a rhetorical question for his Figure Instructor. "What would you do when you're needed to step down or stop figure skating?"

"Oh geesh . . ." That hurt Ally's heart.

Immediately, she stopped skating backwards with a back stop. She closed her eyes and had her right hand over her heart.

Daniel did an open mohawk turn to stop gliding with a forward snowplow stop. His ears did hear Allison softly cry. Warm tears were falling from her eyes and rolling down on her cheek.

"I'm sorry for asking." He sadly spoke. "I was only wondering about your opinion on what would happen if it did happen to you."

Ally opened her teary brown eyes and sniffled, "What would happen if my time on the ice was over? I honestly can't bear the thought of letting that happen to me. I got years before that time would come. For now, I just keep on skating."

Then she had a thought.

She did tell her figure student this: "I do know is I don't want to do anymore competitions until I reach twenty-five years old. That's my retirement from doing routines and big skating events. After that, I wouldn't mind to be a figure skating coach and teach others how to be good on the ice by starting with the basics and move up."

"Ally-Loop. Ice skating teacher." Danny teased. "Has a nice ring to it."

The figure friends began skating forward.

"I am glad my coach is nothing like Joy Hunt." Ally sighed happily.

Daniel asked, "I have seen Joy Hunt with Sally at Regionals, but not from her skating practices. How is she a coach to Sally during off-season?"

Allison replied, "As I said before, 'Joy only wants the gold.' She's a harsh, strict coach to Sally on the ice. She never wanted her daughter to start off slow and then progress to pro skills. For example, let's say Joy Hunt wanted to teach a six year old how to do a double salchow jump after the six year old just made it into the first freestyle level. That level was not needed to do double salchows. The six year old should learn how to do a waltz jump rather than a double spin jump."

The Figure Instructor seriously put in, "My point is Sally's mom doesn't take the time rethink the basics and move up in the skating levels properly. I wish I knew why she wants the gold so badly."

Now that he thought of that statement, Daniel Gray was very curious himself on why Joy wanted the gold too. He definitely needed to ask either Sally or Paul.

"My passion is pretty simple. To dance on ice and show people that figure skaters can be hard-core athletes."

"Does everyone have passion?" Danny asked.

"Yes." She did a right inside three turn to skate backwards.

Ally then explained, "If you want to find your own passion, you have to discover it within yourself, Daniel. Ask yourself these three questions: What makes you happy no matter what goes on in life? Why does it make you happy? And most importantly, how do you keep that passion alive?"

Daniel thought, *Such good moral questions. Not only Ally is a good figure skater, she understands passion.*

He told her, "I'll let you know when I figure out the answers."

"Take your time." She calmly said.

Danny asked, "Didn't you want to do college or something other than figure skating?"

He tried to do a right inside three turn himself and ended up hitting against a wall on his back. He pushed away from the wall and skated backwards.

Allison deeply sighed and answered, "I'm not that smart to get into college and I have some big goals to do in ice skating. One of those goals is something I've been working very hard for Nationals next January. I love this sport so much, I can't picture myself of doing something beside ice skating around a big patch of ice."

The figure student wondered, "What kind of skating goals do you have?"

"Well, there's the most obvious one. Win an Olympic gold medal." Ally giggled. "But for this year-"

She so wanted to tell someone other than her coach what she wanted to accomplish in competitive figure skating, but stopped herself after realizing if she did say something, she would not nail her challenging jump combination.

"This year what?" Daniel waited with anticipation.

Allison shut her mouth and did a backstop with her right blade.

Her figure student turned around from a right open mohawk and stopped himself. He nicely pressed her, "Aren't you going to tell me?"

She looked at him and shook her head firmly.

"How come?" He asked.

Her voice nervously spoke, "It's only for me and my coach. I'm afraid if I did tell someone else, I would jinx it."

"I understand, Ally," replied Danny.

They both started to skate around the center part of the rink and worked on backward crossovers for both ways.

As a song ended and a new one came on, Ally instructed Daniel, "Why don't you skate around and see if you can dance to the flow of the music's tune."

The figure student was a little unsure on how he should groove on ice like Ally-Loop. He did feel grateful it was only the two of them instead of facing a huge crowd of people on the ice.

Danny did not glide or move. He just stood in one spot.

Allison figured out why her student decided to not dance.

He's scared. She thought.

She asked, "Can't you dance?"

Daniel shook his head.

"Have you and Sally ever danced together?" Ally wondered.

"Never did." He confessed.

The Figure Instructor told her figure friend, "Daniel, I know this may come as a shock to you but to be a good figure skater on ice, you need to learn how to dance."

"Like ballet stuff?" He nervously questioned.

"A little." Ally stated. "Except dancing on ice can be fun and enjoyable. Joy Hunt really likes male figures who can dance well on and off ice."

Danny thought Ally was trying to butter him up so he could be shown how to ice dance. Truth of the matter was: the Figure Instructor was not buttering up her student to dance.

He gave in. "Okay. How do figure skaters dance?"

What Allison decided to do for Danny was show him some easy dance steps. The mohawk combination.

Forward stroke left, then right, left again, right inside mohawk turn, glide backwards on the left blade, right blade steps on the ice and outside mohawk turn for a forward left foot glide.

Ally would show Daniel how to skate to the music some other skating time. Their feet practiced with turns until it was time of step off the ice for a resurface to start afternoon public session.

The figure friends took off their skates in the lobby area and continued to do step-by-step figure turns. Daniel was getting better and better at it.

While the two practiced, lots of people came inside the arena's building. Kids with birthday parties or teenagers or adults came to the rink for dates or get-togethers.

But that day, a huge group college age girls wearing turquoise color jersey shirts and acting all happy and flirting strutted in the big rink's lobby.

The Pet trainer curiously wondered, "Why are there a lot of girls, Ally?"

She firmly explained, "I've heard from Jessica some of the PHL guys are coming here for a little practice session. You know squealing girls. They love cute professional athletes."

And sure enough the front doors opened and thirty PHL players with serious looks on their faces and dressed in their turquoise jersey shirts or black soft shell team jackets headed inside the arena. They carried their gear bags and their coaches walked with the group.

Like Allison Rigden predicted, the girls squealed and raced up toward the hockey dudes for autographs or wish to get a number from one of the players. All the PHL guys were unhappy to be surrounded by stuck up bitches who would not let them be. Instead of going to the big rink, the hockey team went to the small rink. The girls followed them.

Ally scoffed, "Typical non-loyal fans."

Danny had to agree with his Figure Instructor's point view about those brainless girls.

Both figures ignored the PHLs and the sneaky ladies at the small rink to work more on dance steps and basic turns.

It was one-thirty in the afternoon when public session was ready for the big rink. Allison and Daniel's figure boots were back on and ready to skate more on the ice. They both stroked forward around the rink. After gliding a few times a round, Ally slowed down to do a mohawk turn to glide backwards.

Danny decided to do the same thing that his Figure Instructor did. He slowed down his speed, lifted up his left blade from the ice, stepped it close to his right blade and did a perfect switch feet turn. He stood up straight and all and kept on wiggling his hips and feet.

Ally told him, "Good job."

Her eyes saw a small group of teenage girls chattering and giggling at each other as they skated on the ice and wearing rental skates. The Figure Instructor turned herself around to skate forward.

Danny noticed Allison looking unhappy before she wanted to skate forward. He asked, "Are you okay?"

She sadly confessed, "I would trade in my skating talent just to have friends."

He questioned his instructor, "How come you don't have any friends?"

Both their ears heard, "I think Number 65 likes you, Rachel."

Allison angrily responded, "It's hard for famous athletes to have faithful friends when they're not competing or trying to be a normal person."

She's mad. The Pet trainer thought.

Like Daniel Gray predicted, Ally glided around the ice as fast as she could. She looked happy and at peace by skating all by her lonesome self.

After she skated the whole rink circle three times, Allison stopped at the center. Danny skated for the center.

He had not let go of his concerned question. "Why, Ally-Loop?"

She rolled her brown eyes and unhappily sighed. She thought her pupil was going to let go of that topic. Her mind remembered back to her grade school years.

"I only had one friend in my whole life. Her name was . . . Donna." She did have a hard time saying that name.

The two figures started to skate around the rink forward.

"Oh . . ." Danny sighed, "What happened?"

Their blades were crunching and scraping on the solid ice floor.

Ally told out her not-so-lasting friendship tale. "Before fifth grade, Donna and I were inseparable in and sometimes outside of school. Fridays before lunch during fifth grade class were library time. That was when I first found that skating book. I was reading the book so much, I started to ignore Donna and did not want anymore play dates with her. She and I fought a lot-" The Figure Instructor felt a chill from the cold air. Her arms were getting warm after her hands rubbed them.

"In and outside of school because I was too obsessed from reading that figure skating book and all I wished to talk about was figure skating. Donna grew tired of wanting to be friends with me. I don't blame her for thinking that way of me, but I could not let go of my own special little passion spark. Our parents, teacher, and principle tried to settle out our differences, but Donna and I could not get alone anymore. She was sent to another class and I acted like she never existed."

Daniel was surprised at the silly, childish rivalry. He insightfully spoke, "I think you may have occupied yourself too much with that book more than being with people."

Allison relieved, "I figured that out a few years after I first started this sport. So when me and Donna's friendship was really over, figure skating became my best friend and I skated as much as I could. I am sorry and still feel bad that my old friend and I had not rekindled or make up, except I can't let go of my purpose in life."

"And what is your purpose?" Danny wondered.

"To beat your fiancee in her own skating game." Ally-Loop stated strongly.

Daniel's heart did feel hurt after listening to his instructor's claim. The fact was: Allison Rigden was a more passionate figure skater than figure champ Sally Hunt.

He reluctantly understood his Figure Instructor's point of view.

When the time reached four-thirty that afternoon, Daniel Gray was all skated out. He had to admit, Ally did give him some really simple pointers on how to improve his skating skills. He was also glad he was not alone on trying to be a good figure 'male' for Joy Hunt. Their next session would happen the Wednesday before going to Sectionals.

He did figure out what he wanted to do for Sally later that night for their date.

Danny made it back to his unit, took Butch for an hour long walk, showered, put on some nice outing clothes, and left his unit for Sally's mansion home.

Behind the closed door of the mansion house, sunshine Sally Hunt was shocked to see Daniel with a beautiful bouquet of blue and white color flowers in his left hand.

"Oh, Danny . . ." Sally slowly grabbed the floral grouping with both of her hands.

Her honey voice gasped, "You brought me Delphinium, Hydrangea, and Hymenocallis for the bouquet's decor. Such a wonderful combination."

She let her fiance in the house and went for the kitchen. His right hand went for his jacket's side pocket and pulled out her dark blue dvd case.

Danny told Sally, "I brought back your skating dvd."

He handed back her case.

Sally had her floral grouping in her right hand and her case in her left hand. "Thank you, Daniel. I Love You."

His heart made him say, "I Love You too."

In the kitchen, Sally found a small flower vase and filled it with cold fresh water. Her flower gift was safely placed in the vase. Daniel waited for his love in the room while she rushed up to her bedroom and put her flower bouquet on her nightstand.

While Sally was in her room, Joy was dressed in long white slacks and a deep maroon color dress shirt. She saw her future son-in-law in her house.

She greeted him, "Hello, Daniel."

"Hi, Mrs. Hunt." He uncomfortably spoke. "Just waiting for Sally."

Joy told him what the travel plan was, "Paul will pick you up at your place at three a.m. and bring an overnight bag."

Then she gave Danny his round trip tickets in a paper billfold. "Please keep them safe."

"I will." He kept the billfold close to him.

The blond figure champ rushed down stairs.

Joy spoke to Sally, "Be careful."

"Yes, Mommy."

Mrs. Hunt went upstairs for the master bedroom.

Sally & Danny gave each other a 'Miss You' kiss' and left the house for a yummy Mexican dinner and talked about skating stuff during their date.

Sunday went slow for Daniel.

Sally told him the night before when Sectionals was over, no more date nights for two weeks. He gave in to Joy's request. He knew it was her idea instead of Sally's.

The Pet trainer did ask his parents if they would watch over Butch for his trip to Salt Lake City. Mrs. Gray said to her son she and her husband would be happy to watch over Butch.

Danny told his mother he would bring Butch and his doggie essentials over Wednesday night and he would pick up his beagle that coming Sunday after his plane flight.

Throughout Monday thru Wednesday, Daniel kept himself busy by taking out Butch for his walks, doing his dog training in the Pet store's booth without feeling scared or afraid of interacting with the dog's owners, worked on his figure moves off ice, and watched more of Ally's skating routines and naming the moves she did.

Ally on Sunday and Monday were the most nerve-wrecking times on the ice. She was trying her very hardest to nail an edge quad-quad combination jump. She and her coach worked and worked with no success.

The figure's teacher assured Ally, "It's okay if you can't nail one before Sectionals. You still have Nationals."

Allison moaned sadly. She wanted the world to know she wanted to conquer something no other figure skater could do before.

The Figure Instructor did practice on her trampoline for her 'in the air spins'. It was a good thing she had blown up mattresses around her jumping tool so she would not injure herself badly. She requested from the staff members at the rink for a Tuesday night private ice session. They granted her request and let her have the small rink.

When Tuesday night arrived, Ally skated and pushed herself as much as she could in the dark small ice rink. 'Vault' and 'The Ace's Wings theme' were pumping her up to nail the quad-quad edge combo.

Sectionals was in two days. She needed to be her ultimate best that night. The brunette figure was long and lean in her spins and spirals. Her feet fast-paced for dance steps. And lastly, her jumps were full of height, speed, and strength.

Her forehead was covered in sweat and her muscles ached her body from practicing two and half hours straight.

Her tired voice called out loudly, "I-want to-win!"

She growled and glided quickly around the small rink once before doing an axel take off and managed to do four back spins up in the air, she checked her landing and took off for a loop jump.

Without even thinking, Ally did not one, not two, or three back spins. She managed to do four back spins in the air after she felt an extra back spin from a normal triple loop.

The landing was strong and perfect.

Allison Rigden could not believe or feel on what she had just done. Her back gliding stopped and proudly stood on the ice. She cried loudly. Her heart felt relief and satisfaction.

"Now that's hard-core figure skating!" She yelled out.

She was ready to work on a new routine for Sectionals and Nationals. Only Nationals will get the quad-quad.

The only thing that could have made Ally-Loop's night was: if tonight happened to be Nationals.

Chapter Eleven

It was Wednesday night and Danny dropped of Butch and his stuff in his folk's home. They were surprised of their son going to a figure skating event because his fiancee was participating in it. What Daniel did not tell his parents was his Figure Instructor was his fiancee's skating rival.

Danny said his 'good-bye and be good' to Butchie-Wutchie. Butch seemed happy to be back in his first home.

The Pet trainer left the Gray's house for the arena.

Allison Rigden's heart was filled with excitement and a mixture of fear too. Less than twenty-four hours ago, Ally nailed the quad-quad combo and no one else knew about it. She did not want to tell her coach until the last day of Sectionals.

She was dressed in her hot pink skating costume and long tan tights that covered her skating boots from her Regional's 'Vault' routine. She stood by the men's locker room with her right hand holding her phone and waited for Daniel to come out.

The locker doors opened.

Out came Danny in his sweat pants, t-shirt, and his suede material boots. He saw Ally and said, "All dressed up for tomorrow?"

She giggled, "Yup, I am. But we are going to use the small rink for the night."

"Why?" He questioned his Figure Instructor.

"Because tomorrow's the Senior Ladies' short program for Sectionals and I would very much like to have my student judge my routine. Interested?" Ally offered.

Danny already saw her short program from Regionals but he would not mind seeing it again and name off the moves she did.

"Lead the way, Ally-Loop." He happily replied.

The two figure friends left the lobby and walked through a long hallway by the building's front door. There was another skating rink in the rink's building. It was smaller than the other one.

He did remember to give back Ally her skating dvd.

"Here's your disc." His right hand presented the red case to her.

She took the case and said, "Thank you. I hope you learned something from the disc."

"I learned lots from yours and Sally's routines and practice sessions." Daniel replied.

Ally walked through the small rink's door first then Danny followed her.

Their blades touched the ice and the Loop glided for her speaker. She placed her phone on an MP3 black speaker, fixed up her routine song, and had the remote in her left hand.

Danny stood by the side to watch his Figure Instructor do her 'Vault' routine. Before she did begin her program, she placed her dvd case by the speaker and skated up to her figure student. She handed him the speaker's remote.

What he held was a small rectangular black and gray color remote with eight different buttons on it.

Allison requested her student, "Press play only once. When I nod my head down, press the button and I'll start out skating."

He responded, "Okay."

Ally skated to the middle and did her short program stance. Her head nod down and Daniel raised the remote for the black speaker and 'Vault' started to play.

Danny whispered, "Back pivot."

Ally-Loop was doing the left toe-pick back spin stance. She stroked around the ice and did an inside right mohawk turn. She did some backward crossovers, both blades were on the ice, and then both blade jumped up together.

"Double loop." The figure student mumbled from watching Ally do two back rotations in her loop jump.

The routine lasted for two and a half minutes. Daniel noticed fans or beginner skaters watching Ally from the glass windows.

When the song ended, Ally did her trademark lunge trick. Danny and the skating fans clapped and cheered for Ally-Loop's routine.

Fans walked out from the small rink's lobby for the rink's steps. Ally did tell them strongly, "You folks can't be here."

A young girl complained, "How come he can and we can't?"

The girl pointed out Danny out on the ice.

He skated to the speaker and placed the remote on top of the speaker.

Allison professionally spoke, "He's my student and has special privileges to be here with me."

A male rink staff member stepped out of the small rink's lobby doors and spoke out, "I'm sorry but no public attendance is allowed here. Please go to the big rink."

The fans left the small rink with disappointing looks on their face. Some of them grumbled with unfairness in their hearts.

The male staff cheered, "Keep it up, Ally-Loop."

He left the rink to leave Daniel Gray and Allison Rigden alone on the ice.

"Sorry that happened, Daniel." Ally unhappily said.

"It's okay. That's what I get for being friends with famous figure skaters." He told her.

His Figure Instructor nodded her head uncomfortably in agreement. She could relate to that too.

She wondered, "How was I?"

Danny replayed Allison's 'Vault' routine in his head and slowly looked at all the moves she did. This was his judgment for Ally.

"Allison Rigden, you're going to rock out tomorrow."

"I'm glad I haven't lost my touch." Ally blushed.

They glided off the small rink for a little break. The two sat on a bench to rest and did talk a little more what was going to happen in Sectionals.

Fifteen minutes later, Daniel and Allison just skated around the small rink, forward and backwards, with music playing from the black speaker. Ally knew she needed a good night's rest for Sectionals the next day.

Their skating time had ended the same time as public session stopped. Walking through the hallway for the big rink lobby, Daniel reminded Ally, "I am going to Sectionals with Sally and her parents."

"Wow, really?" She gasped.

Danny nodded excitedly.

"In Salt Lake City, Utah?"

He nodded again.

"How'd you let Joy do that for you?" Ally curiously wondered.

"She invited me." He candid.

The Figure Instructor had a new concern for Daniel. "What about Butch?"

He assured his instructor, "He's with my folks now and they promised to take care of him until I get back."

"That's a good idea." His Figure Instructor tried to say cheerfully, "Give Sally my best."

"Good lucky for you too, Ally-Loop." Danny spoke to the Loop as a coach instead of as her student.

"Night." They spoke at the same time.

She went for the girl's locker room and he moved into the men's locker room.

At two-thirty the next morning, a sleep Daniel Gray was woken up from his cell's alarm. He lifted up from bed, packed up his things together, and dress up nice for the Hunts. Dark gray dress pants, light brown dress shirt, and black dress shoes. He also brought a nice black coat.

Danny found his black roller suitcase and skating bag. He brought his skates in case he got a chance to do a little bit of skating.

He waited for the Hunt's red SUV five minutes.

When the red car arrived, Daniel walked outside the apartment building and made it for the red SUV. Inside were Paul driving, Joy sitting in the passenger seat, and Sally in the backseat. All the Hunts were dressed super nice for the airport.

"You look very handsome, Danny." Sally squealed.

They leaned in for a long kiss.

Paul drove the car from downtown and went on the freeway for an hour long drive south from both their homes. Then he took the exit for the Mineta San Jose International Airport.

Paul paid for parking in the parking garage and all the figures left the car for their flight to Salt Lake City.

The airplane flight lasted for about three and a half hours. In first class, Sally & Danny sat next to each other while Joy & Paul sat in front of them. The young lovers talked, held hands, kissed, and watched some of Sally's past skating routines from her portable dvd player.

When the plane ride was over, the Hunts and Daniel left the huge plane and walked through the Salt Lake City International Airport. It seem to Danny's point of view that there were some skating fans in the airport too.

He & Sally kept their mouths shut and followed Paul & Joy for the terminal to get their things and to a rental car stand.

Mr. Hunt drove an expensive looking silver SUV from the airport to a hotel not far from the skating rink's building for Sectionals. The SUV was pulled into the hotel's parking lot.

Everyone got out and gathered their things.

The hotel was packed with competitive figure skaters, coaches, family members, and skating fans too. Sally & Danny kept close together by holding their hands.

Joy told them both, "Go to the dining room and wait for us there."

Daniel Gray & Sally Hunt rushed from the entrance to the dining room on the first floor. Their free hands carried their bags. There was an empty table by the far end corner of the dining room. The young couple sat in the chairs and waited for Joy & Paul to come back.

Sally breathlessly said, "You'll get use to it, Danny."

Danny was not sure if he wanted to get use to being surrounded with lots of fans for figure skating. All he wanted was some alone time with his girl before she did her short program that night.

Paul & Joy Hunt walked into the dining room and found Danny & Sally. The married Hunts sat with the engaged couple.

Mr. Hunt gave Sally her room card key and Daniel his card key. "Daniel, you get your own room, Sally has her own room, and me & my wife have ours together."

Mrs. Hunt demanded from Danny & Sally, "We also don't want you two to sneak into each other's room at night. Understand?"

The young couple nodded to Joy's strict request.

A waitress came by their table and asked, "Can I get you folks something to eat or drink?"

Paul replied, "Sure. Menus please?"

She left the table to get four large menus for the hotel's restaurant food selection.

An hour later, everyone at the corner table were tired and full from their late breakfast meal.

Joy suggested, "Why don't we go to our rooms, rest up, and meet up by the lobby at four p.m.?"

"Sounds good, Mommy." Sally yawned.

The time was eleven-thirty a.m.

Plenty of time for a long nap and get ready for Sectionals. Danny helped Sally up from her chair and they went to their rooms.

He was glad Paul Hunt gave him a room next to Sally's. Sally &
Daniel put her things in her room.

They hugged and kissed.

"I Love You . . ."

Danny's heart felt sadness from his fiancee's voice. She was scared.
Scared of what was his question.

"I Love You, Sally . . ."

Their arms dropped from their bodies and Daniel left Sally's guest
room for his room.

It took him a few times to get in his room his key card. Danny
changed out of his nice clothes and into a comfy t-shirt and his black
sweat pants from his overnight bag.

He got on the comfy, newly made King size bed for a long cat nap.

Three hours later . . .

Daniel woke up in his guest room bed's at the hotel. He lifted up
from the messed up King size bed and grabbed his cell to call his folk's
home phone to see how Butchie-Wutchie was doing.

His mother sweetly told her son, "Butch is doing fine. I remember
to give him his morning walk and he's happily sleeping on his pillow."

That made Daniel feel better.

He ended the call and walked toward his overnight bag. He took
out his showering essentials. His arms carried them to the sparky clean
bathroom and placed them on the sink counter.

A warm shower did make Danny feel ready to go with Sally and her
parents to Sectionals. His hair smelled good, teeth were clean, face was
freshly shaven, and his bod was lightly spiced from his body wash.

He dressed himself in a white dress shirt, black slacks, and polished
his black dress shoes. His cell, wallet, and card key were in his left pant's
pocket.

Daniel left his locked up guest room and walked over for Sally's
room. On her door was a white piece of paper.

'Hi Sleepy-head,

I woke up early and just waiting for you in the first floor lobby.

Love,
Sally-babe'

Danny stepped away from Sally's room and rode down the elevator three floors for the first floor.

On the first floor were lots of skating fans crowding around the Hunts for picture taking and Sally signed some autographs for them. Joy was dressed in a light gray suit and black dress shirt with black heels. Paul was dressed in a dark gray business suit with a white dress shirt, dark gray dress shoes, and a silky light gray tie. Sally was dressed in jeans, gold color sweater, and her athletic shoes. Her curly blonde hair was up in a high ponytail.

The Pet trainer rushed through the fan crowd and took Sally's left hand. They left the lobby to stand next to the rental silver SUV.

Sally whispered, "Thank you, Danny."

Their lips meet together for a long soothing kiss.

Paul & Joy hurried out the hotel and made it to the SUV. They all got inside the car. Sally & Danny in the back, Paul & Joy up front. They were buckled up and Paul drove out of the parking lot.

Joy gave her husband a very special red, blue, and white color plastic parking pass. His right hand took it and placed it on the dashboard.

The rink that held Sectionals' event was a short drive from the hotel and was packed with cars, fans, and competitors. Paul drove to the rink's special parking area. He lowered the driver's side window, showed a male security guard the parking pass, and drove right on through for his assigned spot.

Sally and her Mommy left the SUV with her pink roller suitcase. They walked quickly over for the rink building's back entrance. Paul and Daniel went for the front entrance. Mr. Hunt handed his future son-in-law a V.I.P. pass badge.

He slipped on the thick red and blue color lanyard around his neck. The badge did say, 'All-Access'. He got special privileges to see Sally before her program.

Paul wore his badge too and the two men walked through the large crowd of people wanting to get in with tickets and the two men went for the V.I.P. doors with two big security guards there. They showed the guard their badges and let them through.

Mr. Hunt walked in front of Danny to the rink's stands. They sat in the front row and the Pet trainer was starting to feel cold by sitting close to the ice.

Paul did whisper to Daniel, "After the girls finish practicing on the ice, go down the walkway to good luck Sally."

"Thank you, Mr. Hunt." Daniel happily said.

He was wondering where Ally-Loop was.

His eyes did see his fiancee wearing her sunshine skating dress and her blond hair in a French braid with her color matched headband. Her left hand also wore her engagement ring too.

Danny was very proud of his love by wearing her ring.

He did notice Allison out on the ice too.

She was dressed in a very dark green, long sleeved skating dress and her brown hair was tied back in a low bun.

Ally's eyes saw Daniel at the stands and she winked at him for showing up.

The time was five forty-five p.m.

A lady announcer spoke into her mic that practice session was over and the girls needed to get ready for their short routine program. Daniel got up from his seat to see Sally. He walked on the walkway and Joy let him join her and Sally for their long walk in a hallway to the girl's locker room.

Danny & Sally held hands.

Even though Joy did not like seeing them be physically close, she kept her mouth shut and let them be a couple after all the learning he did from Ally-Loop.

Joy Hunt walked in the locker room first.

Sally nervously told him, "I Love You . . ."

Daniel held his blonde girl tightly. Her arms wrapped around his spicy smell bod. "Oh, Sally . . ."

His loving voice whispered, "I Love You too . . ."

They let go of their embrace and Sally went inside the locker room. The doors closed. Daniel walked back to the stands where Paul Hunt was sitting at.

"Is she okay?" The concerned father asked.

"She's nervous." Daniel told him.

"That's typically what all skaters feel just before they do major events." Paul expressed.

The dog trainer nodded his head in agreement.

Just like Regionals, Sally was up first in her light blue, silky bodysuit dress and a light blue color headband with her hair in a French braid. But when she tried to step out on the ice to do her figure strokes, Sally Hunt misused her left toe-pick and fell flat on her face on the cold ice.

The audience and judges gasped out loud. Photos were being taken of the incident. Sally crawled on the ice to the open gate door. Joy got her daughter's cold wet hands and helped her off the ice. She kept Sally to her side in her arms.

Daniel got up from his seat. He wanted to comfort his love from her fall.

He yelled out, "Mrs. Hunt, let me help!"

He quickly followed the Hunt girls in the hallway for the girl's locker room.

They stopped walking in the hallway.

Joy softly told to Sally only, "You know the plan."

Sally whispered, "Yes, Mommy . . ."

"Sally?" Danny concernedly asked, "Are you okay? Can I help?"

"Danny, please don't come closer." The blond figure champ insisted.

Danny was shocked. He demanded, "Why not?"

"Daniel, get back!" Joy yelled. "You don't know how to treat figure injuries!"

Her left hand caressed Sally's French braid. She soothed to her little girl, "Mommy will make you feel better, Sally."

The girls started to walk again.

Daniel protested, "She can't be with Mommy forever!"

"I'm not going to tell you again. Get back to the stands!" Mrs. Hunt growled.

She and Sally were close to the doors.

Danny questioned his fiancee, "Sally, who do you want?"

She turned her head to see Daniel Gray and softly told him, "Mommy can make me feel better for my routine."

Her head was back to face Joy and mother and daughter walked through the locker light blue doors.

As the doors closed, a male announcer stated, "Looks like a five minute delay for Ms. Hunt to do her program."

Danny moved closer for the doors. He wanted to hear what Joy and Sally were saying or doing in there. His left ear heard Joy Hunt's voice yelling at Sally.

"Sheesh, Sally! No wonder why you can't skate. Someone's been tampering with your special skates! Must be Ally-Loop!"

Sally argued back, "Mommy, not this again! Ally would not be that kind of skater."

"Hush, child!" Mrs. Hunt shouted.

Then Danny heard sharp slapping noises and Sally was crying her hardest. He so wanted to get his loving fiancee out of her mom's sharp claws and into his safe arms.

He rushed out of the long-stretched hallway and back to the stands before Joy or Sally saw him in the hallway. Danny sat in his seat next to Paul Hunt.

"How's Sally?" Mr. Hunt wondered.

Daniel answered, "Joy's taking care of her."

"Good."

Instead of paying attention or listening to the process of the skating event that night, Daniel had three important facts to think over. Why did Sally need 'special skates'? If she did, what could make Allison Rigden do that to Sally Hunt? And should he continue his skating lessons with a cheating figure skater just win over the blessings of a very violent mother-in-law?

Then again, Ally was right about what Joy Hunt was like behind closed doors. Wanting her daughter to be the best and not worrying about the basics in figure skating. Sally received harsh punishment because she did not go first or started out doing a first place routine.

When he got the chance to be alone with Ally, they had a lot to talk about. Daniel hoped Allison was not a cheater.

It was midnight and the window showed the black night sky. Daniel Gray was laying in his guest room's bed. What he learned during the drive back to the hotel was Sally won first place and Ally second. He was getting the feeling that his fiancee did not deserve the gold if she had 'special skates.' And yet, he had a bad vibe that Ally-Loop should not compete herself if she 'tampered' Sally's figure skates. He did not know who to trust in the world of figure skating.

In fact, there was only one figure he could trust in the mean time. Paul Hunt.

Danny made a mental note in his mind for the next day. If he can, he was going to have to talk about Joy's rival with Ally-Loop with Paul secretly.

Another hurtful feeling came inside his heart.

Joy was not giving him the chance to be a loving man for the woman he loved. He could not believe that Sally, his cute fiancee, would want her Mommy more than him. The girl who said, 'Yes' after he popped the question to her did not want to let go of her Mommy's love and support.

That really made Danny feel depressed and lonely. If he & Sally did get married, he wondered if she would still have Joy Hunt as her rock when she competes, or from the man who loved and adored her more than a figure champ.

The Pet trainer closed his eyes and let sleep take over his body for the rest of the night.

Knock-knock . . .

Knock-knock . . .

That made Daniel Gray open his eyes.

He moaned softly and rolled onto his other side to see if he could sleep some more.

Knock-knock . . .

"Uhhhh!" He growled.

Danny angrily lifted himself up from the Kings size bed for his door. His right eye looked through the little see-through glass on the door to see who was knocking on the door.

He immediately unlocked and opened the door for Ally-Loop.

"Hi, Dann-!"

His right hand grabbed her left arm and pulled her into his room. Ally fell on the carpet floor from that strong jerk. Daniel closed and locked the door.

"Hey, what the hell's wrong with you?" She protested.

She got up on her feet to face a pissed off, tired Daniel Gray.

He demanded, "Did you tamper with Sally's skates?"

Ally was shocked and confused.

"What? I may despise your fiancee's skating skills, but I would never cheat or stoop down to her mom's level."

"I'm not going to ask you again. Did you mess up Sally's skates last night?" Danny shouted.

"Daniel, what the fuck are you talking about?" She wondered.

He told Ally, "How could you, Allison? Sally could've hurt herself if you did something selfish and unfair."

"Unfair?" Ally barked back. "Unfair?"

"That's right." Danny thought over of a theory. "You got so sick and tired of coming in at second place, you decided to hurt Sally by doing something to her skates. What did you do to her skates?"

Allison Rigden knew Joy had gone too far with her stupid rival against her. Getting her student to think she had anything to do with Sally's special skates.

She strictly told Danny, "You want to talk about 'unfair?' How about Sally getting special treatment wherever she goes because she's the champ. She's only a figure champ because her last name is Hunt! Yes, I agree that Paul Hunt was a wonderful male figure during his competitive years, but Sally's not up to par with her own father! But if you think I had something to do with Sally's fall last night, then you have no idea what happens in the locker room with Joy and Sally!"

Danny strongly implied, "I heard Joy say you've been tampering with Sally's skates before her short program."

"Ha! That's Joy Hunt! Always blaming me for her own shitty little problems. Listen here, Daniel Gray: Joy and Sally always have the locker room to themselves just so little miss sunshine can have an extra ten minutes to get herself ready for her time to shine for the judges!" Ally huffed.

Still feeling tired, Daniel calmed himself down and sat on his messed up bed. He questioned his Figure Instructor, "So, you really didn't 'tamper' or caused something to ruin Sally's figure skates?"

"Look," Ally lowered her voice, "I have nothing personal against the Hunts. I just wonder why would Joy pressure her daughter so much to win the gold in figure skating. I do notice in Sally's eyes that she has fear. She is petrified to be on the ice and tied to her Mommy all the time."

"You're not the only who can see past her smily face." Danny solemnly stated.

He got up from the bed and gave Ally an apologetic hug. "Sorry I was bastard."

She wrapped her arms around him. "It's ok."

Their arms dropped and Daniel did feel relieved that the Loop was not a cheater. He wanted to make up for his little misunderstanding with Ally.

He asked her, "What are you going to do today?"

The Figure Instructor thought over her schedule. "Well, my coach and I are going to do a lesson this afternoon. But nothing this evening."

Danny requested, "Could we skate tonight?"

"Sure." She said. "Do you have your badge?"

He pointed out his lanyard 'All-access' badge on top of the nightstand.

"We'll sneak in around nine p.m. and we should be able to skate as much as we want tonight." Ally snickered.

"Sounds good to me." He went for his overnight bag and picked out the clothes he wanted to wear for the day with Sally. Nice khaki pants, a button up light green shirt, and brown dress socks and shoes.

Ally left Danny's guest room quietly.

Before he could take a shower, his ears heard a girl argument in front of his door.

He quickly exit his guest room and closed the door to see Ally and Joy using fighting words against each other.

His voice loudly spoke, "Hey! Quit it!"

Running Paul came to the group too.

Joy demanded, "Why did she go into your room?"

"To talk." Danny calmly explained.

"Listen to me, Ally-Loop. Daniel Gray is engaged to my daughter and I don't want you to butter him up so he can get into your pants." Mrs. Hunt strictly spoke.

Unimpressed Ally sighed, "You know, Joy, I don't have any feelings for Daniel at all. I was only being a coach to him, nothing more."

"I saw you two hugging each other from the little see-through glass on the door." Joy snarled.

Paul unhappily replied, "Oh, Danny . . ."

Embarrassed Daniel looked at Paul.

"Why?" Mr. Hunt asked.

"I got mad at Ally because she woke me up. I jerked her into my room and yelled at her for no reason." Danny explained sadly. "We only gave each other a friendship hug as an apology."

Joy Hunt had an idea.

"Daniel, there's only one way for me to be sure that you don't have feelings for Ally."

His brown eyes eyed at her upset green eyes.

"And what's that?"

Her voice spoke, "Kiss her."

"Huh?" Ally and Danny questioned Joy.

"Kiss Ally as if she were Sally." Mrs. Hunt requested. "I've seen you & my daughter kiss with love and affection. Show me that you can with another girl."

Daniel gulped.

He knew Sally was not going to like this.

He stood in front of his Figure Instructor, did his best to look lovingly into her strange dark brown eyes, and leaned down to softly kiss Ally's smooth lips. To make Joy Hunt happy, Ally kissed Danny back.

Their kiss was short.

When their lips split, Ally confessed, "Sorry, Daniel."

He wondered, "Why sorry?"

"I felt no spark from your hug or kiss." She answered honestly.

"Neither do I, Ally." Danny happily told her.

Joy was disappointed.

She scoffed, "That was an awful kiss from you two. I guess you really have no feelings for each other."

Paul took his wife's right hand and respond, "Sorry my wife bothered you guys. We'll meet you in twenty minutes at the dining room, Danny."

The married Hunts went back to their room to clean themselves up.

Allison still felt chagrin from that little outburst episode with Joy Hunt. She suggested, "So, eight-thirty tonight by the lobby. Have your skates ready."

"Sounds like a plan." Danny replied.

Just when he wanted to turn around for a shower and change of clothes, he realized he left his card keys in his room.

The Pet trainer groaned, "Aahhh . . . Ally?"

"What's wrong?" She asked.

He sighed, "I left my card in my room."

Ally offered, "You want me to go down to the front counter and see if I can get you another card?"

"Sure."

Allison's figure form rushed from the Daniel's room door for the stairs and ran down the staircase.

It took her faster than she thought to get a spare for Danny's room. Her long legs dashed up the stairs and handed the dog trainer a spare card.

He thanked her. "Thanks. I still owe you from that misunderstanding this morning."

"I can wait." She said.

Ally walked back to her room on the other side of the third floor.

Danny got inside his room for a quick shower, changed into the clothes he picked out, and took his wallet, cell, and card keys.

He met up with Joy & Paul Hunt in the dining room.

He sat in a chair and asked nicely, "Where's Sally?"

Paul told him, "She's at a bookstore now. She needed some time away from the fans and media."

"I can imagine." Danny stated.

Then he nervously questioned her parents, "Does Sally need to know about what Ally and I did?"

"No, Daniel. She doesn't." Joy assured her daughter's fiance. "I guess I was wrong about that. I am sorry for treating you like crap ever since I first met you. My only concern was you & Sally were going to ruin each other's live if you two had gotten too close."

Danny firmly told Joy & Paul, "I Love Sally and want to give her the good things in life."

Paul replied, "Let's see if you're going to be true to your word after the wedding."

A waiter came by their table for their morning meal.

Fifteen minutes later, the food arrived and the Hunts and Daniel Gray completed their breakfast within twenty minutes. They left the dining room for a SUV ride to a huge, two-story tall bookstore a few miles away from the hotel.

Inside the bookstore, Daniel found Sally looking at some gardening books on the second floor. He sneaked up behind her and tickled her.

She gasped out loud and turned to see Danny.

He grabbed her in his arms for a long, long 'I really Missed You' kiss.

As they kissed, Joy & Paul found them by the gardening section. The married figures' arms held each other with pride.

Mrs. Hunt softly snickered to her husband, "Now that's what I call 'a good kissing couple'."

"Me too, Joy." Mr. Hunt agreed.

They walked away from the engaged couple for some privacy and went down to the first floor.

After their bookstore visit, Paul drove himself, Joy, Sally & Danny to a shopping mall for some carefree fun. They bought some clothes, had a fabulous lunch, watched a movie, and talked and laughed together for some off ice time.

In the SUV, Sally told Daniel, "Mommy told me I need to get to bed early tonight."

His arms were wrapped around her tightly. He kissed her blond hair and whispered, "I understand, babe. You need your rest for tomorrow."

"I Love You, Daniel Gray . . ."

He leaned his head down and kissed his love's lips. "I Love You, future Sally Gray . . ."

They softly giggled from hearing her new name in the next few months.

The SUV made it to the hotel's parking lot.

Paul & Joy went to their room while Daniel escorted Sally to her room. They kissed and hugged again before they part for the evening.

Danny went inside his quiet guest room. He got his cell and called up his parent's home phone to check on Butch.

His father answered the call and explained to Danny, "Butch is fine. He seems to miss you."

"Why?" The Pet trainer wondered.

"Your mother told me this morning that the tri-bastard kept coming in your old room." Mr. Gray chuckled.

Danny requested, "Well, give him a big hug for me."

They talked a few more minutes and ended their phone conversation. Danny's eyes looked at the time on his cell. It said quarter after eight p.m.

He needed to get ready for his skating time with Ally.

Daniel changed into a white t, black sweat pants, his normal skating socks, and tennis shoes. He put his cell, wallet, and key cards in his right pant's pocket. His left hand carried his skating bag and his 'All-Access' badge was around his neck.

The guest room was clean and locked up when Danny left for the elevator ride for the first floor's lobby.

At the lobby, he saw Ally-Loop there with her badge and roller suitcase.

She spoke, "Hey, there."

"Hi, Ally." Danny said.

The figure friends left the hotel and Ally pointed out not a nice rental car, but a beautiful long stretch black limousine. "That's our ride."

"Wow." Daniel gasped.

The limo's chauffeur, a black male in his late 50s, took care of their skating bags and placed them gently in the trunk. He opened the back right passenger door for Ally and Daniel.

Both of them sat on opposite ends of the back leather seat. Windows were tinted black, there were two extra long leather seats in the limo. One on the right side and the other was facing in front of the back seats. The floor was all black color carpet.

There was also a little flat screen t.v. on the left side with a little refreshment table and an MP3 player speaker for Ally's phone.

The driver drove into the rink's deserted parking lot.

The chauffeur opened the back door and Danny and Allison exited the car. They got their skating bags from the trunk.

"What time shall I come back?" The dark colored chauffeur asked Ally-Loop.

She whispered something that only the man could hear.

He tipped his uniform hat and got in the limo.

Ally said, "Let's go, Daniel."

They walked from the cold dark night and into the cold air ice rink.

Inside of Ally's suitcase was her black speaker and polished figure skating boots.

She set the speaker up on the announcer's desk by the ice. She and Danny laced up their skates at the stands. He did want to ask more to his Figure Instructor about Sally's special skates.

His heart made him decide to wait until after he & Sally's wedding ceremony. That way he would be part of the family and get to learn the ins and outs with the family's trust and hidden secrets.

For the next three hours, Allison and Daniel skated the night away by talking about skating terms, working on figure tricks, and singing and strutting on the ice.

Morning came and Daniel Gray was happy in the King size bed. He felt refreshed to face the last day of Sectionals after he and Ally's skating session.

He got himself ready by taking a long warm shower, changing into a navy blue dress shirt, khaki pants, and dark brown dress shoes, got his wallet and room key in his pants pockets, and slipped his lanyard badge around his neck.

Danny stepped out of his room.

He wondered if Sally was up.

There was a note on her door.

Danny,

Meet me and my parents for breakfast in the dining room. I Love You . . .

Sally-babe

He ran for the elevator and made it to the dining room in good time. Sally and her folks were there having a comfortable breakfast.

Daniel greeted them, "Hi."

Sally happily replied, "Good morning, Danny."

She got up from her chair to kiss her love.

They sat in their own chairs and Daniel ordered his breakfast when a waitress came by their table.

Joy explained the plan for the day and tomorrow. "Senior Ladies start at five and will end at six-thirty. Then the big award ceremony and press conference will end shortly after eight. Tomorrow, we'll leave the motel at ten-thirty a.m. so Paul can drop off the SUV and we'll have plenty of time to make it for the one o'clock flight back to Santa Jose."

They all to Mrs. Hunt's plan.

Breakfast was done at ten that morning.

Joy and Sally left the dining room for Sally's room. Paul and Daniel went to the lobby and waited till the girls came back. Off they went for the skating rink's last day for Sectionals.

Sally was up first and did not fall down after going through the open gate's door. She pretended to skate her heart out in Danny's eyes. As her routine ended, Paul stood up and cheered for his little girl. He was surprised to see Daniel still sitting in his seat and was deep in thought for some odd reason.

Next up was Ally-Loop.

Daniel stood up and cheered for the Loop skating out on the ice wearing what it seemed to be a dark brownish green costume that was imitating an Air Force dress uniform but was made into an ice skating dress.

The lady announcer did speak into her mic, "I have word from Ally-Loop that she will be doing a very special jump combo for her long program in Nationals. Good luck, Ally!"

Danny did see Sally and Joy walking toward the girl's locker room. Except, Joy stopped in her tracks and listened closely to what the lady announcer said. She did look very curious on what the Loop wanted to the show the world for Nationals.

The Pet trainer saw a sly look from Joy Hunt's eyes. He had a feeling that Ally may need some help to protect her secret jump combo from Joy.

His ears heard 'The Ace's Wings theme song' playing for Ally's long program. No wonder why she wanted to dress up like someone from the Air Force.

Ally's long program was remarkably flawless in Danny's figure judgment. He had a feeling Ally-Loop was going to win the gold that night.

When he saw the scores, Allison Rigden only came in second. Sally Hunt won Sectionals with her boring classical routine.

Daniel's insides felt hurt.

He knew the judges were wrong about Sally's performance scores.

He and Paul left the stands and watched Sally be all bubbly and happy talking to the camera crews and reporters. His eyes were looking for Ally. He did find his Figure Instructor's coach and she explained that Ally already left for her plane ride home.

Danny got his cell and tried to get a hold of Allison.

The call only made it to her voicemail.

He decided not the bother the Loop until they met up at the rink for the following Wednesday night at the small rink.

Chapter Twelve

Daniel Gray was very relieved to get his Butchie-Wutchie back and go to the dog park after that four hour flight from Salt Lake City's airport to San Jose's airport. Butch did look happy to have his owner back. They stayed at the dog park for an hour and then went on home for dinner.

The Pet trainer and his faithful pal missed each other so much, they slept on the twin size bed together that night. Danny's right hand petted his pooch's white fur as he thought more on why his fiancee choose Joy over him.

Mommy can make me feel better for my routine. His ears heard Sally's voice spoke that statement.

The next voices he heard were of his and Ally's from their fight.

You have no idea what happens in the locker room with Joy and Sally!

I heard Joy say you tampered with Sally's skates before her short program.

Ha! That's Joy Hunt! Always blaming me for her own shitty little problems. Joy and Sally always have the locker room to themselves just so little miss sunshine can have an extra ten minutes to get herself ready for her time to shine for the judges and audience!

The Pet trainer wanted to know what the Hunts were hiding or really doing for Sally's skating career.

He asked Butch, "Why would Sally turn to Mommy in her time of need instead of me, Butch?"

His sweet loving beagle was too tired to hear or answer his master's question. The cute dog just slept.

Danny closed his eyes and fell asleep himself.

A broken heart dream woke Daniel up six a.m.

He sat up in bed without Butchie-Wutchie by his side. He laid his back on his bed. His eyes shut to think of the dream he just had.

Sally & Danny just married on ice and Joy Hunt was controlling Sally's moves on the ice from the laptop on her lap. He was still spooked of the wires his blonde wife wore all over her body. As the ceremony ended, instead of going with Danny for their honeymoon Sally was forced to go with Joy & Paul to their home.

The blond champ told the Pet trainer, "Mommy thinks its best for us to stay in separate homes until my competing years are over. I'm so sorry, Danny."

She went with her parents and Daniel Gray was stranded at the ice rink parking lot again.

Danny's eyes opened from watching the hurtful image. He hoped Sally would not tell him that for real.

He got his cell and decided to phone Sally.

"Hello, Daniel."

Joy answered her daughter's phone.

"Hi, Mrs. Hunt. May I please talk to Sally?" He requested nicely.

"No, you can't." Joy spoke strictly. "Sally and I have lots of work to do for Nationals and cannot be disturbed till Nationals. Please don't call her cell or give her emails because I will answer them first."

She instantly hung up on him.

Daniel was more heart broken than he felt after waking up from the dream he just had. He knew what was going with Joy and Sally. Super intense skating sessions because of Allison's secret jump combo she would show at Nationals. Sadly, he got ready to take Butch out for his morning walk.

Even though his heart was still depressed, Danny's work day went really well that Monday.

He did a group instead of individual teachings and was very successful from doing it for the first time.

The Pet store's training booth sure looked different than it was a month ago. The booth had only Daniel doing obedient training for the dogs. Now, it was full of dogs and people learning Pet training.

He did feel much happier and calmer by coming into the Pet store as an overall dog trainer. His goal was to have Jack, the Pet store's manager, to tell him he was 'an overall dog trainer' for his next employee evaluation. His heart pleaded that Jack was closely watching the training booth.

Daniel would give the dog and their owners a welcome smile, the owners smiled back and told him successful stories about their dog being misbehaved about something and no longer doing it, and the dogs acting well-behaved toward other dogs, customers, or animals in the store.

It was time to close and clean up the booth for the next day. Sweeping the floor, wiping the swing door and see-through glass above the wooden wall and chairs for people to sit on, and organizing his schedule folder. Danny's little booth was sparkly clean and filled with fresh supplies of dog food, play toys, and cleaning essentials.

He gathered his personal belongings from his locker box and left the store for his car. Outside the store and in the parking lot, Daniel's brown eyes noticed a new store was being built not far from the Pet store. There were no signs or clues on what type of store it was going to be. He wondered of the kind store it would be when it would open.

Danny got inside his car and drove back to his unit.

Butchie-Wutchie waited for his owner by the front door. Danny quickly changed into street clothes, got Butch's retractable leash, attached it to Butch's collar, stuffed his back left jeans pocket with plastic baggies, and they exited the unit for a forty minute walk.

He could not get over the fact that he was not allowed to see or talk to his fiancee until Nationals. He had no clue when that would happen. A question for Allison to answer.

For Tuesday and Wednesday, Daniel felt worse than he did before. At least he could talk to Ally Wednesday night. He naturally did his dog training work, chores, and his very best to make his heart and mind feel better.

After taking Butch out for his evening walk and changing into his skating clothes, Daniel left his apartment unit with his skating bag. He was looking forward to a night of blowing off steam from his hurt and pain of not seeing Sally for weeks, maybe months.

In the men's locker room, Danny laced up his skates and his feet did feel comfortable in his suede material boots. He stored his bag and personal belongings in his locker box. He walked out of the room for the cold small ice rink.

Danny did feel a little weird to be at the old rink building and not the rink in Salt Lake City from Sectionals. He watched Ally skate around the patch of ice first and then other skaters got on too. He went for the crowded rink.

His blades touched the ice and stroked around the rink forward. After going around once, he did a smooth right mohawk turn and started to skate backwards.

Allison saw Danny on the ice and left him alone so he could warm himself up on the ice. She worked on some dance steps at the center.

No matter how fast he went or tried to ignore it, Daniel Gray could not let go of the fear that he might be losing Sally to her Mommy. He loved her so much, he just wanted her to be happy for her. Even if it means if she wanted to be with Joy so much, he would let her go willingly.

He made it for the center.

"Hey, Ally." He spoke loudly.

"Good evening, Master Gray." She teased. "How are you?"

"I need to let out some anger tonight." He explained.

Ally wondered, "Why?"

Danny began to skate around his Figure Instructor backwards. "Joy's being a bitch."

"She's always a bitch." Ally spoke.

"A bitchy-bitch to me & Sally."

Allison sighed, "I see. I'm sorry to hear that."

He desperately asked, "When's Nationals?"

She thought in her head and told Danny, "January 22-29. But Sally and I compete on the 26th and 28th."

"Ah, shit." He angrily cursed.

"What's wrong, Danny?" Ally concernedly questioned her troubled student.

From the top of his lungs, Daniel yelled out, "I can't see my fiancee for two whole months!"

"Is Joy locking up Sally again?" Ally demanded.

"Again?" Shocked Danny shouted. "She did that before?"

The Figure Instructor confessed, "Long ago, Joy did lock up Sally."

Daniel had had enough of figure skating in his lifetime. He could not be a loving man for Sally or never earned Joy's trust with her daughter off ice. There was no reason for him to continue on his skating lessons with Ally-Loop.

"Ally," Danny stated, "I can't do figure skating anymore."

"Why not?" She sadly spoke. "You've been doing such a good job within six weeks of learning. Lots of beginners and first timers are jealous of you."

"I don't care!" He bursted out.

He calmed down his voice to say, "Figure skating is a fuckin' waste of time. I can't do it anymore."

Ally had such great respect for her student and other figure skaters, she told him, "Danny, it's ok if you want to stop your lessons and skating all together. Do you remember why you wanted to ice skate in the first place?"

Daniel Gray stopped moving backwards with a right blade, back stop. He thought back his very first time on the ice wearing the worn out brown rental skates, meeting Ally-Loop, and receiving ice skating lessons from her for free. But his heart went further than that tough public session. He got his reason back.

"Yes, I do."

He sighed and his right hand ran through his short brown hair. "It's only because I want to impress my future skating-in-laws. Not for the passion to dance, glide, jump, or dance on ice."

His heart did feel a bit better for letting out his secret guilt instead of burying it deep inside of him like garbage. He started to skate forward around cold air rink. Ally caught up with him.

She expressed out, "I already knew that. I am your Figure Instructor after you asked me for help. I don't want to pressure you into something you don't want to do."

Ally thought more why Danny wanted to stop his skating lessons. *Joy does not want to let Sally go. That stuck up bitch went inside of Danny's heart to kill it. Badly. Now he thinks figure skating is not worth for the Hunt's blessing in marriage.*

She told him, "You have free will. All you have to is how you want use it in life."

Danny was still upset from the fights he went up against Joy from the first day of Sectionals and last Monday morning. He did not feel like a man in love by being a male skater at all.

"Then I will use it to get the hell out of here!" Angry Daniel declared.

He stoked away from Allison and stepped off the ice quickly. He went for the men's locker room to get his personal belongings out of the box and bag. What he left behind were his cleaned blade figure skates and other essentials in the locker box. He did not want to bring his skating stuff home.

Danny marched out of the locker room and the skating rink's building for a long car ride back to his apartment unit.

Inside the unit, Butch ran up toward his owners for a welcome home greeting.

Daniel spoke tiredly, "Hey, Butch."

The boys went for their bedroom and both of them slept all night long.

The next day happened to be Thanksgiving.

No work for Daniel at the Pet store for four days. It was a perfect time to relax, clear his mind, and try to figure out a way to get some alone time with Sally.

He felt Butchie-Wutchie on his chest. His left hand stroked the dog's white fur and whispered, "Off, Butch."

The beagle looked up at his owner's sad brown eyes. He stretched out his tri-color body and leaped off of Daniel and the bed. Butch's clawed paws tapped, tapped, tapped on the wooden floor. He went to the kitchen for his breakfast.

Daniel slowly got up from bed and followed his pooch. He gave Butch fresh cold water and some dry kibbles. Danny fixed himself eggs, toast, and warm coffee.

Butch knew what time it was when Danny finished his morning meal. Morning walk for the pooch.

The Pet trainer took a long shower, dried himself, donned some warm clothes, and thought about what he should do that day. He did not want to walk Butch alone.

He decided to go over to the Hunts' mansion and see if he could talk to Sally in private. His eyes noticed the time from his cell. It was almost ten in the morning.

Danny's mind constructed an idea.

He put on his jacket for the cold weather outside. He also gathered some baggies, his wallet, keys, and clicker.

"Butch! Park time!"

The cute beagle immediately ran toward Danny. He sat on the floor and his owner leaned down to connect the gray retractable to his brown collar.

Daniel and Butch left their unit home for a half hour car ride to the Hunt's home.

At the mansion's driveway, Danny saw Sally's light blue convertible there. He was glad the red SUV was not there too. His left hand opened the driver's door.

He commanded his pooch, "Stay."

Butch stayed on the passenger seat. His owner exit the car and walked to the large cream color mansion.

Standing in front of the door, Daniel knocked on the tan wooden door with his left fist. The door opened to reveal his cute sunshine Sally dressed in jeans, light pink sweater, and pink slippers.

"Danny!" She squealed. Their arms hugged each other tightly.

"Hi, Sally . . ." He whispered happily. "I Love You . . ."

"I Love You too . . ."

Hearing those words did let go more of the anger he had from Joy's controlling mind for her daughter.

Both their heads moved to look in their loving eyes and their lips kissed longly and sweetly.

She asked her fiance, "What brings you here?"

Danny had only one thing to say, "Breakout."

Sally hastily got out of Danny's arms and ran up for her bedroom to put on her tennis shoes and light blue coat. Her right hand took her keys and purse. Sally was back by the front door under a minute.

She questioned her love, "Where are we going?"

"To a special dog park for Butchie-Wutchie." Daniel remarked.

"Oh," she sweetly breathed out, "you brought Butch?"

She walked out of the house, closed and locked the door, and her blueish-gray eyes was looking for the loving beagle.

"He's in my car." Danny stated.

"Let's take my car." Sally insisted.

She let Daniel go to his car and brought Butch out of the vehicle. They walked toward Sally's convertible.

Sally nicely said, "Come on, Butchie-Wutchie."

But Butch did not want to go to Sally or her car. His nose was sniffing on the grassy ground. His owner announced, "I think someone needs to go potty."

The cute beagle walked around the Hunt's front lawn for a few seconds and did his business. Danny got out a baggie bag to clean up Butch's poopy mess. He handed Sally the retractable leash so Daniel could throw away the baggie full of poo. He found a garbage can behind the mansion's driveway and placed the dirty bag in the can.

Daniel, Butch, and Sally got in the cute little blue car and drove off for the dog park Daniel suggested of going to. They arrived at the park within twenty minutes. Danny let Butch run wild in the leash-free section. The dog played and wrestled with a few other dogs around the sandy gravel ground.

Sally & Danny walked around the park hand-in-hand while Danny kept a close eye at his beagle friend.

The Pet trainer did want to talk something important to Sally. He gave her the real reason why he showed up unexpectedly at her home.

"Sally, why I decided to see you is I need to tell you that I-" He forced out, "I can't figure skate anymore."

His fiancee wondered, "Did you and Ally have a fight or something?"

"Not with Ally." Danny confessed. "The argument your Mom and I had from Sectionals got the best of me when I couldn't come in to your rescue. I feel figure skating was not making myself better, or at least a better man for you. On and off ice."

Sally tightly held her heart aching dog trainer's hand and soothed him, "Mommy never wanted me to get involved with a guy after I accomplish all I can in competitive figure skating. That's why she wanted me close to her and Dad. She did not want anything bad happen to her only child."

Danny told her, "I tried to call you last Monday, but Joy told me I can't talk or see you again until Nationals. That's like two freakin' months away. I can't bear not to see you in two months without knowing if you still love me and want to marry me."

"She's more mad at you because Ally-Loop is teaching you figure skating." Sally sighed disappointedly.

Butch ran to Daniel & Sally with a worn out tennis ball in his mouth. He dropped it on the sandy ground.

Sally leaned down for the ball and threw it behind Butch. The beagle ran after the tossed tennis ball.

"Why doesn't Joy like Allison?" Danny questioned the figure champ.

"Sometimes I hear her admit Ally-Loop has more passion on the ice than I do. Except, Mommy just wants me to win like she did when she was young." Sally expressed.

Danny's sweet dog came back for another ball toss from Sally Hunt. Her feminine fingers picked up the slobber ball from the sandy ground and tossed it behind Butch's back. His short legs ran after the thrown tennis ball.

Daniel Gray thought back of his long chat with Ally about Joy Hunt wanting the win the gold.

All she wants was to win. But what's her reason to make Sally win so badly?

Then it was time to leave the dog park.

Butch was attached to his retractable leash and Danny & Sally left the park arm-in-arm. They all were happy from their carefree fun.

When they reached Sally's closed top convertible, someone dressed all in black stood next to the car and was trying to break in with a long thin metal pole at the driver's window.

Daniel yelled out and his arm dropped from Sally's waist, "Hey! What the hell are you doing?"

He quickly ran to the car thief and his right foot kicked the thief's back hard. The thief fell down on the gravel ground.

Sally found her cell in her purse and called 9-1-1 for help. Butch was kept close by her.

The thief wore black pants, boots, jacket, leather gloves, and a very long wool ski cap with holes for his eyes, nose, and mouth. It got up from the ground and wanted to beat up Danny for kicking it.

Daniel had a feeling the thief was male because his body form looked male and was willing to fight against him. The car thief lifted up his leather fists to defend himself.

He started to charge at the Pet trainer.

Danny was not scared or nervous to go up against the thief. His mind thought of a plan.

The car thief had his right leather fist up so he could punch Danny's face, but the fist missed after the Pet trainer spun around his right foot like a three turn and his left elbow punched the thief's side very hard.

The thief fell on the ground again.

While he was lying on his stomach, the car thief's left hand dug inside his left jacket's pocket for his Swiss Army knife. He lifted his body off the ground a little to flick the 3.5 inch sharp blade. His left hand moved the blade toward his chest and kept it hidden and close.

Danny stood closely the laid down thief until help came to the park. His head hovered over to watch the man carefully. The car thief made his move by slowing lifting up off the sandy ground.

The thief's left hand swiftly slashed his knife at Danny's forehead and formed an inch long cut on his head. The Pet trainer cried out in the pain and fell on the ground.

Daniel's head was feeling the stinging pain from a metal blade cutting into his head. His fingers felt blood oozing from the cut.

The car thief wanted to get back at Danny with his blood stained knife, but he was stopped in his tracks when his ears heard sirens and a cop yelled out, "Freeze! Sir, drop your weapon!"

At first the male dressed all in black did not drop his knife. The cop shouted, "I'm giving you ten seconds to put down the knife!"

He started to count and reach down for his gun in its holster, "1 . . . 2 . . . 3 . . . 4 . . . 5 . . ."

Sally and other dog owners at the dog park were scared and nervous on what was going to happen next.

When the officer was about to say '10', the dressed in black car thief dropped his knife on the ground and surrendered.

The officer moved in to handcuff the car thief.

He forced the criminal into the backseat of a squad car. Another cop wore latex gloves and picked up the bloody knife to put it in an evidence plastic bag.

Sally and Butch ran toward Danny.

The pretty blonde sat on the dusty ground to help her fiance sit up. He was feeling dizzy and tired. His eyes saw sweet Sally next to him.

"How many times do you have to save my life?" He curiously wondered.

The blonde champ laughed and Butch yelped out loud.

Her mind remembered the first time she & Daniel first met when she and her friends saved him from hefty Walter. She could not believe it had been so long since they had been together.

Both their eyes saw an ambulance driving up to the injured Danny. Two male paramedics helped Daniel up on his feet and into the back of the ambulance van.

Sally & Danny gave their statements to the police officers. The car thief was immediately transported to jail.

Danny got cleaned up and his head was bandaged up.

He & Sally were grateful his cut was not deep enough for some stitches. One of the medics told him to keep it clean, ice it, take some Aspirin, and rest was essential too. Danny felt very happy that Sally was the driver instead of him.

The engaged couple and Butch left the ambulance for the unhurt light blue convertible. All the police cars and ambulance van drove away from the dog park.

Sally helped Daniel get inside her car. Butch jumped in for the back seat. Then she settled in the driver's seat.

Before starting up the convertible, Sally only had one question for her fiance during his fight against the car thief. "How did you miss that guy's punch?"

Danny remembered exactly on what he did in that moment. He explained, "From the skating lessons Allison showed me."

He had to admit. Sometimes doing figure skating moves were helpful off ice. Especially when it came to fighting against bad guys.

Sally softly replied, "Maybe Mommy was wrong about Ally teaching you how to ice skate."

She turned on her light blue car and drove back to her parent's home. Daniel fell asleep during the drive.

When the drive was over and the car reached the driveway, the Hunt's red SUV was there.

She gently woke Danny up by whispering in his left ear, "Danny, wake up?"

His head stirred a little but he was still sleeping.

At the backseat, Butch yelped out three times.

Sally turned her head to see the cute beagle sitting happily in the middle of the black comfy seats. She giggle softly while Daniel finally woke up.

The figure champ had her head turned back to yawning and stretching Danny. He shifted himself in his seat. His forehead was still hurt and his bandage did not come undone.

Sally's right hand softly brushed Daniel's soft brown hair. They both leaned in for a long relaxing kiss. Their arms were wrapped around each other tightly.

Daniel uncomfortably asked his fiancee, "What are we going to tell your parents about my head?"

"I'm not sure, Danny. What I do know is if you feel too tired or lightheaded to go back home, Mommy & Dad would let you rest in the living room until your ready to drive back home." She answered.

Their arms dropped and exited the car with Butchie-Wutchie. Sally & Danny went toward his car. But Butch needed a potty break again and did his pee business. Then he was walked to Danny's car. He jumped in and his owner shut and locked the door.

Danny took Sally's hand and they headed over for the Hunt's mansion. Together they stood by the front door. Sally got her key out from her purse to unlock the door. They walked inside and went for the living room.

In the living room were Joy & Paul Hunt discussing Sally's skating routines for Nationals. Their heads turned to see the young couple back in the house.

Joy sternly spoke, "You have a lot of nerves to show up here, Daniel Gray."

"Shit, Danny!" Paul gasped. "What happened to your head?"

The young lovers sat on a couch together.

Danny candid to Sally's parents, "I, I was attacked at a dog park."

"Ha!" Joy huffed sarcastically. "What, did a small, helpless dog get you?"

Sally defended her love.

"Mommy! How could you say that to him after he saved my life from a car thief?"

Paul Hunt was stunned.

Joy showed very little emotion for Danny being brave for her sunshine daughter.

The red haired woman stood up from the sofa and angrily told her daughter, "Sally, this is why I asked you not to leave the house without us! I knew something like this was going to happen! Danny, you should've listened to me last Monday when I specifically told you 'no contacting Sally until Nationals'! Come along, Sally. Please leave, Daniel."

Mother grabbed her child's left hand jerked her off the couch from Danny. Both girls hastily went upstairs.

"Let's go." Mr. Hunt ordered Daniel.

The guys left the living room for the kitchen. They stayed quiet until the front door opened and closed.

"Danny, first let me say, 'Thank you for protecting my daughter.'" Paul gratefully spoke.

"You're welcome, Sir." Daniel's tired voice relieved. "It would kill me if something bad were to happen to Sally."

"You really love her, don't you?" Paul stated.

Daniel firmly nodded his head.

"Do you want some water?" Mr. Hunt offered to the Pet trainer.

"Sure."

The mansion owner walked over to the fridge and handed Daniel a plastic bottle of cold water.

The tired Pet trainer was strong enough to unscrew the top and drank some of the cold liquid down his dry throat. His cooled mouth said, "Thanks, Mr. Hunt."

An interesting question came to Paul's mind.

He asked Daniel, "How did you go up against a car thief?"

Young Gray licked his lips and answered, "I remembered the figure moves Ally-Loop taught me and used some of the moves to defend myself."

Paul Hunt was impressed.

He solemnly apologized to his future son-in-law. "I am very sorry that my wife's stubbornness caused such a misunderstanding against you. And Allison."

"I only wanted to help Sally, Mr. Hunt." Danny honestly respond.

Paul spoke back, "I can relate to that. And please call me 'Paul.'"

"Okay, 'Paul.'"

Paul walked over to a side window and announced, "Looks like Joy took Sally to Garden Park. They'll be gone for a while."

Now was the time to ask his future father-in-law his most curious question about why Joy Hunt wanted to win the gold in figure skating so much.

He sipping some more water and asked, "Why is your wife like this?"

Paul sighed, "I'll tell you in the living room."

The two men left the kitchen and went for the living room. Mr. Hunt was in the room first. Daniel moved to the front door and walked over for his car to check on Butch. The cute beagle was sleeping in the passenger seat.

Danny's legs marched from his car and back to the mansion house. He closed the front door before he met up with Paul in the living room.

Paul asked, "You okay?"

Daniel replied, "I'm fine. Just needed to check on my dog. He's in my car."

They sat in separate comfy couches.

Daniel took another big gulp of water to listen closely to the story Paul was going to tell.

Sally's father explained, "My wife was once a skating champ like Sally. She had dreamt of going for the Olympics, but she couldn't."

"What happened?" Daniel wondered.

He waited patiently for the whole story.

"During the last two years of her competing years, the rink she skated at regularly changed clubs. There were different technical scorings and new basic skills and maneuvers she and her coach had to learn fast. She did not qualify to do big skating events in time and ended up doing small rink competitions. The judges and fans were not wowed or impressed to see Joy's new skating moves. Many young skaters got better than her and she quit at age 18."

Daniel was starting to understand why Joy Hunt wanted Sally to win the gold. He knew there was more of the story that Paul needed to tell.

Mr. Hunt added, "Her coach and staff members felt sorry for Joy's unfinished career that they offered her a job at the rink as a cashier for the admission and skating store desks. Sometimes she and her coach did work on the new moves but Joy felt like a failure for not being a talented skater with stricter rules on the ice. She never wanted to be defeated or out smarted in figure skating."

The Pet trainer finally comprehended Joy's obsession of Sally's skating career. She wanted her daughter to do what she wished she could have done decades ago.

Paul continued on with the story, "I first met Joy when I was 18 and she was 20. I was going for Sectionals at the rink she worked at. She sure was beautiful and I overlook her temper just to have her love. We got to know each other, dated, and I did my best to teach her the club's new moves. Problem was: Joy did not have the talent to do future competitive figure skating events."

"What was different from the clubs?" Daniel curiously wondered.

"The new club states that all spins must be centered, fast, and artistic from fingertips and blades. Legs needed to be straight from jumps, checks, landings, and freestyle positions. And Joy had a skating trademark skill that happened to be an illegal move in figure skating today. Her way of doing backward spiral." Paul told out.

Danny questioned, "Why was her spiral illegal?"

Instead of telling the Pet trainer about the spiral, Mr. Hunt stood up from the chair he sat in and found an old VHS tape from the dvd shelf. He put the tape in the VHS box player, turned on the flat screen t.v., and the tape began to play.

Daniel's brown eyes saw a young Joy dance on ice with the spotlight on and dressed in a sparkly navy blue skating dress. He listened what Paul told him the moves Joy was doing on the ice in the early-80s Junior Championship competition. Then they both saw her illegal backward spiral move.

She was moving backwards and her left hand was holding her left blade up so the pose could look like a long leg spiral.

Paul explained, "The reason why the move was illegal is because the judges, coaches, and skating fans think Joy could not handle her own leg lifts without the use of her hands. Figures need natural flexibility in almost all the freestyle moves they do from poses and spins."

"Okay. That makes sense to me." Danny agreed to Paul's skating judgment. His mind thought back of Allison doing her split spiral stretch while holding the little blue ball in front of her from their first pilate workout.

Mr. Hunt got up from his chair to rewind the tape in the player and put the VHS tape back on the dvd shelf.

Danny did want to ask Paul about Sally's 'special skates,' but Paul spoke before he could.

Paul politely told the young Pet trainer, "I think it's time for you to go home, Daniel."

The Pet trainer could not argue with that idea.

He did not want to make Joy Hunt even more mad at him. He finished his water bottle drink and handed it to Paul. They both went for a short walk to the front door.

"Have a good Thanksgiving, Danny, and take it easy." He encouraged him.

Daniel spoke, "Thank you, Paul. And do tell Sally 'I Love Her . . .'"

"Will do." Mr. Hunt promised his daughter's fiance.

They shook hands and Daniel Gray left the mansion house.

He walked on the front lawn to reach his car. His key in the driver's door woke up Butch. He sat patiently for his owner to start up the car.

Danny sat in the driver's seat and petted Butch for a few long seconds. Then the car was turned on and Daniel drove him and Butch back to their unit home.

The boys arrived in the unit around two-thirty that afternoon. They had a very long day together. Danny thought Butch was very good that day, he decided to treat the pooch something very special.

For their late lunch, Daniel fixed up some hot dogs for them to share. Butch felt pleased to have something in his hungry tummy. Content Danny did feel better by eating something and resting up from the crazy incident that happened at the dog park.

His heart was glad after remembering that there was no work the next day because of the Thanksgiving holiday. He could just rest and rest some more for his sore head.

Daniel decided to take some Aspirin and drink more water to help heal the cut on his forehead and get him some sleep. He popped the pills in his mouth and gulped down lots of cold water.

He slowly made it to his bedroom, changed into comfy sweats, and fell on his bed. His eyes closed for a long nap.

He only hoped Sally was doing okay.

Daniel Gray did not wake up from his deep sleep until 11:00 p.m. that night. He lifted his tired body up from bed and went for his bathroom. He stayed there for a half hour for a long warm shower, cleaned and dried himself, and slipped on some clean street clothes.

He did have a very late meaty dinner with Butch in the kitchen first and then living room. He asked his furry pal, "Walk?"

Butch barked and ran for the unit's front door.

Daniel put on his tennis shoes, heavy coat, got his cell, keys, baggies, and the gray retractable leash. Butch was leashed up and ready to go.

They walked around the dark of night for half an hour. Danny let his dog be a dog around the neighborhood.

Butch lead his owner back to the apartment building. They were both getting sleepy from their walk. Silently, they slowly made their way to their unit without disturbing their neighbors.

Danny took Butch's leash off and his extra layer of clothing and shoes. The sweet beagle pranced over for his pillow after he had a nice long drink of water. Danny took off his jeans and into clean sweat pants.

Before going to bed, he checked on his head. His hands were clean after washing them in the bathroom. He carefully took the bandage off and checked on the cut he got from the car thief. The cut did stop bleeding, but he placed the bandage back on for the night.

Slipping inside his comfortable twin-size bed, Danny thought on what he should do the next day. He could not talk or call Sally till Nationals came. His heart wished to have her in his arms that night.

Then he realized on what he needed to do for Friday evening. Ice skate. Whether his Figure Instructor was there or not.

The next mid morning, Danny woke up feeling better than the day before. He stretched his body and called out, "Butch?"

He woke up from his pillow and jumped up onto his owner's messy bed. Danny petted and caressed his dog's short white fur.

They left the bedroom for some breakfast in the eating area of their unit home. It took them twenty minutes for them to finish their meal and got ready for their walk.

Daniel did check his cut again. It did look more healed than it was before. His fingers took off the bandage and threw it in the bathroom's brown trash bucket.

Butch waited for his master to come out of the people's business room and to the front door so he could do his business outside, even though he had his fake grass.

The Pet trainer located the retractable leash and connected it to Butch's collar. Off they went for a two hour walk around the neighborhood.

When the time reached six p.m., Danny was waking up from a nap in his bed after his long walk with Butch, doing some shopping errands, and cleaned up his unit. He was in his normal skating clothes and gathered his personal belongings.

"Night, Butch." He said to his sweet beagle by the unit's front door.

Butch looked at him and laid down on the couch in the living room.

Door was closed and locked behind Daniel Gray. He went down to the garage for his car. Got inside the car, turned it on, and his mind thought of the things he wanted to do out on the ice.

He made it to the rink's building a little after seven p.m. He walked for the admission desk and paid for the evening's public session.

The lady at the front desk was a little baffled why Danny did not pay for rental skates since he did not have his skating bag with him. He knew he left his bag in his locker box a couple days ago.

Daniel went for the men's locker room. His eyes saw his temp locker number. He turned on the lock's number combinations. It unlocked and Danny opened the box. His skating bag was still there.

He sat on a chair to lace up his skates. His feet did feel very happy to wear the suede material figure boots again.

When he finished, Danny stood up, put away his personal stuff in the locker box, and locked it. He strutted from the room for the cold air ice rink.

The ice was just resurfaced as Daniel made it to the gates. He opened the gate's door, took off his red plastic guards, and smoothly glided on the 'freshly cut' ice. His head was not bothering him by going ice skating.

Danny started that Friday night by skating forward and backwards with three turns and mohawk turns. His mind reminded himself, *First work on the basics and then do some advance skating moves.*

His brown eyes saw a figure male skating at the center part of the rink doing incredible centered spin positions. He had short light brown hair and was dressed in black sweat pants and a turquoise shirt that was well-fitted for his buffed chest and arms.

Damn, he's really good. The Pet trainer thought. *Almost as good as Ally-Loop.*

When the mysterious figure male finished his camel, sit, scratch spin combo, he checked and happily glided forward around the ice fast. The guy did look familiar to Daniel Gray. It was like the Pet trainer saw the figure male before at the rink not too long ago. When was his question.

Danny noticed the figure male had quick reflexes as Allison Rigden. Maybe, just maybe, the figure skater knew Ally or got some tips from her.

Is that Ally-Loop's first figure student five years ago? He had to talk to that dude.

But instead of the dog trainer skating up to the male figure, the male figure surprised Danny by gliding backwards next to him.

"Hey." He spoke tiredly.

"Hi," replied the caught off guard Gray.

With that close up, the Pet trainer realized that the figure male was the same beefy hockey dude who did hockey lessons with Ally-Loop. But why would he do figure skating as well as hockey?

"Nice suede boots." The male skater stated.

Danny quickly glanced down at the other skaters boots. They were the same type of boots as his. "Thanks."

While the figure hockey dude glided backwards, he did a left outside mohawk turn to skate forward.

"What brings you here tonight?" He asked Daniel.

The dog trainer candid, "Need to blow off some steam."

"Good answer."

The incredible male skater sped up and really went fast around the crowded ice rink. Then he quickly did a right inside mohawk to lithely skated backwards.

Danny went to the center to practice forward and backward crossovers. When he wanted to work on turns, the figure male was at the center too preparing for a long back spin. He did a right inside three turn and spun around in one spot with his arms crossed over his buffed chest.

Jealous Danny stopped paying attention to the guy to focus what Ally wanted him to practice when he decided to go back to her for more skating lessons. A realization came to him as he glided. He did feel alive and happy to figure skate again.

He thought, *Allison was right about passion.*

He skated that night because he was enjoying himself being out on the ice with grace and strength from the moves he could do. He also knew he and Ally had some more work to do if he wanted to be a good male figure skater for Sally Hunt. On and off ice.

Chapter Thirteen

After a good night sleep from skating the pervious night, Daniel Gray had some breakfast, a shower, checked on the cut on his head, put on jeans, his gray sweater, tennis shoes, and took Butch out for his morning walk. He did feel lonely without being Sally, but his heart was mostly bothered of the fact he needed to make up with Ally and get her back as his Figure Instructor. Doing the lessons and off ice training would keep Daniel busy and a little distracted from thinking Sally would stop loving him.

He and Butch made back to their unit before nine a.m.

Daniel knew now was the time to face Ally at the rink and apologize. He took his jeans off and into his black sweat pants. His wallet, cell, and keys were stuffed in his left pant's pocket. He did leave his skating bag in his locker the night before.

The drive to the ice rink was making Danny feel better. He looked forward to have another skating lesson with Ally-Loop. He only hoped Ally could forgive his rude attitude last Wednesday night.

In the rink's parking lot was Allison's white Horundi convertible and a few other cars. Danny parked his car to go inside the arena's building. He walked through the front doors, felt the cold air swirl around him, and moved from the doors for the rink.

His eyes noticed that Ally was not out on the ice. He turned his head to find a rink employee. There was a lady cashier at the admission desk.

He asked her, "Excuse me? Do you know where Ally-Loop is?"

The lady answered, "I think Allison's in the ballet room, Daniel."

Her right index finger pointed out where to go for the ballet room. His right side for the little hallway to the small rink.

"Thank you." Daniel rushed from the admission desk and turned around quickly to run for the ballet room.

He headed over where Allison was located at.

There was a sign above two closed door from the opposite side of the small rink. It said 'Ballet room'.

The Pet trainer's left hand the gold knob on the left door. It was unlocked. He slowly pulled the door toward him, sneaked inside the music playing room, and closed it softly.

In the room was Ally dressed in a traditional black ballet bodysuit, pink tights and ballet shoes. She was doing some leg stretches on the bars.

She looked at the mirrors. She stopped stretching her body after seeing who was in the ballet room with her.

Danny.

Her head turned around to see him. She asked him, "What brings you here?"

He replied, "I'm sorry about my outburst behavior a few days ago. Sally & I talked and I found out what my problem was. I guess I thought figure skating was not helping me be the kind of man Sally Hunt deserved in life."

Ally walked to her black speaker. She picked the remote and paused her music player. She listened carefully at her figure student's apology.

"I was wrong." He confessed.

"What do you mean?" Ally-Loop wondered.

Danny pleaded, "I want to be a wonderful male figure skater. Ally, please help me win over my girl's uptight mother?"

The Figure Instructor sat in a dark green cushioned chair. She lifted up a water bottle in her right hand and sipped some water. Her mind made a drastic decision.

"Daniel," she started off. "I knew at some point you wanted to stop doing figure skating because it wasn't cool or fun. I was surprised you lasted more than six weeks. I forgive you since you were not directly mad at me, but at bitchy Joy Hunt."

Allison put in, "Are you sure you still want to skate?"

Danny explained, "Well, I can't see my girl for two months and I need to prove to my future in-laws that I am a good male skater for their champion daughter."

Ally-Loop stood up from the chair she sat in and took her phone out from the black speaker. She declared, "Then, I will be happy to be your Figure Instructor."

The Pet trainer's heart was filled with glee and excitement. *Ally-Loop is my instructor again.*

He requested, "Can we have a session now?"

Allison thought over Danny's reason to stop figure skating. *So, Daniel Gray really figured out that ice skating was making him a better man for the woman he loves. I think it's time to show and treat him with my secret place.*

"Yes, we can have a session." Ally announced happily. "But not here."

She leaned down to unlace her ballet shoes. The shoes were in her left hand. She spoke to her student, "Get your skates and come with me."

The figure friends left the ballet room and went to their gender locker room for their skating stuff.

Five minutes later by the front doors, Ally changed her clothes and had her roller suitcase with her. Danny was waiting for her after he got his skating bag from his locker box.

"Forgive me for being nosy, but what happened to your head?" Her eyes carefully looked at his cut on his forehead.

"I defended myself against a car thief Thanksgiving Day." Daniel explained. "Someone was trying to break into Sally's car. I did some figure moves so the guy wouldn't punch me in the face. I guess I didn't know he had a Swiss Army knife on him. He suspiciously laid low, I lowered my head close, and he lashed his knife on my forehead."

The Figure Instructor was glad of Daniel using figure moves for his everyday life, even for some heroic times. "I'm sorry to hear that happened. It could have been worse if you did nothing."

Ally-Loop told Danny her plan. "I'm going to drive us to a place that I love going to."

They left the rink building for her Horundi. It was an hour long car ride north from the skating rink. Danny wondered if Butch was okay. He hoped so.

Ally unexpectedly parked her hot-looking convertible by an abandoned building. The building's windows were broken, the front had an enormous sliding door, old pieces of paper surrounded outside the building, the paint walls was dark blue and the chips were peeling off, and there was a very big green dumpster at the right side of the sliding door.

Daniel was confused about Ally-Loop taking him to a place like that. Ally got out of her car first, her student followed her. The trunk opened to get their skating bags.

Ally also pulled out a very heavy brown colored tarp. She opened up the tarp to put it over her car. Danny helped her with the tarp. They gathered their skating bags and walked over to the abandoned building.

The Pet trainer asked his Figure Instructor, "What are we doing here?"

"You're going to love this!" Allison squealed proudly.

Instead of going through the sliding door, the Loop walked over for the left side of the building. There was a lone door. Ally's right hand dug in her right pants pocket for something. The something was a normal size silver key. She unlocked the door and she and Danny walked through the doorway.

The Figure Instructor closed and locked the door behind her. It was dark inside the building. Ally brought out phone to shine in some light. Daniel noticed from the phone's light were stairs that went down. Slowly and carefully, both he and Ally-Loop went down the mysterious stairs for the surprise.

When they reached the bottom steps, Allison turned to her right and Daniel followed her. They walked down a long hallway. Danny was feeling very cold during the walk. He breathed in and could see his breath.

Then lights were starting to light up their path and the Pet trainer's ears was hearing music. He and Ally kept walking, lights shined on them and the music was getting louder and louder.

Ally proudly kept on walking.

Danny was stopped dead in his tracks when his eyes saw an ice rink from his left side. The rink looked fairly new and on the ice was a huge surprise to him.

Ten average looking guys skating on the new ice rink, listening to 'Delusional Madness', and they were doing figure skating. The guys looked happy. Happy enough to be enjoying figure skating.

Even though the night before at the public big rink was a shock to him, this was something Daniel Gray was not expecting for his surprise from Ally-Loop.

His brown eyes noticed at the guy's skating moves and listened closely to the metal's notes. The male figures danced and glided naturally to the song's energetic passion. Jumps were taken off or landed from the sound of drums beats. They did some advanced single spin positions or combinations of three or more spin positions.

So, this is what Ally wanted to show me. You can rock out and skate like a perky ballerina on ice. Daniel thought.

The biggest surprise was the kind of clothes the male skaters wore. They were not wearing tights, spandex bodysuits, or colorful sparkling male figure outfits for competitions. In fact, these male figures wore normal guy jeans or sweat pants, t-shirts, sleeveless shirts, or sweaters and in their male figure boots.

From Danny's point-of-view, these guys acted like they were at a bar and chilling out like the typical horny bastards they appear to be.

Ally whispered to Daniel, "These 'male figures' also play for the PHL."

Her student's eyes were wide-open.

They play pro hockey and practice figure skating moves too? He wondered. *How would Ally-Loop know those guys?*

One of the guys dressed in a white t-shirt and navy blue sweat pants noticed Ally in the building with a new male figure.

He skated up to a gate door close to them and tiredly asked, "Hey, Ally-Loop! What brings you here?"

"Hi, Evan! This 'figure' needs some hard-core skating techniques." She explained and added, "Would you guys care to help him?"

"Sure! Anything for the Loop!" The male figure exclaimed. Evan then wondered, "What's his story?"

"This is Daniel Gray and he needs to learn how to figure skate because he's engaged to Sally Hunt. In order for him to get Joy Hunt's blessing is to learn how to figure skate. He is getting good and I want you guys to show him how to be a hard-core figure in spins, jumps, dance steps, and freestyle poses." Allison expressed.

Another male figure skated up to the open door and questioned Ally, "What can he do?"

She did not tell. She let Danny tell them.

The Pet trainer gulped. The second figure hockey dude was the guy he saw the night before. That made Danny scared.

"Um, stop, forward and backward crossovers, strokes, basics figure turns, and getting up after a fall." He nervously replied.

"Well, this is going to be fun." Evan said excitedly.

Ally knew that code. She told Danny, "Get your skates on and the guys will show you hard-core skating."

They stepped away from the gate's open door and sat on the steel benches to put on their skates.

Ally stepped on the ice first. Then Danny got on the ice. He skated around once forward and did a mohawk turn to skate backwards. The PHL players watched Daniel skate.

Allison skated up to the group and asked, "What do you think of Daniel Gray?"

Danny did not hear their comments. He was getting into his skating groove to the heavy metal shit that was playing from the rink's speakers. He too was enjoying his time being out on Ally's special rink.

Five of the PHL figures skated up to Daniel and they chatted for a little while before they showed him some male skating skills. Ally laughed at the group when one of the hockey players was teaching Danny the 'bunny hop.' It was the very first jump a figure skater needed to do.

How to do the 'hop' was glide forward on the right blade, swing the left boot forward, jump up with the right toe pick and land forward on the right blade.

Danny started off slow. He practiced it with the small group of PHL guys for fifteen minutes. By then, the Pet trainer was ready to some upper level jumps.

They worked on waltz jumps for ten minutes.

Some of the guys traded turns to practice with Danny that way all the guys could have a chance to skate and talk to Ally's new figure student and talk and work on some stuff with Ally-Loop.

Danny began to do spins easy by doing pivots and two foot spins. He did laugh after his twentieth try of pushing around and managed to do a good long, centered two foot spin.

Then the guys taught Daniel about speed and being alert on the ice. The dog trainer did get faster and could glide more smoothly in all the moves he could do. With more practice, Danny would have fast-paced feet on and off ice.

Allison Rigden was very proud to have her all her figure students teach other about hard-core skating. She skated around and other hockey players would glide up to her for a chat or get some skating tips.

For three hours, the PHL players, Ally-Loop, and Danny skated and skated as much as they could. He was taught a great deal for easy jumps and doing wind-up spins.

Edge jumps were jumps that were taken off from the blade and toe jumps from the toe picks. Waltz, salchow, loop, axel, and split jumps were edge jumps. Toe-loop, flip, and lutz were toe jumps.

When wanting to do a spin from going backwards clockwise, imagine yourself in an invisible circle, wind up your shoulders and hips, have your left boot step into the circle, and then let go of the wind up to spin around on the left blade.

The trick part of going faster and longer was practice, let the arms and free leg move toward the body at the same time, and smoothly glide into the wind up without doing any extra pushes if the spin's speed decreased or from losing the spin itself.

Danny had trouble doing a scratch spin for his first few tries. The hockey dudes showed the dog trainer the step-by-step way to do good scratch spins. He did get better after doing it step-by-step.

Then it was time to go.

Most of the figures stepped off the ice to clean up, take off their skates, and head out of the building. Ally and Danny sat on the steel benches. They cleaned their blades and bottom part of their figure boots from rags.

Daniel noticed the figure hockey dude driving the Zamboni truck and that puck chaser seemed to stare and admire Ally-Loop from a far. But when his hazel eyes looked at Daniel Gray, he looked very jealous.

Now was the perfect time to ask his Figure Instructor why she was friends with puck chasers. "Ally, how do you know those hockey players?"

She put her skates in her roller suitcase before she answered the question. "I taught them all how to skate. Hockey and figure. The dude driving the Zamboni was my first five years ago. Why he wanted to learn how to ice skate was he wanted to see if he had what it takes to play professional hockey. I was shocked. I knew very little about hockey around that time and gave it a chance. Now Rich is one tough PHL player."

Danny realized then why the Zamboni driver looked familiar. It was Number 65, Richard McCarthy, Captain of central California's hockey team. The dog trainer also wondered why the hell McCarthy would want to be in an abandoned building and have Ally teach him hockey instead of being in a beautiful hockey rink with his teammates and well-trained hockey coaches.

And why would Number 65 want to do figure skating too?

Then it was time to leave the building.

Allison and Daniel gathered their skating bags and walked down the long dark quiet hallway for the staircase to exit the abandoned building.

The Figure Instructor continued on with her figure tale, "After a year of working with Rich on and off ice, he tried out an open hockey draft pick and made his current team. Many coaches wanted him to be part of their team. He wants to stay in San Jose because he loves the area he grew up in."

Danny was surprised of Ally's skating teachings for Captain Richard McCarthy. Then again, it made sense from McCarthy's figure skills the night before. And Ally learning about hockey with her competitive skills was strange too.

"It wasn't long before other 'guys'-I mean regular dudes who like baseball, football, wrestling, and race cars-who wanted me to teach them how to skate too." Ally expressed. "My boys and I are a skating family."

"That's real cool of you, Ally-Loop." Daniel complimented. "Skating and being friends with hockey pros."

She laughed loudly and they made it for the staircase.

The figure friends started to walk up the steps while Ally added twist to her tale, "True. But I faced a real big problem to be friends with ten wonderful PHL players. We cannot hang out in public."

"Why not?" Daniel wondered.

Their tired feet made it to the top step. Allison turned the door's knob, slowly pushed the door to open a little, and she and Daniel quickly left the building.

She huffed and locked the side door, "The press and the media would invade our skating sessions."

So, that's reason by saying she had 'no friends'. No one would pester her or constantly question about her PHL friends. Daniel thought in his head.

Both figure friends walked over to her tarp hidden convertible.

Ally put in, "Their hockey coaches could not bear of hearing the news that their boys were taking figure skating lessons from a competitive ice skater. The coaches and players would have second thoughts to accept them as part of team because figure skating and hockey plays don't mix together. But I taught the guys not to do figure moves in hockey skates."

"What's the difference?" Danny questioned his Figure Instructor.

Their hands lifted the tarp off the car and into the trunk with their skating bags.

"Hockey skates have a thicker blade than a figure skates and it's curved with no toe-pick." She started out.

Danny and Ally made it inside the car. The car was put into drive for their ride back to the skating rink.

"The moves hockey players do on the ice should be done from traditional hockey maneuvers for turns, skating forward and backwards, stops, edges, and play ideas the coaches have in their play books." Her voice explained. "For example, figure skaters do one to two crossovers for edges or going around corners while hockey players tend to do more because of their curved thick blade or to glide faster. They can't do three turns, dance steps, or have the use of their toes during practice or games."

Danny was understanding hockey standards pretty well with Ally around. He insightfully stated, "You've done some research about hockey, didn't you?"

"Yes, I did." Ally admit. "I had to if I want those 'men figures' to be skillful and determined hockey dudes."

He had a new question for Ally-Loop. "How did you find that abandoned building?"

"Two years ago, I was looking for a deserted place so the guys and I could catch-up and skate privately. We couldn't do it at a public rink because of the risk of exposure. I searched around the area for a few days and found that building. Richard came with me to check the place out. First, we inspected the room behind the sliding door. It was big, but the floor's foundation was not supportive enough to construct an ice rink. After finding out why, Rich found the staircase behind the left side door that went down to the building's basement. The temperature was cold. As cold as an ice rink."

Ally took some deep breathes and continued on her story a minute later.

"With the money I earned from skating competitions and major events, and the guys generous donation, I bought the building and got permission to make the basement into a private ice rink for me and the PHL players."

That's a real nice thing for a figure skater to do for professional hockey players. Danny thought.

"Richard not only plays hockey, he also takes care of the building and ice. He is licensed to drive and maintain a Zamboni truck. When he's traveling with the team and I want to skate in my rink, I have a secret helper who would do Rich's jobs. Some of the other players were taught how to do some of his jobs, but I trust him the most after all the hard work he's done to the building and the rink." Ally explained happily, "So far, the guys and I are happy to rock out on the ice as hard-core skaters, not just 'hockey dudes and a figure girl'."

The Pet trainer requested hopefully, "Could I come here too?"

Allison sighed disappointedly, "Not by yourself, Danny."

"How come?" He sadly asked.

"I do not want the Hunts to know what I've been doing with my earnings and let them know I like hanging out with stick dudes instead of other figure skaters." She firmly spoke.

Daniel understood what Ally was trying to tell him. *That must be her reason to have her special rink at an abandoned place. So no one would break in and destroy it. Joy wants to crush Ally's passion for figure skating so Sally could win easily.*

He promised to his Figure Instructor, "I won't say a word about it."

Ally relieved happily, "Thank you."

She did tell him some good news for his request. "You can come to my rink, but only if I'm with you. All you have to do is ask."

The figure student nod his head for her agreement. His heart still felt a little bad after yelling and ditching his figure lesson from a true figure skater.

Allison's Horundi arrived back at the skating rink.

The two figures scheduled their next skating session together. That coming Wednesday night at the small rink. They left the convertible, Danny got his skating bag from the trunk, and they went their separate ways.

Daniel walked to his car. Ally got out of her car for a stroll over to the ice rink's building.

The Pet trainer put his bag on the passenger seat and turned on his car for a ride back to his apartment unit. He did tell Butch all about his hard-core skating time with ten PHL hockey players and Ally-Loop during their lunch time and walk around downtown.

After a good night's rest, Daniel Gray opened his eyes and moved out of bed to spend a relaxing morning with Butch. A tasty breakfast, warm shower, long walk to downtown's dog park, and he let his mind ease off the pressure he had from fighting against Joy Hunt during Sectionals.

Skating with Ally-Loop and her PHL friends did make him feel better to be back on the ice. He had come so far from being a first timer to a new freestyle figure in so little time, Danny regained his strength to do more figure lessons.

His strength came from the love and passion he had for Sally Hunt.

For four years, Daniel saw and felt her love as a woman, not a skating champ. After all that time, his love for her grew stronger and stronger. He was being like Paul Hunt for his wife.

I overlook her temper just to have her love. Danny's ears heard Mr. Hunt's voice.

The Pet trainer thought Paul Hunt was not only a good male figure skater, he also was a very brave man to love someone like Joy Hunt.

One of the problems he had with Joy was why he expected to do so much just to have the love of one special girl for life. His heart felt a little sad because he could not feel that way for another girl. He did imagine what it would be like to be with someone like Allison Rigden. He would do nothing strenuous to do to earn her love, and having special figure skating treatments would not be a bad thing to him.

There was only one problem with that idea: his mind reminded his heart when he hugged, looked, and kissed Ally's lips that he felt no special spark or loving feel from her and neither did she with him. He could only receive the sparks from Sally.

Danny and Butchie-Wutchie made it back to their unit home. The cute beagle drank some cold water while his owner drank some fruit juice to quench his thirst.

The dog trainer thought over the other problem he had since Sectionals. He needed to understand the Joy Hunt vs. Allison Rigden rival story.

Off to his desktop in his bedroom.

Daniel sat in his computer chair, turned on his computer, and opened his net service. He searched online for some news stories about the two.

He decided to type 'Allison Rigden' in the search bar.

The search page showed results of figure skater Ally-Loop from pics, blog pages, fan sites, and news clips dealing with her skating career.

His mouse clicked on the news clips result bar. What popped up were some positive headline titles of Ally-Loop. There were also negative headlines too. He looked up the negative clips.

The first one happened when Ally was fifteen years old and the latest was a year ago. All of them contained Allison telling the press that Sally and her parents were cheating in competitive figure skating and had proof.

Joy would argue back by telling the media that Ally was a ridiculous and stubborn kid who did not know better in figure skating. Mrs. Hunt did state her daughter was a special skater and needed 'non-cheating' figure training.

Danny knew that Joy was lying if Sally was forced to wear 'special skates' instead of normal female figure boots like Ally-Loop. And why did Sally have to wear the same costume style, always had her hair in a French braid with a headband, and went first in all the competitions and events she did?

He wished his Figure Instructor would tell him what she knew what goes on in the girl's locker room between Joy and her daughter.

The dog trainer could not ask Ally immediately Wednesday night. What he should do first was look up all he could about the rival story before questioning the Loop her side of the story and see if there was anything he could do to help out the problem.

During the last days in November, Daniel worked hard at the Pet store's training booth, was a blessed dog owner with his sweet-loving beagle by his side, and did lots of skating reading from the figure books and rereading the news clips about Ally and Joy. He even looked up Joy's past skating career, Paul Hunt's competitive years until he was twenty-two years old, and Sally's skating updates from fans.

There were no clues or hints to the answer of the inside scope behind his fiancee's cheating success.

When Wednesday night came, Danny and Ally had a swell time practicing jumps and spins for the first few freestyle levels on the small rink. He also learned some easy dance steps from the spiral bound figure book.

The novice skater wanted to do a little challenge at the Pet store with Ally and Butch. He offered, "Ally, would now be a good time for you and Butch to come to the Pet store for dog training sessions?"

"Sounds like a good idea to me. But we'll talk about it Friday night that way I'll get my schedule from my coach and have lots of time to talk things over." She replied.

"No problem." He replied.

Ally had an idea herself before the session came to an end. She suggested, "Actually, do you want to do an early gym session on Saturday instead of a skating lesson Friday night?"

Danny liked that idea. "Sure. What time?"

"Lets meet at the rink's building seven a.m." She answered.

He sealed the plan by doing a wobbly scratch spin.

When he did his check from the spin, Ally concernedly asked, "How are you really doing?"

The dog trainer knew what Ally meant from that question. She did feel sorry for him because of his separation time from his love.

He sighed unhappily, "I miss Sally and long for her more than ever."

The Figure Instructor left it at that and they went to their own homes.

Danny Gray was finally glad the weekend came.

He could keep himself busy by planning out his teachings with Allison Rigden and Butch in the Pet store's training booth. For Saturday morning, he woke up early, ate a light breakfast, changed into street clothes, and took Butch out for his morning walk. They made it back to the unit before six-thirty a.m.

The Pet trainer changed into his skating clothes and brought his skating bag. He drove to the skating rink to meet up with Ally-Loop. It was a little before seven when Daniel's car pulled up in the rink's lot. Ally's Horundi convertible was already there and Ally was sitting the driver's seat.

A new concern hit Danny's heart.

He was bothered of the fact that the Loop did not have close friends she could trust off ice or could have much of a life besides figure skating.

He exit his car with his skating bag in his right hand. The car was locked up and he headed over for the cute white German car.

"Hi, Ally," Daniel greeted to her when he got inside the convertible.

"Morning, Danny." She spoke back cheerfully.

The Horundi was turned on and Ally drove off the lot for the gym.

In the gym's building, both figure friends had a wonderful warm-up run and pilate workout. While doing legs for pilates, Danny requested, "Do you have an idea on how you and Butch can come to the Pet store for training time?"

"This is what I can do: I'll come by every other weekday for two weeks before one in the afternoon." Ally explained.

"That won't be a problem with me." He responded and struggled on his reps, "I could-give you-spaaareee keyssss—forrrr-the buuildiing-and miii uunnnitttt-" he breathed in "after the training session so-Butch could be at home-rather than with you-till my shift ends."

"Good thinking . . ." Ally strained loudly.

They finished legs and went on for arms. Bungie cord and blue ball time.

Danny wondered, "What time could you come to the apartment building?"

"Um . . . like eight to eight-thirty in the morning." The Figure Instructor answered. She placed the cords around her running shoes.

So did Danny.

"Sweet," he sat on the wooden floor and placed the little blue behind his back.

Ally snickered, "That way Butch would 'pretend' to be my dog when he and I come into the store with a behavioral problem."

They started to do arm curls.

"Yup, that's the idea." Danny reminded Ally, "The training booth opens at eleven in the morning and I normally close it at three or four in the afternoon so I could be fair with Butchie-Wutchie."

It was ten a.m. when their workouts ended and left the gym building for the skating rink. The figures did some private ice time and skated during the afternoon public session.

Skating around the center to do easy dance steps, Danny had few new questions for Ally-Loop after public session started. "What days were you thinking on coming or when's the first day? Do you need directions to the Pet store I work at?"

She offered, "I can come to the store this Tuesday and alternate on for the following weekdays. And I do know which Pet store you work at."

"How?" He wondered.

While Ally worked on advance turns, she snickered, "I found it a month ago when I wanted to see you in action with the canines before going to the dog park with Butch."

Danny suspiciously questioned her, "Why?"

The Loop stopped moving to explain to her student, "I needed some 'behind-the-scenes' look of your old training technique to help out your Pet training problem."

Anger left the Pet trainer after he thought, *Only for instructional purposes.*

He calmly said, "I understand."

"I'm sorry if I said it like I was trying to stalk you or something." She sadly apologized.

"Nah, it's cool." Daniel replied.

Then he requested, "Could you show me how to go through a wedding ceremony on ice?"

Allison was surprised. "Um, I never went to a wedding on ice. I'm sure it would be like any other proper ceremony, but on ice."

"Okay."

"I'm sure Paul or Joy would tell or show you what to do for the Big Day." The Figure Instructor assured her student.

Danny nodded his head and would wait till he would see the Hunts again.

The two figures skated more throughout the session with great success from Daniel Gray's improved skating skills.

Their next session would happen Wednesday night.

Sunday went slow for Danny.

It would have a good day if he could see or talk to Sally again. He constantly wondered if she was okay during her 'lock up' with her Mommy and if his fiancee still loved him.

He did give Butch his morning walk and did some reading from his figure skating books. By mid-afternoon, Daniel had a sudden urge to look at the Pet store's website and see if there were any new reviews on the post boards. He went for his bedroom, turned on his desktop and his net service.

His fingers typed the Pet store's web address on the search bar. The page popped up and the arrow went for the blog page. The mouse clicked it.

All Danny wanted to see if the new posts had said anything about the training booth. He did find something from a username called 'Smokey_Squid67.'

"Let me start by saying what a difference Jack Randell's dog trainer was like a couple months ago just because he did not want to lose his job position. The Pet trainer did not show the dog's owners what kind of training their dogs need to be well-behaved outside the training booth and I too detest the idea of having my dog be in the hands of a non-proper dog trainer. My pug had a problem of barking at people coming by, loud noises, or when I wanted some peace and quiet in my home. At first I told the Pet trainer my dog and I were not going come back, then he suddenly had the heart to show me the type of obedient training my pug needed. After being taught of simple commands from the Pet store one month ago, my dog will stop barking when I want him to and I keep him busy with fun training exercises. I only have one question for Daniel Gray: What changed your mind from being a nonchalant employee to an overall dog trainer so quickly?"

Danny was surprised at the post. Then he realized who 'Smokey_ Squid67' was.

"Bob . . ." The Pet trainer gasped.

That made him happy.

He was also glad Smokey was being a good behaved pug to the retiree Squid. His eyes looked at the date of the post. It was added to the review board the day before. He would have to show and tell Bob and Smokey sometime at the booth.

He noticed other posts about him and the training booth. All were positive reviews of him working hard in the training booth with the dogs and their owners, kept the booth clean and stocked with food and play toys, and they were all happy to do special individual or group training.

The Samoyed owner's post was still there. That did not matter to Danny Gray. Lots of owners liked his changed training technique.

What he decided to do next that night was he started by calling out, "Butchie-Wutchie!"

The cute little beagle ran for his loving owner in their bedroom. He jumped into his lap.

Danny petted his loyal friend and asked him, "Do you want to go to the beach and pig out on some hot dogs?"

Butch answered with lots of happy yelps. He leaped out of Danny's lap and went for the front door.

The Pet trainer looked the fridge for meat dogs.

Nothing.

His heart felt sad. He remembered there was a dog stand at the beach. He got the short leash, baggies, wallet, cell, and keys.

Patient Butch sat by the door.

His owner told him, "We're getting the dogs at the beach, okay, pal?"

The clever beagle stuck out his left paw and he and Daniel shook hands. The boys left the unit for a night of playtime on the beach.

Chapter Fourteen

Work day on Monday went by smoothly for the young Pet trainer. He was looking forward to Tuesday morning when Allison and Butch would come in the Pet store's training booth. His heart continued to ache for his beloved Sally Hunt. Before going to bed that night, Danny found some old pics of he & Sally in his nightstand's middle drawer.

Tears were rolling on his cheeks from realizing how much he missed her and longed to be with her again. He whispered a soft pray that his fiancee was all right. He could not wait for this two month separation to be over. Because when it does, Daniel Gray would take his girl in his arms and pleads to fate that he & her would not be apart ever again.

He also knew if she and her parents were cheating, Sally would not do it voluntarily. Mom must have forced her into doing it. Maybe that was why Sally Hunt feared so much of being alone with Joy and competing on the ice.

An image of Joy Hunt physically beating up her daughter came into Danny's head because she did not do a flawless routine or out skate Ally-Loop. That killed the dog trainer's heart badly. So badly, he almost went for his cell and call up Sally's cell. He knew he could not call her or Joy was going to find out and torture Sally even more.

That was it.

Keeping himself away from his sunshine girl would protect her from her mother's killing claws and hurtful criticism. He had to do it for their future's sake.

Daniel went for bed. He settled in while his sweet beagle pooch was sleeping in his comfy pillow. He closed his tired brown eyes and fell asleep.

Time was 6:23 a.m.

The sound of a dog barking woke Daniel up. He groaned, "Mmmm, Butch. Can't you wait?"

The dog trainer flipped on his right side and tried to go back to sleep when the sweet beagle jumped on the twins size bed. His wet nose tickled Danny's face and his floppy pink kissed his owner's cheeks.

Danny's brown eyes opened and teased, "You know what today is, don't you, fuzzy butt?"

He laughed and his left hand grabbed the small wagging tail for a little playful tug.

Butch's face pushed his owner's right shoulder to get his ass out of bed and off for their morning walk.

"All right. I'm up." He gave up in utter defeat to make his pooch happy.

Daniel lifted up from his warm messed up bed and did his normal morning routine with his behaved beagle dog. Butch was extremely happy to have his morning walk and potty breaks along the way.

The boys' walk was done by seven thirty-five that morning. Danny showered, changed into his work clothes, got his extra spare keys, Butch's short leash, baggies, and other essentials. His dog was connected to his short leash before they left their unit home.

Half an hour later, by the apartment building's front doors, Daniel and Butch waited for Allison's car to arrive. The beagle's heart was very excited to see Ally again.

A familiar white Horundi pulled up and parked on the side of the street. Butch yelped out.

His owner said, "Yup, I see Ally, boy."

Daniel opened the door on his left and walked out the building with Butch.

Ally got out of her convertible. Her figure student was waiting outside for her. She was dressed in a pretty purple long sleeved shirt, jeans, and her N+ running shoes. Her cheeks did look flushed and pink. The Pet trainer thought his Figure Instructor was at the rink early that morning.

"Good morning!" She tried to speak cheerfully.

"Hi, Ally-Loop!" Danny greeted.

"How's Butchie-Wutchie?" Ally kindly wondered.

Butch yelped two times at her question and was jumping up from all four legs.

The figure friends laughed at Butch's excited attitude.

"I guess that answers my question." Smily Ally replied.

Daniel stood in front of Allison. He handed her Butch's short leash, a few plastic baggies, and two keys. A large gold key for the building and a small silver key for his unit.

He told her, "Butch had his morning walk and some breakfast. All that's left is for you and Butch to come to the Pet store around eleven or so."

Ally's left hand held the fray resistant nylon leash and her right hand stuffed in the keys in her right jeans front pocket. "That's good. We'll see you at the training booth, right, Butch?"

Her brown eyes looked down at the cute loving beagle. He had his left paw out. She was a little confused of the dog's body gesture.

Daniel explained, "He wants to shake hands with you."

"Oh." Ally sighed happily and got on her knees. Her right hand took the padded, furry paw for a gentle shake.

"Good shake, Butch." Daniel's instructional voice spoke.

Ally and Butch let go of their shake.

The achy figure girl lifted up from her squat to lead the beagle to her Horundi. Her left hand dug in her front left jeans pocket for her car keys. Her fingers found them, pulled it out, and deactivated the car's alarm. The convertible's lights flashed and two fast bleeps were heard.

Even though he trusted her with his faithful friend, Danny requested from Ally, "Take care of him."

She promised, "Butch will be in good hands."

The passenger door opened. The happy beagle leaped into the beautiful German car. Ally shut the door and walked over to the driver's side. She sat in her seat, turned on the convertible, and drove off.

Daniel whispered, "Be good, Butchie-Wutchie."

He turned around to walk inside the apartment building. He made it for the parking garage and drove over to the Pet store.

The dog trainer's car reached the store's lot at precisely nine in the morning. He walked out of the car and went for the store building's back door.

What he did during his morning chores was training his mind to act like he never seen Butch before. That would be a very difficult task to work since his dog could recognize his owner anywhere. From his scent, the way he walked, talked, and dressed, Butchie-Wutchie would know where Daniel Gray would be. As cute as he may be, Butch the beagle dog was a good hunting dog.

The Pet store was clean and ready to be opened.

10 a.m. and the front sliding doors were unlocked.

Danny went to the training booth for another thorough clean, had treats and toys stocked up, and calmed down his excited heart. He did wonder if Bob and Smokey would come by for a visit. That would help make his day if they did show up.

After finishing the booth, Pet trainer employee was told from another Stock Boy to help out a delivery that morning. He helped out carry in huge bags of animal food, boxes of new dog toys, and care-take essentials for certain animals.

Eleven o'clock.

Daniel's heart raced and he smiled a big smile. He did one last check of the booth. From the corner of his left eye, he noticed a small gray dog attached to a short leash coming into the store with it's owner. He turned his head to look at the sliding doors.

The dog trainer was really glad to see Smokey and Bob enter in the Pet store. The sweet pug barked cutely at the friendly dog trainer.

Bob grandly spoke, "Nice to have you back, Daniel."

The dog trainer unlocked the gate door and let in Bob and Smokey in the booth. "Thank you. Where have you two been?"

"Oh, Smokey and I took a trip to see family on Thanksgiving and we stayed longer than I wanted to." The elderly man dressed in loose jeans and an orange-brown color sweater chuckled. "Why did you disappear the week before Thanksgiving?"

Danny explained, "I went to see my fiancee's figure skating competition in Salt Lake City, Utah."

"Figure skating?" Bob was confused. "Not something I would expect a man your age would do for fun."

He chuckled some more and sat in a padded chair. Smokey sat-stayed by his owner's feet.

The Pet trainer gave the little pug a little piece of biscuit and Smokey ate his treat. Danny told Bob about his figure quest, "I have to learn how to figure skate to win my girl Mother's blessing for marriage."

Smokey's owner sighed, "Wow . . . your fiancee must be a really good ice skater."

"Her name is Sally Hunt." Daniel whispered in Bob's right ear.

"No kidding." The shocked elder man spoke.

Then the dog trainer secretly said, "Between you and me, Allison Rigden is a much better skater than Sally."

"Why do you think like that behind your fiancee's back?" Bob strongly asked.

"I don't see any passion when Sally skates." Danny candid. "I don't know, Bob. Her skating attitude looks fake, an act, and there's no life when she does her routines. I have been taking lessons from Allison and I like to ice skate more than Sally does."

"Everyone's entitled to their own point-of-view." Bob concernedly wondered. "Do you have any-feelings for Allison?"

A ping of deja vu his Danny's heart.

The dog trainer honestly respond, "No, no, no-nothing at all from Ally. I mean she's a nice girl, but Sally Hunt? I just love the woman, not the figure champ."

"Good." His aged voice backed him up.

Daniel professionally questioned, "So, what can I do for you and Smokey today?"

"Actually, we decided to watch you teach other dogs and their owners." Bob chortled.

"I appreciate it." The dog trainer happily replied.

There were other dogs and their owners coming into the store for the training booth. Danny told to Bob only, "Not only Ally teaches me figure skating, she did give me wonderful tips on how to be an overall dog trainer."

His left aged eye winked at Daniel for answering his question from his post.

A total of six more dogs and owners came inside the wooden cube. Just when he wanted to ask the owners what kind of training they wish to do that day, his brown eyes saw Ally-Loop and Butch coming inside the Pet store and heading for the training booth.

Daniel smiled happily to see his sweet beagle in the Pet store for the first time.

Acting like a concerned pet owner, Allison asked, "Hope we're not too late."

The Pet trainer warmly welcomed the late comers, "Nope. You're right on time."

Ally and Butch were in the booth and she sat on an empty padded chair.

Some of the owners, especially Bob, were surprised to see figure silver-medalist Allison Rigden in the Pet store. A few dog owners wondered, *When did Ally-Loop get a dog?*

Danny started off the session by telling all the owners to do simple basic obedient exercises. Treats and clicks were their rewards. Butch and his 'owner' were having a ball. Lots of talking and playing with dogs happened in the cube booth.

It did not take Bob long to understand why Allison was there in the first place. He remembered what Danny told him earlier. *She's there to help him in his dog training sessions. Such a nice thing for her to do. Wonder why is his fiancee not there instead of Allison?*

Ally was really glad to come to the Pet store with Butch for training time. She still wanted Daniel to do an ice skating lesson full of little kids. That would be a good instructional test for him.

The time was one in the afternoon and Danny, Butch, and Ally walked out of the booth for her Horundi in the parking lot. By her convertible, Allison said, "Good job, teach. We had a wonderful time today."

"I'm glad you and Butchie-Wutchie had fun." Daniel replied. He picked up his sweet beagle for a tight hug.

He promised to Butch, "I'll see you in a few hours."

The loving dog's floppy tongue kissed the Pet trainer's right cheek.

"I Love You too, fuzzy butt." He lowered Butch back on the ground.

Ally reminded him, "Skating lesson Wednesday night?"

"I'll be there."

The Figure Instructor and Butch got in the beautiful white German car. The dog trainer turned around and headed back for the Pet store.

After walking through the sliding doors, Bob and Smokey surprised him there. He questioned Danny, "So, how come Ally is teaching you figure skating instead of Sally?"

"Her mother locked up Sally for Nationals." The young trainer sadly respond.

"So, you can't see your fiancee?" The Senior man wondered and kept hold his dog's short leash.

Sad Danny nodded his head and spoke, "I can't even talk or email her."

Bob felt sorry for his pugs' trainer. "I'm so sorry, Danny. Doesn't seem fair for you. A nice young man like you should get to see his girl."

"I can't. Joy wants her daughter to win. It gets worse." The brown haired Pet store employee looked as if he was going to cry.

"What?" The retiree Squid spoke. "What can be worse than that temporary separation?"

Daniel lead them over to his training booth. "I'll tell you at the booth."

The booth was empty. The two men sat on padded chairs while Smokey laid down on the floor.

"It's like this: I had a couple of bad dreams of Sally not being free from her mother. I don't think Joy wants her daughter & I living together until Sally's skating years are over."

"Oh, Danny . . ." The elderly man sighed. "It's a shame you have to go through that."

Young Gray's brown eyes were full of tears and he started to cry softly. He whimpered, "Bob, I don't know I can last that long without the love of my life . . ."

The wise pug owner gave him a bit of advice, "I can relate to that. I was in the Navy during 'Nam and my wife & I were apart a lot. We had very little ways to communicate during our separation time, but we always remembered why we fell in love in the first place."

"Thank you, Bob." Danny sniffled. "I do Love Sally. I wish her mom weren't so hard on me or her."

"It's okay, son. I'm sure you can find the strength to wait a little more patient for your fiancee." Bob encouraged the twenty-one year old. He got up from the padded chair and he and Smokey left the Pet store.

Danny cleaned himself up to do two more hours of obedient training.

That Tuesday work day made Daniel Gray really satisfied professionally. He was super happy to see Butch in the unit all excited and full of energy for his afternoon walk. The only thing that could make it better was have a date or another chance to talk to Sally.

While he changed out of his work clothes and into jeans, black t-shirt, tennis shoes, and synthetic jacket, his mind thought of something ironic. His work life was going swell, but his love life was awful.

Funny how life seem to work that way.

A couple months ago, Danny's love life was promising after proposing to his girl and had a tough time struggling with his dog training job. Now, he was more comfortable of going into the Pet store and teach the dogs and their owners obedient training, but he had not seen or heard of his fiancee in almost two weeks.

He knew it would not be long before he & Sally got married. Then again, Danny hated the idea of he & his wife not living together after their big date because her Mommy thought it was best for her competitive years. What he wish was a solution to make Sally Hunt stop figure skating forever.

Butch and his owner went out for a long walk around downtown.

Wednesday afternoon at the Pet store was a huge surprise to Daniel Gray. The surprise was someone was not expecting to see again. It all happen twelve-thirty p.m.

Danny was busy helping out the owner of a two year old German Shepherd. The owner wanted its dog to do some tracking exercises by doing the Pet trainer's hide & treat game. As the shepherd got better and better at the game, Daniel's brown eyes saw a familiar brunette lady with a white fluffy, struggling Samoyed dog in her arms.

The first thing that came to mind was, *Ah, shit. What's she doing here?*

He wanted to ignore her request, but her voice called out in the store, "Ceinwen! Ceinwen! Come back here!"

Danny knew then he had to help the stuck-up lady and her dog. He politely told the other owners, "Excuse me."

He left the wooden booth to help out the lady with her Samoyed dog.

The lady kept calling out her dog's name, "Ceinwen? Where are you? Ceinwen?"

Daniel spotted the white dog in the toy aisle and did his best to speak out her name. "Hey, Ceinwen."

The fluffy little cloud ran towards the Pet trainer. He leaned down and his hands picked up the soft toy-like dog. He was standing up straight when he decided to give Ceinwen a little piece of biscuit to calm her down. She contently ate it.

Ceinwen's owner found her dog in the arms of the lazy Pet trainer.

"You!" She demanded. "Put my dog down!"

Danny sadly placed the cute Samoyed dog back on the floor and Ceinwen ran for her caretaker.

"I was only trying to help." He insisted.

The lady kept her dog close to her and strictly replied, "I see. I am shocked the manager had not replaced you for a much more better Pet trainer."

Deja Vu stuck his heart big time.

Then again, Ceinwen's owner was not the first bullheaded woman he ever met. He knew how to fight back.

"Ma'am, for the past few weeks I was taught how to be a good dog trainer from a wonderful figure skater and now the booth is full of well-behaved dogs and their owners." He firmly explained.

The angry lady requested, "Prove it."

Without fear or nervousness, Daniel Gray lead the lady and her struggled white fluffy cloud to the training booth. What the lady saw had caught her off guard.

Her brown eyes saw seven different dogs and their owners doing obedient training without having any problems of the dogs or owners getting along. Owners were talking and playing with the dogs by doing training exercises.

Danny's heart smug. He knew the Samoyed's owner would change her mind about him from their first encounter that happened more than a month ago. Him not talking or giving training advice to the dog's owners and only he was in the booth and training the dogs.

The lady had to admit. Jack's lazy Pet trainer had grown up and changed his training technique in so little time.

Daniel offered, "Care to join with us in the booth?"

"All right." She tried to say calmly. Ceinwen was not acting positively in her owner's arms. "Could you also show Ceinwen to be calm when she's in my arms?"

"Absolutely!" Exclaimed the Pet trainer.

This would be a good instructional test. He thought. *Too bad Ally isn't here to watch this.*

They walked in the cube booth. The lady sat in an empty padded chair and her Samoyed dog sat on the floor.

Daniel told the group, "Thank you for keeping yourselves busy."

All the dogs and their owners stopped doing their obedient training and cleared the floor so the Pet trainer could do the session. People sat in the padded chairs. Dogs either sat-stayed or laid on the floor. And Daniel Gray stood in the center.

He calmly spoke, "This nice lady and her Samoyed dog has a problem. Let's see if we can help them out."

The 'nice' lady did know what to tell the group. She explained, "My name is Ruth and my sweet Ceinwen does not like to be held, would not be told keep quiet, or control herself around people."

"If you saw what happened earlier, may I ask what Ruth was doing wrong with her dog in the Pet store?" He asked the owners.

A dark man spoke out, "She paid attention to her dog while the dog was acting in a negative manner."

"Couldn't have said it better myself." The Pet instructor smug.

Ruth pondered, "Why should I ignore her inappropriate behavior?"

The young dog trainer's mind thought over the 'not focusing on your dog's angry attitude.'

He explained, "If someone gave their full attention to something they don't want their dog to do, the dog think its okay to do it because you are focusing them and they'll keep doing it just to have someone's attention. If they ignore it, the dog would think, 'Oh, this does not get people's attention. I should stop and do something else to get some attention.'

The Pet trainer turned his attention to the Samoyed dog's owner. "Ruth, all dogs want love, attention, and be part of the family. You need to make sure everyone in the house give love and attention to Ceinwen only when she did something good or positive. The more you do it, she will let go of her negative behavior."

His eyes looked at all the owners and dogs in the booth. Then he added, "Rewards don't have to be-"

Ceinwen started to bark at other dogs and customers. Ruth listened to Danny's advice by not looking at her white fluffy cloud. The other owners and dogs did not focus their eyes at the Samoyed's annoying barking.

"As I was saying, rewards don't have to be treats or new toys. It can be a pet, a click from the clicker, hug, play time, car ride, an extra long walk, special place to go to for free leash fun, or do something together as a team for your bonding time." Daniel finished his interrupted speech.

No one see to mind the barking Ceinwen and she decided to stop yelping after closing her muzzle mouth.

Ruth's head tipped down to look at her fluffy Samoyed and whispered, "Thank you for not barking, Ceinwen."

She picked up her dog and had Ceinwen on her lap.

The Pet trainer requested, "Ruth, let's have you and Ceinwen step up for a little basic training exercise."

Ruth stood up from her chair. She let her dog stand on the floor. Both girl were in front of Daniel. The brunette lady handed the trainer Ceinwen's pink nylon jacquard leash.

A question came to his mind. Danny wondered, "Ruth, what does 'Ceinwen' mean?"

The Samoyed's owner expressed, "'Ceinwen' in Welsh means: fair, lovely, white, and blessed. I thought I was blessed with a fair and lovely dog. I was wrong."

"Ceinwen can be a fair and lovely Samoyed dog with a few simple training tips to work with." He encouraged to Ruth.

Daniel lowered his eyes and eyed at the dark eyed fluffy pooch. He commanded her, "Sit."

Ceinwen sat.

The trainer slowly leaned down to her muzzle and gave her a small piece of biscuit from his left work pants pocket. She ate it happily.

"Down." He spoke to the sat-stayed dog.

The white fluffy cloud slowly laid down on the floor. She was presented another piece of a biscuit for her reward.

Danny let go of the pink leash for a little challenge for the Samoyed dog. He reached down for Ceinwen's small soft body. After being a foot off the floor, the Samoyed dog growled and started to struggle. She was immediately placed back on the floor.

Ruth curiously questioned the dog trainer, "Why did you do that?"

A woman answered, "Because Ceinwen was not calm when Daniel was lifting her off the floor."

Ruth understood the woman's answer. *Ceinwen acted mean toward the trainer's love and affection. She deserved to be ignored if she wanted to be rude.*

"I'll try it again when Ceinwen's calm." Daniel replied.

She did her sit and lie down commands from the Pet trainer again and received her biscuit treats. A minute passed by without any movement or noise coming from the fluffy Samoyed dog.

Danny carefully reached down to the cute white dog. His fingers touched the soft fur. She did feel calm to him. He opened up his hand, slide Ceinwen on his palms, and slowly lifted up the white dog off the floor.

Surprised Ruth was impressed of the Pet store's dog trainer picking up her once misbehaved fluffy cloud without a fit or struggle coming from her.

The Pet trainer offered Ceinwen another small piece of biscuit for a 'good job' treat. She ate it quickly.

He suggested to Ruth, "Why not try it yourself?"

Ceinwen was placed back on the floor and the leash was in her owner's left hand. Her new friend handed her owner some more biscuit pieces. Ruth stuffed in her right coat pocket.

Danny instructed, "Be calm, happy, and fair with Ceinwen."

Ruth kindly said, "Hi, Ceinwen."

The other owners watched and learned what Ruth and her white dog were doing right and wrong. So far, both girls were doing positive steps for their training exercises.

Ceinwen had her owner's attention.

Ruth commanded, "Sit."

The Samoyed dog did a beautiful sit and was presented a piece of biscuit from her owner.

"Now, Ceinwen knows what a 'sit' is from her owner." Danny stated to the group. "It's important for the dog to learn simple commands from its owner."

"Lie down." Ruth sweetly said to her dog.

Ceinwen slowly lied down on the floor.

Ruth bend not in front of her white dog, but to the side and handed Ceinwen another treaty reward.

The dog trainer made another statement, "Ruth did a good thing to Ceinwen by not hovering over the dog's face or Ceinwen would be scared of being dominated from her owner. Dog's don't want to be dominated, they want to be equal with their family."

An idea came to Ruth's mind. While sitting next to Ceinwen, she lifted her hands and gently caressed her dog's soft white fur.

Her voice whispered, "Good dog, Ceinwen."

Her hands felt her dog's heart slowing down. She knew what to do next.

Like handling a breakable China doll, or dog in this case, Ruth slide her hands under the Samoyed dog's body and lifted up off the floor. There were no peeps or any sudden movements coming from the cute fluffy cloud in her owner's arms.

To all the owners surprise, Ceinwen was napping.

Ruth was very glad to come to the Pet store after all.

Everyone in the training booth gave Ruth soft applauses for her hard work.

Daniel whispered to Ruth, "Just keep ignoring her negative behavior and continue to do basic training then Ceinwen will be a fair, lovely Samoyed."

"Thank you, young man." She softly spoke happily. "I'm so sorry for saying those awful things about you."

"Actually, I'm glad you did." He chortled. "I needed to be taught a lesson if I want to be an overall dog trainer. Thank you for coming to the booth."

Ruth replied, "We will come back for another session. Now, it's time for me and Ceinwen to go home."

The Pet trainer opened the gate door.

Ruth carried her Samoyed dog out of the Pet store building and into her car.

Daniel Gray went back to work with other dogs and their owners until his shift ended at four that afternoon. He was really looking forward for his skating lesson with Ally-Loop and tell her all about his most successful dog training day ever. But his heart was sad of the fact that he could not tell Sally his ironic day in the training booth with the rude lady and her Samoyed dog.

Danny went to the rink later that day with satisfaction in his heart. He proudly told Ally his day in the training booth with Ruth and her Samoyed dog, Ceinwen.

The Figure Instructor was very proud of her student to face a past mistake and learned not to do the same thing again for a future encounter.

Allison's mind thought, *He really did a wonderful job at the Pet store today. I wish there was some way to treat him. Maybe I could show him my very special quad-quad combo jump one day. I could trust Danny with that secret after he promised not to tell Joy Hunt my special skating rink and my PHL friends.*

When their session for the small ice was over, Ally asked, "Tomorrow morning?"

"Yup." Daniel agreed. "I'm glad Butch likes you."

"He is a sweetheart." She sighed. "Have a good night."

"Night, Ally-Loop." Danny said.

He headed out of the skating rink for his car. He drove to his apartment unit, had a little bonding time with Butch, and changed his clothes for bed.

For the next week and a half, Daniel Gray got more and more successful in his Pet training job with and without Allison Rigden and Butch in the store's training booth to show their support. Ally was really glad to come to the Pet store. Sometimes owners talked to her about figure skating and she was kind enough to do some autograph signing.

What happened behind the figure friends' backs was someone spying on them. Someone desperately had to know Ally's special combo jump for Nationals.

In a white SUV with dark tinted windows and wearing disguised clothes and wigs, the snoop would follow the figure friends from the skating rink to their units, the gym where they worked out, and sometimes to the Pet store where Danny worked at. The undercover SUV driver had spot the Pet trainer and Ally-Loop with a familiar beagle in her arms at a parking lot. Both of them were talking to each other longer than they should.

The secret informer was curious on why Ally would be nice to Danny at the Pet store with his dog. It thought, *They're up to something. I just need to do some more digging.*

After Friday afternoon's dog training session, which was Allison's last visit to the Pet store's booth, she offered, "Danny, would you like to come to my loft tomorrow for a special off ice training in my ballet room?"

"Sounds good to me." Danny said.

"We need you to get into spin jumps. My trampoline would be a very helpful tool for you." She explained.

Butch yelped and jumped up for Ally's idea.

"Seems like Butch wants to come over too." She teased.

"Sorry, pal." His owner sadly replied, "A trampoline is not a safe play thing for dogs."

The Figure Instructor lead the sweet beagle to her Horundi car. She turned around and told Danny, "I'll be at the apartment building eight a.m."

"See you tomorrow then." He responded.

Ally got in her car, drove off from the parking lot, and headed back to Danny's apartment unit to bring Butch back home. She did leave the spare keys in his unit before leaving Butchie-Wutchie alone.

Daniel was done with shift three-thirty p.m.

The booth was clean and stocked up for his next dog training shirt Monday morning. He clocked out and made it for his car.

During the drive, his heart was bothered of two things: was Jack seeing the new and improved Daniel Gray the Pet trainer, and how was Sally doing?

It was the middle of December, Christmas was going to come up, and so was New Year's Day. The end would pass by quickly with busy holiday shoppers.

After walking through the unit's front door, Danny was greeted by Butch. His dog yelped loudly with excitement as he closed and locked the door.

He asked, "Was Ally good to you today?"

Butch smiled big at his owner with his pink floppy tongue sticking out. The beagle walked to the kitchen and waited patiently for his dinner.

Daniel headed for his bedroom. He changed out of his work clothes and into jeans, navy blue long sleeved shirt, and tennis shoes. Then strolled over for the bathroom to clean himself up from a wonderful training day at the Pet store.

He left the bathroom for the kitchen.

As he reached the living room to cross through, his eyes noticed something shining on the coffee table. It was the spare keys he gave to Ally.

The boys chowed down their dinner in the kitchen.

Butch knew was time it was when dinner time was over. Time for their evening walk.

Danny connected his faithful beagle to his retractable leash. They left the locked up apartment unit for an hour long walk around the neighborhood.

Chapter Fifteen

Saturday morning arrived.

Daniel Gray woke up from bed six-thirty and he and Butch were ready for their morning walk. Their stomaches were full from having breakfast. The Pet trainer changed into jeans, a t-shirt, and his tennis shoes. He attached his sweet beagle to the gray retractable leash.

The boys set off from their unit home for a long stroll around the city's downtown.

It was seven-thirty when they reached back inside the apartment unit. Butch was feeling tired. Danny, however, did not feel tired at all. Maybe after doing two months of pilate workouts and ice skating sessions got him in better shape.

He changed into his normal skating clothes. Black sweat pants and a white cotton t-shirt. Then he gathered his skating bag and his keys, cell, and wallet. Before leaving his unit, Danny made sure Butchie-Wutchie was okay on his own with food, clean water, and fixed his Bong toy.

The dog trainer reached the apartment building's front doors a little before eight o'clock. He saw Ally's Horundi pulling up in front of the building just when he made it for the doors. His right hand turned the building's right door knob and pushed the door away from him. He stepped outside with his skating bag in his left hand.

Inside the cute German convertible, Ally sat in the driver's seat in her casual skating outfit and unlocked the car door's for Daniel. Her eyes saw and her ears heard him get in the car.

"Morning, Ally," Danny greeted cheerfully.

"Morning, Danny," she greeted back.

She hoped her student would like her test idea for a short afternoon session at the small rink.

They sat in their seats and Ally drove off to her loft's building. She parked her convertible safe and sound in the secure parking garage.

Allison and Daniel exit the Horundi for an elevator ride to her luxurious loft. Inside the loft, it had not changed since Danny's last visit a month ago. He followed his Figure Instructor to her ballet room. He was getting nervous of the idea to jump on her trampoline and try to do spins in the air. He was more scared if he fell off the trampoline with a broken bone or two.

He did remember that her trampoline did have lots of big inflatable mattresses around it. His heart was a little relieved that Ally had plan ahead.

Ally-Loop went to her black speaker in her ballet room and placed her phone on the speaker's dock. Music was playing from the phone's music player. She took off her purple N+ running shoes. Danny took his tennis shoes off as well.

She instructed to Danny, "Almost all figure jumps are done from back spins. The only forward spin jump is salchow."

The Pet trainer remembered what a 'salchow' was from his skating time with the PHL players. Starting on his left foot, he took three forward steps, did a left outside three turn, and jumped up from the left foot but landed backwards terribly on the right foot. His arms and left leg were out of whack from not standing up straight and nearly fell forward on the hardwood floor.

Allison stood in front of Danny and offered him a little landing tip. "Land on the balls of you feet. That's when you get better balance rather than on the heel."

Danny stepped back a few feet from Ally.

While doing his figure pose, his left foot did an outside three turn, popped up from his left foot, his right leg crossed over his left leg for the forward spin, and landed strongly on the ball of his right foot backwards. He stood up straight with his arms out and a smile on his face.

"Now that's a salchow, Figure Gray." The Figure Instructor smug.

He bowed forward to thank her.

She added, "But all the other spin jumps are for back spins."

"Why does it have to be back spins?" Danny wondered.

"I see you have not paid attention to all the step-by-step set-up for all the jumps." Ally insightfully stated sadly.

Now Daniel Gray knew he had not done what his coach requested him to do from reading the figure skating books and watching Ally and Sally's dvd skating discs.

"No." He disappointedly admitted. "I guess I haven't."

Ally-Loop decided to teach Sally's fiance a lesson when it come to advance figure jumps.

She found and held her speaker's remote from her right pant's pocket. Her right index finger paused the song that was playing. She walked to the speaker's table and opened the table's cabinet doors. What she pulled out were a white board and colorful pens to write on the board.

The Figure Instructor explained to Danny with a red pen in her hand, "Okay, let's say I want to do a salchow. Salchows are forward spin jumps because-"

She waited and drew the step-by-step trace of the jump on the board with the red pen.

Daniel thought for a minute.

"Because-" he sighed in utter defeat "-I give up."

Ally answered kindly, "Because you're taking off from the left blade. You normally spin 'forward' on your left blade, don't you?"

"Ooohhhh . . . I get it!" Danny exclaimed. "Which ever 'blade' the skater 'takes off' from is the spinning blade!"

"Well," she replied, "almost like that."

The Pet trainer curiously questioned her, "What do you mean?"

"I'll explain that later." Ally promised. "Let's do some more examples."

A new thought came to Danny's mind. "Then why do the lands have to be the right blade backwards?"

The Figure Instructor's answer was, "When you're doing full spins or jumps, you land backwards because it will be a full circle jump instead of a half-circle jump if you land forward. Folks who are left handed would land on their left blade for the comfort of their spins and jumps."

Those are good tips. He thought.

"Here's a good blade-change-spin-jump." She spoke and had her focus back on her white board. "Toe loop. You do a right outside three turn-" she drew a long stretched red three turn, "then you have your left toe pick on the ice behind you," there was a small red dot not far from the three turn, "you do take off from the left pick but you do a back spin from a doing a right hip turn in the air," her right hand drew a check edge from the toe loop jump, "and finally, you land on your right blade backwards. Simple as that."

Daniel did get a much better idea on what a top loop was like without having to practice it on ice. He understood Ally's point of view of him going slow for his skating lessons.

All the basics I learned are combined together to do advanced figure skills. From edges, going forward and backward, doing turns, and the 'bunny hop,' I can do spins, jumps, dance steps, and freestyle poses. He relieved happily.

Figure skating was making more sense to him.

"I understand it now." Danny remarked.

"The loop usually come after the toe loop." Ally-Loop spoke. "It is an edge jump, you glide backwards, and both your blades are on the ice for the take off. Except, you are spinning backwards while you're in the air from doing a right hip twist and your left leg cross over your right leg in the air. You still land backwards on your right blade."

She did tease, "Your left leg would not be much of help if you spin on your right blade and your left blade was your checking blade or people would think you're left handed or doing an opposite salchow jump."

"That's understandable." The dog trainer said.

Ally went on to show Danny the flip, lutz, and axel jumps on the white board.

"Now the flip is not a body twist trick like the gymnasts do. You glide forward on your left blade to do an outside left three turn, pause for a second, dig your right toe pick on the ice after the three turn, take off from the right pick to do your back spin, and land backwards on the right blade."

Her red pen drew the flip jump trace.

She continued on with the lutz jump.

"Lutz is tricky to do because the take off is from back left outside edge, but you land on a right inside edge."

"How's that tricky?" Danny questioned Ally.

"Almost all jumps are on the same edge, from take off to landing. The lutz starts out from a backward clockwise edge," she drew a small clockwise half-circle on the white board with the red pen, "there's the take off," a little dot was on the board on the same edge as the clockwise's half-circle trace, "for the right pick and then the land for the right inside edge." The last thing was added for the lutz trace. A counter clockwise half-circle was the right inside edge.

Danny saw that Ally was right about the lutz jump. "So, it's like a clockwise to counter clockwise toe jump?"

"Something like that."

He did look a little worried about doing a lutz jump. He carefully examined at all the other jump traces Ally drew on the white board. Only the lutz was an opposite edge jump.

Allison was not done there.

"The only jump left with spins is the axel jump. It is one of the few jumps with no special blade trace to determine the axel jump. You take off like a waltz jump, but in the air you do a back spin and land on your right blade backwards." She warned in the end, "It is the hardest single rotation jump to nail."

And Daniel thought the lutz was going to be tough, him to do an axel jump was going to be a total pain the ass.

The Figure Instructor saw her student's face in absolute fear.

She assured him, "Daniel, I will help you in every step of the way. I did it with my PHL friends when they were learning how to skate and I'll treat you the same way. You too can be a grand male figure for the Hunts."

His fear was let go from her encouraging words. He smiled from ear to ear after knowing he would not be alone in his figure quest.

"What do we do first?" He wondered.

Allison went over to her ballet bars. "First, we stretch."

With her right hand, she found her speaker's remote and pressed play at the speaker's dock for the phone. Pumped up music was playing from the phone's music player.

Danny joined her at the bars and Ally showed him some simple stretches for legs, body, arms, and feet. They worked on spiral stances and some spin positions with the figure pose. Scratch spin, combination forward, back, and forward spin, sit spin for left and right foot with, layback, the sword, cross-foot, and camel spin.

Doing the camel stance looked weird and funny to Daniel Gray from looking at the mirrors. His right hand held on a bar for support. Allison's hands corrected his arched back, his pulled back right shoulder, his straight right leg behind him, and right foot flat and pointed.

"That's how your body should feel when you're doing a camel spin." She proudly stated.

"Can I let go?" Danny requested tiredly.

"No!" Ally teased. "You must stay there for the next five months!"

"What?" He cried out and lost his concentration by falling down on the hardwood floor.

Ally just giggled hard at her student's facial reaction and fall to the floor. "I was kidding!"

Danny got up from the wooded floor and fixed his shirt and sweat pants.

"Let's do some jumping on the trampoline!" She declared.

He walked with her to the trampoline. She stepped onto the black taut and both her legs were bent forward. She spring herself straight up to the ceiling like a rocket was blasted up into space.

Ally bounced and bounced some more before her right leg crossed over her left and twisted her left hip to do a full forward spin in the air.

The Pet trainer was impressed with the Loop's trampoline tool idea. He watched his instructor do some more forward spins.

"Now, watch the-next spin!" Bouncing Ally announced and did three big straight bounces. Then she did her next spin.

Danny's eyes saw Ally do a forward two spin rotations in the air and safely jumped off the trampoline. She tiredly replied, "That's a double spin jump."

He answered, "Because you spun around two times?"

"Good to know you're catching up." Ally happily complimented.

Daniel sadly explained, "I did watch the dvds, but what I did not do was closely watch or comprehend the step-by-step moves in all the advance terms."

The Figure Instructor sincerely spoke, "I am glad you are comprehending figure terms now."

"Better than I did a month ago." He chortled. "Better than a week ago. Yesterday. Hell, an hour ago!"

Both figure laughed.

Allison got back on the trampoline and explained to Danny, "Okay, I am going to do some back spins!"

Daniel saw Ally do some straight bounces and then her left leg crossed over her right and did some right hip twists for some single back spins. She bounced up higher to do doubles and triples.

The surprised dog trainer was amazed at Ally's ability to do beautiful multiple spins in the air.

An idea came to Ally's mind.

She jumped up even higher than before and presented her student a quadruple spin rotation jump. She jumped off the trampoline without any problems.

Danny swore the last jump Allison did not look like a double or a triple. The height was higher than the rest and the spin was longer than a triple.

He asked, "What was that?"

Panted Ally turned down the speaker's volume to tell her student, "That-was a-quad spin."

The Pet trainer was shocked. "Why do you want to do quads?"

I guess I can't keep this a secret any longer. Ally thought in her head.

"Daniel Gray, I want your damnest word that you will not tell this to anyone. Especially to Sally or Joy."

It must be that serious to her. He seriously promised to his instructor, "I won't tell anyone anything about it."

Allison Rigden professionally spoke, "I'm going to be the first figure skater in history to nail an edge quad-quad combo jump for my long program in Nationals."

Danny heard some crazy shit in his life, but Ally's mind was beyond crazy, shit as hell to him.

He furiously wondered, "Ally, that's not a practical figure skater's mind. That's suicide!"

"Look, I am fuckin' tired of coming into second while your fiancee's talent are bought, not earned! I know I can win the gold with a quad-quad to get back at Joy Hunt!" Ally yelled out from the top of her lungs and cried out the pain she had in her heart.

Daniel thought, *That's why the announcer spoke of Ally's special combo jump from Sectionals.*

But hearing that Sally's skating skills might be 'bought' hurt his heart.

"Do you really think Sally's skating talent are fake?" The Pet trainer questioned Allison.

She sniffed, "Yes . . ."

Danny then got on the trampoline and started to do some straight up bounces on the taut. He had to admit. Ally really knew something that he or others did not know about the Hunts wanting Sally to win the gold.

While he continued to bounce, he decided to not ask Ally on what she knew until he got some real proof that Joy was 'buying' her sunshine daughter to the top in competitive figure skating.

Allison went back to her ballet bars for some more stretching. She was feeling much better to do practice her earned skating skills.

By looking at the mirrors in front of her, Ally suggested, "Danny, try to do a forward spin in the air."

He bounced up high in the air and tried his best to do a right over left leg forward spin. He did feel a little twist, but fell on one of the inflatable mattresses.

Ally saw Danny fall on the mattress he was laying on. She did remember her first tries on the trampoline. She laughed and giggle from all the falls and mess ups she faced.

Daniel slowly moved off the blown up mattress and hurtfully asked, "What's so funny?"

"I was not laughing at you, Daniel. Just old memories of me falling on the mattresses from my first tries." She tried to cheer up her figure student. "It's ok. It took me a while to get use to do spins in the air from my trampoline without falling down."

"I figure." He sighed and walked to the trampoline to try again.

For twenty more minutes, Danny bounced up and down on the trampoline and really tried his hardest to do forward or back spins in air with no success. He did fall down a lot on all the inflatable mattresses around the trampoline.

He decided to give up for the day.

Ally decided to help Danny do some figure dance steps. She turned on pop dance music to make Daniel happy.

To Danny's surprise, he was having fun by doing figure steps. Kinda like what ballerinas do up on stage, except he did not have to dance on his toes and listen to boring classical tunes.

The Figure Instructor was unimpressed with Danny's dance moves. *No wonder he was embarrassed to dance out on the ice before Sectionals.*

She knew how to help the dog trainer be a better male figure for Joy Hunt.

When it was eleven-thirty that morning, with her heart filled with excitement, Ally announced, "Let's go to the rink."

"Okay." Tired Danny answered.

They rested in the living room for ten minutes with chats and drank some cold water.

After they rested, Danny and Ally gathered their skating gear and left the Loop's loft. The figure friends rode down the elevator for the parking garage.

They made it to her car and rode off for the ice arena.

Ally questioned Danny, "What do you know about music?"

Before he answered, his mind thought of his music knowledge. He spoke, "I like music. That's pretty much what I know about it."

She had an idea.

Ally suggested, "Why don't you turn to your favorite radio station?"

Daniel's brown eyes looked at the Horundi's radio player. It was a touch screen to use the radio, GPS system, MP3 player for music deceives, phone conversations from her touch screen phone, and internet service. His left index finger touched on the blue rectangle for the radio and selected his favorite station.

Ally was not surprised that a rap song was playing. Her face cringed and closed her eyes quickly to the singer's lyrics and the song's too fast rhythmic pace.

Typical. She scolded in her head.

She turned off the radio by pressing the 'off' button on the car's touch screen.

"Why'd you do that?" Danny protested.

"I can't handle rap," said Ally strictly.

He remarked, "But you like heavy metal."

"That's different." She snarled. "Heavy metal is pump-style music. Rap is a pop-style music. A genre that can be used in any kind of situation that happens in life if the person wants to show off their reputation."

The figure student sighed, "I guess you're right."

"You have to understand that figure skater's attitudes are not like that. On and off ice," explained Ally, "not many skaters want to skate to rap because it would be hard to dance, spin, jumps, or do freestyle moves with it. They also don't have kind of reputation-"

"I get it." Danny curtly spoke.

"Sorry." She softly apologized.

They arrived at the rink's parking lot.

There were more than thirty parked cars that Saturday afternoon. It was normal to see a bunch of cars in the lot during a weekend day.

Both figure friends left Ally's Horundi and went to the locker rooms with their skating bags. Ally finished first and stood by the men's locker room for Daniel to finish. She wanted to explain their skating plan for the day to him.

The men's locker doors opened.

Danny walked through the doorway and his eyes spotted the Loop by the doors.

He asked, "Big rink?"

Ally shook her head 'no' and told him, "We're a little early for public session. What we are going to do is head over for the small rink."

Daniel and his Figure Instructor traveled from the big lobby for the hallway to the small rink. He did think on what she had planned at the small rink. The narrow hallway to the small rink's lobby was filled with lots of kids and adults standing around and talking.

The Pet trainer looked at the scene before him.

It could not be a birthday party since there were no decorations, party hats, colorful table cloths, balloons, cake, presents, snack foods to munch on, or anything that indicated it was a birthday party.

"Hi, Ally!"

A voice called out behind her and Danny.

Ally turned around and greeted, "Hi, Barbra!"

Barbra was a middle-age woman in a big black comfy coat, blue sweat pants, and worn-out white figure skates on her feet. Her head wore a dark blue baseball cap and her light brown hair was in a ponytail from the cap's hole in the back.

Ally and Barbra hugged each other.

Daniel recognized Barbra from Regionals and Sectionals. He thought, *Ally's coach. Or maybe I should say, her Figure Instructor.*

Figure coach and her student let go of their embrace.

Allison smug, "This is Daniel Gray. My figure student."

"I hope Ally's been treating you right." Barbra kindly replied. She stuck out her right hand and Danny's left hand took her hand for a hand shake.

"Ally's a wonderful coach, Barbra." Danny honestly complimented.

The hand shook stopped and Ally's coach questioned her, "So, are you ready?"

Allison declared, "Yes, we are."

"Wonderful." Barbra beamed. "I will take the adult group and you'll take the kid group."

The Loop's coach walked out of the small lobby and was gliding out on the ice to the other side of the rink.

Danny wondered, "What do you mean by that?"

Some of the kids and adults were out on the ice when Ally answered, "Oh, I'm not going to teach the kids today."

She snickered, "You are."

"Huh?" Speechless Daniel Gray spoke.

Allison suggested, "I am going to test you on how well of an instructor you are in figure skating. You already passed from seeing you in the training booth at the Pet store. I got curious on what you'll be like in ice skating."

Then all the kids were out on the ice skating around one half of the ice while the other was for the adult group.

Danny could not believe he was once a beginner couple months ago and now he was practicing spins, jumps, dance steps, and some freestyle moves. It seemed his first timer days happened a very long time ago when he thought of his first time out on the ice, falling on his ass, and meeting Ally-Loop.

He realized that Ally was out on the ice when that little flashback of his ended and after looking through the see-through glass screen window. She was with the group of kids and waiting for him to come out.

Daniel moved from the lobby and was out on the ice with Ally and the group of beginner kids.

"This is Danny." Ally announced to the kids, standing by the wall. "Today, he's going to be your instructor."

The Pet trainer nervously glided in front of the kids and looked at all fifteen kids with in the group. It was a cute mix of boys and girls dressing warmly and wearing their own figure skates or rental skates.

Ally stood by the side from the group.

"Hi there." He greeted to the little kids.

A little boy with blond hair and light green eyes asked in his high-pitch voice, "Can you do a triple axel like Ally?"

All the kids and Ally giggled.

"Um, I'm not that good." Blushing Daniel replied. "Why?"

A dark skinned girl cutely answered, "Ally-Loop normally does one before our lesson."

"I'll do one." The Loop offered.

She glided around the small rink forward fast and turned around backwards after passing the adult group. Then she did a back right outside edge, stepped on her left blade to go forward, jumped up high from her waltz set-up and did three back spins in the air before landing on her right blade backwards.

Ally smiled proudly and everyone on the small rink clapped and cheered for her amazing triple axel jump. Barbra had tears in her eyes from her student's wonderful axel jump. Even thought that was the kid's tenth time to see Ally do a triple axel, they still thought that was the coolest thing they had ever seen.

"Okay," she panted and stood up straight with her hands on her hips. "Lesson time."

The Figure Instructor stood away from the kid's group invisible circle and watched Daniel Gray be an ice skating teacher for the first time.

Danny knew he had to start out slow to pass Ally's instructional test. His mind created an idea.

"What have you been taught on the ice?" He kindly asked the kids.

A dark haired boy respond, "Skate without falling down."

"How to stop." An Asian girl spoke and skated forward to show Danny a snowplow stop.

"Forward stokes and crossovers." A sunshine blond girl told the group. She stroked away from the wall forward and did her crossovers on a painted circle three times around. The she glided back to the group.

The sunny little girl reminded Danny of Sally.

He wondered, "What about backward crossovers?"

All the kids shook their heads 'no.'

Danny glided around backwards and did his crossovers three times around the same painted circle the sunny girl did. He stopped and questioned the kids, "Would you like to?"

The little figures nodded their heads 'yes.'

Just when he wanted to show the beginners 'side-steps', he turned his head at Ally and she gave him a small smile and a left thumbs up. He had his focus back at his group and taught them how to skate backwards exactly how he first learned to go backwards with Ally.

Some of the little figures did well.

Others struggled and Daniel was there to help them up after a fall and gave them all some simple pointers to do better. He even showed them how the wall could help them move backwards.

He actually learned figure skating from the inside out. Allison thought in her head. *That's amazing. Too bad none of the Hunts are here to watch this.*

She was wrong.

Up on the building's second floor, in an office room, a shadowy figure was watching all the action at the small rink. It could not believe what Daniel Gray was doing. The snooper was there when Ally did her triple axel jump, but nothing from the Loop's special combo jump for Nationals. Just be more patient and maybe something would come up.

A cell phone rang and answered it.

The shadow quickly walked out of the arena's building for a twenty minute ride in a white SUV not to its home.

The group lesson lasted for a half hour and the little figures thanked the Pet trainer for being their teacher. They rushed off the small rink for the lobby. Some hugged their Mommies and Daddies while others headed off for the big rink alone. All their skating stuff were packed up to leave the building or move to the main lobby.

"Hey," Ally spoke, "good job, teach."

He blushed again and told her, "I-I was acting the same way that you would teach me how to skate."

"And you did a wonderful job, young man."

It was Barbra who spoke. She glided pass the figure friends for the coach's lounge room by the big rink.

"Couldn't have said it better myself." Ally smug on her coach's behalf.

They put on their guards and went to the rink's snack bar for a little something to eat before public session started on the big ice.

When they finished their lunch, Allison and Daniel skated and worked on some figure moves. Danny worked more on his spins, especially spin positions, jumps, dance steps, and how to improve his speed to go into spins, jumps, dance steps, and freestyle moves from forwards and backwards.

"So, what is my reward?" Daniel pestered Allison once more in her moving Horundi car at seven o'clock p.m.

She was driving to her special rink for a special Monday night skating session, and was getting a little annoyed of hearing that repeated question since their last skating lesson Saturday afternoon.

"Daniel, it's a surprise." She strongly stated.

She had a feeling he was going to ask her again.

Ally stepped on the break in a deserted street and warned her student, "If you dare to ask me again, you have to walk home and you won't get another lesson for the rest of the week."

The dog trainer closed his mouth and let Ally drive to the abandoned building.

She parked her car and they both got out the of top-up convertible for their skating bags and the brown heavy tarp in the trunk. The Horundi was hidden and the figure friends managed to get through the left side door surreptitiously.

In the cold, quiet basement, Ally and Danny laced up their skates at the bleachers. The Loop set up her phone on the speaker's dock. Daniel glided around the ice smoothly.

He questioned Ally, "Are we the only ones here tonight?"

Music was playing from the speaker.

She answered loudly, "Yup! We're going to be here till eleven, then Richard will be here after a special Christmas dinner with the team to take care of the building and ice!"

Gotta bless that man's heart. Her heart thought.

The two worked on spins and a little on spin jumps.

Another helpful tip Sally Hunt's fiance learned from doing spins was if he did not feel ready, he could do a few more backward crossovers until he felt confident enough for the wind up and spin.

Daniel's mind imagined what that tip meant.

When he would the wind ups, it would either be a good spin for being alert and ready or a bad one because he did not focus on the spin.

He was really improving his figure skills.

A couple hours later, 'The Ace's Wings' song came on and Ally pretended it was Nationals.

She shouted to her figure student, "Your reward is seeing my quad-quad combo jump before anyone else does! Not even my coach had seen me do one!"

Ally skated just like her long program for Sectional, but the ending would be different. She started off with a quad axel and then a quad loop. But her tired right foot made her lose the second landing and she felt a painful crunch in her right ankle.

The Figure Instructor fell down hard on the ice.

Lying on her side, she cried out in pain, "Danny!"

The Pet trainer skated up to her. He asked, "What happened?"

"Fuck!" She cursed. "Oooowwwww! God-damn, muther-fucker! I hurt my ankle!"

"Can you walk?" He wondered.

"No . . ." Ally whimpered and pulling her right leg toward her chest. She tried to move it. "My foot feels numbed and aahhhhh!"

She added, "Hurts like shit!"

Daniel offered, "Do you want me to call out for help?"

"Don't call 9-1-1!" She screamed out in pain.

Then she requested strongly, "Call Richard from my phone."

Chapter Sixteen

Danny Gray was puzzled.

Why would Ally want Richard McCarthy to come over to help her instead of an ambulance full of trained paramedics?

Then he thought, *Because her secret rink might reveal and McCarthy could help out her and the rink. Good enough reason for me.*

The dog trainer skated quickly to Ally's phone from the black speaker on a table in a cube box that was surrounded with see-through screen windows. He paused her music player and pressed the home button to find the phone button on the touch screen.

His ears did hear Ally crying hard and softly moaned shitty words for being so stupid to do the quadruple-quadruple with tired, achy feet.

Daniel did find the little green button for phone. His right index finger pressed on it, went to contact, and scrolled to Number 65's private number.

The Pet trainer gently pressed Richard's name on the screen and the phone began to ring. Danny's ear heard four rings until Rich answered it.

"Hey, Ally . . ."

To Daniel, he knew then McCarthy longed to talk to Allison in a non-skating way. "Richard, it's Daniel."

"Where's Ally?" The hockey Captain demanded.

Danny solemnly replied, "She's hurt at her rink."

McCarthy angrily questioned Ally new figure student, "What the hell happened?"

"She was doing her special combo jump and hurt her right ankle pretty badly from the second jump's landing." The dog trainer hastily explained.

From the top of her lungs, Ally demanded, "McCarthy! Get your fuckin' ass down here and help me!"

She cried out more in pain and tried to comfort her injured foot with little use of her hands.

"I'll be there in twenty minutes!" Richard promised and hung up first.

Daniel pulled Ally's phone away from his ear and his right thumb pressed the home button. Then the side of his left index finger pushed a small rectangular silver button to turn the phone off. He placed the phone back on speaker's dock and glided over to the injured Ally, crying out in pain.

"What did-Richard say?" She struggled to say clearly.

"He said he will be here in twenty minutes." Danny spoke.

Still on her side, Ally whimpered, "I'm sorry this happened."

He offered, "Is there anything I can do?"

The Figure Instructor was getting very cold and wet for being on the ice a little too long. She slowly flipped on her back and looked at Daniel to tell him, "Get me some blankets."

"Where?"

Ally's weak voice replied, "There's some in the office room over there."

She pointed out a small gray cube room off the ice in front of them. Her left hand went in her left pant's pocket to dig out a black and pink key.

Daniel leaned down to get the oddly colored key from Ally's cold fingers. He skated off the ice, put on his guards, and rushed to the gray cube office. He slipped in the p&b key on the door's lock. It was unlocked and Danny walked in the dark room. He found a switch for the lights to turn on.

Inside the small gray office room were a wall to ceiling bluish-gray color cabinet door and a normal size gray file cabinet by the door. Behind the filing cabinet were a small tan computer desk, a black padded chair next to the desk, a really nice silver desktop computer with a dark green all-in-one printer, dark gray office phone, and black desk lamp.

His eyes did see some photos of Allison and her PHL friends. There were hockey sticks placed at a corner against one of the walls, a plastic bucket, and the walls contained ten posters of each PHL player in Ally's figure group. Including Number 65.

Careful Daniel searched and searched for blankets in plain sight, the desk drawer, or the filing cabinet, but could not find anything. The only place he had not looked was in the wall to ceiling cabinet. It was locked and the key Ally gave him did not work. Then he remembered seeing a small gold key in the computer desk's top drawer.

Maybe that's the key for the cabinet. He thought.

He found the small gold key and used it on the cabinet door's gold padlock. The padlock came undone and Danny's fingers slipped the lock out from the door's hook holes.

Sure enough, he found the blankets that Ally wished to have. Big, comfy, and really soft blankets to cuddle in. He carried a few in his arms and raced out of the office cube for the rink.

Daniel's ears heard, "Ally!"

He saw Richard McCarthy dressed in his dark turquoise color hockey jersey, jeans, and N+ turquoise, black, and white running shoes. Captain Number 65 ran for Ally.

"About time fuckin' you got here, McCarthy!" The Loop yelled out.

Danny offered to Rich the blankets, "Here, you'll need these."

The hockey dude took the blankets into his arms.

"Thank you." He gratefully respond.

With three blankets in his arms, Richard stepped out on the ice slowly and toward the injured figure.

Daniel went to the stands and sat on the bleachers. He unlaced the laces on his suede material figure boots, cleaned the blades and bottom part of the boots with his rag, and his eyes watched almost everything that happened between Allison & Richard.

Rich spread out two of the folded blankets on the ice. He helped Ally sit on the dark blue and royal purple blankets and placed a cozy white blanket over her cold, shivered body.

"I'm soorr-soooorrrrriiieeee-" freezing Allison spoke from her chattering teeth, "y-y-yoooouuuu'rreee mmmmiiisssing-"

"Don't worry about that, Ally." McCarthy assured the Loop. "The guys and coach understands my 'other job'."

He softly snickered, "To tell you the truth: they're jealous."

Ally rolled her eyes. She was starting to ignore her wet, cold body from his little tease. Her shivering lips told the puck chaser, "Thhhaaannnxxx fffooorrrr cccooommmmiiinnnng, Caaaappptaiiin."

Richard smiled and blushed a little. "Well, couldn't have been Captain without your help."

"TTTrrruuuueeeeee."

Ally made her mouth stop moving in fast pace and she winced from feeling her hurt, twisted right ankle.

"Come on. Let's get you off the ice." Rich suggested.

She agreed. "'Kay."

At the bleachers, Danny laid on his back and closed his eyes, pretending to nap.

The hockey Captain stood up on his feet first and then helped Ally stand up on her blades from the blankets she sat on. They were standing close in front of each other. Richard slowly leaned over Ally to lightly kiss her left cold cheek.

While he pulled back, Allison firmly whispered, "Richard, we can't, I-"

"Just hear me out," he interrupted her.

Number 65 strictly spoke, "I am not going to hear you say, 'no' about us being together anymore, Allison Rigden."

Ooohhhh . . . this is getting good. Danny thought.

Ally's arms and hands kept her white blanket close to her cold body for warmth.

Rich's hazel eyes looked deeply into Ally's dark brown eyes and confessed, "I Love You, Ally-Loop. I have for four years now and I'm tired of waiting."

She tried to skate away from McCarthy, but he stopped her by holding on to her cold, numbed hands. His hands were warming hers up by rubbing them.

"Give me one damn good reason why we can't work out?" The stick dude demanded.

Ally was feeling uncomfortable to stand on her hurt foot in her figure boots. She pleaded softly, "Can I sit so my ankle can heal?"

"Ohh . . . sure." Sympathized Richard McCarthy.

He kept Ally close to his right side with his arm wrapped around her waist for support. They carefully made their way off the ice.

Allison still had her white blanket around her tired, cold body.

The two old figure friends stepped on the wet foam floor and headed over to the bleachers. Daniel continued to nap on the bleachers' third row.

Ally sat down on the second row and Rich sat in front of her to unlace her figure boots very slowly. Both boots were off her feet. Still shivering, she was starting to feel better with her cold, wet hands rubbing over her comfy blanket.

Richard cleaned the Loop's boot and blades with her light blue rag. The figure boots were stored in her roller suitcase. He had an idea on how he could make Ally feel much better from her incident.

Both of her nylon feet were on his lap and he began to massage her sore feet with his strong, soothing hands. He was gentle with Ally's right twisted ankle.

"You really twisted your ankle badly, Ally-Loop." Richard stated sadly.

Allison was not used to being treated nicely. Except, being around McCarthy was making her heart feel happy. Maybe she could get use to it.

Richard's right hand lifted up her sore foot and his lips kissed the nylon foot.

"Rich," she disappointedly spoke, "it's not a good idea for us to be together."

He solemnly sighed, "It is because I'm a PHL player and you're a silver medalist USIS?"

"No." She nervously caressed her white blanket with her fingers.

"You don't have feelings for me?"

"No . . ." she shook her head.

The hockey Captain's hands kept on rubbing Ally's feet. He softly pleaded, "Then what?"

She felt the need to cry again. Her blanket covered right hand wiped away her tears.

Sad Allison Rigden explained, "I'm-I'm afraid to love someone more than figure skating."

That's all? Daniel Gray wondered thoughtfully with his eyes still closed. *Trading in a sport for someone else's love would not be a bad thing to happen for Ally-Loop.*

"Ah, honey." Richard breathed out. He carefully lifted her feet off his lap to sit on the same row as Ally.

He added, "I will never take away your passion for figure skating. I just can't stand to be alone without you."

Ally's cry questioned him, "You really love me?"

"I do." Their eyes looked at each other.

His arms reached around her blanket form for a loving embrace.

"Ally . . ." his head was on her right shoulder and he whispered, "I was nothing before I first met you. Remember?"

The Figure Instructor pulled back from the embrace. Her sad eyes were locked to her old figure student's beautiful golden brown eyes. She nodded and used her blanket to wipe off more tears.

She sniffed, "College drop-out, looking for a reason to live, and using up your last ten dollars to ice skate and a chance to meet me."

She lightly giggled at the end.

Richard joined in her laugh.

Daniel's heart was laughing too and kept himself quiet. He did not want to ruin the scene or a chance for Ally to be happy with someone.

"Best ten bucks I ever spent on." The hockey Captain confessed.

His left hand stroked her messed up brown hair.

"I think it's time to get you guys home." He insisted.

"All right."

Ally turned her head and yelled out, "Wake up, Daniel!"

His brown eyes were wide open and he slowly sat up from his napping position.

"Sorry . . ." he yawned without faking. "I am getting sleeping."

Danny gathered his and Ally's skating bags and the three figure friends made their way out of the abandoned building with the left side door closed and locked up.

They were heading not for Ally's cute white convertible, but to Richard's hot-looking, shiny black truck with four doors and a small flat bed in the back.

Rich helped Ally into the backseat. Daniel went for the passenger seat. The skating bags were on the backseat's floor. Ally was very tired and she stretched out on all three leather backseats with her white blanket over her body. The hockey Captain sat in the driver's seat to start up his truck.

Danny told Richard where his apartment building was.

Rich drove off from the abandoned building and Ally's tarp hidden Horundi.

During the drive, Daniel decided to act like a fan by asking Captain McCarthy, "Did you really want to play hockey to get close to Ally?"

Rich chuckled, "One of the reasons."

I normally don't tell anybody the real story, but Danny's a good guy and involved with Sally Hunt. Number 65 thought.

"What's the other?" The dog trainer questioned the truck driver.

"I've always been a good athlete, but I didn't know which sport was meant for me. I tried out for almost all different types of sports in high school and college. I never made the team." Richard sighed disappointedly.

"Really?" Shocked Danny was puzzled. "I hear you're one hell of a good hockey player and an athlete poster boy. What changed?"

The hockey dude said, "Not a lot of people, even my teammates and coach, know that part of my life."

Daniel replied, "Because hockey and figure skating don't mix?"

"It seems to be that way." Rich answered and continued his secret past tale, "This is real the beginning of my hockey career: One day while I was in college, there were no classes and I had nothing to do, I decided to go out for a drive. While I was waiting to pass through a car accident, I turned my head to the right and saw an ice rink building. I felt a weird urge to ice skate."

Danny was confused and yet understandable with McCarthy's story.

Rich told out more. "Luckily for me, I was just in time for a public skating session and watched the last five minutes of a drop-in hockey hour. I thought, 'Maybe I could play hockey. Now all I need is someone to teach me how to ice skate.' I slipped on some worn-out brown boots and that was when I first saw Ally. She and her coach talking and laughing in the lobby. The first thing that came to mind was: Damn, did I get lucky today."

The Pet trainer related a little to Richard's first time out on the ice and meeting Ally-Loop.

"After Ally's skating lesson that day, I took the chance by asking the Loop how to skate." The hockey Captain chuckled a little. "She was very stubborn and told me 'no' because she was focused on her rival battle against Sally Hu-"

Richard stopped talking after he remembered Danny was engaged to Ally's competitor.

Daniel was not offended of Rich's ego for the Hunt vs. Rigden ice competition. He said, "It's ok. I kinda knew Sally never had any passion for figure skating."

"That's good." The hockey dude relieved. "She sucks on the ice."

"I'm with you, man." The dog trainer agreed.

While Rich was doing a left turn, he told out, "It took me a while and Ally reluctantly decided to help me ice skate during that public session. We practiced and a few days later, she helped me get a job at the ice arena. I dropped out of college and quit my job not far from campus."

Then he added, "I was shocked when I asked how old she was. 15."

Daniel remembered Allison telling him the first time she & Rich met at the rink five years ago and he wanted her to teach him how to ice skate so he could play hockey.

"How old were you?" The dog trainer wondered.

"Twenty." Richard sighed and kept his eyes at the dark road. "How could a 20 year old fall heavily for a cute high school girl who does figure skating?"

Danny was baffled from that question too.

"Anyway, my heart told my brain: age is a number and she was not going to be 15 forever. I made my move when she reached 18, but she did not show any interest for me. I tried dating other girls. Except, Ally has this sweet, loving aura I cannot receive from another girl." Number 65 sounded like a high school boy who got dumped from his first crush.

There was one other puzzling thing in Danny's mind. "If you play professional hockey in the PHL, why do you like to figure skate?"

Richard replied, "As much as I love to see Ally, I do figure skating more than just for her. Me doing figure would let go of the stress I get from practice, drills, and pro games. I mean, skating forward and backwards fast helps, but sometimes it's nice to challenge myself with new figure skating skills instead of doing the same hockey moves over and over again. Figure skating does help improve my balance and gain better strength in my legs by practicing spin jumps and doing centered spins. I am quick on my blades from doing lots of dance steps."

"Make sense to me." Danny gave in to Captain McCarthy's fun figure time out on the ice.

"Daniel, what should I do about winning Allison's heart?" Rich's eyes looked at the rear view mirror and saw sleeping Ally-Loop in the backseats. "In fact, how did you win over Sally?"

The surprised Pet trainer answered, "Nothing special. I was being myself and treated Sally with love and respect."

"Was that your real reason to figure skate?" The hockey Captain wondered. "To win the Hunt's approval for marrying Sally?"

"That really is my real reason to figure skate. At one time I wanted to give up because Joy is not letting me see or talk to Sally till Nationals. I thought figure skating was a waste of time." The dog trainer confessed.

"What made you come back?" Richard wondered.

"I took a chance on Thanksgiving Day to 'break' Sally out of her home. Sally & I went to a dog park with my dog. When we wanted to leave, there was a guy dressed up in black trying to break in her car." Daniel explained. "I defended myself against the car thief by doing figure moves, but he slashed my forehead with a Swiss Army knife. Sally, my dog, and her car were unharmed."

Rich cursed, "Damn, shit . . ."

Then the Captain stated, "I did wonder about the cut you had on your head. I thought you accidentally misused one of your skate blades or something."

"Nope." Danny firmly said. "Just trying to protect those I love."

"That's good." The stick dude added.

"Look, Rich, I might be losing my girl too." The Pet trainer sounded defeated.

Richard breathed out, "Joy Hunt is the devil's bitch."

"Can't argue with that."

The hockey dude continued the drive and his eyes on the road. "Have to admit, I was jealous when Ally brought you to her rink and seeing you and her together."

Danny laughed out, "You should go to the gym with her. Guys would be howling at her."

"I know." Angry Rich McCarthy responded and gripped the steering wheel tight. "The rest of the PHL guys wanted a piece of Allison until I stepped up and beat all of them in their own hockey game."

"Sweet revenge." Figure Gray pointed out.

The black truck reached Daniel's apartment building.

The dog trainer got his skating bag slowly and carefully from the backseat behind him so he would not wake up Ally's peaceful slumber.

He whispered to Richard, "Thanks for the lift. Hope Ally feels better soon."

"Oh, she will. She's a tough, hard-core skater who turned me into a kick-ass hockey Captain from a guy who once had nothing to live for. And I'll make sure she calls you when she's ready to be back on the ice." Rich softly stated.

Danny exit the truck.

Richard drove off and went back to the abandoned building.

Young Gray went inside the apartment building and his unit. Butch was happily waiting for his loving master to come back home.

The boys got themselves ready for bed.

What happened next to Ally-Loop was a real surprise after she twisted her ankle.

As Richard McCarthy drove back to the abandoned building, Allison Rigden continued to sleep on the comfy black leather seats and snuggled up in the white blanket covering her body.

Number 65 would keep looking at Ally from the rear view mirror. His heart smiled from knowing the Loop was going to be okay.

He arrived at the building and parked his truck next to the tarp hidden Horundi convertible. He got out his truck after remembering the ice needed to be taken care of.

Richard sneaked inside the building, went down the dark stairway, and made it for the rink. He moved into the Zamboni box and started up the snow truck to resurface the ice. He finished it in fifteen minutes.

Captain McCarthy did his closing routine for the rink and left the abandoned building. He safely made it back to his truck. The inside of the shiny black truck was all quiet and blissful for sleeping Ally-Loop. But the sad thing was: he needed to wake her up.

To make Allison wake up from her slumber, Richard turned on his music player on the entertainment touch screen and picked out a pumped up metal song. The volume was turned up.

He snickered from knowing how the figure skater in the backseats was going to react.

The loud noise of an electric guitar startled Ally and she was fully awake. Pounding drums were pumping too much from the speakers. She sat up in the backseats, reached forward for the volume's knob, and her tired left hand turned down the sound of his team's theme song, 'Look & Annihilate.'

"Shit, Rich! That's too loud!" Ally screamed.

The song's sound was lowered enough to be background music.

Richard laughed, "I thought you love 'Annihilate!'"

Ally went for the right back door to escape. Just when she was about to step out from the black truck, she forgot her right ankle was still twisted badly and she fell down on the cement ground face down.

The hockey Captain watched Allison fall out of the truck. He sighed unimpressively, his right hand turn off the music player, and got out of the driver's seat to help the Loop get back on her feet.

Rich stood by the fallen down All-Loop. He leaned down, lifted her off the ground, and carried her in his arms to set her on the truck's passenger seat.

"Oww . . ." she moaned in pain.

Her right foot felt very sore and numbed.

Richard closed the passenger door and the open side door. He walked around his black truck for the driver's door. He sat in his seat and the door was shut.

The inside of the truck's cab was silent for a minute.

McCarthy wondered, "Why did you call me?"

Sniffled Rigden spoke, "Who else could I trust to help me with a twisted ankle?"

"Daniel was there." The hockey Captain suggested.

"The rink needed to be taken care of." The Figure Instructor importantly stated. "Besides, Danny wouldn't be able to cheer me up like you can."

Richard felt special.

He asked the injured figure skater, "What do you want to do for your 'healing time' off the ice?"

"I wish I can skate . . ." she hopefully wished.

She laid back in the comfy black leather seat.

Richard's right hand was raised up to Ally's tired face. His fingers were stroking the figure's tousled brown hair.

"Why did you push yourself so hard tonight?" He requested from the Loop.

Heart broken Ally breathed out, "I want to win so badly and show bitchy Joy Hunt a thing or two when it comes to competitive figure skating."

Number 65 wondered, "With what?"

Allison was not sure if she should tell Richard her combo jump secret. She did tell and almost showed Daniel her quad-quad edge jump for Nationals.

"You can trust me, Ally . . ." Rich softly said.

He leaned forward and his lips kissed her lips.

She did not kiss him back, nor pushed him away. Her mind and heart were confused. She was not sure if she should give in by trusting someone or continue to keep her heart safe.

From the one-sided kiss, Rich asked, "What are you thinking about?"

Allison Rigden shook her head and softly confessed, "Why I always have such a hard time to have a clear mind around you."

Chortled Richard McCarthy replied, "Sometimes I'm that way too. Wonder why we both feel that same way?"

"I don't know, but-"

"Ally, you don't have to be afraid to add a different kind of love in your life." The hockey dude added, "I know you're scared to face the ice alone. You have been since we first met. Please let me in your heart and share each other's love."

His right arm reached over for Allison white blanket form and let her lay on his muscular chest. Her heart opened for Richard and instantly felt different from the inside out.

To his surprise, the Loop started to cry and her tears were making his hockey jersey wet. He did not mind that.

Her weak voice complained, "I am so fuckin' tired of working so hard on my skating career by myself."

"Thank you." Richard relieved.

His arms held her tighter and kissed her forehead.

"For what?" Ally sniffled loudly.

"Trusting me." He simply answered. "And thinking I am not a selfish, arrogant, horny pig."

Tired Allison questioned the hockey Captain, "Did you get that from Danny?"

Richard teased, "I didn't have to."

She slowly moved her arms around her first figure student and snuggled more closely to Rich.

"Good." She grinned, "Because you're not."

"It's a start." He raised his right hand and lifted up Ally's teary face.

He kissed her again. This time, Ally kissed Rich back.

Their lips part together and smiled sweetly at each other.

The hockey Captain had an idea how to specially treat Ally. "You wanna come to one of my games?"

"Like I haven't heard that one before." She giggled.

She calmed down to tell the stick dude, "All right, Captain McCarthy. I'll go and watch you get tackled down by other stick boys."

"Would you care to be my 'coach' for the week?" He teasingly offered.

Her arms dropped from the embrace by thinking what Rich meant from that kind of request. She hesitantly asked him, "What kind of 'coach' did you want me to be?"

His arms let go of Ally's body and explained, "A 'coach' on the ice, and a loving 'partner' in bed."

Ally sat up and cringed at the thought of sleeping with someone. "Rich, I'm a-"

"Hey . . ."

He placed his left index finger over her lips. "I was not expecting us to fuck and do everything in bed all in one night. I just don't want to sleep alone."

"Okay. I can go for that." She agreed.

Ally added, "Where did you want me as your 'coach'?"

Rich suggested, "My place?"

"Sounds good to me." She softly spoke and leaned forward to kiss Rich again. "But what about my Horundi?"

The hockey Captain thought of a plan.

Talking to Ally-Loop like a teammate, he huffed, "I'll drive your Horundi. We'll stay at your place tonight and then my place tomorrow. My truck will be fine in the building overnight with the front door locked."

"Let's go." She handed him her car keys.

Richard hopped out his seat first with her keys in his right hand and his left hand carried the Ally's roller suitcase from the backseat's floor. He went for the tarp hidden convertible.

He pulled the heavy tarp off her car, disarmed the car, opened the trunk, and neatly folded up the dark brown tarp and her skating bag in the car's trunk. Then he went back to his truck and helped Ally off the truck's passenger seat for her car's shoot gun seat. She was comfortable enough to be alone for a few minutes.

Rich headed for the building's sliding door. He unlocked it from a chunky silver padlock and with all his might, he pulled the sliding door to the right side of the building.

The hockey dude panted, "Shit. This thing's getting harder to move from not being used in a couple of years."

He walked to his truck and looked at sleepy Ally-Loop in her car. He sat in the truck's driver seat, turned on the ignition, and slowly drove the truck into the abandoned building.

McCarthy exit the big truck and turned on the alarm.

He left the building to slide the heavy door to the left side of the building. He placed the padlock back on the door's hook holes for the padlock's arms. Door was locked up and his truck was secured for the night.

He turned away from the sliding door and went to Ally's white convertible. He sat in the driver's seat, turned on the car, and slowly drove to the Loop's loft building.

Richard found the building and in front of the building's secure garage door. He noticed a special door opener with her car keys. His right hand raised the key chain alarm and pressed the button at the door. The garage door slowly slide up the ground.

Ally's Horundi rolled into the garage lot.

From the dim lighted garage box, he located her assigned parking spot number after looking closely at a number on her key chain. The car was parked and the garage door was back on the ground.

Richard got out the driver's seat, went to the passenger door, opened the door, unbuckled her seatbelt and leaned in to lift to carry the sleeping figure off her seat and in his strong, comfy arms. He was feeling pretty happy with Ally in his arms.

They rode in the elevator, he walked out of the elevator box and managed to unlock and open her loft's unit door without dropping Ally. He located her bedroom. He gently laid her on her hot pink & black theme bed and placed an extra pillow under her hurt ankle. Then he took off his shoes and jersey shirt before cuddling next to Ally in her bed.

Richard slept comfortably with his Figure Instructor for the first time.

The next morning, Allison Rigden was surprised to be in her bed and see Captain McCarthy in bed with her. Shirtless, if she may added. His arms were warm and comforting to her.

She slowly made her way out from his loving arms and up from her bed. Her legs limped over for her bathroom. She decided to take a long soothing bath in the tub so her body and achy foot could heal from the night before.

Her was being filled with warm water, her hands and fingers slowly took her clothes off. They were tossed on the tile floor. Naked Ally-Loop got in the warm water.

She softly moaned. Her tiresome body was feeling much better in her steamy tub. She gently moved and stretched her right foot. It was still a bit sore and swollen from doing her quad-quad jump and bad landing.

The Loop was glad Daniel was there to help her out.

Richard, however, was the most helpful of all. She would be grateful of the kindness and love he had for her.

The bathroom was covered in warm steam.

Her eyes were closed. Her mind went blank. Her heart was satisfied.

A few minutes later, her lips felt someone else's lips kissing them. She kissed back with a big smile on her face.

The Figure Instructor pulled away from the kiss and opened her eyes. Her brown eyes saw hot-stud Richard McCarthy leaning over Ally and sitting on the tub's rim.

"Hey, Rich . . ." Her voice softly greeted him.

"Hi, Ally . . ."

He got up from the tub's rim and took off his jeans and undershorts off.

Ally blushed brightly to see sexy Number 65 with nothing on him.

"Move forward." He insisted.

Feeling the warm water's gentle waves, Ally sat up in the tub and slide herself forward to give Rich enough room to sit behind her.

The hockey Captain got in the tub with Ally-Loop in between his legs and his well-sculpted arms wrapped her warm body. The two were very relaxed in the steamy tub.

"Mmmmm . . . what are we going to do today?" She whispered.

"Well," Richard snickered in her left ear, "we could go to the rink and let you watch me practice."

They chuckled lightly together and snuggled deeper into their blissful embrace.

His lips touched her soaked hair. "Or have a free day from skating by spending the day in San Francisco."

His lips kissed the nape of her moist neck a few times.

"No skating or talk about the rink?" She slowly woolgathered.

"Pretty much, yea." McCarthy leaned his head forward and his right cheek laid on Allison's right shoulder blade.

Ally turned her head to her right side. Their lips met for a long loving kiss.

When their lips part, the Loop requested, "Could you wash my back?"

"Will you wash mine?"

"Mmmmm-Mmmmm . . ."

Richard bent his legs close to Ally and he pushed himself from the warm tub. Ally was slowly lifted up with Rich's help. The tub's water went down the drain.

The Figure Instructor fixed the shower head for their soothing, shared shower. From the steamy showering area, he body washed her toned, lean figure and shampooed her long soft brunette hair. She lathered his buffed muscular bod and cleaned his short brown hair with her shampoo.

Both lovers dried each other's bodies before they left the loft for an hour long ride to San Francisco.

Chapter Seventeen

Allison Rigden & Richard McCarthy were not the only ones having a special get-togethers off the ice.

Daniel Gray had to wait not one figure, but two figures in the world of competitive figure skating. Sally Hunt, the love of his life. Allison Rigden, the Figure Instructor he needed to prove his love for Sally's parents.

He hoped both girls were all right.

All through the rest of December, he kept himself busy with work, practicing figure moves on his own, giving Butchie-Wutchie lots of walks and love, and reading more of the figure books. Sometimes Ruth and her Samoyed dog, Ceinwen, would come to the store for a little visit. Bob and Smokey also came by for short visits too.

Danny was doing lots of help around the store instead of dog training around the Christmas holidays since customers were too busy to stop for dog training. His boss, Jack Randell, decided to close the training booth and let Daniel do stocking jobs and working the cash registers.

He was missing Sally more than ever. He did pray and asked fate if there he could have a chance to see or talk to his fiancee again. Skating was helping him, but he did left out with Ally not there to help him on the ice.

The dog trainer was worried about Ally-Loop too.

It had been more than a week since her ankle accident on her skating rink and she did not call him saying she was better and wanted to skate again.

Danny had an idea on what was going on with Ally.

She & Rich are now together and 'tending' to her extremely long recuperation from the ice. Oh, well, at least she's happy and having a life off the ice.

When his Friday shift ended, it was the last one for the year. Danny went to his apartment unit. Butch was waiting for him behind the front door.

They had dinner, their evening walk lasted for an hour and a half, and turned in early for bed.

The next morning was New Year's Eve and Daniel woke up from his twin-size bed. He did have a good night sleep. Even Butch, Danny's beloved beagle, slept well on his comfy pillow.

Breakfast happened in the kitchen and Danny had a long hot shower. He remembered what he needed to do later that night. It would be Butch's special bath time.

Just when he stepped out of the shower with a green towel wrapped around his waist, his cell phone was ringing. His legs quickly moved to his bedroom.

What he saw on his cell's caller ID was a gift from the Heavens. It was Sally.

"Morning, babe." He said cheerfully.

"Hi, Danny . . ." She weakly answered.

"Something wrong?" Concerned Danny asked his fiancee.

Scared Sally hastily spoke, "Mommy's been acting very strange since my long program from Sectionals and she's been wearing me out on the ice. Can you come here now? I'll be waiting by the sidewalk so you can pick me up."

"Okay, babe." Danny assured her. "Butch and I will break you out and we'll talk about anything you want."

"Sounds wonderful to me."

"I Love You . . ."

"I miss and Love You dearly, Danny . . ."

Their phone conversation ended there.

Daniel changed into jeans and a nice brown sweater with his tennis shoes, and gathered his keys and wallet in his jeans pockets.

Butch was happy on the couch in the living room until his owner spoke, "Butch, beach time."

Daniel and his sweet beagle exit his unit for his car in the building's garage.

The car did make it to Sally's neighborhood in good time and sure enough, he saw his blond fiancee walking out of the mansion house with an upset look on her face.

She was dressed in tight jeans, tennis shoes, and cream color sweater with her gray purse on her right arm. Her blond hair was back in a ponytail. It looked to Danny that Sally had lost at least ten pounds since the last time he saw her.

His eyes met hers and she ran toward his car.

Sally opened the door, sat in the passenger seat, and softly told Daniel in a stern voice, "Just drive."

He stepped on the gas pedal to drive as quickly as he could from the neighborhood.

All he did was drove and drove to a beach. The first five minutes during the drive, Sally kept her mouth shut and then started to bawl like there was no tomorrow.

Danny knew her mom had something to do to make her all upset. He had one very important question to ask his love.

He puck up the courage and spoke, "Are you going to live with me after we're married?"

His ear heard Sally gulp hard. Immediately, his heart fell out of his chest and down to his feet.

"Um, Mommy and I have talked about it and-" Sally paused and then spilled out, "she does not want us to live together during my competing years."

A bomb was set off inside Daniel's heart. His dream was right all along. He had to do something to make Joy stop controlling her beautiful daughter.

"But, Sally," He started to protest.

Sally strongly stated, "Danny, I need to be strong if I want to go to the Olympics. I'm so sorry to break the news to you. At least I told you before we actually got married."

"That's not fair." The dog trainer argued. "Do you really want to skate in the Winter Olympics?"

Sally thought for a minute and hesitantly answered, "Yes. I want to conquer up to the top."

Danny knew she was lying. It did sound like Joy made Sally rehearse on what to tell others about her splendid skating career and goals in competitive figure skating.

She added, "I have to. It is my purpose."

No, Sally-babe. That's what Ally-Loop want, not you. Don't give in to your Mommy's desire. His heart pleaded secretly.

"Are you sure?" He wondered.

"I'm very sure." Sally acted excitedly. "We'll have a good life after I win the gold."

Danny was disappointed in Sally.

He was doing well himself with his Pet trainer earnings. Maybe he would get a raise from Jack if he knew his dog trainer was improving in his job with the dogs and owners.

"If it makes you happy, go for it." He pretended to cheered for Sally.

"I'm so glad you understand my job." Sally happily sighed. "I Love You . . ."

"Love you too, Sally." He spoke with no satisfaction.

He made it to the beach's parking lot. Then he requested, "When can we see each other again?"

Right when he parked the car, Sally stormed out of the vehicle and rushed toward the coastline.

The car was turned off. Danny followed after his fiancee. He called out, "Sally?"

He and Butch just ran and ran for Sally.

The blonde figure champ kept on running on the sandy ground. Her legs were feeling very tired from practicing on the ice with her horrid mother. Her voice whimpered and kept cried out loud. She tripped on the sand face down. She lifted herself up and sat on the sandy ground.

Butch ran around the beach and kept close by Daniel & Sally.

The Pet trainer joined his blonde girl by sitting next to her. His left hand caressed her hair. Her sunshine face was messed up with tear strains and sand dust.

"Hey, come here." He whispered.

His left hand took her into his arms and held her tight.

Her wet tears touched his sweater.

When she was finally ready to tell her love what was wrong, Sally softly complained, "I'm just so tired from being out on the ice yesterday."

Danny wondered, "How long did you skate?"

"Fourteen hours total." She tiredly respond.

"Ahh, Sally. What made your mother do that?" He moaned.

As scared as she was, Sally whimpered, "Because of Allison's surprise announcement from Sectionals. Mommy wanted me to be better than her. I don't think I can from the Loop's last long program."

"I thought Ally's long program was flawless and more entraining than your routine." Danny admitted.

"That I don't blame you for liking hers more than mine." Sally's tearful voice snickered.

The Pet trainer did have a concerned question for his love. "Do you have your cell with you?"

Sally said, "No. I didn't bring it."

Daniel happily breathed out, "Good."

"M-Mommy took my cell. It took me forever to find it. I put my cell back where she hid it from me." The blond girl replied sadly.

The Pet trainer groaned, "It sucks that we can't talk or see each other till Nationals."

"I am sorry about Mommy's behavior." Heart broken Sally sounded very alone after being 'locked up' from Joy.

"Well, doing my skating lessons does keep me busy." The Pet trainer assured his fiancee.

"Daniel," she did put in, "in the car, I lied."

He guessed, "That you don't want to go to the Winter Olympics and get the gold?"

"You're a good guesser." She relieved.

"I'm not the only one who thinks that way." He confessed. "Ally-Loop knew it too."

"She knows figure skating better than my mother & father put together." Sally said.

Danny wondered, "Then why do you have to ice skate if you don't want to?"

Sally sniffled, "To please Mommy. It is all I know."

That's not true, Sally. He thought in his head. *You know about flowers and love to create beautiful floral groupings.*

"Then we'll need to find something you can be good at after your skating years." He cheerfully replied.

"That'll be years from now." Her broken voice spoke hopelessly.

Danny told her, "I will always be here for you, babe."

His right hand lifted up her head from her chin and their lips kissed. Smoothly and lovingly.

From their parted kiss, Sally sighed, "I do Love You, Daniel . . ."

"For better or worse, I will Love and Cherish you, Sally . . ."

Their love was sealed with a sweet kiss.

For their New Years' Eve night, Danny and Butch brought Sally to his apartment home after having a very big late lunch at a Pizza parlor. The same one where Danny and his old homies went to for his 17th birthday. Sally was looking and sounding a lot better after having something to eat and laughing with him.

Danny asked Sally, "Would you like to help me give Butch a bath?"

"Sounds like fun!" The blonde figure champ giggled.

"Butch!" His owner called out. "Bath time!"

The three of them went for the bathroom. Daniel got out Butch's doggie shampoo and towels. Sally ran the bath tub's water. It was getting warm and soothing for Butchie-Wutchie.

Sally lifted up Butch and placed the sweet beagle in the warm water. She was on her knees and her hands and fingers gently moist Butch's short tri-color fur coat with the water.

The loving beagle was enjoying his bath.

Danny knelt next to Sally. He squirted some of the liquid shampoo out of the bottle and began to rub it on Butch. The wet, soaked dog did not make a fuss or stubborn on trying to get clean from his bath.

"Does Butch like baths?" Sally wondered.

"He sure does." Danny smug. "The bastard really likes the water for some reason. Don't you?"

Soapy Butch looked at his owner and smiled big at him & Sally Hunt.

Daniel rinsed his hands in the water, stood up for the shower head, brought it down close to Butch, and the head sprayed the water on the beagle and the shampoo was being washed away.

Sally rinsed her hands in the water too. She wanted to dry off Butchie-Wutchie in his special light blue, wet-doggie towel. She dried her hand and sat on the toilet seat.

The Pet trainer lifted his wet dog out of the tub and on Sally's lap. The blonde girl rubbed and rubbed Butch's soggy fur coat.

"Mmmmm . . . don't you smell good?" Sally sweetly teased Butch. Her feminine hands kept on moving up and down all over the cute beagle with his towel.

Daniel cleaned the tub from the soap and water by using the shower head, putted away the doggie shampoo, and needed to do a few more things for Butch.

He requested, "Keep him on your lap."

Sally nodded her head and her arms lightly hugged her fiance's loving dog.

The dog trainer went to a drawer and got out seven things. Two blue bottles, one for ear and another for eye cleaner, a black high tech toe nail trimmer, a small wash cloth, a little green tooth brush with a two-sided bristle facing each other, a small tooth paste bottle, and a dog brush.

"I like to have a clean Butchie-Wutchie for the New Year." Danny spoke.

"Ah." Sally replied.

He did add, "It's kinda nice not having to do this alone."

"Then, I am glad I called you, Danny." She happily respond.

Butch was sure pampered from his owners. His teeth were sparkly clean, toe nails were trimmed perfectly, eyes and ears were cleaned, and next up was the brushing.

The clean beagle went to the bedroom with Danny & Sally behind him, hand-in-hand. The little tri-bastard jumped up on the twin-size bed. The humans joined with him too.

All of them laid on the bed and Danny & his fiancee each had a turn by brushing Butch's soft, clean fur coat.

When they were done, the time was ten o'clock.

Sally knew she had to get home for her Mommy & Daddy. But she did not want to be out on the ice for more skating time, or face Joy again.

"Daniel," she started.

His brown eyes had her full attention.

"I'm going to tell Mommy & Daddy I'm quitting figure skating."

That made Daniel Gray's day. He lifted himself up to hug Sally tightly.

Then she started to cry.

Concerned Danny asked, "What's wrong?"

They pulled away from their hug. Both of them sat in front of each other. Eyes looking at one another with love and devotion.

"How am I going to tell Mommy?" Sally softly cried.

Daniel knew tonight was not the time to worry about answering Sally Hunt's quitting news. He answered, "Let's talk about it tomorrow after a good night's sleep."

She whimpered, "I guess you're going to have to take me home."

That was it.

The dog trainer firmly respond, "No."

"What?" Sally curiously wondered.

"I am not going to take you back to the devil's bitch." Danny spoke up like a man in love. "You are going to stay here with me tonight, discuss about the problem, and then face your parents. You need a peaceful night from your horrid mother."

The blond champ could not believe what she just heard.

She happily expressed, "Oh, Danny . . ."

Sally collapsed into her love's arms.

"Thank you . . ." She cried out.

She was letting out happy tears.

"You're welcome."

Both their arms held each other tightly for support.

The clean beagle was off the bed and went to his pillow. He walked around on it a few times, gently laid his small furry body down, curled himself up, and closed his eyes for a good night sleep.

Danny & Sally let go of their loving embrace and decided to go to bed themselves. Then he turned his attention to his cell on his nightstand.

On the cell's cover, he had eight missed calls. He flipped the cover and most of them came from Joy Hunt's cell. One was from Paul.

The Pet trainer listened to all of Joy's messages. She did sound very angry and pissed off for taking Sally out of the house and not bringing her home. She even threatened to call the cops.

His ears did listen to Paul's message.

"Hi, Danny. I know you did not intend to get Sally out of the house by force. But please, bring her home. She has special needs she cannot get from you. And um, Joy's serious about having the police be called over to your unit and take Sally back home. Do the right thing, son."

The voice message ended. Daniel flipped his cell shut.

"Paul's right." He mumbled to himself, "I have to bring Sally home."

He got his keys and called, "Sal-"

His eyes saw blissful Sally sleeping on his bed without him knowing it. "Awe, they can wait one night."

Daniel got up from his bed and changed his clothes in his closet. He wore sweat pants and a gray t-shirt for bed.

The dog trainer walked back to his unoccupied bed. He slowly took Sally's shoes, socks, and her cream color sweater. She was wearing a light pink tang top under her sweater.

There was one thing that he wondered from Paul Hunt's message. *What special needs that Sally has at the mansion that she could not get here?*

I think it's because Joy's afraid of her daughter to be with me in bed. Stupid, bitch. I would never betray Sally that way.

He flipped the bed's covers for him and Sally to sleep in all night long. His arms were wrapped around her body. He kissed her soft lips and whispered, "Happy New Year, Sally . . ."

And he kissed her lips again.

His heart was very, very satisfied to have his fiancee in bed with him.

It was the morning of New Year's Day.

Daniel Gray opened his dark brown eyes.

His arms felt sleeping Sally Hunt lying comfortably in bed with him. His lips smiled. He tightened his grip on the love of his life. And his nose smelt her fruity flavor blond locks.

So, this is what it will be like to be in bed with Sally. He thought happily. *Being married to her will be a joyous one for me. And her to me. Ah, hell . . . for us.*

Danny was feeling Sally shifting herself in bed. Her body moved up and her tilted down head raised up. Her eyes opened. She smiled big at the person who protected her all through the night.

Their lips met for a long, loving kiss.

They part when Butch whimpered at the lovers in bed for his morning walk. The beagle sat on the floor next to Danny's bed.

Daniel's tired voice spoke, "All right, fuzzy-butt. Sally & I will take you out for you walk."

He got up from bed and went for the bathroom.

Sally stretched her lean figure form as she sat up in twin size bed. She contently waited for her fiance to help her up from bed.

While the Pet trainer walked out of the bathroom, he noticed Sally was still in bed. He asked, "Aren't you going to get up?"

She requested, "Could you help me?"

That's kinda strange from Sally. His mind curiously wondered.

"Sure. I'll help." He obliged.

Butch yelped out three times loudly by the unit's front door.

Daniel walked back to his bedroom.

Standing by his bed, he leaned down, kissed Sally's lips, and scoped her in his arms. Her arms wrapped around Danny's neck.

He questioned her, "Where to?"

"Bathroom first." She chagrin.

"No problem." He blushed a little.

They traveled to the bathroom.

Just when Danny was lowering Sally to the floor, she immediately pleased, "Don't lower me!"

"Huh?" He asked.

Sally gulped, "Carry me to the toilet seat?"

Butch was barking and barking some more.

What is up with Sally? He insightfully thought.

Daniel reluctantly moved toward the toilet and lowered Sally down to let her sit on the seat. He turned around, closed the bathroom's door, and went forth the barking beagle.

"Butch . . ." the dog trainer's commanding voice spoke out loud.

The noisy dog sat on the hardwood floor and closed his muzzle mouth.

"Good boy," Danny sighed.

He rushed to his bedroom's closet. He changed out of his night clothes and into jeans and a dark gray t-shirt as fast as he could.

After leaving his bedroom, he heard, "Danny?"

He dashed to the bathroom's door, opened it, and the blonde figure champ was still sitting on the toilet seat with her jeans all zipped up. Her feet were not touching the floor.

"Pick me up?" She sweetly asked from her bright white smile.

Butch started to bark again and began to scratch the wooden front door with his trimmed claws.

Danny yelled, "Butch!"

This time, the once good beagle did not listen to his owner's command. He was misbehaving because he was not getting his morning walk.

"Danny?" Sally's honey voice complained.

She stuck out her arms in front of her like a little kid wanting to get her way.

The Pet trainer firmly replied, "No, Sally. You can walk yourself."

He excused himself from the bathroom's doorway for his bedroom. He found his clicker on the night stand to get Butch under control. He rushed out of the bedroom for the yelping and jumping beagle. Behind Butch, Danny clicked the clicker three times. But the beagle continued on his negative barking behavior.

A knock was heard on the door. Then they heard a voice coming from behind the unit's front door.

"Daniel Gray?"

He answered nervously, "Yes?"

"Santa Rosa police officials." The voice called out again. "Open the door."

Daniel thought, *Damn, Joy Hunt was serious.*

He unlocked the door and four uniformed officers was standing in the hallway.

"What's the problem?" He calmly questioned them.

The speaking officer requested, "Is Sally Hunt in your unit?"

"She is." The dog trainer candid.

"We were told from her mother that she needs to come back home." The police man firmly explained.

Daniel decided to do a drastic measure. His legs stood strong at the doorway with his arms crossed over his chest. He was not going to let his fiancee go back to that violent woman.

"And what if I don't let her go?"

The officer pulled out his silver shiny handcuffs and his professional voice stated, "Then you'll be charged of kidnapping a minor."

"What the fuck?" Danny yelled out. "Sally is 20 years old and I'm her fiance!"

"Well, her mother said-"

"A pack of shitty ass lies!" The Pet trainer argued.

Butch was growling and barking loudly.

Daniel stepped away from the door and went for Sally's gray purse in the living room on the coffee table. He opened the bag, then all the guys heard a big THUMP! coming from the bathroom.

"Danny!" Sally screeched out loud.

The four officers ran to the bathroom while Danny continued to look for Sally's license.

What the policemen saw in the bathroom was Sally Hunt lying faced down on the tile floor with her lower legs and feet sticking up in the air.

One of the officers questioned Sally, "Ma'am, can you get up?"

"No . . ." Sally softly whimpered.

The officer leaned down and asked, "Did Daniel Gray hurt you?"

Her head raised up and sniffed, "No, officer. Danny has not hurt me or kidnapped me."

"Do you need some help?" The police man offered.

The blonde nodded her head 'Yes'.

The officer grabbed her hands to lift Sally off the floor. But as she stood on her feet, she screamed out in pain and fell on the floor on her butt.

"I can't stand!"

One of the other officer's shoulders was tapped by Daniel. He showed the police man Sally's drivers license.

"See?" He pointed out Sally's birthdate. "She's 20."

The officer spoke, "Looks like we need to have a chat with Joy Hunt."

"Daniel?" Sally pleaded, "Please take me home?"

He made his way into his bathroom and carried her to his bedroom.

The officer who knocked on the unit's door asked the blond girl, "Sally, would you like an escort to your home?"

She was placed on the messy twin-size bed.

"Give us a moment?" She answered.

All four officers left the apartment unit and went back to their squad cars.

When they were finally alone Danny's bedroom, he sat on the bed and asked his fiancee, "Sally, what's going on with you?"

"I didn't want you to know this." The figure champ whispered. She found her sweater and slipped it back on.

Butch was still barking and yelping.

"Butch!" Danny shouted. "Go use your grass!"

The beagle unhappily scampered to his fake grass in the bathroom to do his doggie business.

Before Sally could speak, Daniel's cell phone rang.

His left hand picked up his cell in his left hand to answer it. "Hello?"

"Hi, Danny!"

His voice breathed out, "Ally . . ."

Sally was glad it was Allison Rigden who called Danny instead of her parents.

"How are you?" Ally asked.

Danny gulped, "I think Sally & I are in trouble."

An idea came to his mind. "I need your help."

The Loop offered, "All right. Rich & I will come to your apartment building."

"I'll met you in a little while." Daniel agreed.

The call ended.

Sally relieved, "Thank goodness for Ally-Loop."

"I Love You . . ." Danny replied.

"I Love You too . . ."

They kissed each other's soft sweet lips.

He reached down to the floor to hand Sally her socks and shoes. She only put on her socks.

The Pet trainer told Sally his idea. "You are going to wait here and Ally will help us get you to my car."

"Sounds good." She said.

He left his bedroom with his wallet, keys, and cell in his jeans pockets. He got Butch's short leash and attached it to his dog's brown leather collar. The two boys left the unit to go downstairs for the building's front doors.

Daniel did not see Ally's Horundi being pulled up. It was Richard's black shiny truck that came.

Out from the passenger side was Allison dressed in a long black sleeved sweater, jeans, and her black snow boots. Her hair was fixed up in a braid with a black hair tie at the bottom.

Rich exit his truck too. He was dressed in his team's black jacket, dark green t-shirt, jeans, and running shoes.

Danny invited the two new lovers in the building.

Inside, Ally-Loop wondered, "Hey, Danny. What seems to be the matter?"

"Sally needs help by going home." He uncomfortably told the two softly.

"Did you & Sally get it on in bed?" Rich snickered.

Allison snapped, "Rich, be nice."

The hockey Captain closed his mouth.

All three figures and Butch went up the stairs for Danny's apartment unit. He explained, "Ally, take my spares and why don't you & Rich go to the dog park with Butch while Sally & I deal with her parents?"

"Okay, Danny." She agreed to the plan.

Richard replied, "Sounds good to me."

They reached the apartment unit's floor.

"Hope Sally's okay." Allison prayed.

Danny nodded his head and kept on holding Butch's short leash. At last they made it for the unit's front door.

All three figures walked inside, Danny handed Ally Butch's short leash, his car and spare keys. Then they made it for the bedroom. Sally was still sitting straight up in bed.

The Pet trainer asked her, "Ready to go?"

"Yes, I am." Her voice sounded tired. She had her purse and shoes on her lap.

"Let's go then." He announced.

The blond figure champ was surprised to see Richard McCarthy there too.

"Hey, McCarthy." She greeted.

Danny picked up Sally and carried her in his arms.

"Nice to see you again, Hunt." Rich spoke back with his right arm slid across Ally's shoulders.

Allison's left hand kept her grip on Butch's short black leash and Danny's keys.

"How do you two know each other?" Daniel suspiciously questioned his fiancee.

As they left the bedroom and went through the hallway to the front door, Sally whispered into the Pet trainer's right ear, "A few years back, McCarthy tried to get me and other figures to tell him what Ally's taste in men were."

"Really?" Danny surprisingly asked.

He was out of his unit home.

Sally added, "I am glad they're together."

"Me too, babe."

Allison, Richard, and Butch stood behind to close and lock up the unit's door. She handed the hockey Captain the beagle's short leash so she could help Danny to his car.

The boys went down the stairs for the black truck.

Ally walked behind the engaged couple down another stairway to the parking garage.

Daniel softly asked Sally, "Why can't you walk out of bed?"

"Not here." She voice was raised a little too high from a whisper.

"Okay."

Ally huffed sarcastically to herself at Sally's feet problem. She opened doors and unlocked Danny's car doors.

They arrived at the Pet trainer's car.

Shotgun door's was opened and Daniel lowered Sally down on the seat. Her lap still had her purse and shoes.

Ally handed back his car key.

The Pet trainer walked around his car.

Allison left the garage to go back to Richard's truck. The three went to the dog park.

Danny's car drove out of the garage lot with two police squad cars driving behind them. They traveled to the Hunt's mansion.

Sally's heart was sad and scared to go back home. She wished Danny would drive her somewhere else. Some place special and private just for the two of them.

The drive went faster than she thought it would be. Danny parked his car. The ruby red SUV was in the Hunt's driveway along with Sally's convertible up front.

Silence was heard inside the car.

Daniel's right hand took Sally's left hand and his thumb played with her three stoned engagement ring.

He whispered lovingly, "I Love You . . ."

Her bluish-gray eyes were full of worrying tears.

"I'm afraid to be here." Her terrified voice respond.

"Sally, you have to tell your Mom you want to stop figure skating. Be strong." He encouraged her. "Just try, please? I'll be with you."

You can't be with me when Mommy hurts me like there's no tomorrow. Or comfort me after facing her. Sally thought.

She nodded her head and relieved, "All right."

Their faces leaned forward for a minute long kiss.

As their kiss ended, Daniel got out of the car first and then made it for the passenger side to carry Sally out of the car. They traveled together toward the Hunt's mansion home.

The four police officers stepped out of their squad cars and walked behind the loving couple.

Sally Hunt dug inside her purse to hand Daniel Gray the mansion's front door keys. He held the keys in his left hand and slipped the front door key in the key hole. He twisted it. The door unlocked. His right foot gently kicked the door to open up the doorway.

Danny headed for the living room while the police men stayed by the front door. He lowered Sally on one of the couches and she sweetly thanked him. Her shoes and purse were dropped on the rug. His left hand placed the keys on the coffee table.

"Get the hell out of my house, Daniel Gray!"

He turned around and saw Joy Hunt walking quickly for the living room.

One of the officers got a hold of Joy's left arm with his right hand. He sternly told Joy, "Take it easy, Ma'am."

"Arrest him for kidnapping my baby!" She demanded.

"Lady, Danny showed us that you're daughter is not a minor and he is her fiance." He stated.

Joy barked, "My daughter is a famous gold medalist figure skater who should be home with her Mommy & Daddy!"

"Joy!" Outrageous Paul Hunt shouted from the stairway. "You lied to the police? About Sally?"

"Paul, I did what I thought was right." She softly told her husband.

He made it to the bottom floor when his wife said, "Sally needs to be here with us. It's not safe for-"

"Is she going to be charged of reporting false information?" Paul questioned the officers.

All four police officers formed a little circle and mumbled amongst each other.

Danny sat close by Sally on the rugged floor. He held her hands and caressed them smoothly and gently.

"Maybe I need to leave." He whispered.

"Danny, don't go . . ." she pleaded.

She softly cried again and sat up to hug Danny tightly. His arms held her tight.

Paul slipped past the police gathering group for the living room. He softly said to Danny, "Daniel, thank you for bring Sally home, but please leave. I'll make sure Joy will let you see Sally a week before Nationals."

Daniel let go of his fiancee and answered, "Okay. I Love You, girl . . ."

"Danny, I Adore You . . ."

They shared a short kiss and Paul lead Danny through the back door.

The Pet trainer ran past the backyard, the drive way, and through the front lawn as fast as he could. He did feel like he was running on the track again. He reached his car before Joy could yell at him from the front door.

He immediately drove to the dog park.

It was ten after eleven a.m. when Daniel Gray arrived at the dog park and parked next to Richard's shiny black truck. His dark brown eyes immediately spotted Butchie-Wutchie playing happily with other dogs, big or small.

He also noticed the Loop & Number 65 walking around the dog park, hand-in-hand, and acting like a normal couple instead of big famous winter athletes.

The Pet trainer felt good to have Rigden & McCarthy together.

Daniel did cry a little in his car. His broken heart was hurting him like crazy. Lots of thoughts came to his mind.

Why does Sally need help to get up from bed? Why can't she walk on her own? Are the Hunts really buying their daughter's skating talents so Joy can have the gold?

He needed some way to get proof from inside the Hunt's house without getting caught. Maybe Sally could help. He would have to wait for that plan to be put into action. Just until thing between Joy & Paul, the police, and Sally cooled down from that misunderstanding.

Danny exit his car and walked through the dog park's gate. He reached Ally & Rich.

"Hey," he greeted them.

Looking surprised, both figure lovers spoke back in unison, "Hey."

Ally let go of Rich's hand grip and asked Danny, "How are things?"

The dog trainer lost focus of Ally and paid attention to Butch and small brown furry dog playing tug-a-war with an old dirty play rope.

Danny answered to Ally, "Bad."

He sighed and sat on a wooden bench to calm down his hurt heart. Rich & Ally sat on the bench with their sad friend.

"Joy is worse than ever." Daniel started out. "Yelling at me, the cops, and her husband. Paul told me he will find a way for me & Sally to be together the week before Nationals."

"Better than nothing." Ally assured him.

The Pet trainer questioned the two figures, "How's Butch?"

Richard proudly spoke, "He's surprisingly a well-behaved dog."

"Good."

Ally wondered, "So, now what?"

Danny explained, "I guess I keep on skating and work hard off ice when Nationals come."

The Loop offered, "You guys want to go to my rink and skate this afternoon?"

Both male figures liked the idea. They did need it after going through that hare-raising experience earlier that morning.

"How long have you guys been here?" Daniel asked.

Ally reached in her jeans' pocket for her phone. She replied, "Like forty minutes or so. Give or take."

"I think Butchie-Wutchie could use some food in his tummy and a long nap while we're out on the ice." The dog trainer suggested.

Allison handed back Butch's black short leash to Danny. She told him, "We'll meet you at your apartment building in an hour."

He nodded his head for the plan.

Richard & Allison lifted themselves up from the bench and left the dog park. They rode off in McCarthy's shiny black truck.

"Butchie-Wutchie!" The Pet trainer commanded at his loving beagle.

Butch was acting like a behaved dog by listening to his owner and ran toward him. He sat on the sandy ground. Danny squatted down to attach Butch to his short leash.

The two boys left the dog park together and had a nice car ride back to their unit home.

Butch and Danny got settled in their home. Ate some lunch, rested a little in the living room, and the human went for the bedroom to change out of his street clothes and into black sweat pants and a blue t-shirt. His left hand grabbed his skating bag and stuffed his cell and keys in his right pants pocket.

He was ready for some skating time with Ally & Rich. The dog trainer headed out the bedroom for the front door.

"See ya later, Butch." Danny told his pooped out beagle on the living room's sofa. He smiled contently at his sweet pooch.

Daniel left his apartment unit and went down the stairway for the building's front doors. He waited five minutes for Richard's black truck to arrive.

The Pet trainer exit the building and got in McCarthy's truck from the right back door. He sat in the back seat behind Ally's seat, buckled himself, and placed his skating bag next to him. He felt a little deja vu after his eyes did not see the figure couple's skating bags in the truck.

Richard drove off for the abandoned building.

Danny asked, "Where are your skating bags?"

"On the flat bed." Ally stated.

"Ohh . . ." the dog trainer relieved.

The Loop had an idea why he asked that question. She thought the Hunts would tell him why Joy never brought Sally skating things during competition time years ago. Guess she was wrong.

A new curious question came to Danny's mind. "Are you two officially seeing each other?"

Ally let out a good laugh.

Richard answered for her, "If you mean 'us dating and sleeping in bed together,' then yes, we are."

"Well, what's the story?" Danny pleaded for the couple's juicy details.

"Rich & I do love each other and want to wait for marriage in a few years." Allison explained. "We both have skating goals to conquer before settling."

The dog trainer spoke, "That's understandable."

Good ol' McCarthy smug, "And it's really special to have another 'coach' and a more loyal 'fan' at the stands."

Ally replied. "Richard had been pestering me to take me to a game of his for the past three years. Ever since my sprained ankle incident, he took me to his team's practices and games."

"So that's why you did not contact me sooner." Danny gasped. "I kinda knew something was up between you two, but I wasn't sure if I was right."

Rich chortled, "You guess right, Figure Gray."

The truck arrived at the abandoned building. All three figures got their skating bags from the truck and headed down the stairs for the building's cold basement.

Inside the basement and in their skates, Ally and Danny worked on some figure moves while Rich practiced his edges and special hockey maneuvers in his hockey skates. He also wore his black color team jersey.

An hour later, the figures helped Richard get a hockey net set up on the ice. McCarthy got out his hockey sticks and fixed up new tape layers on the wooden stick's handle and blades.

Ally carried a white plastic bucket and poured out lots of black pucks on the ice from the bucket.

"Have fun, McCarthy!" She announced and tossed the bucket off the ice and it banging loudly on the wet foamed floor.

To keep himself busy, Danny was enjoying himself doing scratch spins. Doing figure spins was feeling more natural and comfortable to him.

Richard's hockey sticks were ready for his stick drills with hockey pucks. He got up from the bleachers and stepped out on the ice. He sneaked up behind Ally and locked her in for a hug with his hockey sticks in front of her.

Number 65 whispered, "You're the best, babe."

She turned around to give him a kiss on the lips.

McCarthy let Rigden go from his prisoned hockey stick hug and skated toward the net.

Daniel was thinking how to make his spins be more centered from doing wind ups and figure spin positions. He saw Richard skating at the other end of the rink.

The dog trainer did feel a little spoiled to watch a PHL player practice his hockey drills at a private ice rink for free. He wondered what the rink would be like with Ally's other PHL friends playing against McCarthy in a hockey game.

Chapter Eighteen

After three hours of being out on Ally-Loop's private skating rink, Daniel Gray was really getting some helpful tips. For his spins, he made sure he started out slow, let his arms and free leg move toward his body at the same time, and his feet felt comfortable for the wind up, spinning, and check.

Not only his spins were getting better. His jumps, dance steps, and freestyle moves improved a lot too.

Ally did turn on her music player from her phone in the black speaker dock. Both her male figures had become hard-core skaters after listening to music. It was good of them to be wonderful ice skaters with musical tunes swirling around the ice rink.

Richard's slap shots dazzled Ally.

Daniel's jumps and spins were flowing to the music's notes perfectly from Ally-Loop's musical instructions.

The three figures were getting tired and needed some time off from the rink.

"When's the next lesson?" Danny questioned Ally.

They were getting off the ice and went for the bleachers. Richard stayed on the ice to put away the hockey net in its special box and picked up all the pucks and into the plastic bucket.

"Um, Friday night at the big rink?" She wondered.

"Sure." Daniel answered.

The figure friends sat on the bleachers.

They cleaned their blades, stored away their boots, and put on their street shoes back on their sore, tired feet.

"Captain McCarthy offered to take me to his out of town games tomorrow and Wednesday night." She explained.

"I'm cool with that." Danny agreed.

Richard rushed off the rink while he carried the bucket off the ice. He sat next to Ally, placed the bucket by his feet, unlaced his hockey skates, wiped the blades clean, slipped on his running shoes, and turned to the Loop for a quick kiss.

The hockey Captain walked from the stands to the gray office and put away the bucket full of pucks in the office room. He went out of the office for Zamboni truck's gate box behind the gray office room.

Danny told Ally, "I need some time alone this week."

"Because of what happened between you and Joy?" Allison concernedly asked.

He sighed, "No. I have a feeling my next dog training evaluation scores are going to be read soon. I want to be the best for Jack and not lose my job position."

"I know you're going to pass with flying colors, Daniel Gray. You sure changed a lot since the first time I met you on the ice." Ally commented her figure student.

"What about Richard?" He wondered.

Ally saw McCarthy driving around the Zamboni and making the ice be smooth again for the next time they skate.

She admitted, "Number 65 and the other PHLs were difficult for me to teach. You were an easy student because you didn't like me or wanted to have sex with me."

"Ah." Danny replied. "What made you decide it's ok to be close to McCarthy?"

"That goes back when he & I first met."

And Ally-Loop started out her attitude change in figure skating.

Five years ago . . .

Fifteen year old Allison Rigden and her coach, Barbra, were heading for the big rink after finishing some ballet training in the ballet room.

Ally was dressed in a silk black skating dress, light pink tights, and white athletic shoes. Her left hand carried her ballet shoes while her right hand held her polished white figure skates from the guarded blades. Her brunette hair was pulled back in a bun.

Barbra wore jeans, a dirty white sweater, and tennis shoes. Her light brown hair was in a ponytail.

Both girls were laughing and chattered about the ballet session and what to work on the ice.

It seemed like a normal Thursday afternoon for Ally-Loop, but when the girls entered in the arena's main lobby, the Loop's brown eyes noticed a really cute guy with brown hair and hazel eyes looking at her and then back down at the floor.

The guy looked at least a few years older than Ally. He wore jeans and a dark blue sweater with red lettering on it. He was sitting on a bench and lacing up crappy brown rental skates on his feet.

Scolded Ally went in the ladies' locker room.

Five minutes later, her skates fitted comfortably and she was ready for her lesson with Barbra for the next half hour.

The ice was freshly cut.

A few people came out for public session.

Ally was standing by the main gate door. She opened it and waited for the Zamboni driver to scrap the extra snow, water, and ice into a huge drain. She oddly looked for the cute, hazel eyed guy around the lobby. She could not find him. Her shoulders shrugged and kept her focus on her lesson time with Barbra.

The teenage Loop leaned down to take off one of guards from her blade. She did place her right blade on the smooth patch of ice.

The Zamboni gate door closed.

Ally took off her other guard and began to glide around the ice like a lithe figure skater. She skated forward once around and did a right inside mohawk to skate backwards. She did cross edge change around the ice three times.

When she finished doing her cross edge warm ups, Ally spotted Barbra at the center. She glided for the center. Show-stopped in front of Barbra and the figure student and instructor got to work. Figure dance steps, turns, adding height and speed for jumps, and be more graceful in figure spin positions were Ally's topic lessons.

"Looking good, Ally." Her coach complimented. "See you tomorrow afternoon."

Barbra glided off the ice.

Allison was practicing some bracket turns at the center when her eyes saw the cute guy in the dark blue sweater with red lettering and wearing the horrifying brown rental skates on his slanted feet. He was standing at the center rink.

"Hi." He said to her.

She felt a little uncomfortable of the hazel eye guy being there in the first place. She nervously respond, "Hi."

The guy slowly requested, "I know this-um, silly for me to ask you this, but could you show me how to ice skate?"

Ally was delighted to hear that kind of request. Except, she needed to work on her figure routines instead of taking the time to show someone how to skate.

"Forgive me for saying this, but I'm going to have to say, 'no.'" She decided to skate away from the guy and see if he would stop bugging her.

From doing a right inside three turn, Allison skated around the rink backwards.

The guy tried to follow the Loop, but he misused one of his toe-picks and fell hard on the ice. He was having a hard time trying to get back on his blades.

Ally skated and skated backwards while she watched the hazel eyed guy struggling to stand up after his fall. She did sigh heavily and felt sorry for him. Her skates changed her edge from going counter clockwise backwards to clockwise forward. She headed for the first timer.

Standing next to his laid down body, she offered, "Need a hand?"

The guy asked, "How do you fuckin' work these things?"

"Novices with weak ankles should not be wearing brown boots." Ally stated.

She leaned down with her arms stuck out in front of her. The guy's cold, wet hands grabbed hers and he was back on his rental blades.

The pretty hazel eyed guy questioned her, "What did you call me?"

"A novice." She replied. "Someone who's new to something or someone and you're obviously a novice to me."

"Thought that was a shitty word you figures use to criticize people's skating skills." He breathed out and rubbing his cold hands together.

Innocent Ally spoke, "I don't have the heart to insult people easily."

She turned around and glided backwards for the center.

The guy moved slowly toward a wall. He watched the pretty brunette skate her figure moves. From spins, jumps, freestyle moves, dance steps, and skating forward and backwards fast.

Ally's eyes looked at the cute guy too. She wondered why the guy wanted to come to an ice rink if he was not going to skate. Then she glanced at some hockey players come out of the locker room with huge hockey bags on their backs, wooden hockey sticks in hand, and leaving the rink.

A few minutes later, three more players came out of the room and got on the ice for some more skating.

She sighed unimpressively at those stick boys.

One of them had a huge crush on Ally. He was also twice her age.

His name was Mike and a show-off in hockey skates because he could do figure tricks. He could manage to do centered spins and nail doubles in spin jumps.

He casually glided up to Ally.

"Hey, Allison." Flirtatious Mike stuck out his tongue and wiggled it like a snake.

"Mike." She spoke indifferently.

The brown hair and hazel eyed guy felt jealous of the hockey dude talking to cute brunette. His eyes looked at another first timer's feet. She was wearing blue rental skates and skated much better than he was.

The hazel eyed novice understood what the brown hair figure meant about him in brown rental skates. *Maybe the blue ones will make me glide on ice than these shitty brown skates.*

He got off the ice to get some blue rentals.

Back on the center of the ice, the Loop was bugged by the stupid hockey dudes.

"So, you going to be busy tonight?" Mike pestered.

Ally told him, "Look, dude, I'm not interested in dating anyone. Especially you, you horny pig."

"Is that a fact?"

"It's the damn truth, pervert." Ally hissed.

Mike thought of a plan to get back at the Loop. The blackish hair and dark brown eyed hockey dude skated toward his teammates. They were talking amongst each other.

Resurfacing time came.

Ally wanted to skate off the ice, but one of Mike's teammates grabbed her right arm and Mike snickered, "Let's go to the locker room and I'll show you what you're going to be missing out on."

The other teammate got Ally's left hand and both dudes were pulling her off the ice. She struggled her hardest to get loose, but she could not break free from their tight, tough gripped hands.

Standing in the big rink's lobby with blue rental skates on his feet, the hazel eyed guy did walk much better in the blue skates than the brown boots. He saw the brunette figure was being forced off the ice and into the locker room by the hockey players. He knew what to do to help her.

Mike opened a gate door and the hockey locker's room. Lights were turned on. Ally was pushed inside the cold room.

One of Mike's teammates, Robert, teased, "Have fun with her, Big Mike!"

With a big grin, Mike closed and locked the door.

Allison leaned down to unlace her skates. She threw both of them at him. They missed him after he ducked.

"Now, Ally, don't be like that." He unhappily said.

He leaned down to unlace his hockey skates.

The Loop tried to escape from the locker's door when Mike grabbed her arms and carried her on the black matted table. He pinned her on the table with his hands.

"Come on, babe," he struggled to say, "Just-one time."

Mike's ears were hearing his teammates arguing with some other son of a bitch. He did not care about his friends' problem. He got Ally-Loop in his grasp.

He quickly climbed on top of her.

Ally's body was wiggling to break loose. Her hands were trying to push Mike away from her. She was unable to get up from Mike's strong bod.

He kept pressing himself on top of her. His hands quickly pushed down her skating dress and sports bra off her body.

Half-naked Ally tried to knee Mike's groin, but she screamed out in pain for her hurting right knee.

"Ally," the hockey pervert laughed, "I'm still wearing my cup."

His rough lips pressed against her soft lips and his cold left hand was rubbing in between her wiggling thighs. His hand went in deeper and got inside her tights.

"Let go of me, muther-fucker!" Ally demanded.

"I will." He lowered down her pink tights to her knees.

Then Mike promised her, "After I get my pussy treat."

Her hands grabbed his face and pushed it away from hers. She tried to use her hand to push him off of her from his chest.

The hockey perv's body towered over hers by squishing her harder on the matted table.

"I am not going to repeat this, Ally-Loop." Angry Mike warned her. "If you don't do what I say, I'll tell everyone that you're just a figure skank wanting to fuck all the hockey players with your innocent charms and girly-girl voice."

Ally fell under Mike's sex spell. She was so relaxed and lightheaded she could not have a clear head or think about escaping from the hockey pervert.

Mike's right hand took her left hand down to his hard rock cock and balls.

"You like that, don't you?" His lips kissed her lips. "Mmmmm . . . you're hot and wet, baby."

He took his right fingers out of her tight pussy hole and showed her his wet sticky fingers. His fingers went to his mouth to lick her cum.

"Awwww . . . Ally, Ally, Ally. My cock needs you . . ."

His wet hand took her hand off his cock and balls and he lifted himself up.

The locker door opened. Mike was pushed off the table and his body was slammed against the cement wall before he went inside of the relaxed teenager's tight hole.

Scared Allison pulled herself up on the table and saw the hazel eyed guy standing by the matted table. Naked and with a shocked look on her face, she started to cry and brought her knees to her chest to hide her shame. The left side of her face was stinging badly and her right knee continued to bother her.

Some of the staff members rushed in the room and saw nude Ally-Loop in the locker room bawling.

"What the hell is going on here?" A male staff sternly questioned Mike.

"Um, Ally and I were-" he chortled "trying to fuck in here."

The well-hung hockey player stood up, took off his cup's straps, and pulled up his underwear and jeans on his waistline.

The guy with the hazel eyes handed tearful and terrified Ally her black skating dress and sports bra. He helped her off the table. She was shivering and felt petrified of what she went through with Mike.

"Does that look like she wanted to have sex with you?" The staff demanded from the hockey perv.

Mike's brown eyes had sexual urges for Ally-Loop. "She's still delicious for me to fuck."

"Let's go." The male staff's hands grabbed Mike's arms and hauled him out of the hockey locker room and was brought into the lobby area.

In the locker room, shaky Ally slowly pulled up her panties, tights, black sports bra, and her black skating dress. She was shocked and speechless.

Her scared mind kept thinking, *I was almost raped! Raped! In my own rink! And I thought this was a safe place for me. Guess not . . .*

20 year old Ally-Loop paused her story to take a breather. She stood up from the bleachers and walked around the hallway.

Daniel could not believe that the Loop went through something like that. It also made sense why she had to be strong, defensive, and never opened up her soft side easily. He did feel good from thinking that Joy Hunt was probably not told of Ally's almost rape experience. If she knew, Joy would call the Loop a 'whore figure tramp.'

After a ten minute breather, Ally moved back to the stands and sat next to Danny.

"You ok?" He wondered.

"I'm good." Her voice were full of fear.

What he wondered next was, "How did you get the strength to go back to the ice rink after going through something as horrifying as that?"

Allison's answer was not spoken at first. Her loving eyes watched Richard coming toward the stands from the Zamboni box.

Daniel scrutinized Ally's facial expression at McCarthy. Then the dog trainer understood why Ally had special feelings for the hockey Captain long before he was Number 65.

The cute guy with brown hair and hazel eyes took off his dark blue sweater and slipped it over Ally's cold, numb body. Good thing he wore a comfy black t-shirt under his sweater.

Petrified Allison could not move.

The guy softly asked her, "Do you want some help?"

Her stunned head moved up and down slowly without looking at him.

His sore hands lifted the cute figure skater off the wet foamed floor and carried her in his arms. He heard her whisper, "My skates?"

A female staff member picked up Ally's skates and followed the guy and Ally for the lobby area. When the three were in the lobby, Mike and his bruised up teammates were being handcuffed and taken out of the building by the police.

The brown haired guy placed Allison on a bench and the lady staff put the Loop's skates next to her. The guy sat next to Allison on the bench.

"Is there anything that you want, Ally?" The lady employee kindly offered.

Ally opened her mouth.

What came out were, "Hhhh-hooottt-cccoooo-cccccc-" gulp "hoootttt cccooocccooaaa? And-um, ice pack?"

"I'll be right back." The lady spoke quickly and left for the snack bar.

Allison's hands were rubbing a strange sweater over her body. She touched her left cheek. It burned and stung badly from her touch. She stretched out her achy right leg. Her heavy sad heart made her cry again.

The hazel eye novice sitting next to Ally held her tight in his arms. He hoped the 'horny pig' would get the kind of punishment he deserved. *Taking advantage of a young sweet girl like Ally in a hockey locker room? What the hell was wrong with 'Big Mike?'*

Ally's broken voice gratefully said, "Thank you."

The guy pulled back and asked her, "For what?"

"Protecting me." She sniffled.

He blushed and breathed out, "You're welcome."

Their eyes looked longingly at each other.

The lady employee returned with Ally's cup of hot cocoa and a small plastic zipped up bag full of cold snow in it.

"Thank you, Jessica." The Loop replied and holding the small paper cup. She breathed in the hot brown liquid.

"No problem." The nice strawberry blond woman stated. "If there's anything else you want, just ask."

Ally nodded her head and Jessica went for the front desk.

The Loop slowly took a sip of the warm hot cocoa beverage. Her throat and tummy did feel a little happier. She did press the ice pack on her hurt cheek.

The guy with the brown hair and hazel eyes was rubbing his bright pink colored knuckles with his fingers.

He wondered, "Are you going to be okay if I left you alone for a few minutes?"

"Yea, I'll be fine." Allison whimpered and drank some more of her hot cocoa.

Her brave rescuer got up from the bench to head for the men's room.

The ice pack was making the Loop's cheek feel better. She pulled it away to let the coldness settle in.

Ally's brown eyes spotted the guy's walking feet.

Her mind thought, *He's wearing blue rental skates instead of the shitty brown kind. Not many novices could figure out that problem.*

She waited on the bench and two police officers stood in front of Ally. They both sat down to write down her statement between her, Big Mike and his teammates. Her left hand would ice her hurt cheek a few more times during the story telling.

When the confrontation ended, the cops left Ally alone and the hazel eye guy came back.

"Hi."

She looked up and said, "Hi."

Her head turned to her left. She set aside her hot cocoa cup and the cold plastic bag on her right side. Both her hands picked up her skates to slip them back on her feet. She carefully laced them up.

As she finished, Ally stood up and asked the guy, "Did you want to learn how to ice skate?"

The guy was shocked.

"Shouldn't you take it easy for the rest of the day?" He concernedly wondered.

Strong, determined Ally-Loop turned her head to look at the freshly cut ice. Her voice announced, "No. I love figure skating so much, nothing can keep me away from the ice."

"Wow . . ."

The guy was surprised at the pretty brunette haired figure skater.

"So, do you want to or not?" She offered again.

"Yes, I really want to." The hazel eyed guy firmly respond.

The two skaters stepped out of the lobby and skated around the smooth, glassy ice.

Ally glided and asked the struggled first timer, "What's your name?"

"Richard." He spoke. "Richard McCarthy."

He was having a hard time to stand up straight while he moved in the blue rental boots.

She curiously questioned Richard, "What made you want to skate?"

He replied, "Looking for my purpose in life. I am a good athlete and I want to see if I'm meant to play hockey."

Ally giggled, "I see."

Her blades did a left outside three turn to skate backwards.

"Why do you think you have what it takes to be a stick boy?" She asked the novice.

"I beat up the horny pig's teammates while you were locked up in the hockey room." Richard solemnly admitted. "I wanted to teach those dicks a lesson."

Allison did remember seeing Mike's friends bruised up and tired. She was very shocked that Richard was the one who gave Big Mike's buds the bruises.

"You beaten up two PHL lackeys just I could I can be safe?" She breathlessly asked.

Richard was caught off guard. "Those were PHL players?"

"Yup." Ally confessed, "Robert Jones and Alex Banks."

Rich could not believe what he heard. *Maybe I do have what it takes to play hockey.*

The Loop questioned her rescuer, "How did you get so fast? Those guys wouldn't let you survive after a fight on the ice."

"I just felt so pissed off, my inner tiger came to life and followed their lead." The novice growled.

"If you want to be a hockey player, you need to practice the basics and then some hockey plays." Ally suggested. "After that, I guess you'll be on your own."

"When do we start?" Richard asked.

Her hands pushed the novice down on the ice.

Standing next to his body, Allison stated, "We've already begun."

The flashback ended with Danny, Ally & Rich laughing together at the stands.

Daniel explained, "You told me that same thing."

"Yup." Cheerful Ally spoke.

"That story never gets old, Ally-Loop." McCarthy said happily.

The figure lover's heads turned for a long kiss.

Their lips part and Daniel wondered, "What happened after that?"

Rich told the Pet trainer, "Ally and I made a flexible schedule to do on and off ice training. She did ask the rink's manager to get me a job at the rink. The manager gave me a staff position only because I saved Ally's life and saw that I have the heart to be a hockey player. At the rink, I was taught how to take care of both ice rinks, offered maintenance training for the Zamboni truck, sharping and repairing skates, and Ally & I learned a lot about hockey from reading books and watching hockey players practice."

"Cool." Danny replied.

"After a few months of mastering the basics, the rink's owner bought me hockey and figure skates. I was pretty happy to get both boots." Happy Richard sighed.

A new curious question came into the dog trainer's mind. He bravely asked, "Okay, have you told anyone how you really got to be part of a PHL team?"

Richard & Allison chuckled a little and McCarthy expressed out, "A few."

His left arm went behind Ally's waist. He smug, "But only one figure skater saw the truth."

Allison smiled big and respond, "I was with Richard McCarthy when his future PHL coach was doing some draft pickings for his team four years ago."

"I walked in the arena just like any other ordinary workday and what took me by surprise was a crowd of big tough guys surrounding the big ice rink wanting a shot at the pros." Rich started out.

"I noticed Richard looking at the wanna-bees from the small rink's hallway. I went up to him and-"

She stopped and thought of a better idea how to tell Daniel the real story.

Ally's left hand took Rich's left hand off her waist line and giggled, "Let's show Danny how the story went."

The hockey Captain got up from the bench to stand in front of Figure Gray.

Allison got up and walked down the hallway from the rink. A minute later, she started to walk toward Richard.

"Hey, Rich."

"Hey, Ally." He breathed out, pretending to look at the thong of guys. "What's going on here?"

Ally whispered, "The PHL Tiger Shark's head coach is looking for some new hockey players."

"Damn . . ."

A flashback came alive.

"It's an open draft pick. You should try-out." Sixteen year old Allison happily encouraged her first figure student.

Twenty-one year old Richard sighed sadly, "I don't think I'm that good, Ally-Loop. Besides, I don't have any hockey equipment."

The lady staff member, Jessica, saw Richard & Allison looking at the hockey wanna-bees from the store's window doors. She went to the back for something.

Ally walked through the big crowd. Richard followed behind her. They saw guys in proper hockey gear, skating with hockey sticks, and chasing after pucks for drill times.

Coach Hartman, a man in his late forties with grayish brown hair and dressed in his white shirt and navy blue sweat pants coach uniform. He was standing on the ice and yelling at the guys: 'keep up the pace', 'eyes on the puck', 'look out for other players', and 'breath when you skate'.

Jessica spotted Ally & Rich by the big screen windows.

She tapped on Ally's shoulder and softly told her, "He'll need these."

The lady staff winked her left eye at the Loop.

Richard turned around and noticed a big surprise in Jessica's hands.

"McCarthy, you should try-out and show Hartman what Ally taught you on and off ice." The strawberry blond lady encouraged and handed him a bran new blue and black hockey bag.

Ally & Rich stepped away from the window to sit on a bench and look inside the bag. What was in the hockey bag were a new black helmet, body pads and warmers, two strong wooden hockey sticks, two rolls of black tape, dark blue and black color hockey gloves, protective cup, mouth guard, three pucks, and a really cool flamed designed jersey shirt. It was all the essentials he needed to play hockey.

The hazel eyed rink worker announced, "All right! I'll do it!"

Richard went for the men's locker room and put on his new hockey equipment.

Twenty minutes later, he came out looking like a real hockey player. His left gloved hand held his helmet to his side and his right gloved hand carried one of his hockey sticks.

Some of the other guys looked at Richard. They were surprised and feeling jealous to see him at the rink. They all wondered who the late comer was.

Ally was feeling proud of herself to make Richard McCarthy into PHL's next greatest hockey player.

She & he made it for the line and waited his turn.

Just before Richard got on the ice, he whispered, "Thank you, Ally-Loop."

He leaned down to kiss her lips for the first time.

Ally did not kiss back and left him for the stands.

"Richard McCarthy." One of Hartman's assistant coaches called out. "You're up!"

He stepped on the ice, put on his helmet, and skated around the rink like a hockey dude instead a figure male. He glided fast and strong. He worked his wooden stick with five different pucks at a time. He missed the other players chance to knock him down or slam him against the glass screen windows. But he got them back by tackling them down instead. His hazel eyes looked around 360 degrees at all the players and the pucks. He also listened to the coaches' instructions too.

Ally-Loop cheered for her figure student.

Twenty minutes later, Coach Hartman was impressed with Rookie Richard's hockey skills. "McCarthy! Hustle with the Tiger Sharks!"

Richard hustled against the other PHL players, shoot the pucks, and his body slammed at some of the Tiger Sharks. He was having the time of his life being a puck chaser. He smiled and kept on bustling during drills.

For a half hour, Rich played with some of Hartman's boys for a practice game. He sure got the PHL player's attention when he was on the ice with a puck and hockey stick.

The open try-out ended.

Coach Hartman and his assistant coaches were on the ice with fifty other hopeful hockey players kneeling on the ice with their hockey sticks. Hartman's boys were standing behind him. Standing proudly in their turquoise jerseys and their sticks by their right side.

The coach yelled out, "Rookies, today was a good try-out! You all had a wonderful opportunity to show me what you can do on the ice and some played against my Tiger Sharks! Unfortunately, most of you will not be one of my boys and play pro-hockey! I made my decision and will only call out those who are invited to be part of my team's training camp!"

Tired and exhausted Richard slightly turned his head at Ally-Loop, who was at the stands' bleachers. She gave him a big smile and a thumbs up.

The coach was calling off the name of the guys who made his team. Only three were chosen.

Breathing in deeply, rookie McCarthy looked strongly at Hartman.

The first guy was called out. He stood up and skated to stand with the other Tiger Sharks. The second guy was called out too and glided to his new teammates.

Coach Hartman called out the third guy's name . . .

"And finally, Richard McCarthy!"

Allison stood up and cheered from the top of her lunges and clapped her hands.

Richard got up from his kneel, skated to Hartman for a handshake, and stood by his new teammates.

"That's it, gentlemen!" The Head Coach called out. "Thank you for coming!"

The wanna-bees complained about not making it to the team's training camp and left the rink with disappointing hearts and angry facial expressions.

Hartman walked in front of all the players and exclaimed to his boys, "Men! Veterans and rookies, you showed me you are relentless, determined, swift, agile, bright and fearless! Those are the qualities a Tiger Shark should have when you're going up against other PHL teams! We've got a lot of work to do! Do fifty sprints between the blue center lines!"

The coach blew his silver whistle.

Richard and the rest of the Tiger Sharks sprinted back and forth in the center part of the rink. He was much faster than the team's current Captain.

Allison was very happy for her first figure student. She silently left the big rink to go the small rink and had her figure lesson with her coach, Barbra.

During the Loop's walk, she unhappily thought, *He got his wish to play professional hockey. He does not need me anymore.*

The story tale ended.

Speechless Daniel stated, "It's amazing how fate works out for those in need."

"True." Allison sighed.

She looked at her phone from her left sweat pant's pocket. "We need to get going, guys."

"All right, babe." Richard grabbed his hockey bag.

Ally got her roller suitcase.

Danny carried his skating bag in his right hand.

The three figure friends left the chilly basement for Richard's shiny black truck.

Inside the moving truck, the Pet trainer asked, "What happened between you two after McCarthy became a PHL player?"

"At first, we went our separate ways." Allison started out. "I was busy with school and competing against Sally. Richard traveled, worked hard with the team through training camp, games, sport promotions, received lots of offers from other coaches, he dated other girls just to get me jealous, and being the newest PHL Captain for the Tiger Sharks."

"When Ally became an adult, I did ask her out, but she turned me down repeatedly because she did not want to date anyone. Especially after what happened to her from Big Mike." Rich explained. "So, I left it up to fate by being friends with her and see if she could open herself by loving me. It start out when she wanted to have her private rink. She called me to check out the abandoned building with her. Then the build of the ice rink, running it day and night, working with the Zamboni truck, the guys and I practicing at the rink with Ally, and alway remembering why I wanted to play hockey."

He put in, "I am glad I did wait."

Allison's left hand took his right hand and caressed it. "Sorry it took so long, McCarthy."

His right hand turned around so he could hold her left hand better.

"At least you really had a friend all along, Ally." Daniel softly stated.

"I had to keep it a secret, Danny." She strongly spoke. "Can't tell the Hunts about this."

Daniel Gray promised, "I won't tell them anything."

The Pet trainer was let out the truck by his apartment building. He got his skating bag and took care of his beloved Butchie-Wutchie for the rest of the day.

A new week began for Daniel Gray.

His heart was chemically mixed with happiness and fear at the same time. He was glad he could come into the Pet store and be an overall Pet trainer for the dog's owners. The other side was hearing the results of his second dog training evaluation scores.

Danny thought back when Ally told him that he was going to pass it with flying colors. Maybe, just maybe, she was right about what the Pet store's manager would tell him on his evaluation day. That did make the Pet trainer a little better.

He continued not contact or receive any calls or emails from Sally Hunt. Each day was a battle for him to go through without knowing how his fiancee was doing and if she was thinking about him. He really missed and dearly loved her.

The dog trainer hoped Joy would get in trouble with the cops after lying to them about Sally. But Joy Hunt probably talked her way out from getting in big trouble by lying to police officials.

Sometimes Danny's mind continued to wonder, *If Joy was really 'buying' Sally's skating talent, how is she pulling it off?*

He did remember certain clues:

Sally's always going first for skating events
Her costumes were about the same
Her hairstyle did not change for the past six years
Her skating bag was not with her for skating events
Sally not getting up from bed in the morning
And what were her 'special skates'

He needed answers from Ally for their Friday night skating session. She must know something from the Hunts some time ago if she figured Sally was cheating in competitive figure skating. Danny had to be true to his word for Allison with the ugly side of his loving fiancee.

Chapter Nineteen

It was the first Thursday morning of January.

Daniel and Butch had breakfast, their morning walk, and a little chill time in their unit home. Then it was time for the human to go to work.

The Pet trainer put on his work clothes, gathered his cell, wallet, his synthetic coat, and his keys. Professionally, he was ready for work. He was no longer afraid of talking to the owners about what kind of trainings their dog needed.

Personally, he felt sad and lonely without talking or seeing Sally Hunt. Even if she and her parents were cheating, he just wanted to be with his love. He wished he could call her up, but her controlling mother forbid her to see or talk to Danny when she should be practicing for Nationals. Or in Ally's case, cheating.

He left his bedroom and headed for the unit's front door. His head turned to look at the living room. Butch was on the sofa, having a little puppy nap.

The Pet trainer whispered, "Sleep well, Butchie-Wutchie."

Danny exit the apartment. He closed and locked the door. He made it down to the parking garage, got in his car, and drove to the Pet store.

Twenty minutes later, the dog trainer stepped out of his parked car for the Pet store's back entrance. The door was unlocked and opened from the employee's work key. Danny stepped inside the building to go to the employee room.

He past by the owner's office room and was about to go in the staff room when a voice called out in the hallway.

"Daniel Gray . . ."

Brown eyed Danny turned his head to his right.

His boss, Jack Randell, was the one who said his name. Jack's head was sticking out from his office room with a stern look on his face.

The nervous Pet trainer walked over to Jack's office door. His hands were getting sweaty and his heart was beating very fast.

"I've been waiting for you." The boss replied.

Jack, who was dressed in his manager uniform, invited Daniel into his office cube.

Deja Vu hit the young man's heart.

The boss sat in his leather chair behind his computer desk. On the desk was a cream color folder file. The dog trainer looked at the folder's tab.

'Daniel Gray'

He gulped hard and was even more nervous than before. It was the reading of his second employee dog training evaluation.

"Have a seat, son." Jack offered.

Danny sat on right padded chair in front of his boss' dark brown computer desk. He breathed in deeply to calm his fast-pacing heart.

The Pet store manager noticed the young man being scared to be in the office again to hear his new evaluation scores.

Jack kindly asked Daniel, "Well, how are you doing?"

Instead of pretending to put on a smile, Danny honestly answered, "Struggling, Sir."

The older man questioned, "Oh, how so?"

"I'm not allowed to see or talk to my fiancee for two weeks." The Pet trainer stated sadly.

"Why?" Jack wondered.

Daniel explained, "Joy 'locked up' Sally so she can beat Allison Rigden at Nationals."

His boss did feel sad for Daniel's lonely heart for his fiancee, but understood Sally Hunt's mother to be extra protective of her daughter for a very big figure skating competition.

"I can comprehend on how you feel, Daniel. Except, if Sally wants to win the gold in figure skating, you should accept her heart's desire in the sport." Jack expressed like a fair judge with his hands folded on his computer desk.

Daniel sighed, "Jack, Sally does not want to ice skate or compete."

"How would you know?" The boss asked his employee. "Did you ask her?"

"Yes, I did." The angry Pet trainer spoke.

He added, "Sally & I talked after breaking her out of her house New Year's Eve and had a very long talk about her competitive years and plans after we got married. Her mom told Sally we can't live together until her skating career was over."

"Why would Joy want to pressure her daughter into doing ice skating if she doesn't want to?" Stunned Jack wondered.

"Paul, Sally's father, explained to me about Joy's skating past. When she was young, she was a champ and then the world of competitive figure skating changed clubs during her last two skating years. The new style did not make her a star and she quit." Daniel replied. "She still has the heart to win an Olympic gold medal. Now, she's forcing Sally win the gold for her."

The Pet trainer began to cry.

He lowered his head to his lap and tears were coming out of his eyes.

Jack thought of something else to ignore Danny's cry.

A minute past and Daniel looked terribly sad from his red eyes, hot tears staining his cheeks, and quivering lips.

"I think I'm going to lose the love of my life, Jack."

The manager stood up from his leather chair to leave his office room. He wanted Danny to be left alone and let him cry till there were no more tears.

Five minutes later, Jack opened the door to ask Danny, "You okay, Daniel?"

The young man sniffled, "A little."

"Come take a walk with me." The Pet store owner requested from his dog trainer.

Broken hearted Danny Gray got up from the padded chair he sat in and left the office room with Jack Randell.

They went into the employee room so Daniel could put his things in a locker box. His things were stored up and the two men left the room for the store's main entrance.

They walked out of the store.

Daniel Gray was a little confused why Jack wanted to bring him out here. Maybe the boss wanted his young Pet trainer to think outside the box from he had in the past and think about the future possibilities he want with his girl.

His heart was hurt after he thought what he might be losing. He really was not losing Sally for good, but he longed to see his love again. Like what Ally told him a few days ago, *Better than nothing.*

Danny should accept the changes he was going through in life with Sally Hunt if he waned to have a life with her, even as her competitive figure skating self.

He spoke, "Jack."

The Pet store's owner turned to look at his dog trainer. He waited to see what the youngster wanted to tell him.

Daniel Gray got the courage to tell his boss, "I'm sorry about my behavior in there."

He did want to act-no, not act. He had to be a man about his mistake in the office room.

"Do you know why I brought you out here?" Jack Randell questioned Danny.

"That I should be patient with Sally and her parents and not get to dwelled in it when I'm at work?" The dog trainer professionally explained.

Jack was shocked.

He laughed. "No, not that at all. Good try though."

Danny was puzzled from his boss's laughter and what he told him. "What should my answer be?"

"Um, I was not thinking about what's going on between you & Sally's relationship status." The store owner said. "I thought I give you a surprise."

A surprise?

It was supposed to the reading of his new Pet training evaluation results. Not a day of surprises for Daniel Gray.

"What are you talking about, Jack?" He asked.

"There's your surprise."

Danny saw a big colorful truck coming into the parking lot. He noticed that the truck was a dog equipment delivery truck.

The truck parked and two mustached guys wearing light blue overalls and baseball caps came out of the truck. One of the guys was much taller than the other one.

The tall guy asked in a deep voice, "Where do you want to set up, Mr. Randell?"

"The center would be wonderful!" He exclaimed.

Both truck boys went to the back to unload something from the back. They brought out a big multi-colorful fabric material gate that stretched out forty feet wide. They also unloaded fifteen huge buckets of dog treats and play toys.

Danny could not believe what was happening.

"Dog training outside?" He questioned his boss.

Happy Jack announced, "Thought you could use a change of scenery and grade you out here."

The Pet trainer's heart fell down to his feet.

"You-yoooo-youuuuu-"

"Take a deep breath, young Gray." His boss advised him.

"You have not graded my results?" Danny gasped out hastily.

Jack simply shook his head.

He explained, "I realize employees are always in fear when they see their employee folder that contained their scores. I have watched you secretly of working with all the owners in the training booth for the past couple of months. My mind wanted to do the traditional way, but my heart thought it was best to let you have fun in your job instead of overwhelmed with fear on your evaluation day."

Danny figured out why Jack talking that way.

"Where's Ally?" He suspiciously asked.

"Actually, the question should be 'where's my Figure Instructor?'" The short guy spoke in a disguised voice.

The delivery boys undressed themselves and under their mustached disguises were Allison Rigden & Richard McCarthy.

"Hahahah!" Rich laughed. "Got you, Gray!"

Danny laughed along with the two figures.

"And you were in it too?" He asked his boss.

The store owner replied, "Well, I am surprised you know two grand figure skaters and a PHL player. I could not turn down their offer of treating you special in your job."

Eight cars drove in the lot.

The drivers and passengers came out the cars with their dogs. A woman asked, "Is this the Dog Picnic?"

Jack smug, "Yes, it is, folks. Step in the fence and Daniel Gray will be your host for the day."

"Dog Picnic?" Danny spoke to Rich & Ally.

"Yup." Ally yelled out, "Oh, Butchie-Wutchie!"

The cute beagle jumped out of the truck and ran toward the three figures.

Danny squatted down to get his beagle in his arms.

"Awe, Butch . . ."

He held his dog tighter. "I sure miss you, fuzzy-butt."

His head raised up to look at Ally-Loop. "Thank you. How did you get him here?"

"I did not give you back your spares when you took Sally back to her parent's mansion." Allison expressed. "A few days ago, an idea came into my head and Rich & I began planning the 'Dog Picnic' with Jack."

Danny stood up on his feet with Butch in his arms.

"You're full of surprises, Ally-Loop." He stated. "I don't know how you can keep up with her, McCarthy."

"Couldn't do it by myself." The hockey Captain admitted. "Ally taught me how to groove with her."

The Loop smug, "And I'm surprised you have not lost your touch, Number 65."

"It's in my hustling nature, baby." The hockey dude teased and took her in his arms.

Danny and the figure couple went to the training fence. More cars were showing up at the parking lot. Twenty minutes later, a total of fifty cars were in the Pet store's parking lot for the 'Dog Picnic.'

Many dogs and their owners were having special training sessions with Danny and Butch. Kids were playing with dogs and play toys. Ally & Rich were having the time of their lives playing with other dogs and doing a little dog training. Other Pet store workers helped in the fence and inside the store too. Loud music was playing from the truck. And a hot dog stand van came to the lot for the picnic event.

Jack watched the entire event. It looked like a dog fun park. Some customers came in the store to get some stuff for their dogs. Either than that, more than seventy people came to the Dog Picnic.

The store owner was secretly grading Daniel Gray's training performance. His Pet trainer was smiling, interacting with the owners, and showed them the rope and tools to bond and experience the joy of having a dog.

Danny was doing a flawless job. In fact, he really had passion for being an overall dog trainer.

When the time reached one in the afternoon, Jack stepped into the fence and asked the large crowd of people, "How are you folks doing?"

Then the noise of chattering and barking were lowered down to let Jack Randell talk.

"I have something to tell you all about Daniel Gary." He started out. "He first started at my store five years ago as a Stock Boy and then moved up to be a Pet trainer. He was not an overall dog trainer a couple months ago. Somehow, with a Figure Instructor teaching him how to figure skate, he managed to understand what a dog trainer should be with the dogs and their owners."

Jack was full of pride for Mr. Daniel Gray.

"Danny, you are an overall dog trainer in my eyes. You got a perfect score." He shook hands with Daniel.

All the folks in the lot clapped their hands and cheered for Danny.

Daniel felt a huge piece of weight being lifted out of his heart, mind, and soul. He felt his eyes being filled up with tears. He let go of Jack's hand to turn his attention at all the happy dog owners.

He happily asked, "Anyone up for another training session?"

Twenty owners stood up from their seats and walked in front of the dog trainer.

Jack silently went back to the Pet store and into his office room for some peace and quiet in his leather chair.

The Dog Picnic ended three p.m. that day.

Everyone had a good time and they all started to leave the lot in their cars with their dogs.

The Pet trainer clocked out and grabbed his things in the locker box from the employee room. Some of his co-workers told Daniel he did great that day at the Dog Picnic. That made his day much better.

He returned outside to do his chore.

Ally, Danny, and Rich cleaned up the messy lot. Butch was put in Daniel's car. The three figure friends loaded up the colorful truck, picked up dog poo or littered food or other garbage essentials in trash bags and tossed them in a big brown metal garbage bin.

They all felt tired when the cleaning task was done.

"So, Danny, did you get what you wanted today?" Ally giggled.

"I was not expecting this." He honestly said. "This work day was better than I thought it was going to be."

Allison handed back his spare keys and responded, "I'm glad I made you happy."

She walked over to the colorful delivery truck.

Rich spoke up, "Ally knew you deserved something like this. Do something fun, relax on the job, and show your passion to others."

"Did she do something like that to you?" Danny questioned McCarthy, holding his spares in his hand.

"Yes, she did." The hockey dude admit. "A few months ago when I was named Captain, Ally surprised me and the team to fun filled day at an Amusement Park. All-expense paid."

Danny stuff his spares in his left work pant's pocket and wondered, "Is she really that rich?"

"Ally did a lot of savings for her career and did pretty big promotions in figure skating." Richard add softly, "She also does teachings during off season."

"Pretty awesome of her."

"I am proud of my baby." McCarthy replied. "Sorry Sally's a figure phony."

"Me too." Danny sighed unhappily.

Ally shouted, "Rich! We need to take back the truck and get you ready for tonight's game!"

She was sitting in the passenger seat in the truck with her head out the window.

"Coming!" Richard McCarthy called out and ran for the truck's driver seat.

Danny waved his hand at Ally & Rich.

Ally waved back.

The truck left the Pet store's parking lot and was out of sight. Daniel relaxed a little from the Dog Picnic. He did notice the little building was being a lot more renovated than the last time he spotted it weeks ago. The building still did not have a sign or gave Danny a clue on what it was going to be.

He headed back to his car and drove himself and Butchie-Wutchie to their apartment unit home.

Daniel's Friday work day went really well for him after his boss told him he was 'an overall dog trainer.'

The dog trainer was a lot more confident and ready to deal with any problem dog owners had with their misbehaved dogs. But his heart longed to talk and see Sally Hunt once more. He would feel like half a man without her by his side.

He went back to his unit for a fresh change of clothes, taking Butchie-Wutchie out for his walk, dinner, gathered his skating gear, and headed off to the ice rink. He was happy to do some skating after his first week of the new year.

Danny walked inside the rink's building. He paid for public session admission and went to the men's locker room. Skates were on and they fit his feet comfortably.

The figure student stepped out of the room for the ice rink. He did notice Allison & Richard skating together on the smooth patch of ice. The Pet trainer moved through the doors and glided out on the cold rink.

He started off by skating forward fast with crossovers and strokes. Then he did mohawk turn to skate backwards. He was very happy he could skate backwards fast and without falling down.

After going around the rink backwards twice, Daniel made it for the center. Ally was there to meet him.

"Good evening, 'overall trainer Gray.'" She teased.

"It is a wonderful evening, Figure Loop." He smug.

Danny did remember what he wanted to ask her about Sally and her parents cheating their daughter in figure skating.

"Can I ask you something important?" He requested.

Allison stood close to her student.

"Ally, how did you know that Paul & Joy Hunt were buying Sally's skating talent?" He quietly whispered in his Figure Instructor's left ear.

The Loop was surprised.

She knew Danny was smart and was learning that Sally Hunt's skating career seemed fake to her fiancee.

"Not now, Danny," she whispered back, "You will know the whole story before Nationals. Now is not the time."

The Pet trainer was disappointed, but he understood the secret should not be told out that soon. He let the subject go and concentrated on his figure moves.

Ally began to glide on her right blade with her left leg in front of her and did an inside turn. Danny had never seen his Figure Instructor do that kind of turn before.

Allison skated back to her turn trace.

Her eyes carefully examined the mark on the ice and whispered, "Perfect."

She looked up at Danny to tell him, "Tonight, I am moving you into special figure turns. Brackets and choctaws."

"What are brackets and choctaws?" He wondered.

"Let's start with brackets."

She did a left inside three turn and bracket turn to show Danny the difference.

"To put it mildly, the points in a three turn are done inside of an invisible circle while bracket points are pointing outside of a circle."

They both kneeled on the ice to see the turn traces that Ally just made.

"The first one is a normal three turn." She pointed out. Three turn's little point was inside an invisible circle.

Both of them moved to the second turn trace.

Ally spoke, "That's a bracket."

The instructor's bracket trace point was sticking away from a circle. Who would have thought something so tiny could be the answer to a big, complex question?

"It reminds me of the 'brackets' that you see on computers or in math books." Danny insightfully said.

"Yes, that is true, Daniel." The Figure Instructor replied happily. "Good remembering."

The dog trainer asked, "So, how do you do it?"

"Doing brackets is almost the same feel from doing a three turn, but you turn with the free leg in front of you instead of behind you." Ally explained.

Danny did an inside three turn first. Then he tried to do a bracket from his right foot and fell down on the ice after his first try.

Ally did give him a helpful tool idea.

"It's ok with me if you want to use the wall. I'll join with you and we'll also work on choctaws too." She offered.

Daniel was back on his blades. He questioned Ally, "What about Richard?"

Her eyes watched her hunky skate around the rink in his hockey skates. She replied, "He trusts me with you."

"Just didn't want to get you into trouble." Danny said nervously.

"Richard may be the jealous type in his heart, but he would not let out his anger outside of drills or pro-games." Ally assured her figure student.

"That's good."

Both of them went for a wall.

Danny practiced doing brackets with Ally. He asked her, "And what are choctaws?"

"They're like mohawks, but like a lutz jump, you glide on a different edge after the turn." She respond.

"I see." He uncomfortably said.

Allison Rigden smiled.

"You know I'll be with you when you want help during your skating lessons." She assured him.

Danny Gray relieved sadly, "I know. Just so many things to remember."

She encouraged him, "I believe you can comprehend all the terms better than Joy, Paul, and Sally Hunt. All you have to do is go slow and practice."

The dog trainer nodded his head. He went back to practice brackets and choctaws during the first skating hour. After that were jumps and spins. He did learn and got really good by doing jump and spin combinations.

Ally's tips were practice combinations slowly from finishing one skill and into another, practice each trick by themselves, get use to timing from completing each maneuver, and never over do it.

The Pet trainer followed Ally's lead for doing combination jumps and spins slowly and step-by-step.

Skating that Friday night was what Danny needed to make himself feel better from the loneliness of not being with Sally. He was looking forward to do his off ice training with Ally the next day at the Gym, her loft, and then back at the rink. She was going to pick him up in front of his apartment unit eight in the morning.

The next morning, Danny woke up in his bed and called out, "Butch."

Butch the beagle got up from his fluffy pillow to stand next the messy twin size bed. He watched his tired owner getting up from his bed. The human yawned big when he got on his feet and headed off for the bathroom.

Sweet Butchie-Wutchie went for the kitchen. He sat next to his green ceramic bowls. He was hungry.

Danny exit the bathroom and walked to the kitchen for some food too.

Ten minutes later, the cute beagle ate some dry dog food, clean water, and dog flavored beef and chicken medley meat for his meal. The Pet trainer had yummy waffles without syrup, a banana, and orange juice to drink. He did not want a fattening breakfast before doing a workout morning with his Figure Instructor, Ally-Loop.

Both boys left the kitchen and Danny was preparing himself for Butch's morning walk. He changed his clothes, slipped on his tennis shoes, gathered some baggies, and attached his beagle to his gray retractable leash.

They strolled out of their unit home with the door closed behind him. A few minutes after leaving the apartment building, in Daniel's bedroom on his nightstand, his cell phone was ringing. Who was trying to get a hold of Danny?

When Danny and Butch arrived back in their unit, they each had a drink of cold water. The human went to his bedroom for his skating bag, wallet, and his cell phone. As his eyes took a glance at the front cover. He had a missed call.

His left hand flipped the cover to check the recent call. The person who left him a voicemail was not someone he was excepting to hear.

It was Joy Hunt.

"Daniel Gray, Paul & I talked about you seeing Sally and you can see my daughter if you do something in return. You owe me a thousand dollars for the fee I had to pay for giving police officials false information!" Mrs. Hunt shouted.

I owe her? No, no, no, no, no. I owe her nothing. Danny thought.

"My money should not be used to clean up your messes! I hope you're happy by ruining Sally's skating career! Call me when you made your decision." Joy added.

The message ended.

The Pet trainer was hurt. He knew the real reason for Joy's excuse of him owing her. Because she did not want to lose her wealth so Sally could be kept in the figure world.

The Hunts are much more wealthier than Ally-Loop. Why would Joy be so upset about losing a thou for Sally's skating competition fees? Daniel wondered.

He did keep thinking about that question after leaving the unit with his skating bag. His legs walked down the stairs for the building's front door.

Allison's Horundi convertible was there when he arrived the first floor. Danny exit the building and rushed toward the cute white car.

Inside the car, Ally greeted him, "Good morning, sleepy head."

"I didn't oversleep, Ally-Loop." Angry Danny stated while buckling up. "I got held up from an unexpected call."

"You don't have to sound mad at me." The Figure Instructor snapped a little. She turned on her car and drove off for the gym.

Danny calmed himself to tell her, "Sorry. I'm not upset with you."

His hurt heart made him say, "Joy called."

"Uh-oh." Ally gasped. "She must mean business if she called you."

"She claim I owe her a thousand dollars after she paid a fee for giving false information to police officials." Daniel tried to tell Ally nicely. "That's her fault! Not mine!"

Allison felt bad for her student to go through Joy's schemes. All he wanted was the love of her daughter, not use Sally for money. The Loop wondered what to do for her figure student.

"Danny, did you tell her that you don't want to give her a grand?" She asked.

"I didn't directly talk to her. She left me a message while I took Butch out for a walk." Daniel Gray sighed sadly, "She said if I don't, I can't see Sally before Nationals."

Ally cursed out, "That shitty, stuck-up bitch!"

"Whoa, Ally." Danny calmly replied.

"I can't believe she's pissed off of losing a little bit of Sally's skating investment after committing a crime." Ally strictly told him.

To let go of her anger, her brown eyes just kept looking at the road and ignored the subject.

They arrived at the gym, went for the second floor indoor track, and Danny and Ally ran their hardest to get rid of the hatred they both felt about Joy Hunt. The figures did feel much happier after the twenty minute run and went down to a studio room for an hour long Pilate workout. Another twenty minute when they finished their strength training time.

Ally's Horundi convertible drove from the parking lot to her loft building's parking garage. Car was parked and locked up.

Danny and his Figure Instructor rode in the elevator to her loft floor. Both figures made it inside for the ballet room.

First thing they did was some stretching at the bars. Danny felt he was getting more flexible than he did a couple weeks ago from the first time he and Ally did off ice training in her ballet room.

Next up was doing some dance steps to some cool metal and pop tunes. Ally and Danny were smiling and having a ball by dancing figure moves and yet looking cool.

Through the third song, he asked the Loop, "How did you get into kick-ass tunes and be a hard-core dancer?"

Ally laughed, "Ah, Richard hated my old school type of music and introduced me to heavy metal. I was a little uncomfortable about metal shit at first. After a few songs, I started to like it and Rich & I began to groove and head bang out on the ice. We are pretty good together when 'Delusional Madness' or 'Look & Annihilate' would play at the rink."

"Now that make sense." Danny spoke while doing some bracket turns. "I'm surprised metal works for you while you skate."

"Like I said before, 'heavy metal music is pump-up music'. I like being strong out on the ice and I remind myself that an ice rink is not a safe place for people to have fun. I always have my guard up." She firmly explained.

Danny remembered her almost rape story. He knew that was her reason to be strong.

Half an hour later, Danny practiced some 'in the air' spins on Ally's trampoline. He was getting better than before and did some forward spins and back spins. He only could nail one spins instead of two. He was okay with that.

Ally had her turn on her trampoline and did single, doubles, triples, and some quads.

When they were done, the Figure Instructor told her student, "We need to think of a routine to wow the Hunts."

Danny was confused. "Why?"

"I assume they want to test your skills from doing a skating routine. And I have some ideas for a good routine to learn fast and yet be impressive for Joy to enjoy watching from you." The Loop replied happily.

"I could go for that." The Pet trainer agreed to her idea. "When did you want to start that?"

Ally suggested, "Today at the rink?"

"Sounds good."

They left her loft and headed off for the skating rink.

Tired Danny Gray came back to his barking apartment unit with his skating bag in his left hand. Behind the door was Butch, waiting impatiently for his owner to enter their home.

The human asked his dog, "Hey, fuzzy-butt. Wanna go for your walk?"

The cute beagle did a sit with his muzzle mouth closed and his white tail wagging side-to-side on the hardwood floor.

"Good boy."

Danny lumbered to his bedroom.

He placed his skating bag in the closet and slowly went for his bed. He laid on his back for a little breather. His heart was satisfied after the skating session he and Ally had at the rink. She gave him a sample of the song she picked out for his routine and a list of moves he needed to do for the routine.

Butch jumped up on the twin-size bed and snuggled with his owner on his sweaty shirt. Danny's right hand petted his dog's short white fur coat.

"Give me a moment, Butchie-Wutchie." The human mumbled softly.

His brown eyes closed and both boys slept on the bed for an hour.

When Daniel woke up from his short nap, he was ready to give his beagle dog his dinner and a walk. As the boys ate their meals, Danny was looking inside of the red folder that contained two white sheets of paper. One of the papers was his step-by-step skating moves while the other had a drawing diagram on where to do each move on the ice.

He was going to have fun with this skating project.

He did remember Ally telling him she was going to help him with all the steps during their lesson times. Except, they could not be on the ice all time and he needed to do some alone training.

The Pet trainer got himself ready for his evening walk with Butchie-Wutchie. Butch was eager to go on the walk too. They left their unit with the front door closed and locked.

Sky was dark and street lights were shining on the best buds as they walked around the neighborhood for an hour. Danny thought more of his not-so lonely heart since he had something important do to for the Hunts before the big day. He was grateful that Ally gave him a skating routine to keep himself happy for a little while.

Eight p.m.

Danny and Butch arrived back in their home.

They both chilled in their bedroom on the twin size bed. Butch laid down to nap on Danny's pillows and Danny was flat out on his bed and studying the skating moves. He read each maneuver out loud.

After reading it three times, he was getting an idea on what Allison had in store for his routine. He could not wait to get on the ice the next day and try it out.

For the rest of Daniel's evening, he practiced the steps in the living room. He went slowly and carefully remembered the moves.

Butch seemed interested in his owner's skating routine. He sat outside the living room and watched the human dance around the room for the rest of Saturday night.

Sunday arrived and Daniel Gray was happy that the new day was just starting. He and Butch had their breakfast, morning walk, and resting time in their living room together.

The time was eleven in the morning.

Danny showered, changed into his skating clothes, had a little snack to munch on, carried his skating bag and skating routine folder.

He said to Butch, "Be good."

The behaved beagle sat on the hard wooden floor and his left paw was raised up in the air as his 'I'll be good' sign.

The human smiled big at his good dog.

He left the unit, closed and locked the door, and went down the stairs for the parking garage. His car drove him to the skating rink. He arrived there a little after eleven-thirty that morning.

In the rink's lot, Danny could not find Ally's Horundi convertible anywhere. He was worried. His Figure Instructor had always been punctual. That did not settle the Pet trainer's stomach. Something was not right. He hoped nothing bad happened to Ally-Loop.

Danny went inside the rink's building and it was a little crowded for a Sunday afternoon skating session. His mind kept thinking, *Maybe Ally's running a little late or needed to do something important before my lesson.*

Jessica, the strawberry blond lady, noticed Danny looking a little confused and lost. She called out, "Daniel?"

His eyes met hers and he walked up to the admission desk. "Hey, Jessica. Is Ally here?"

"I haven't seen her come in this morning." Jessica replied sadly.

The employee went back into the rink's store.

Danny looked around both rinks for Ally. There was no sign of her anywhere.

He went forth to the men's locker room. Before he went through the doors, his cell was ringing in his skating bag. He unzipped it and found his ringing phone. His eyes saw it was Ally calling him from the caller ID. He flipped over the cell's cover.

"Hi, Ally." He relieved.

"Hi, Danny." She softly spoke.

"What's wrong?"

Ally whispered, "Go to the front of the ice rink's building."

Danny went for the front doors.

He noticed Richard's black truck waiting for him.

The Pet trainer stepped outside the building and made it inside of Number 65's truck from the left back door. Ally & Rich were sitting up front, being quiet. Daniel put on his seatbelt and placed his skating bag on next to him.

Richard slowly drove away from the parking lot.

The truck went south from the ice arena's building. They were not going to Ally's special rink or staying in town after the truck made it on the freeway.

At last, Ally sternly spoke, "Danny, we need to keep a low profile for the next two weeks."

"What's going on?" He suspiciously wondered.

Richard huffed, "Joy's been spying on you guys."

"What?" Daniel growled. "Why?"

Ally disappointedly replied, "She's trying to find out what my special combo jump is for Nationals."

The dog trainer was very angry at Joy Hunt.

He was glad he kept his mouth shut by not telling out Allison's quad-quad jump combo secret when he was with Sally at the beach and never saying a word about Ally's secret rink and her hanging out with ten PHL players.

"How do you know that someone is spying on us?" Danny wondered.

Ally explained, "Last month, when I went to the Pet store for dog training or us going to the rink, the gym, your apartment building or my loft's building, I noticed a white SUV following me. It was the same model and with the same license plates. Then Joy made her mistake by going into the rink building's office floor during your teaching lesson with the kids on the small rink. While I skated around, I saw a shadow behind the big screen window before my triple axel jump."

"So, why do you think it was Joy?" The Pet trainer questioned Rigden.

"I can recognize her shadowy figure anywhere. And she's one of the few figures who has keys for the whole rink's building." The Loop pointed out.

Danny still had his doubts.

He spoke, "Anything else?"

Richard told him, "There was another reason why Ally did not contact you sooner after she twisted her ankle. We were trying to get proof that Joy really was doing some detective work on Ally."

Behind her seat, Allison handed Danny a long tan envelope. His fingers found the little silver hooks on the envelope and pushed them off the flap. The flap was lifted up, the envelope was opened, and inside contained photos.

Daniel's brown eyes saw the photos.

The first three showed pictures of a white SUV in three different familiar spots. The ice rink's parking lot, in front of the Pet store, and not far from Danny's apartment building. His scrutinized eyes did see a pattern. The plates letters and numbers were the same.

What he saw next was a disguised Joy Hunt looking out the driver's window. He looked at the rest of the photos. They were of Joy wearing wigs, hats, sunglasses, and sometimes scarfs on her head and sitting in the driver's seat or walking out of the white SUV.

Daniel Gray was shocked.

"How did you get these?" He asked.

"I took them from a secret camera built in my rear view mirror." Richard replied. "Ally and I did some secret driving around town."

He touched his dash board entertainment screen with his right index finger and touched one of the rectangular buttons. The camera was on.

Rich put in, "See that?"

Danny's brown eyes looked at the camera screen first and then up on the freeway. They were the same. He was impressed.

Ally announced, "So, today we're going to another rink for a lesson."

"Why not your private rink?" The dog trainer wondered.

"It would be safer at a public rink rather than my rink during the day. At night, Joy would not be out spying." The Loop added.

Danny told them, "I understand. She hardly likes to go out at night."

Then he thought, *Does Sally or Paul know Joy was doing this?*

His heart was mixed with anger and loneliness.

He longed for Sally Hunt, but he was very upset that Joy wanted to be sneaky by learning Ally-Loop's special quad-quad combo jump before Nationals.

"Where are we going?" Danny wondered.

"My team's rink." McCarthy smug. "Got it closed for the afternoon for your lesson time with Ally."

Daniel felt honored.

The Tiger Shark's team rink? With Number 65? Shit, maybe I should try out for hockey and Rich & Ally could be my coaches. He pondered.

Acting like an eager kid, he did ask them both, "Hey, McCarthy, do you think I have what it takes to play hockey?"

Ally & Rich laughed together.

"Um, sorry for laughing at your request, Danny, but honestly, you're not cut out to play pro-hockey." Rich tried to say calmly.

Danny was a little disappointed.

Tears were filling up Ally & Rich's eyes. Their laughter stopped after taking deep breathes and focused more on Danny's hockey question.

"Hadn't Ally and the PHL guy's teachings made me a good, hard-core skater?" He pointed out.

"True, except you would not last five minutes by going up against pro-skaters who are like football players on the football field." Rich explained. "Your body gets bruised up, you get into fights with other players thinking they're tougher than you or you made an unfair play, receiving bloody noses, teeth would fall out, pucks would fly everywhere, and you're always hustling your hardest on the ice."

Danny had seen hockey games before and he thought about what McCarthy just told him. A Pet trainer would not last a minute against pro-hockey players during a hockey game.

"Maybe I should stick with figure skating." He slowly said sadly.

"Good for you, Danny." Ally happily replied.

The dog trainer teased, "So, you're not gross out of Richard's body after being beaten up from playing in a pro game?"

Ally smug, "That's one of our favorite times together."

"Her being an undercover coach and a nurse for me on and off ice is a lifesaver." Rich chortled. "Massages, hot baths, and talking about the game plays does make me a better player and I do recover faster from practices and games."

Daniel felt good that Ally could make Number 65 feel recharged and refreshed to play future games.

The Loop had a question for her figure student, "Do you think Joy will invite you to Nationals?"

"I don't know." He sighed sadly. "I hope so."

"If you don't, Ally & I would drive you there ourselves." Richard offered.

Danny relieved, "Really? Wow, thank you."

Ally told him, "If the devil's bitch does not say a word about it before the twenty-third, give me a call and don't tell the Hunts that you're going. You'll come as my guest."

"Sounds great." He replied happily.

In her Figure Instructor attitude, Ally asked, "Have you been reading and learning your routine moves?" Danny took out his folder and the two figures chattered on the figure moves he needed to do for the Hunt's skating test.

For the rest of their car ride, the three figure friends discussed more about figure terms and some of McCarthy's hockey maneuvers. He even smug about some of his past games with his teammates.

As they reached the huge rink's gated parking lot, Rich got out his Tiger Shark badge and showed it to the guard and let McCarthy pass. He parked his truck by not far from the enormous silver rink building.

They all got out the truck with their skating gear and headed up the stairs for an entrance. Rich showed a security guard his badge from the front doors' windows. The guard let all three figures inside.

McCarthy lead Ally and Danny to the ice rink.

Danny was amazed of the big, big, big cold rink.

The biggest he had ever seen.

"Shit, it's huge."

All the figure friends walked down the rink's stand stairs for the locker rooms.

It was getting cold for Daniel Gray. At least he was dressed warmly for the ice, and he could get warmed up by skating on the big, smooth, glassy ice.

Richard went for the Tiger Shark's locker room while Ally and Danny went to the first rows. They slipped on their skates quickly.

When they finished, McCarthy had on his black color jersey shirt and his hockey skates. He let Ally and Danny out on the ice.

Music started to play.

It was 'Vault!'

Ally smiled big and she just skated around the rink like she owned the rink. High jumps, centered and fast-paced spins, long and lean figure moves, and fun dance steps were her moves for her song.

Rich and Danny would cheer and applaud the Loop's fantastic skating routine.

As 'Vault!' ended, a soothing pretty song was playing.

The Figure Instructor said to Danny, "This is your routine song."

He practiced the routine five times.

Danny was glad Ally & Rich were there to help him with his first skating routine.

The figure friends just skated and rocked out on the tough Tiger Shark's domain arena.

Chapter Twenty

Daniel Gray, Allison Rigden & Richard McCarthy were tired from skating their hardest three hours later. They all chilled at the stands and talked more. Laughter and chattering could be heard from the figure friends.

A rink employee walked around the hallways and heard laughter.

From a door way entrance, the worker noticed the three young adults looking happy at the stands. To his surprise, one of them happened to Richard.

"Hey, McCarthy!" The worker called out.

They all turned around in their seats to see who was talking to them.

It was a black male in his mid 30s, medium height and built, wearing black sweat pants and a white work shirt.

"Hey, Dave!" McCarthy responded back.

Dave walked down the stairs and asked the Tiger Shark's Captain, "So, what brings you here today?"

The Captain answered, "My friends and I are having a break from skating."

"I see." Dave suspiciously said. "How are you doing, Ally-Loop?"

"I'm good, Dave. Thank you." She replied happily.

The worker wondered, "And who's this?"

He was asking who was the other friend.

The Pet trainer slowly stood up nervously.

He remembered what Paul Hunt told him about pretending to belong in figure skating when he went to Regionals for the first time. But Danny did not have to pretend or act like a pro. He had learned so much from Ally-Loop, he could master all the figure terms without doing a trick.

He eyed at the worker and introduced himself. "I'm Daniel Gray and Ally-Loop is my Figure Instructor."

"What for?" Dave curiously questioned the newcomer.

"I am Sally Hunt's fiancee. I have to learn how to figure skate in order for me to win over Joy Hunt's approval by marrying her daughter." Danny explained.

The African-American worker was surprised that Hunt had a lover. He told Daniel, "Well, good luck with that and, Rich, did you need the Zamboni?"

"Now would be a good time to use it." Number 65 gave Ally a kiss and stood up from his folded chair. He headed for the locker room.

Dave went for the rink's Zamboni box.

Ally and Danny found their bags to take off their skates and clean them.

She suggested to her student, "How about a skating lesson this Wednesday night at my rink? I will pick you up around seven p.m."

"I'll be ready by then." Daniel said.

Their brown eyes saw Number 65 driving the Tiger Shark's Zamboni truck on the ice. Captain McCarthy looked really happy to make the ice be 'freshly cut' again.

The enormous ice was smooth again.

The Zamboni truck was back in its box and was locked up. Richard headed for the team's locker room to grab his hockey bag. He and his figure friends left the rink's building for his black truck.

After going through another two hour drive to his parked car at the previous rink for his car and another short car ride, Danny was back in his apartment unit with Butchie-Wutchie. They ate dinner and had a long walk that night.

For the three work days, Daniel Gray did his work, took care of Butch, read and practiced more on his routine for the Hunts, and did not call Joy Hunt about his decision because there was no reason to compromise a deal just for him to see Sally again.

The dog trainer was relieved when his shift completed Wednesday afternoon. He needed a long skating session with Ally-Loop in her rink. Daniel went for his car and drove to his apartment building. Butch was there to greet him from walking through the doorway. The human took his uniform off and put on jeans and a long sleeved dirty gray color shirt.

They had a quick dinner in the kitchen, an hour long walk, and rested on his bed together for half an hour. The dog trainer did imagine more of his first skating routine.

After their rest, Danny showered, dried himself, put on his skating clothes, and gathered up his skating bag. Not from his closet was Butch was on his fluffy pillow.

He told his beagle pooch, "Sleep well, Butchie-Wutchie."

The human left the unit and went down the stairs for the building's front doors. He waited a few minutes for Ally's white Horundi convertible.

When his eyes saw the cute white car, he left the building, walked down stairs, and made it inside of the top up convertible.

Happy Ally said, "Hi, Danny."

"Hi, Ally." He spoke back. "Where's Richard?"

The Loop started up her car and told her figure student, "He and the Tiger Sharks are traveling to Canada for a game tomorrow night."

"Oh." Daniel breathed out. "Must be hard for you."

"Nah, I'm good." Ally replied and pulled up her phone. "We always have our phones to talk to each other."

The Pet trainer thought back when Bob, Smokey's owner, told him about being in war and had limited communication to talk to his wife. Rich & Ally were lucky to have video chat on their phones.

They went to her rink and skated the night away by judging each other's skating routines and moves. Danny was struggling to remember all the moves he needed to do.

Ally gave him some tips on when he should do certain moves by listening closely to the song's tune and lyrics. He tried her tips and he improved a little better than before, but he still needed some work on it.

As Danny's lesson came to an end, their next meet would take place Friday night at the small rink.

Work went well for Danny Thursday and Friday.

Regulars and newcomers would come to the training booth for Daniel's passionate teaching technique with dog training. He was really glad to be an overall dog trainer in Jack Randell's eyes.

During his time in his unit, Daniel would practice more of his figure routine in the living room. He saw Butch sitting and enjoying his master dance. The master would smile at his dog while he performed.

For Friday night, Danny wanted to practice a little on his routine and left the unit for the ice rink. He drove himself. He was feeling proud that his figure skating journey was coming to an end. He sure came a long way from being a first timer three months ago and now he was being an overall male figure skater. His heart felt happy that his Figure Instructor was in every step of his skating lessons.

He arrived at the rink's parking lot in good time.

Paid for admission, went to the men's locker room, laced up his skates, found his folder, stored his stuff in his locker, and carried the folder in his right hand. He stepped out of the locker room to walk toward the small rink.

Through the small hallway, Ally was waiting for him. She was not wearing her skating clothes or her figure skates. Just jeans, her maroon sweater, and her N+ running shoes. Her brunette hair was back in a long braid.

"Evening, Danny." She replied in a little frustrated voice.

"Hey, Ally." He told her. "What's wrong?"

She whispered, "Joy's been checking up on me yesterday and today." Danny's heart felt angry at Sally's mother.

Ally added, "I don't feel safe anywhere without Richard around. We talked an hour ago and he suggests I should only skate at my private rink."

"Why don't we go there?" The dog trainer wondered.

"It doesn't feel safe to go there now." She sadly stated. Her cautious eyes looked around the rink.

Poor, Ally-Loop. I wish Joy Hunt would stop spying on her. Danny thought in his head and heart.

"So, tonight, I won't skate and we'll work on your routine for a couple of hours." She offered sacredly.

"Of course." He said and handed her his folder.

The folder in her hands, Ally promised, "I'll make it up tomorrow afternoon after off our ice training in my loft."

"Whatever works for you, Ally." Danny assured her.

The figure friends were on the smaller rink and Danny skated around and around for two long hours. He did not mind skating by himself and working on his routine. Ally taught him more on advance figure moves. He wanted to show Joy Hunt what kind of skater Ally made him to be.

Saturday morning arrived.

Butch was full and tired from breakfast and his morning walk. He was napping on the living room's sofa.

Daniel hastily got himself ready for his off ice training time with Allison. Clothes on, skating bag all set, and his pooch would be good on his own for the next few hours.

The Pet trainer left his unit and went down the stairs for the front doors. It was eight a.m. and Ally's Horundi pulled up by the building's front doors. Danny left the building for the beautiful German car. Except, he did forget something really important for his skating lesson and failed to remember what it was.

Ally drove off to her gym.

The figure friends had a wonderful run, pilate workout, and rest time after the second run. The instructor was impressed that Danny was getting better in running and pilate workouts with her.

Next stop was Allison's loft.

Inside her loft, Danny and Ally did stretches on the bars, loosened up their bodies with some dancing time, and worked on her trampoline with their 'up in the air' spins.

Daniel's spins were getting much better from bouncing on the trampoline. He was hardly falling down or messing up his spins. Forward or backward. He felt content to do singles instead of doubles or triples. Or quads in Ally's case.

When the time was eleven-thirty, it was time to go to the rink. Danny and Ally were heading over to her car when he remembered what he forgot.

"Ah, shit."

"What's the matter, Danny?" Ally asked.

He looked inside his skating bag for his folder. It was not there. He moaned, "I left my routine papers in my unit."

Allison suggested, "I'll take you back to your unit and why don't we meet at the big rink?"

"Why can't you wait?" Danny questioned the Loop.

She respond, "If I do, who knows if Joy would be out spying on us and thinking something was up. We really need to keep a low profile, Daniel Gray."

"No problem." He tried to say cheerfully. "I'll check up on Butch."

"How is he doing?" The Figure Instructor wondered.

They reached her car when he answered, "He's happy."

"Good. He's such a nice beagle."

Both figure friends got inside the convertible and left the garage lot for Danny's apartment building.

The time was ten till twelve.

Danny exit out of Ally's Horundi with his skating bag in hand. He got inside the apartment building as the white German car drove off.

He rushed up stairs for his unit floor. Unlocked and opened the door. Who he saw was Butchie-Wutchie looking surprised to see him home so early.

"Sorry, pal. Forgot my folder." He explained to the sweet pooch.

Danny moved onward for his bedroom and located his folder on his computer desk. He took it, left the unit, and went down the stairs for the parking garage. He drove his car to the rink.

What Daniel did not know was someone was actually following behind him.

Ally noticed Danny's car pulling in the rink's parking lot. She got her bag out from the trunk when her student got out of his car with his folder and skating bag in hand.

They went inside together before they received disappointing news about the smaller rink. The figure friends were told to use the big rink since the small rink was being used for a private party.

Both instructor and student were a bit uncomfortable to use the big rink. They realized no one showed up in the big rink's lobby. Their hearts were a little happy.

Allison went for the ladies' locker room and Danny headed to the men's locker room. The Loop changed her clothes and slipped on her figure boots. The Pet trainer stored his skating bag in his temporary locker box and laced up his suede material skates.

While the figure friends were in the rink's building, a mysterious white SUV pulled into the parking lot. The driver parked and got out the car. It walked toward the rink's building front doors, moved inside, and decided to hide in the rink's second floor.

The sly SUV driver waited and waited to see who was going to skate at the small rink. Its eyes noticed the skaters were a bunch of little kids who were part of a birthday party. Failure filled its heart.

The driver moved to see who was at the big rink. Its eyes saw Ally and Danny skating on the rink. The person smiled. "There they are."

After being in the rink for ten minutes, the SUV driver saw something it was not expecting. Allison Ridgen did not a double, not a triple, but a quadruple axel jump. Then the quad single jump was turned into a combo with a quad loop jump.

"So, a quadruple-quadruple edge jump is Ally-Loop's special combo jump." It whispered.

The sneaky shadow quickly turned to leave the rink's building.

Danny and Ally were happily having the rink to themselves and the Loop decided to do her quad-quad jump. She began with a quad axel jump and added a quad loop jump.

The Pet trainer applauded Ally's beautiful combo jump for Nationals.

But the Loop was not happy after doing her second landing. Her head looked up and saw a shadow behind the second floor's glass window.

Ally skated off the ice and slipped on her guards.

Daniel went after her.

The figure friends raced out the building and saw a familiar white SUV in the parking lot. The SUV left the lot in a hurry.

"Joy saw my special combo jump." Ally sadly spoke.

Danny felt sad for his Figure Instructor and knew what he needed to do for Ally and Sally. He sat on the cement ground to untie his figure boots.

The Figure Instructor added, "Now she's going to make Sally do it first."

Her student had his skates off and he replied, "I'm going after her."

In his socks, Danny went back to the men's locker room to put his skates in the locker box, gathered his keys and tennis shoes. With his shoes on, he raced to his car, drove off from the lot, and headed south.

It did not take him long to find the white SUV with the same license plates Danny saw from the pics of Richard's secret rear view mirror's camera. He laid low as he followed Joy's mysterious white SUV without her noticing him.

Joy drove for twenty minutes from the previous ice rink to another ice rink. She turned the SUV off and rushed inside the other skating rink building.

A few minutes later, Danny's car reached the second ice arena's parking lot. The car was parked and the dog trainer exited the car for the strange new rink.

He was inside the mysterious building. The lobby was totally empty and it felt cold to him.

As cold as an ice rink. He could have sworn his ears heard Ally's voice when she told him about her private rink.

The ice arena's building had a huge screen window and a lot of benches, some tables, five video game stands, a few vending machines filled with snack foods, soft drinks, and a coffee maker. There was also a skate shop, and a single glass and metal frame door. Behind the glass door showed stairs that goes downward.

Just when he wanted to go through the glass door, Danny noticed Joy Hunt talking to a skater who was not his fiancee. This skater had brown hair and her hair was fixed up just like Sally's skating hairstyle. French braid and a jeweled brown color headband.

The two girls stepped away from the rink for the bleachers. Their backs were turned.

This was the dog trainer's chance to go down the stairs unseen.

Danny slowly pushed the door away from him and made his way down the red metal stairway. As he reached the last step, he ducked down on his knees to see from the lower part of rink wall's screen windows.

Joy and the brunette haired figure were back on the ice. They were arguing about something.

Daniel's ears heard, "Look, I pay you to get my daughter to the top!"

That's Joy Hunt, all right. His mind snickered.

She yelled out, "I demand you to nail a quad-quad edge combo jump!"

The young brunette with blue eyes and wearing a long sleeved lime green turtleneck shirt and black stretch pants protested tiredly, "I can't! No skater-can do it!"

Joy was being Joy when she raised her left hand and slapped the right side of the figure's face hard. The girl gasped out loud and her body was turned to her right side.

"I seen the Loop do it. You can too." She spoke in her calmed coach voice.

"Get to work!" She sternly announced, "We'll stay all night if you have to!"

The hurt figure skater stood up straight to glide around the rink and cried out tears of sadness. She was flowing around the ice with her French braid floating behind her head.

Danny could not believe that Joy would be mean to the figure and her own daughter. He could not wait till Sally's competitive years were over.

He did hear a man shouting out, "I'm ready to get her MMMs!"

"Good!" Joy angrily said. "Keep spinning in the air!"

The harsh skating coach turned on a soothing classical music with a stereo system's remote control.

What Daniel realized was Joy seem more interested in the young strange figure girl rather than Sally. This skater was really good and yet, she did look very tired and exhausted from Joy Hunt's highly-trained, strict figure teachings.

Young Daniel Gray was glad Joy was not his Figure Instructor. Something did not seem right to him. He wondered why his future mother-in-law would want to teach that figure girl instead of his fiancee.

Maybe it has to do something with Sally's feet problem. He wondered.

Danny's knees were achy from kneeling too long. He crawled on the wet foamed floor for a better hiding spot by the bleachers. His brown eyes saw a man with a laptop on his lap and sitting at the stands.

The man looked in his early 40s, salty hair, round glasses, wearing gray pants and a navy blue dress shirt, and brown laced shoes were on his feet. He did not seem to care about the cold ice rink's temp or being around Joy Hunt.

Joy continued to yell her instructions harshly to her student to improve her spin rotations from her jumps. That hurt Danny's heart more than ever. He knew his sunshine girl must have went through that kind of abuse the brunette with blue eyes was going through.

The Pet trainer found a good hiding spot under the stand's wall after slithering on the floor like a snake. He found a secret stairway entrance to the top of the stands. He climbed up the wooden steps.

There was a good view of the man's laptop screen before leaving stairway. Two different software programs were running. There was a tiny web cam at the top of the laptop. The program on the left showed the brunette girl being taped on ice while she did her figure tricks.

The program on the right had a black background with a pink and red color form of the brunette figure's muscles. It also showed silver dots flashing on her major muscle groups. There were two at her feet and one on the top of her head. The top page of that program said 'MMM software.'

The silver dot on the figure's computerized head must be from the headband. Danny thought in his head. *But what the hell are 'MMMs?'*

Slowly and being inconspicuous, the brave dog trainer made it down the stand's stairs, crawled down low on his belly, and managed to walk up the red metal stairs to get out of the Joy's secret hideaway rink. He drove in his car to head over for the rink Ally was skating at.

Daniel returned back to the rink in good time.

He ran out of his car and into the rink's building. His scared brown eyes watched Ally-Loop skating her heart out to a kick-ass metal song. He was not sure how to break the news to his trust worthy Figure Instructor.

She waved at Danny from the rink with her right hand. He hesitantly lifted his left hand and waved back at her.

Ally knew something bad was up from the look of her student's disappointing eyes. She glided to the walls. He left the lobby to talk to his figure friend.

Danny's mind kept thinking that Joy Hunt was really doing a cheating scheme not only with her daughter, but with another figure skater just so Joy could have the gold.

He breathlessly spoke to Ally, "Hey . . ."

"Daniel, are you okay?" She concernedly asked.

He sucked in courage and let out, "You were right."

The Figure Instructor was puzzled. "Right about what?"

"All this time . . ." He mumbled. "You were right about the Hunts' cheating scheme."

His voice sounded regretful.

Allison's brown eyes were instantly full of tears. Her strong running legs felt like jelly and sat on the cold, cold patch of ice. She cried out loud.

Finally, someone else believed her tale about Joy's cheating secret to make Sally win the gold. She knew Danny was going to be on her side.

The Pet trainer sat next to Ally on the wet foam floor. He let her cry for a few long minutes. He figured her heart was full of pain after being called a 'fool or liar' that Sally and her parents were cheating in competitive figure skating.

Now was the time for her to let go of the hurt she experienced for years.

When her tears stopped and sniffled a little, Ally and Danny got up and went inside the big rink's lobby area to sit and talk. They sat on the benches to have a private talk.

He was finally going to get the answers he had been waiting for three months. Sally's foot problem in the morning, her going first in skating competitions, same style costumes, and why they needed to go for the back entrance.

Daniel asked, "How did you know?"

Allison Rigden started off with Sally's foot problem story that happened six years ago . . .

Sally and Ally were a wonderful teen rival team on the ice. Sally was always placed first and Ally second.

When Ally turned fourteen, she wondered if Sally had a dirty secret when it came to figure skating. She got an unexpected wish in the girl's locker room one day.

She was getting ready for practice when she heard a girl wailing from the top of her lungs. Ally-Loop hid herself in a full-figure locker box and closed it.

From the thin rectangular holes on the metal door, the young Loop's eyes noticed Sally Hunt was crying and whimpering. The cute blonde was in her father's arms. He placed her on a matted table to let Sally rest up.

Ally was feeling happy.

Sally may not compete again. Her heart snickered.

As Paul Hunt was taking off Sally's figure boots, Joy stormed into the locker room. She yelled out, "What's wrong with Sally?"

"Just wait for the doctor, Joy!" Paul shouted.

"Stop fighting!" Sally demanded. "Ooowwww! My feet hurt!"

The teenage Hunt continued to cry out in pain.

Ally was enjoying to see Hunt be in so much pain, maybe the Loop would place first in future skating competitions and events.

Then a male doctor entered the locker room. He was in street clothes and carried a black leather doctor bag in his left hand.

He stepped toward the matted table and kindly questioned Sally. "Now, honey, where does it hurt?"

Sally's bluish-gray eyes looked at the male doctor with blond hair and green eyes. She whimpered, "My feet."

The male doctor noticed the teenage figure skater's flinched feet in her tan tights. Her arches were being difficult to lay out flat on the table.

Like a foot doctor, the blond man stood by her feet and fingers quickly felt the problem on the bottom part of Sally's feet.

Inside the locker box, Ally wondered what was wrong with the blonde figure too.

What the doctor felt from his fingers and hands were Sally Hunt's extremely tight arches, the muscles were really inflamed, and the ligaments were starting to tear from both of her heel bones.

The blond man made his diagnose of Sally's injury case. "Mr. & Mrs. Hunt, Sally's feet has plantar fascia."

Both of Paul's hands held his daughter's right hand to give her comfort. She softly moaned in pain.

He asked the doctor, "What's that?"

"Your daughter's feet bands are strained and being overly used from, I would say, too much skating lessons and being trained more than she can handle. If this keeps up, her bands would snap or break apart and would need surgery for new bands to grow on her heel bone." The man with green eyes strongly explained.

He put in, "I recommend Sally to not ice skate or do anymore super active exercises."

Allison's heart was filled with glee. Having to hear the words 'Sally Hunt cannot ice skate anymore' was victory news to the teenage Loop.

The blonde hair doctor got his bag and left the locker room.

Joy firmly questioned Paul, "What are we going to do?"

Mr. Hunt looked down at Sally's sad face and hurtful eyes. He would hate the idea to see his loving daughter be in so much more pain than what she felt.

Sally's voice continued to whimper that her feet were still in pain and softly cried out loud.

Paul's left hand let go his daughter's right hand. His left fingers stroked Sally's soft blond hair and leaned over her face to kiss her forehead.

He stood up straight after making his 'what was best for Sally' decision. He gave his full attention to his wife and put his foot down.

"Having Sally not figure skate anymore would not be a bad idea." Paul stated.

Ally giggled a little from that response.

"But . . . what-Paul!" Joy Hunt stammered loudly. "You're . . . you want Sally to . . . surrender?"

Sally's red haired Mommy gulped at the end of her sentence. She detested the word 'surrender'. Especially in figure skating.

"Yes." Her husband replied. His comfort eyes gave Sally love. "She'll forfeit and surrender her skating career."

Sally was glad her father was on her side. He did not want his daughter to have foot surgery or be in anymore pain.

"No, no, no, no . . ." Joy eyed at her 'puppet girl.' She declared, "I will make you an ice skating champ, Sally. I promise."

The blonde gave in to her Mommy's promise. "Yes, Mommy . . ."

Allison was heart broken. She did not want to compete against Sally again.

"Joy, Sally's been limping after waking up from bed and sometimes she does not walk properly." Paul sighed sadly.

The Loop was happy to hear that argued statement.

"Then we'll just have to do something to decrease her 'plantar fascia' problem." Joy was creating a plan.

Sally nodded her head in agreement and tiredly requested to her figure parents, "Can we go home?"

Paul Hunt lifted Sally up from the matted table and all three Hunts left the skating rink with Sally's skating bag and gear. They went on a long ride back home.

When the girl's locker room was empty, Ally came out of the locker box and left the room for her skating lesson. Her heart hoped Sally Hunt would not heal or return for competition season.

Seven months later, Ally-Loop was wrong about the sunshine blonde not coming back to compete.

Daniel Gray was shocked to hear that Sally's foot problem was 'plantar fascia' and she had been battling against it since she was a teenager.

That must be the reason why she could not get out of bed on New Year's Day. Her body was asleep and cannot put pressure on her tighten up ligament muscles. Kinda like when someone has arthritis. If you don't move, the pain would increase. But if you keep yourself active, the arthritis would be less noticeable. He thought.

He did wonder how Ally knew that the Hunts were really cheating for Sally's skating competitions.

Bored Ally declared, "I need to skate some more."

The Pet trainer like that idea too.

The Figure Instructor stood up from the bench and left the lobby. Her student lifted himself up for the men's locker room. He took off his shoes to put on his figure boots. He was ready to rock out on the ice with the Loop. He was gliding on the ice and feeling glad he could skate gracefully from his blades instead of his toe-picks like a novice would.

His mind thought more on what 'MMMs' was.

The Figure Instructor let her student skate around the rink while she worked on some figure turns at the center part of the rink. She waited until Danny was ready to talk some more.

When he glided up to her, he asked, "What made you think Joy had found a cheating way to get Sally to the top?"

"Probably the same things you noticed from going to Regionals and Sectionals with them." Ally explained to him. "Why Sally goes through the back entrances, never seeing her skating gear, same costume styles with different colors and materials, her tacky French braid and headband trade mark, the way she walked on ice is so much different than off ice, and not staying long after her routines were over."

Danny thought he was the only one to notice those things. Ally did long before he & Sally met. He and his Figure Instructor skated around the rink and talked some more.

It was a good time to tell the Loop where Sally Hunt got her skating talent from.

"Ally," he gulped, "I found out what Joy was doing after chasing her from the skating rink."

She stopped gliding.

Daniel stopped too.

He spoke unhappily, "She went to another rink not far from here."

The Figure Instructor asked, "Was Sally there?"

"No." He spoke. "I saw Joy with her real student and she is not Sally. It's some other figure girl."

"Is it someone from Regionals or Sectionals?" Ally demanded. She hoped it was to comprehend why this 'skater' was more important to Joy than Sally.

Danny thought back on the mysterious skater's description. Tall like Ally with long, light brown hair, blue eyes, and in good shape to be skating for Joy Hunt.

"I have not seen that figure girl before." The Pet trainer explained. "There was also a man with a special laptop a the stands telling Joy he was ready for the 'MMMs'."

"Did you see what was on the man's laptop?" Allison curiously wondered.

"I did." Young Gray candid. "The screen had two programs running. On top of the laptop was a camera and one of the programs was recording the girl skating out on the ice. The other showed a chart of the girl's muscle figure. The muscles had some silver dots flashing. There were two for her feet and one silver dot at the top of her head. The page was called 'MMMs software'."

Puzzled Danny sighed, "I wonder what that means."

Just when Ally wanted to skate again, she paused and thought of something.

"Muscle Memory Microchips." She breathed out.

Her feet started to skate again and Daniel followed his instructor around the rink. What her student told her made sense and was able fill in all the missing pieces she was missing for her theory.

Ally pointed out, "A few years back, I did sneak into Sally's skating bag and saw some stick-on microchips, flexible wires, and what the inside of her 'special skates' was like."

Danny shuddered at the thought. His dreams were right about Sally's true figure form.

Allison spoke up, "I think the skater that's with Joy now wears memory muscle microchips and Sally must be wearing some sort of muscle mimic chips during practices and competitions."

The dog trainer listened closely and knew Ally was right with that idea of Joy Hunt's cheating scheme for Sally to suffer through. Then things were coming together of the clues he learned from the Hunts.

That was why Sally needed 'special skates' for her plantar fascia feet problem. She would be tired and unable to win the gold from her own skating moves if she did not go first or wear her headband or her 'special figure skates'.

Both figure friends turned backwards when Allison had a new question for Danny.

"What is Joy doing with her 'figure puppet'?" She asked.

He sadly answered, "She wants her 'puppet' to . . . nail a quad-quad edge jump."

Immediately, Allison Rigden's heart was crushed.

Joy Hunt was stealing her skating ideas to let her puppet do one, save it on the laptop, and transfer the figure moves to Sally's mimic chips before Ally had her chance to do it at Nationals.

The once hard-core Ally-Loop started to cry and did a show stop. She leaned against a wall for support.

Danny stood next to his upset Figure Instructor. He kinda wished McCarthy was here to comfort his girl.

"I give up!" She shouted out loud in the quiet rink.

She glided toward an open gate door as fast as she could.

Danny skated behind her. "Ally?"

"Go away, Danny!" She yelled out and slipped on her guards by the door for the girl's bathroom.

She sat on the foam floor with her phone in her hands. She called up Richard to see if she could talk to him. Her called did not reach him.

Ally's trembling lips whispered, "Damn, stupid time zones. He's three hours ahead of me. Must be game time. I hope he kick ass."

Someone knocked on the girl's bathroom door.

"Ally-Loop?" A voice spoke.

She sniffled, "Come in."

The door pushed and Daniel Gray stood in the doorway. He offered, "You want to talk about it?"

Tears were falling down her face. The back of her right hand rubbed off her warm tears.

"What's there to talk about?" She sternly questioned him.

Her upset voice protested, "Your thieving future mother-in-law is a figure kleptomania bitch who wants to buy skating talent for her golden daughter who does no wrong!"

Ally cried out more.

Danny remembered himself wanting to give up skating because Joy would not let him see Sally, but Ally let him have free will if he wanted to quit. Deep down, she did not want him to lose the commitment he promised to Sally and her parents.

"Allison, don't-don't quit, please?" The Pet trainer pleaded. "What about your fans, coach, and Richard? They don't want you to quit on your passion for figure skating."

He did add, "You never really gave up on my skating lessons when I wanted to quit."

Ally reminded him, "I know. But I let you have a choice of wanting to skate or not and you willingly came back all on your own. I might have to forfeit if Joy is making her 'puppet' steal my special quadruple-quadruple combo jump."

"The 'figure puppet' admitted to Joy she can't do it herself. So maybe you still have a chance to do it for Nationals." Danny hoped his news would cheer Allison up.

"I know Joy well enough that she won't give up until she got what she want." Ally sighed sadly.

We'll stay all night if we have to! Joy's stern voice stung Danny's ears.

The dog trainer admitted, "You're right about that."

The Figure Instructor carefully got up from the wet foamed floor to wash her hands and clean her face. Her lit up phone was on the countertop.

"What does McCarthy say?" Danny wondered.

Ally looked at the mirror and told her figure friend, "He-" gulped "he didn't-I was unable to reach him."

"Why?"

She huffed, "It's probably game time in Columbus, Ohio with the Navy Blue Coats."

Danny looked at the time of her phone.

4:36 p.m.

She was right again.

Before leaving the girl's bathroom, Allison questioned her student, "How can I compete if Sally's going to do my special combo jump first?"

Daniel thought and thought. He stepped away from the doorway to let Ally-Loop pass through.

Then his mind thought of plan after thinking about being at the Tiger Shark's home rink and Richard McCarthy knowing his way around the rink's building. He also got more ideas by remembering Number 65's secret camera in his shiny black truck.

Allison quietly sat on an empty bench.

"I have an idea." Danny softly announced.

The Figure Instructor's head turned to look at the dog trainer with her unimpressed, tearful brown eyes. She was feeling tired and lightheaded from crying a lot. She got up from the bench for the snack bar.

During the walk, he quietly replied, "It's a good plan and maybe Richard can help us."

Sad Ally huffed, "I'm listening."

Just when Danny wanted to tell out his plan, his figure coach ordered some hot cocoa. The teenage snack bar employee turned around to fix up her customer's drink.

Daniel held back his tongue.

Ally got her drink and she and Danny walked to the other side to the lobby room to hear his plan. They sat down on a bench together. Ally had a few sips of her hot drink.

Their eyes looked around the lobby room to see if anyone else was going to come near them. There was no one around them.

Danny leaned in and whispered in her right ear, "We are going to prove to the world that the Hunts are cheating liars in competitive figure skating."

"That's not a bad idea." She gave in and could not wait to plan it out.

"Let's meet Monday evening to talk about it at my rink." She suggested. "Seven good enough for you?"

"Why not tomorrow?" Danny curiously wondered.

"Then Richard won't be there to help us plot out your exposing idea." Ally pointed out.

The dog trainer agreed to her plan.

Both friends went their gender locker room, got their skates off, and left the skating rink for home.

Tired Daniel Gray made it to his unit.

He was glad Butchie-Wutchie was there to greet him. The sweet beagle scampered up to his owner for a big hug. Danny held his pooch tightly.

"How you doing, Butch?" He questioned his pal.

Daniel carried his dog and skating bag to his bedroom. He placed his bag in his closet while Butch leap down from the human's arms for the floor to his pillow.

As the beagle waited, his human friend took off his smelly clothes and headed toward his shower. He showered, dried himself, and slipped on clean clothes.

The boys each had a special chicken dinner.

Danny had fixed up some roasted chicken with mashed potatoes, and green beans with soda. Butch had some dry kibble and doggie meat flavor chicken stew with clean water to drink.

Later that day, a beagle and his owner stepped out from their unit home for a long walking. While they walked around the neighborhood, the owner was thinking what to do on how to expose the Hunt's cheating scheme with videotaping. He also thought about how to make Sally show the judges and audience she was a fraud figure skater.

He knew it was a risky thing to do for the love of his life, but it could help Sally get out of doing her stupid figure skating career forever and let Ally-Loop get the gold in a fair ice skating competition.

Chapter Twenty-One

Daniel Gray's Sunday was blissful for him and Butch.

First, they had breakfast. Second, instead of going for a walk, Danny and his beagle pal went to the park for a play day. Third, they stopped at burger stand for burgers and a soft drink for Danny and cold water for Butch. And fourth, they slept together in his twin size bed.

Allison Rigden's Sunday was not going well for her.

She woke up crying hard from hearing the breaking news Danny told her about Joy was making her 'figure puppet' do her special combo jump.

"It's not fair!" She yelled in her loft's bedroom.

What Ally decided to do was drive over to the rink and talk to her coach. She changed into her skating warm-up clothes. Hot pink long sleeved shirt, tan tights, navy blue stretch pants, and fixed up her long hair in a pony tail.

Her ears were surprised to hear her phone ring. It was placed on her speaker's dock in the bedroom.

Ally rushed to the speaker and answered her phone without looking at caller ID.

"Hello?"

"Hi, baby."

"Richard . . ."

Allison calmly sat on her bed.

"Are you ok?" He wondered.

Her broken voice said, "No."

"What's wrong?" Concerned Rich asked.

"Something bad happened at the rink yesterday." She started off her disappointing tale.

Ally was trying to calm down her painful heart. She panted, "Joy-um, she saw my, my, m-"

354

She began to wail out again.

"Ah, McCarthy . . ."

Her bailing voice let out, "The devil's bitch saw my quad-quad combo jump!"

"Shit . . ."

She heard his curse.

Her right index finger pressed on the phone's speaker button. She fell on her bed and placed her phone on her nightstand. She cried and cried long and hard.

From Richard's end, he was in a noisy airport with his teammates and coaches. Most of them were chattering about the up-coming game that evening.

The team's Captain was sitting in an unpadded leather chair as he listened to Ally's cry. His heart was breaking into pieces from each tear she let out. He wished he could be with her and comfort her.

He suspiciously questioned his lovely Figure Instructor, "What do you think's going to happen in Nationals?"

It took Ally two long minutes to calm herself down.

She sadly explained, "After Joy saw my special combo jump, Danny managed to locate her at another skating rink. He told me Joy is going to make Sally do my special combo jump first."

After breathing some deep breaths, her broken voice continued, "He said Joy's 'puppet figure' thinks she can't do the jump combo herself. Except, I know Joy well enough she's going to wear out her daughter and her 'puppet' to get a quadruple-quadruple edge jump."

"A 'figure puppet'?" Puzzled Rich asked.

"Yes. Joy's using another skater for Sally's skating moves. Danny never told me who the 'puppet' was." She whimpered. "I don't think it's someone who's doing figure events. I think Joy locked up this skater from the public. And from Sally too."

McCarthy let out, "From what you told me in the past, that seems to make sense to me."

Lonely Ally pleaded, "Are you coming back home tomorrow?"

"Yup." Rich stated and got up from the chair he sat in.

His hazel eyes look out the window at four large jet airbuses. The runways were busy with people walking around to prepare the planes' takeoffs. Carts and work trucks were also passing through the runways.

McCarthy put in, "Game time tonight against the Chicago's Sauk Hawks, and we will be back tomorrow afternoon."

He turned away from the window and added, "I really miss seeing you at the stands, Ally-Loop."

"I miss being there for you, Number 65." She confessed sadly. "But you know why I can't go."

"Practicing for Nationals . . ."

Ally sweetly spoke, "It starts next week and I have to be really strong to go up against Joy Hunt's 'figure puppet'."

"There's nothing wrong with that, Ally-Loop." He teased in the end.

"I Love You, McCarthy . . ."

"I Love You too, Rigden . . ."

Richard was thinking how to cheer up the Loop. He smugly reminded her, "At least I'll be with you for Nationals in my team's rink."

That made Ally stop crying and laughter came out from her heart. She giggled and giggled until she finally stopped crying.

"Glad I made you feel better, babe." He chuckled.

"You always made me smile, Richard." Ally said.

From her end, she got up from her bed, picked up her phone to turn off the speaker, and told Rich, "Um, Danny has a plan to expose the Hunt's cheating scheme."

"Really?" McCarthy was intrigued with the idea. "What does he say about that?"

"The thing is: tomorrow night, the three of us are going to my private rink and discuss what we need to do." She explained.

Richard was confused. "The 'three of us'?"

"Yea," Ally spoke, "Danny, me & you. He wants your help too."

"I would be glad to help you guys out." He firmly stated. "It's about time someone out skates Joy Hunt."

Ally praised her hunky player, "Wonderful!"

Then she requested, "Is it all right I meet you at the airport tomorrow?"

"One o'clock at the loading zone outside?" The hunky player requested.

"I'll be there." The Loop promised.

Richard McCarthy had only one thing for Allison Rigden to do for him that day.

Being a man in love, he encouraged her, "Ally, go to the rink. Sounds like you need it badly."

Ally giggled, "I already dressed myself to go and talk to my coach. She still doesn't know I can do a quad-quad."

"Maybe you should tell her." Rich suggested.

Candid Ally-Loop smug, "I'll show it to her today."

"You do that." He paused for a few seconds and sadly said, "Have to go now. I'll call you after the game."

The Loop decided to act like a fan by saying, "Never mess with the Tiger Sharks!"

Both laughed at the same time.

"We usually kick-ass, baby." Rich sighed.

"I better let you go and good luck." She gave him a loving kiss over the speaker.

His heart felt wonderful and he moaned softly. The hockey Captain gave her a kiss back.

They hung up their phones and Allison left her loft for the rink.

Ally-Loop did what her hot-looking hunky player wanted her to do. She showed her figure coach, at the quiet small rink, her quad-quad combo jump. Barbra could not believe what she just saw.

She danced a little on the ice and cheered for her student by doing something no other figure skater had done before.

She gasped, "You are going to make figure skating history, Allison Rigden."

"Thank you, Barbra." The Loop expressed happily.

"Hey, this is all you." Barbra insisted.

Ally blushed, "I couldn't have gone this far without my Figure Instructor."

The two long time friends hugged each other tight.

"I want to do another!" The Loop exclaimed.

She let go of her coach and skated around for another quadruple-quadruple combo jump.

As she skated backwards before nailing another beautiful edge quad-quad combo jump, her heart pleaded, *I wish you were here, Richard McCarthy . . .*

Daniel Gray's Pet training shift at the Pet store Monday went really well for him. Bob and Smokey came to the store for a little fun training time. He did ask the young man if he had any news about Sally Hunt.

"Nothing," was Danny's answer.

Bob told the Pet trainer, "Don't give up on your girl."

"I won't, Bob." Young Gray firmly respond.

His mind gave him idea on how to pull off the exposing plan. He needed to do some research before going to Nationals with either the Hunts or Ally & Rich. The search topic was: where's the nearest rink from Richard's team rink?

He did figure in his head, *I bet Joy, the 'figure puppet,' and the man with the laptop are going too. They would be at the other rink to get Sally's skating moves right before her routines for Nationals.*

When the time was four p.m., the training booth was cleaned, stocked up, and locked up. Danny rushed out of the store for his car. He drove to his unit home.

Butchie-Wutchie was playing with his Bong toy inside the unit after his human owner walked through the front door. His small doggie teeth got the rest of his biscuit and contently ate it up.

Danny saw his dog eating parts of his biscuit from his little red Bong toy.

He spoke, "Hey, Butch."

The cute beagle looked at his master and did a sit without being told to sit. His skinny white tail was wagging on the floor like crazy.

At least the Pet trainer knew what his pal wanted.

Dinner and a long walk.

Daniel changed his clothes, fixed their dinner meals, went on an hour long walk, and came back home feeling tired and happy as the sun was rolling down.

He was ready to leave his unit. Skating bag, check. Keys, wallet, & cell; check. Folder, check.

He softly told Butch, "Sweet dreams . . ."

Butch was sleeping on his soft pillow.

The Pet trainer noticed that the time was six fifty-five. He needed to go. He gathered his things before leaving his unit home. His apartment home's front door was closed and locked up. He walked down the stairway for the building's front door.

Daniel's brown eyes noticed McCarthy's shiny black truck pulling up as he made it for the front doors. He hastily opened them and ran toward the black truck.

Inside were Ally & Rich sitting up front. They were happy to be together again. Danny sat in the middle seat, buckled up, and had his skating bag on his left side.

Richard started up his truck.

They headed to Ally's abandoned building.

All three figures did not say a word during the drive.

Twenty minutes later, the friends got out of the truck with their skating gear and ran for the basement door. Allison unlocked it. They went through the doorway quickly. The door was locked up.

It was dark and cold. Richard & Allison walked down the stairs first with Danny behind them. They quietly stepped down slowly and carefully.

As their feet reached the bottom step and made it for the smooth ice rink, Danny, Ally & Rich slipped on their skates at the stands. Daniel was surprised to see Captain McCarthy put on his suede figure skates instead of hockey skates.

Ally got on the ice first and lithely stroked around her private rink fast. She smiled proudly at her earned skating talents. Her brown eyes saw Danny and Rich get on the ice and they stroked on the ice too.

Even though he only wore hockey skates for the past month and a half, Richard had not lost his touch to skate perfectly in his figure boots. He was faster and better than Daniel, but the Pet trainer did not mind that at all. McCarthy had lots of cross skating training for years.

Loud music was playing from Ally's speaker.

All the figure friends did jumps, spins, dance steps, and worked on freestyle moves. Danny was still caught off guard that Number 65 of the PHL's Tiger Sharks could be almost as good as Ally-Loop when it came to figure skating.

They skated for an hour before gathering around the center to talk about the exposing plan. Music was turned down low and Danny started to tell out his idea.

"This is what I'm thinking what we should do: video tape Joy, the figure puppet, and the man with the laptop during Senior Ladies' first and last days that way the audience would see the 'puppet's' and Sally's similar skating moves before Sally does her long program. I assume Joy would be at a rink not far from the Tiger Shark's main rink to get Sally's MMMs ready for both routines." He explained.

"That's true." Ally said. "Probably why I never saw Joy and Sally with her skating gear from walking through the back entrances. To carefully hide her microchips, wires, and special skates."

Richard told them, "I think I know which rink Joy would go to first before the event starts."

The Pet trainer was glad he did not need to a computer research of San Jose's ice rinks. McCarthy knew the area from the inside out.

Allison did think of something important for Danny to do before going to Nationals. "Daniel, if Joy invites you to Nationals, ask her if you can come over to the mansion for dinner or something."

"Why?" Danny wondered.

"I am curious if there was anything suspicious in Sally's room that could help us with the plan." The Loop stated. "Like old, non-special skating boots, past costumes, or anything she might still had before her plantar fascia problem. That way the world would see Sally's foot problem before doing her routines."

Rich replied, "That may not be a bad idea."

Danny was a little unsure of doing that to his sunshine girl. "I'll try."

Then he put in, "Rich, do you know a place where I can get a secret camera?"

McCarthy slyly respond, "I know the perfect place. I need to be discreet with the employees."

"Good." Danny breathed out.

Ally suggested, "Okay. If Joy does not invite you, we leave next Wednesday morning after Richard gets back from his Tuesday night game, check in a hotel, keep a low profile, and you and Rich will follow Joy to the rink to do the video tapings. If she does invite you, don't say a word or give them any ideas that you're going to do something to ruin their cheating scheme."

Danny promised, "Not a sound."

Number 65 strongly told Ally's figure student, "When you get the taping evidence of the figure puppet, hurry back to the truck and I'll drive us to the rink's lot. For Senior's Ladies last day, that's going to be a tricky part. We'll have to sneak into the security room and show the taping from the rink's score board t.v. screens."

"That sounds good to me. But I'm afraid Joy might do something to destroy or figure out the plan." Young Gray sighed with fear.

"Don't worry about that, Danny." Richard snickered. "Joy Hunt is going to be in Tiger Shark's chomping territory. She has no chance to fight against me and my team to get secret access to the rink."

Daniel felt much better to have the team's Captain be part of the 'exposing Hunt's cheating scheme to the world' plan.

The Figure Instructor offered her students, "Skating night this coming Friday at the public rink?"

Both guys liked that idea.

For the rest of their skating time, Ally & Rich each had a turn to help Danny with his skating routine. They thought he was getting much better in figure skating than before.

All three figures created a pact and were ready for their plan to do underway in a week and a half.

The Figure Pact kept a low profile for the rest of the week. Danny worked hard at his job, practiced his skating routine for the Hunt's skating test in his living room, and took special care of his loving beagle pal. He hoped to get a call from Joy before the week was over.

It was Friday night and no received no call or contact from any of the Hunts. He left his unit for a skating session with his Figure Instructor and a PHL Captain.

Ally had lots more skating lessons with her coach for Nationals. She worked on her 'Vault' and 'Ace's Wings' routines flawlessly. To play it cool from Joy Hunt and thinking too much of the Pact's plan or her skating routines, Ally-Loop went with Number 65 to his home games. She cheered and smiled big at her hunky player being a kick-ass, hard-core skater during drills and game time.

Friday night came and Ally Loop was skating around the big rink alone. She was waiting for her friends to meet her at the rink.

Richard secretly went to a place for a secret technology gadget for Danny. He bought a black baseball with a hidden camera inside and it was able to download tapings to a computer with a UBS cord connection. The cap was hidden in a wrapped up box making it like a birthday present. Number 65 was very happy to see the Loop back at the stands or in bed with him after practice or game time.

McCarthy drove to the public rink that Friday night after doing long hours of drills with the team and coach. He was feeling excited that the exposing plan was coming up soon and could not wait to do it.

He was surprised to see Danny getting out of his car just when his truck was parked in the lot.

The two guys met up and walked in the skating rink together without paying for admission.

Ally saw Daniel and Richard walking inside the building at the same time. They headed for the men's locker room.

In the locker room, figure boots and hockey skates were laced up, their things were stored away, and they talked more about the exposing plan by putting in figure and hockey terms to take out the normal key terms of the Figure Pact's plan. It felt ironic that a Pet trainer and a PHL player could be good friends together. On and off ice.

All thanks to Ally-Loop.

The figure males were on the ice and skated around the big ice rink. While they skated, the Figure Instructor watched them skate. She was also having that ironic feeling too.

Look at those two. They do such different professions and yet managed to be just 'guys' out on the ice together. And sometimes off ice too. Who would've thought people could make friends through ice skating? She thought gratefully.

She lithely glided up to her students.

Richard quickly took her left hand for a kiss on her lips. She kissed him back for a moment and pulled away.

"Shall we skate?"

Both guys nodded their heads and went for the middle of the rink. What they did throughout the night was talk about the exposing plan in code and helped the figures get better their skating routines.

After Allison Rigden hugged, kissed, and dropped of Richard McCarthy at the airport Saturday morning, she drove her Horundi convertible to Daniel Gray's apartment building. It was seven-thirty a.m. when she left the airport's entrance.

At seven-forty a.m., Danny and Butch made it back to their unit home from going on a forty-five minute walk. Both boys were tired and thirsty. They each drank cold water.

The Pet trainer headed for his bedroom and found his skating bag with his red folder. He was thinking that maybe he did not need to bring the fold since he knew his routine by heart. Then again, Ally would not like it if he did not bring all his figure skating supplies with him.

He decided to bring the folder with him.

Butch was comfy on the sofa as Danny exit the bedroom. The beagle's head lifted up to see his wonderful owner with his skating bag and folder.

"Well, Butch. I got to go and be good, okay, fuzzy butt?" The human spoke.

Butch yelped once.

Danny smiled big at his sweet tri-bastard and walked out of his unit home. He was just in time to watch Allison's white car move in the neighborhood.

They went to the gym, her loft's ballet room, and the public skating rink building. Both figures judged each other skating performances. Ally's were flawless even though she could not do her quad-quad during public session, but Daniel still needed to do some more work on his.

It was four twenty-two p.m. when their skating time was over. They would meet again the next day during afternoon session.

Danny was in his unit and took Butch out for his afternoon walk, had supper together, and both rested comfortably on his bed.

Ally went to her loft alone and did her normal bedtime routine. Before she went to bed, Rich called her. They had a video chat in her bright bedroom. Ally sat on her black & hot pink themed color bed.

With a big smile on his tired face, McCarthy told his Figure Instructor all about the drills the team did and that evening's game. Ally was happy to see him be a hunky player.

Then she asked, "Um, do you think Danny's exposing plan can work?"

Richard admit, "It's a good plan with some risks in it. The big thing I'm worried about making the Hunts believe Danny is not a snitch. The best thing for the Pet trainer to do is if he keeps himself away from the Hunts and have us drive him to San Jose."

"You're not bothered about breaking into the big rink's security room?" Ally worriedly wondered.

McCarthy let out a big laugh.

"Ally-Loop, as Captain of the team and doing some maintenance work for the rink's building, I practically have special privileges to get in secret passages inside the rink." He smug. "Besides, I'm sure Dave can help Danny and I during Senior Ladies' long program."

The Figure Instructor's lips gave her puck chaser a sweet kiss.

The puck chaser gave her a kiss back.

"I miss you like crazy, McCarthy." Her sad eyes told him she longed for him again.

"Going to games or practices without you does not make me feel like Number 65, Rigden." He unhappily sighed. "Hold on."

Richard stepped away from his phone to give Allison a little surprise.

What she saw from hot-stud Rich was of him shirtless and laying in his hotel bed. He was acting like they were going to sleep together. That warmed Ally's heart. She blushed and smiled from ear to ear. She laid comfortably in her bed. Snuggled close to a fluffy pink pillow.

A huge yawn escaped from her mouth.

"I think it's time for us to get some sleep." Richard suggested.

Sleepy Allison said, "All right, McCarthy."

Her eyes could barely stay open when she let out, "Kick some fuckin' ass, Captain. I Love You . . ."

"I Love You too, Ally-Loop . . ."

They ended their video chat and both peacefully fell asleep with lonely hearts.

When Daniel Gray woke up Sunday morning, he was feeling sad without Sally Hunt by his side. He could not wait to go to Nationals to see and maybe a chance to talk to his sunshine girl again.

The dog trainer stretched his body before standing up from bed. His whole form was feeling more flexible than ever. He did have a lot of energy and stamina to face another day at the rink with Ally-Loop.

Butch got up from his pillow. Standing on all four legs, his white head looked up at his happy owner.

"Hey, Butchie-Wutchie." The Pet trainer's tired voice said.

The cute beagle yelped once and turned his body around to run toward the kitchen for breakfast.

The overall dog trainer chuckled at his dog while he followed him for a yummy morning meal.

After they finished, Daniel wanted to get himself ready for Butch's morning walk but his cell was ringing. He hastily made it for his nightstand and answered it.

"Hello?"

"Good morning, Daniel Gray."

Danny was stunned.

"Hello, Joy Hunt." He grumbled.

"Don't you use that kind of tone on me, young man." Joy huffed. "At least I was kind of enough to call you on Sally's behalf."

The dog trainer let go of his anger to ask Mrs. Hunt. "What made you decide to call me?"

Joy explained, "Paul & I had another long chat and we wish to invite you to go to Nationals with us to San Jose. Would you care to join us?"

He remembered what Ally told him if he was invited, *Don't say a word or give them ideas that you're going to do something to ruin their cheating reputation.*

"I would be delighted to go." Danny cheerfully replied.

"Wonderful." Joy said indifferently. "We will pick you up at your place on the twenty-fifth at eight in the morning. The event will be over on the twenty-ninth. Make sure you bring nice clothes for the event."

Daniel agreed. "Yes, Ma'am."

Mrs. Hunt added, "And to say, 'I'm sorry' for being rude to you a few weeks back, we wish to invite you to dinner with us tonight."

The Pet trainer's heart was pumped up with excitement. He was going to see Sally that night.

"What time?" He wondered.

"Six p.m." Joy offered.

"I'll be there." Danny said. "Tell Sally 'I Love Her.'"

Mrs. Hunt's voice spoke, "Paul always does."

She hung up first.

Daniel put on jeans, white t, athletic shoes, and his synthetic coat. He found Butch's retractable leash and baggies.

They were ready to go on their walk.

During their walk, Danny could not believe he had enough patience to wait on Sally and Nationals. It was all thanks to Ally-Loop who did make him a better man in his job and lover for Sally Hunt, even though she was a competitive figure fraud.

The boys made it back to their unit home.

Butch had a long drink of cold water. Daniel put on his black sweat pants and kept on his white t-shirt.

He decided to work a little more on his skating routine in the living room before hitting the ice. Butch wanted to play with his owner with his chunky play rope.

Danny got down on the hardwood floor to play tug-a-war against Butchie-Wutchie. Both boys growled and tugged and tugged and tugged for a good five minutes around the living room.

After Butch won in tug-a-war, Daniel got up from the hardwood floor to practice on his routine a little more. He slowly did every step from the diagram. He also spoke out all the figure skills he was doing.

The time was ten till eleven.

Butch and his owner were getting hungry for some lunch. The human fixed up a sandwich with juice and the sweet beagle had dog flavored roasted turkey medley meat, three small pieces of blueberry flavor biscuits, and water.

Danny got his skating things ready for his session with Allison. He was happy to tell her that Joy had invited him for Nationals and dinner at the mansion that evening. He did have a question for the Loop when he does go into Sally's room.

What else could there be to make Sally not figure skate in her room besides the stuff she had in her past?

He told Butch, "See you later, Butch."

The cute pooch went for the bathroom when Daniel left the apartment unit.

Danny walked down the stairs for the parking garage. He kept a tight grip on his skating bag. He saw his car, unlocked it, and got in. He drove to the skating rink's lot.

The car arrived there fifteen till twelve.

Ally-Loop's white Horundi was there.

Daniel got out of his car and walked inside the ice arena's building. He paid for skating admission before making his way for the men's locker room.

Inside the locker room, his fingers were quick of lacing up his figure suede material boots. His skating bag was locked up in his temp locker box. Then he was ready to face the ice.

Ally was on the ice already. She agilely skated around the freshly cut ice. She did feel happy, excited, and a little nervous of the up-coming USIS National's event. She was going to win the gold with her quad-quad combo jump.

Her brown eyes noticed her figure student on the ice with his red folder in hand. She skated for the middle.

Danny met up with the Loop at the center.

"Hey," she greeted him.

"Afternoon, Ally-Loop." Danny teased.

They both giggled a little.

"So, do you want to work on you routine today?" She offered.

"Yes, I do." He smug.

Ally requested, "How about this: we take turns by judging each other's routines."

She opened the red folder and stated, "You can go first."

Danny said, "Sounds good to me."

He stood over the center's blue dot for his stance and started out his routine. He did dance steps, jumps, spins, and some figure poses that went well with him.

Ally had outdone herself with Daniel Gray.

He was looking like a real figure male after watching his skating routine.

As he finished his program, Allison Rigden applauded her student's hard work. She tearfully spoke, "That was beautiful, Figure Gray."

Danny felt tired after doing the routine. He took his folder from Ally's hands and announced, "Your turn, Miss Allison Rigden."

Ally skated to the bottom part of the rink and started off her 'Ace's Wings' routine without triples or quads in all her spin jumps.

Every time I see the Loop's long program, it's getting better and better than before. It's cool she does her moves more flawlessly and perfectly. The Pet trainer thought.

Allison stopped her routine and did her bow in front of Danny. The Figure Instructor was ready to conquer and win against Joy Hunt's 'figure puppet.'

Danny told Ally, "Joy called me this morning."

The instructor asked, "What did she want?"

He sighed heavily, "She invited me to go to Nationals with her and Sally and Paul."

"Okay." Allison firmly spoke. "This is really good."

Daniel added, "And she offered to have me over for dinner tonight."

Ally gasped, "Really?"

"Yes." He put in, "Have to be there at six o'clock tonight."

"Do you remember what I asked you to do if she did invite to the mansion?" The Figure Instructor reminded him.

"Yes. But I have only question about that." He requested.

"And what is it?" Ally wondered.

He stood close to her to whisper, "What else should I be looking in her room beside past treasures of hers?"

Ally thought for a moment as she pulled away.

Her mind had an idea.

"Um, I guess any little details that does not seem normal for a college girl." She explained. "Things like her bed, chested drawers, things in her closet, electronic devices, or what she wears on her feet."

"I understand." Danny sighed.

The Loop told her student, "After dinner with the Hunts, call me and tell me anything that seemed odd in Sally's bedroom."

"No problem." He promised.

When it was four-thirty that afternoon, Daniel left the ice rink with his skating bag and went to his car. He hastily drove back to his unit home.

The Pet trainer rushed inside without greeting Butch.

A fast shower, quick dry, putting on tan pants and dark green dress shirt with his brown dress shoes, and gathering his personal essentials was all Danny could do in his shared home before heading over to the Hunt's mansion for dinner.

He went down the stairs and started up his car.

The car pulled up in front of the large house five minutes six p.m. Danny was feeling nervous to see the Joy Hunt again from their last encounter, but he was very excited to see Sally again.

He got out of his car and walked toward the mansion's front door. His right index hand pressed on the doorbell button.

Ding-dong!

He waited a few seconds before the door opened.

Behind the door was sunshine Sally Hunt dressed in a sleeveless, v-neck shape, white dress with a black ribbon around her waist line and black steams and bright pink flowers at the bottom of her dress.

"Danny!" She squealed and leaped into his arms.

It had been a very long time since they last held each other. Daniel Gray was very satisfied to have the love of his life in his arms once more. He held her tight. So tight he did not want to let her go.

Sally pulled away a little to look at Danny's eyes. Her sad bluish-gray eyes missed him a lot. His loving brown eyes did not care to think about his lonely days.

She's here and that's all that matters. God, I Love this woman. He thought.

His lips and her lips touched each others for the first time in several weeks. They missed kissing each other with love and affection.

At the staircase, angry Joy Hunt saw her daughter and Daniel Gray kissing in the doorway. She wanted to stop the couple's physical touch, but Paul looked at up his wife and silently shook his head.

The red haired woman quietly walked down the stairs and she & Paul headed over for the kitchen.

Both Daniel & Sally let go of their long, long 'I Love You' kiss. She invited him in her home.

"How are you, Danny?" She sweetly asked.

His right hand took her left. He had to look at her ring finger. Her beautiful three gem stoned ring was still there.

"I Love You . . ." His voice was full of pride.

"I Love You . . ." She spoke happily.

They walked away from the door for the kitchen. Something smelled wonderful to Danny's nose. Roast beef with peas and carrots.

All four figures sat at the dinner table with their meals. Sally & Danny next to each other while Joy & Paul sat on opposite ends of the table. Sally was the only without a roast beef meal.

She had a salad with grilled chicken and no dressing. Water was all she had to drink.

Danny wondered, "Did you want some beef?"

Joy spoke up for her daughter. "It's best if Sally didn't have anything fattening before Nationals, Daniel."

He kinda figured that was why his fiancee only had a veggie meal.

During dinner time, Paul Hunt questioned the Pet trainer, "So, Danny, how are your skating lessons?"

Just when Danny wanted to chew a piece of the roast beef meat in his mouth, he swallowed it whole and started to chock on it. He coughed and coughed out loud violently.

Sally turned her head.

"Danny?" She worriedly asked him.

He could not answer his blonde sweetheart. His eyes were watery, it was hard for him to breath, and opened his mouth wide enough to cough out the big piece of beef.

"Sally, take him to the bathroom!" Joy demanded. "I won't have my table be covered in vomit!"

Danny's face was starting to turn pink. He tried to gasp out the beef that was lodged in his throat.

Sally slowly got up her chair and helped him out from his chair. They walked up the stairs to the first door on the right.

The Pet trainer was still gagging and coughing. His fiancee lead him to the toilet and he kneel in front of it to cough out the beef in his throat. Sally knelt with him. Her right hand was patting his back to help him spit out the piece of meat.

What seemed like forever, Danny let out a big cough and the beef flew out of his mouth and in the toilet's bowl.

He coughed and breathed out deep breathes.

"Oh, thank goodness." Sally breathed out and held Danny close to her.

His dry mouth gasped out, "Sally, can I have-some water?"

She answered, "Of course. Just stay here."

Their lips touched each other.

Sally left the bathroom for the kitchen.

Daniel sat on the tile floor with his head up. He felt lightheaded and tired. He also knew the Hunts were mad at him for not being proper at the dinner table. He hoped they would forgive him.

His lungs made him breath strongly once again.

Sally came in the bathroom with a tall glass of water in her left hand. She handed it to Danny.

His right hand took the glass and chugged down a big gulp of the cold water. He was starting to feel better.

The figure champ sat next to her love on the tile floor.

She asked him, "How are you?"

Danny drank some more water.

After pulling the glass from his lips, he slowly respond, "I-I feel . . . embarrassed."

"Why?" Her soft fingers combed his soft brown hair.

He took another sip of water to answer, "Because I was not showing your mother good table manners."

Sally assured him, "She understands that unexpected things happen and Daddy's question caught you off guard."

"Yea, I bet." He mumbled sarcastically.

"Are you ready to come back to the dining room?" Sally asked.

Danny knew he needed to do Allison's request before leaving the mansion.

He lied to his fiancee, "No. I still feel tired and dizzy."

He drank some more water from the glass in his right hand.

"Okay." Sally left the bathroom to give Danny some space. She closed the door.

He waited a minute to slip out of the bathroom. He stood up, flushed the piece of beef down the toilet's pipe, and put the empty glass on the sink's counter top. He also washed his hands and face in the sink.

Quietly, Daniel left the Hunt's guest bathroom to find Sally's bedroom. His eyes looked at the white door in front of him. It was the only door that was closed in the hallway.

"Sally's room." He whispered.

The dog trainer never went inside her room before. His left hand slowly turned on the gold door knob. He moved inside with the door closed behind him.

The room was dark. He found a light switch by the door and flipped it up. Sally's room was now bright with a ceiling light lighting up the whole room. It looked like a normal girl room.

Light yellow colored walls with some figure skating posters on the wall and light pink color carpet on the floor.

In front of Danny was a twin-size bed with light pink and cream color floral bedding sheets and pillow covers and behind the bed was a window with light weight material white curtains. At his left side was white wooden, square-shape vanity, a mirror connected to the tabletop, and a spineless pillowed chair at the sitting area. There was a large sliding door next to Sally's vanity for her walk-in closet.

He noticed a light brown wooden nightstand next to the bed. On the stand were a square shape porcelain white lamp with an oval polyester fiber material to cover the lamp's bulbs, a special picture of him & Sally in a beautiful silver picture frame, and a digital pink alarm clock with large black numbers telling the time.

6:23 p.m.

His eyes saw what was at his right side.

A tan color wooden chest drawer and five silver steel handles on each box door. There were six photos of Sally skating at events or practices. On the other side of the drawer was a big glass case shelf full of Sally's past medals, ribbons, and trophies from figure competitions.

Danny's churned stomach made him feel sick because he knew his fiancee had not earned those awards fairly.

At first the Pet trainer did not find anything out of the ordinary in Sally's bedroom. Then he remembered the two things Ally want him to find.

I am curious if there was anything suspicious in Sally's room that could help us with the plan. Like old, non-special skating boots, past costumes, or anything she might still had before her plantar fascia problem.

Danny walked around the room to get a better view of Sally's things. Nothing unusual on the floor, the vanity, drawer table top, or in plain sight.

He moved over for the walk-in closet. His right hand pushed the door to the right. His eyes saw the dark closet. He found another light switch next to the sliding door. He flipped it on and the closet was lit up.

In the closet box were clothes on hangers, shoes on the floor, and some old figure skating books and magazines in a cardboard box at the far back. He could not find any of her past costumes or old figure boots from past skating competitions in the closet.

Just when he wanted to give up, Daniel thought of the second thing Ally told him to look for.

Any little details that does not seem normal for a college girl. Like her bed, chested drawers, things in her closet drawers, electronic devices, or what she wears on her feet.

Now that he heard the word 'electronic devices', the dog trainer could not find a computer, phone, her cell, t.v., or a stereo system in Sally's room. The only electronic she had was her alarm clock. That was a good start.

What else could he find?

His brown eyes looked closely at Sally's nightstand and behind her silver photo frame. He leaned forward to see three orange plastic tubes with white lids at the top. That was an odd thing to Danny.

Why would Sally need three different type of prescription pills for her foot problem? He thoughtfully wondered.

He slowly stepped away from the nightstand and his head turned to his right to see another odd thing on the other side of the bed.

Daniel walked around the bed. He saw two black and blue, strong plastic, orthotic night splints. He remembered what Paul Hunt told him from the voicemail on New Year's Eve, *She has special needs she cannot get from you.*

The dog trainer figured out how his fiancee goes to sleep without her plantar fascia increase from sleeping in bed. *She wears them as part of her treatment.*

His thoughts continued on, *I wished she and her parents told me about this earlier. I would have understood it. But if they did tell me, I would have known the truth about the cheating scheme and spill out the secret.*

All right. That enough snooping in his fiancee's bedroom. Danny found five unusual things.

Sally had no personal electronic devices, no skating costumes or old figure boots from past skating events. However, there were two orthotic night splints, three orange prescription pill tubes, and the most disappointing one was: no microchips, flexible wires, or her special skates were stored in the sunshine girl's room.

He headed out of the room and went down to the dining room.

At the dining room, all the Hunts looked at Danny.

Joy questioned Ally-Loop's student, "How are you, Daniel?"

He breathed out, "I'm a bit better."

He sat down next to Sally and pushed his plate away from him.

"Aren't you hungry?" Paul wondered.

"No, thanks." Danny stated. "Lost my appetite."

"That's quite all right." Joy softly smug.

She did have a request from her future son-in-law. "Daniel, there is one big thing you need to do for your skating skills. Create a routine to show Paul & I what you've learned in figure skating. If we like it, you may marry Sally."

Ally's right again about the Hunts. He thought.

"That won't be a problem, Mrs. Hunt." Danny happily said.

"Oh really?" Joy did not want to be out smarted in figure skating.

Danny explained, "Yes. Ally fixed up a routine for me to show you guys."

"We can't wait to see it. Right, Paul?" Joy sternly sniffed.

Her husband spoke, "Right, Joy. Do you know when you wish to show us the program?"

"I'm all ready to show it now." Daniel announced.

Sally smiled at her loving fiance. She was proud of her him to fight on the ice for her mother's heart.

Joy thought about it and told the group, "Sally's ice skating wedding ceremony planning is about done. Why don't you show us your routine in three weeks? That way Nationals would be over and all of us will have a little rest from the ice."

Paul suggested to Danny, "The week before the wedding, we are going to look for some special tuxedos you can wear on the ice. I'll come by your apartment building after your pet training shift to get a move on."

"Thank you, Paul." The young man agreed to the idea.

"And before you forget, tell your boss to ask for time off for Nationals." Joy reminded Danny.

He strongly replied, "I'll tell him tomorrow."

Chapter Twenty-Two

After leaving the Hunts early and kissing Sally goodnight, Danny went for his car and drove off for his unit home. Then he remembered he did not feed or give special attention to Butch after coming home from the rink.

He reached his apartment unit and walked inside.

Butch immediately ran toward his owner for attention. The human sat down on the hardwood floor with his loving beagle. His fingers rubbed the dog's soft white fur coat.

"Are you hungry, Butchie, Wuthcie?" Danny sweetly asked his cute beagle.

He barked once.

Arf!

"Okay." Daniel chuckled.

An idea came to his head. He got up from the floor to go into his bedroom. He changed his clothes, found his phone, and called up Ally.

It rang two times and a voice said, "Hello, Danny."

"Hi, Ally."

"What's up?" She asked.

Danny told her, "I went to the Hunts and found some interesting things in Sally's room."

"Really?" Allison gasped softly.

"Yes." Then he offered, "I didn't eat much during dinner and I was wondering if we can meet up somewhere to eat and talk?"

Ally obliged, "Sure. I like that. I haven't eaten a decent meal for the past few days."

Danny wondered, "Because of Nationals?"

"No." She sighed tiredly, "It feels weird to live my skating life without Richard around."

"I understand." The Pet trainer would act the same way with Sally.

"Did you want me to pick you up?" Ally suggested.

Daniel said, "Me and Butch?"

"Sounds good." She giggled. "Where did you want to go to?"

"The beach?"

The Loop stated, "I'll be there in fifteen minutes."

"Thank you."

Both figures hung up their cells.

Danny commanded, "Butch! Beach time!"

The cute beagle went straight for the front door.

The human put on his tennis shoes, navy blue synthetic coat, got Butch's short leash, and baggies along with wallet, cell, and keys.

The boys headed down the stairs after locking up their unit home for the building's front doors. They did not have to wait long for Ally's white Horundi convertible to arrive. Danny picked up Butch in his arms and carried his furry little body down the front door stairs.

In the top up car, Ally was dressed in a comfy white t, long stretched black pants, her N+ running shoes, and her long brunette hair was fixed up in a ponytail.

"Hey, Danny. Hey, Butchie-Wutchie!" She greeted the sweet beagle warmly. "Been a good boy to my figure student?"

He yelped.

The Figure Instructor laughed at Butch's answer.

Danny was buckled up and Ally started up her car. Their car ride to the beach lasted for a half hour.

All three friends left the convertible and walked on the parking lot. Daniel lead Ally to the hot dog stand he and Butch loved to eat at.

They each had a dog while they had their little talk on the sandy ground. Butch was let loose to run around.

"What did you find in Sally's bedroom?" Ally became intrigued.

Danny carefully ate his dog so he would not chock on the dog's meat. As he finished a bite, he explained, "Sally does not have a computer, phone, stereo system, or anything electrical in her room. I found two black and blue plastic foot casts by her bed. Three orange prescription tubes on her nightstand. But no past costumes, figure boots, microchips, wires, or anything that can be used to show Sally's foot disability before the events. Her shoes looked normal to me."

Joy's going the extra distance to hide all evidence from Sally and the 'figure puppet.' I hope she won't know Danny is going to be a snitch. Let's see if he acts like a fan for Sally Hunt. The Figure Instructor's heart thought.

Disappointed Ally breathed out, "I guess we'll have to do your plan instead."

He knew how to cheer the Loop up, "How's McCarthy?"

That question did not make Ally happy.

Her broken heart answered, "Traveling around Canada with the Tiger Sharks. We miss each other dearly."

"Sorry for bringing it up." Daniel felt bad. "Do you feel more lonely after telling him how much you love him?"

Ally shook her head. She told her student, "It's because of Joy wanting to spy on me."

"But she already knows your combo jump for Nationals." Danny argued. "What else can she do to you?"

"Daniel, Joy Hunt is the devil's bitch who wants to ruin a young figure skater's chance at the gold." Allison sternly explained, "Not only she wants to take my moves, she wants torture my love for figure skating so I won't be back on the ice."

The Pet trainer already knew that theory from going to Ally's special skating rink for the first time. He remembered what Sally told him if any of her friends could teach him how to ice skate. *They all quit after last year.*

His mind silently whispered to his heart, *Joy got to them so Sally can win and Joy will have the gold all to herself. What a sly, horrid person she is. No wonder why Ally hates her so much. But in a more honorable manner.*

"Joy tricked Sally's figure friends, didn't she?" Danny asked.

"Yes." Ally sighed sadly. "She's been doing that for years. None of the good local figures wants to come the rink or do skating lessons when Joy's around. How did you know?"

After eating the last piece of his hot dog, he replied, "Sally told me they quit after last year."

The Loop gave the Pet trainer a crooked smile, "I'm glad she did tell you that. Now you know what an ass Joy is."

"It's ok." His found a trash can and threw away his napkins and paper dog holder. Allison threw away hers too.

She was deep in thought of the short program for Sectionals. Her mind was thinking on how to tamper with Sally's skating gear. An evil idea came to mind.

Now, she would definitely need Richard's help too.

After the figure friend's trip to the beach, Danny and Butch were back in their unit home and settled in for bed.

The Figure Instructor was inside her empty loft. Her legs lumbered off for her bathroom. She wanted to take a long warm shower. She took off her clothes and stood in her shower area. Her body was washed and hair was clean. She dried herself and hair.

Fifteen minutes later, wrapped in only a light purple wool towel, Allison went in her closet to put on black sweats and her favorite purple t-shirt. Her phone was ringing on her dock stand at the nightstand. She rushed out of her closet for her phone.

"Hello?"

"You okay, Ally-Loop?"

She happily breathed out, "Sorry, McCarthy. I was in my closet to get ready for bed."

He teased, "Good time to call you then, huh?"

The Loop giggled, "Yup."

She laid on her bed with her phone on her left ear.

"How are you?" Captain McCarthy wondered.

"A little nervous for Nationals and doing the Pact's plan." Her scared voice answered.

"Baby, you know I'll be with you for the entire program." McCarthy soothed her. "I even made arrangements to get out of Calgary, Alberta early for a private flight to San Jose Wednesday morning."

"Ah, Rich," Ally protested, "aren't you going be too tired to do that?"

Richard chortled, "I can always sleep during my flight and sleep some more at the Rink's Hotel with you."

"Good point." She contently spoke. "What time would you be there?"

"I was told the plane would land around eight a.m." The hockey dude explained.

"I'll be there." The Loop added, "There is one important thing that needs to be done without Daniel, Rich."

"What's that?" The puck chaser questioned the figure jumper.

"Could you use some of your 'special privileges' for not just the rink, but also for the Hotel?

Strict McCarthy wondered, "What are you thinking about doing?"

"I want to break into Joy & Paul's room and steal Sally's skating gear." Ally stated.

Richard was disappointed in his girl. "Why?"

She explained, "So the world can see how much of a phony Sally is without her bought talent. Besides, I worked hard with my career while little miss sunshine had the easy way with her parents."

Now that the hockey Captain thought of it, he gave in. "All right. When did you want to do that plan?"

Ally snickered, "The last morning for Senior Ladies' before Danny and the Hunts leave for the rink."

Daniel Gray woke up next morning with glee in his heart. It was the USIS National's week and he would also get to see Sally again and again and again.

He proudly commanded to Butch, "Walk!"

Butch got up from his pillow and his little legs went to the kitchen for breakfast.

Danny got up from bed to follow his cute pooch for the kitchen too. Butch had some doggie meat and kibbles. His owner had orange juice and toast for his morning meal.

After they finished, Daniel traveled to the bedroom. He put on jeans, a black t-shirt, and his tennis shoes. He was ready to give Butch his walk.

The dog trainer reached the unit's front door and saw Butch sitting in front of the door. Danny leaned over Butch to attach him to his retractable leash.

They left together and their walk lasted forty minutes.

When the got back, Daniel changed his clothes, showered, put on his work clothes, and wished Butch a happy dog day.

It was eight-thirty a.m. Danny's car arrived at the Pet store's parking lot. He got out and walked to the back of the store's building. His legs moved through the doorway for the employee locker room. He stored his things in a locker box.

Before he left the room, he did remind himself to ask his boss, Jack Randell, if he could have the twenty-fifth through the twenty-eighth off from work.

Daniel Gray casually strolled over to his boss' office door. His left hand knocked on it. He waited a moment to get a response.

Jack's door opened and there was Mr. Randell looking surprised to see Danny at his office door.

"Daniel. What can I do for you today?" He happily replied.

Danny gulped, "I need to ask a little favor."

The Pet store's owner invited Danny into his office for a more private chat. They sat in chairs and the overall dog trainer was feeling scared to ask Jack for some time off from his job again.

"Sir, Joy Hunt invited me to go with her family to Nationals in San Jose this coming Wednesday and I was wondering if I can have the twenty-fifth through the twenty-ninth off?" The young man slowly requested clearly.

Jack told him, "Of course, Danny."

The manager leaned down for his schedule folder and penciled in Danny's days off.

"Thank you, Jack." Daniel sighed.

The boss stated, "Hope Sally wins."

Not this time, Jack. The Pet trainer snickered. *She really is not a true, passionate figure skater.*

"I hope so too." Danny cheerfully lied.

He got up from the chair and exit the office room. He went for the back utility room to do his normal chores before training time in the booth.

As he swept and mopped the floor, Daniel mumbled to himself, "So, tonight I'll call the house to see if Mom & Dad would look after Butch and pack up some stuff. On the twenty-fourth, I'll drop off Butch at the house after his afternoon walk. And on the twenty-fifth, I'll ride along with the Hunts to San Jose and not say a word about the exposing plan."

He was all set.

Danny hoped Ally & Rich would be ready too.

It was late at night when Daniel got himself ready for bed. His parents were happy to watch over Butch during his time at Nationals and could not wait to go to the wedding.

Ally also called him to ask him if he was getting ready to go with the Hunts. He was and Butch was going to be watched over by his folks.

The Loop felt satisfied that everything was going smoothly for Danny and the Hunts again. They both hoped not to have any more bumps on the road until the big wedding day.

She knew the morning of the last day of Nationals was going to be not a pretty sight for Danny. She really was going to 'tamper' with Sally's skating gear. It was for the best for all of them. Mostly for Sally because that way Ally would see Hunt play, or skate, fair for her last time out on the ice.

Danny's work shift on Tuesday went well and had a big surprise in the training booth. Bob and his pug, Smokey, came by to wish him &

Sally best of luck for Nationals. That made the Pet trainer's day to have a regular be considerate of his personal life.

After the shift, he went back to his unit and took Butch to the park. They played with other dogs. Danny greeted and petted other dogs too. The cute beagle was happy to play in the dog park.

The boys reached back in their unit home six-thirty that night. Danny fixed up burgers for the two of them. Butch enjoyed his share.

Seven-twenty p.m.

The dog trainer gathered all of Butch's supply essentials for his stay at the Gray's house. It was all stored in the trunk of his car.

He made it to his home, attached Butch to his short leash, and made sure the unit's front door was locked up before they walked down the stairs.

Danny told Butch, "You are going to stay with my folks for the rest of the week, Butchie-Wutchie."

The sweet-loving pooch looked a little sad to his owner's brown eyes. He wondered what he did wrong to make him stay with Danny's parents instead of him.

Both of them made it inside the car and drove off.

Seven-forty p.m.

Butch and Danny walked up the stairs to the Gray's front door. The human rang the door bell with his right hand since his left hand held Butch's leash.

The door opened and it was his mother dressed in tan pants and a bright colored multi-splash floral blouse.

"So good to see you again, son." She spoke.

They hugged each other and he gave Mrs. Gray Butch's leash. She held on the leas tight.

Danny turned around to go back to his car. He carried all of Butch's things in one trip.

He set up the fake grass on the second floor's bathroom. The ceramic bowls and dog food in the kitchen, play toys and brush in the living room.

Coming in the house from a late business meeting and dressed in his dark gray suit, white dress shirt, and dark blue tie, Mr. Gray met up with his wife and son the living room.

"Hey, Danny."

"Hi, Dad." He spoke back.

Acting like a proud father, he hugged Danny and told him, "Big day's coming up."

They parted from the short hug.

Daniel nervously said, "Yea, it is."

Mr. Gray gave his son a little bit of advice.

"Remember this, Danny: marriage is a road that man & wife go on together no matter what happens in life. If one does something and the other does something differently, it doesn't mean one has to give up their something so they can be together. All you need to do is remember your loved one in everything you do so you will always be together when man & wife cannot work hand-in-hand."

Mrs. Gray stood by her husband. Her left hand took his right hand and gave it a tight squeeze.

Danny's eyes were full of tears after hearing those wise words. He knew what his father was trying to say. *Just because Sally & I do different job professions, it does not mean we have to be in the same exact place in everything we do. Damn, Dad, I wish you had the chance to tell that to Joy Hunt.*

His speechless voice spoke, "Thank you, Dad."

He added to his mother, "Make sure Butch is happy and loved."

"We always do, Danny." Mrs. Gray promised.

Butch ran up toward his loving owner. Danny got down on his knees to give his dog his full attention. He hugged his sweet beagle with all his might.

During the hug, Daniel whispered, "I Love You, Butchie-Wutchie. Be good to my folks."

His arms let go of his cute pooch.

The well-trained beagle sat on the carpet floor, raised his left front paw, and Danny shook it in agreement.

Young Gray left the house and drove back to his unit.

He cried a little more in his sleep. The fatherly advice really opened his eyes, mind, and heart all together. He hoped that would he & Sally's life together after they were married.

The time was seven a.m. when Daniel Gray woke up in his lonely apartment unit. He had some breakfast, packed up his things in his roller suitcase and his skating bag, showered, cleaned his unit, put on nice jeans, his green t-shirt, tennis shoes, made sure his wallet, cell phone, keys, and everything in the unit was locked up.

He left his unit and felt ready for a two hour car ride with the Hunts to San Jose for the USIS National Champions for Sally Hunt and Allison Rigden.

That was not the only thing he was confident to go through. The Figure Pact's exposing plan had to be done for the last day of Senior Ladies' competition events. It would be the last time the world would hear of Sally Hunt, the sunshine figure champ.

His hands carried his luggage slowly down the stairs. He made it to the first floor without any problems. Standing by the building's front door, he checked on the time from his cell. 7:53 a.m. was said.

Then he looked up and saw the Hunt's ruby red SUV pulling up. It stopped by the curb. Danny got his skating bag and roller suitcase, walked through the front doors, and carefully walked down more stairs.

Out came Paul Hunt in comfy jeans and a light brown t-shirt from the driver's side.

"Nice to see you bright and early!" He happily announced.

To make sure that the Pact's plan would work, Danny decided not to speak to Paul or Joy. He only wish to talk to Sally about the wedding plans and her skating routines.

Both guys walked to the SUV's trunk.

Paul pulled the door up and Daniel put his bags with the Hunt's bags too. He did notice Sally's skating bag was not with the other bags.

His heart pounded forcefully and had a feeling the Pact's exposing plan maybe in trouble.

Mr. Hunt moved to the driver's door while scared young Gray headed for the left back door. Inside the back seat was Sally reading a really thick book.

Daniel got in the car and sat next to his fiancee.

"Good morning, Sally." He spoke softly.

He buckled his seat belt.

The sunshine blonde looked up from her book to see smily Danny sitting next to her. She smiled big and greeted back, "It's a wonderful morning for me, Daniel."

Paul Hunt started up the car.

Daniel Gray knew how to really make Sally more special to him than ever.

Just talk about her and skating terms. That satisfied his heart. *Spend sweet times with her before her routines and also, make sure Joy does not get into our conversations. The further away Sally is from her strict mother, the better she would feel to be on and off the ice.*

The SUV moved down the street and off to San Jose.

As the red SUV drove on highway 101, tired Allison Rigden was standing inside the brightly lit, busy Mineta San Jose International Airport building. She tried to calmly wait for Richard McCarthy's private flight from Calgary, Alberta, Canada.

She barely slept the night before. Her heart raced, her mind was thinking of a million things at once, and could not keep still.

Earlier that morning, when the time was quarter to five a.m., she went to her rink to do some skating. Ally endlessly worked on both of her routines for Nationals.

Nothing.

She even only did quad-quad combo jumps for a half hour and that did not make her sleepy or calm herself down.

Her voice cried out in her special ice rink, "I need Richard . . ."

After giving up skating in her rink, Allison left the abandoned building for her loft. She showered, slipped on jeans, a maroon t-shirt, and her purple N+ running shoes, had a little something to eat, called up McCarthy for a long chat, packed up her skating bag and a smaller roller suitcase bag in her Horundi's trunk, and immediately drove down to San Jose before Danny woke up from his bed.

The Nationals' event was not what scared her. It was Daniel being with the Hunts again. She feared Joy Hunt was going to know and destroy their hard-work plan.

Ally was in more fear without Rich by her side.

He would know how to deal with Joy Hunt on and off ice. What was more, in his team's chomping territory, the devil's bitch would get no special treatments there.

It was precisely eight o'clock when Ally's brown eyes saw Captain Richard McCarthy racing toward her without his team bag.

"Ally!" He shouted.

Their arms caught each other in a tight, tight loving embrace. Both their ears were hearing clicking noises. Their eyes noticed people from the press taking pictures of McCarthy & Rigden hugging each other in the airport.

Rich whispered, "Let's run."

Their arms dropped to their sides and both their legs dashed out of the building. They were running toward the parking garage.

Ally gasped out, "Where's your bag?"

Richard snickered, "I planned ahead and asked a secret helper to carry my bag and meet us by your car."

That's McCarthy. Always thinking two steps ahead. The Loop smug in her head.

The figure couple made it to the Horundi convertible and sure enough, an airport baggage man was standing next to Ally's car with Rich's team bag.

"Thank you, Ed." Captain McCarthy said.

Dressed in his blue and black baggage uniform, Ed quietly replied, "You're welcome, Richard."

The worker left the garage and went back inside the airport building for his baggage carousel station.

Ally turned off her car alarm.

Richard put his team bag in the trunk with Ally's roller suitcase. Then he went to the passenger seat. He sat down and buckled up.

"Ah, shit . . ."

"What's wrong?" Rich wondered.

Ally's brown eyes looked at the rear view mirror.

What was coming up from behind her car were three news station vans. She reversed quickly and stepped on the gas pedal. The cute white Horundi left the parking garage without being followed or bothered by the media.

The car ride lasted for ten minutes and traveled southeast from the airport. Ally's car pulled up at the Rink Hotel's parking lot. She parked her convertible and pushed the trunk's button on the bottom part of her door. Richard rushed out of the car to grab his and Ally's bags from the trunk's box.

Allison locked up her car.

Both figure lovers walked inside the hotel building together with their own skating bags.

The front counter people were not surprised to see McCarthy & Rigden enter in the hotel hand-in-hand. The manager, George, who was dressed in a super nice dark blue suit and tie, saw the figures and greeted them warmly.

"Richard, Allison, welcome!"

"Hi, George." McCarthy replied back as he and Ally stepped up to the marble counter.

"Checking in?" The manager asked.

Ally squat down to dig in her skating bag to get out her print out reserved room in her purple folder. Also in her folder were special check-in forms for Nationals. She zipped up her bag and handed over her reservation forms.

George did some typing on a desktop computer and spoke, "Thank you, Miss Rigden. You're all checked in."

He handed her two cream color hotel key cards.

Ally put one in her right front jeans pocket and gave the other one to Richard. He put his in his front right jeans pocket.

The hotel's manager with dark brown hair and light green eyes offered the couple, "Anything else?"

Before Richard told George his plan, he leaned forward to question him, "Can we talk to you privately?"

The hotel manager looked at his other workers at the front desk. They were busy with their work and it would be all right if he left them alone for a few minutes.

"Sure." George answered. "Let's go to the dining room."

All three left the front desk and went to the dining room. They sat in wooden cushioned chairs around a small circular table. Ally & Rich's bags were on the floor by their feet.

George quietly asked, "Now, what's up, Captain?"

Richard whispered, "We need you to help us break some rules for Nationals."

The hotel manager knew this was a bad idea. Except, Richard McCarthy was a good guy and he would not ask him for something this stupid if there was no other choice.

"Why?"

Ally spoke, "Me, Richard, and Sally Hunt's fiance, Daniel Gray, know Joy is doing a cheating scheme for her daughter's skating career. We want to expose their secret to the world on the last event day for Senior Ladies."

"And where's the 'breaking rule' part?" The hotel manager leaned in close with his crossed arms on the table.

"I need to break into Joy & Paul's hotel room and take Sally's skating gear before her long program." She firmly explained.

George softly sighed, "I kinda knew the Hunts were up to something suspicious during the 2009 Regionals event. They would leave or come into the hotel without Sally's skating bag or gear. I'll be happy to help you guys out."

"Give me a call after they check in and I'll come down to get spare card keys for their room." The hockey dude requested.

"Will do." The hotel manager agreed.

He left the athletic couple to get back to the front desk.

Richard & Allison were left alone at the table.

Both of them did feel happy and nervous of the plan.

"What shall we do now, Captain McCarthy?" Ally tiredly asked.

He replied, "I think we need to take a warm bath."

His right hand held her left hand. His fingers were caressing her soft skin. He continued on, "And then sleep in all day."

The Loop closed her eyes and moaned, "Mmmmmm . . . that sounds wonderful."

They left the table with their bags for Ally's guest room on the third floor.

Inside her room, their three bags were in the closet and the figure lovers were taking each other's clothes off in the bathroom. Hotty Rich McCarthy turned on the tub's faucet. Warm water was filling up the white color tub.

Richard stepped in the warm tub first.

Ally got in next. She sat behind the hunky player with him in between her legs. She was glad she got the Tiger Shark's team Captain in her clutches. Her arms wrapped around his stud-looking athletic bod.

They leaned back happily together in the tub. His head laying comfortably on her chest. Ally felt the puck chaser body's be really relaxed after being in her arms for long five minutes.

"Allison?" He whispered lovingly.

She smiled and her fingers combed his short brown hair. "Yes, Richard?"

He breathed out, "I Love You . . ."

That made Ally's heart feel good.

"I Love You too . . ."

"And you are going to kick those Senior Ladies' asses in both programs." He teased.

Ally squeezed him tighter. "Good."

Rich slightly turned his head to his left with his cheek on the curve of Ally's moist neck. He let his head nuzzle her a little. To him, the best thing to have Ally-Loop in his life was he did not have to be Captain Number 65 all the time.

His hands took her arms off of him. He twisted around in the warm water to see her sad face. She did not want to let him go. McCarthy leaned in to kiss Rigden's soft lips.

From their kiss, the soaked hunky player got up on his feet and pressed down the tub's lid switch. The warm water was going down the drain pipe.

Allison got up on her feet. She exit the bathroom to get her body wash, shampoo, conditioner, brush, and clean comfy bed clothes out of her small roller suitcase.

Richard fixed up the shower head and they both made each other squeaky clean.

When they were both clean and dry from their shower, Ally & Rich climbed into the King's size bed for a long nap.

Outside the Rink's hotel building was the Hunt's red SUV reaching the parking lot. From Joy's eyes, she saw Ally-Loop's white convertible in the lot. Her mind scolded, *How did she get here first? Something's not right.*

Danny & Sally were in the back seat being quiet and holding each other.

Paul announced, "We're here."

Everyone in the SUV got out with their things. Paul & Joy walked in first with the young lovers behind them. They headed for the front counter.

Sally & Daniel waited by the staircase. They constantly whispered to each other, 'I Love You . . .'

The Pet trainer felt bad of doing the plan. But to make Ally win the gold and take Sally out of the figure skating world, he and his figure friends had to expose the Hunt's cheating scheme.

The Hunt couple left the counter desk.

Joy told her daughter & Danny, "Here are your key cards."

She handed them their cards.

"I hope you two will be good. No more mishaps from either of you. Understand?" Joy Hunt strictly requested.

Danny & Sally answered, "Yes, Ma'am."

"Excellent."

Paul jumped in, "I think we all can use a long nap."

The four figures walked up the stairs with their bags to the third floor.

Behind their backs, George reached for his phone to call up a room on the third floor.

Paul & Joy had their own room. Sally's was next to her parents. Daniel's was on the other side of the Hunt's shared room.

The Pet trainer settled in his room by changing his clothes into something more comfortable, cleaning himself in the bathroom, and laying on the King size for a soothing rest.

A few doors not far from Daniel's guest room, Ally was peacefully asleep in bed when Richard answered the cord phone's ringing.

"Yeah?"

It was George.

"Joy & Paul Hunt just checked in." The manager professional said.

"Thank you." Richard replied.

He placed the phone back on the cradle, lifted up from bed, and left the room without waking up Ally-Loop.

When Daniel Gray woke up from a four hour nap, he felt well-rested. He did have dreams what the last day of Nationals was going to be like. He and Richard secretly going to the other rink behind Joy Hunt's red SUV, video taping the 'figure puppet' and the man with the laptop, driving back to the Tiger Shark's home arena, and showing the world Sally Hunt's unearned skating talents.

The Pet trainer continued to feel bad of exposing who his fiancee really was in competitive figure skating. There were times he wanted to let go of his plan and let Sally win like always, but he could not forget what she told him on New Year's Eve in his bed.

Daniel, I'm going to tell Mommy & Daddy I'm quitting figure skating . . .

Those words were all Sally's, not her Mommy's.

The only thing Danny hoped was Sally not going to hate him for doing it. And to Ally & Rich.

Daniel sat up in his hotel bed to stretch his tired body. He did feel hungry for some food. He was on his feet and decided to take a shower.

Ten minutes after having getting clean in his hotel room, Danny was all dried, wearing jeans, a cotton dark green t-shirt, his tennis shoes, and had his belongings in his jeans pockets. He wanted to check up on Sally.

Silently, Danny left his room with his key card and went over to his fiancee's guest room without Joy & Paul's guest room door opening up by his surprise. His eyes noticed there was no note on Sally's door. He raised his right fist to the door and knocked it three times.

The Pet trainer waited patiently.

The door opened and who popped behind the door was Joy Hunt in navy blue sweat pants and a short sleeved bright red shirt. Her hair was back in a ponytail.

His eyes could not see Sally in the background.

"Daniel, we're kinda busy now." Mrs. Hunt hastily spoke to her future son-in-law. "Come back in two hours."

She immediately slammed the door.

He sighed with heavy disappointment.

Danny knew what was going on in Sally's room. *Joy's making the finishing touches for Sally's skating costumes, microchips, wires, her hairband, and her 'special skates'.*

A new question got his attention.

If Sally was wearing microchips and flexible wires, how are they concealed so well under Sally's costumes?

His ears heard another door opening and closing not far from Sally's hotel room. He turned his head to his right and noticed the Loop & Number 65 leaving a guest room together. They were both in jeans and wearing their own team's jackets.

Richard in his soft shell black coat with the team's logo on the left front side and turquoise patches on the sleeves.

Allison in her dark red polyester fleece coat with zipper at the front and zipper pockets at both sides. There was a pair of embroidered white figure boots over her heart.

"Ally, Rich."

Both of the couple's eyes looked at Danny standing in front of a guest door.

"Hey, Danny." Ally spoke.

She wondered, "Locked out again?"

"No." Daniel sighed.

He slumped down his head and breathed out, "Joy's in Sally's room and I'm not allowed to see her."

Captain Richard McCarthy's left arm went across Ally's shoulders and replied, "Don't worry, Danny. In a few days, Joy will get a run on her money when she mistreats a good friend with the Tiger Sharks in their home rink."

That did make Danny feel a little better. He raised his head up and tried to smile.

"We're going to downtown for some fun. You want to come?" Allison offered.

The Pet trainer knew if he did, he would feel left out to be around Ally & Rich and not be close to his fiancee. He answered, "No thanks. I think staying here would make things better for the Hunts."

"That's ok, Danny." Richard add annoyingly, "They probably have a schedule for you to follow tomorrow."

"We'll get together tomorrow morning in my room and detail the plan more," suggested Ally-Loop.

Daniel replied, "I'll be there."

He turned around to go back to his guest room.

After a short nap and calling up his parent's to check up on Butchie-Wutchie, Danny heard a knock on his hotel door. He walked to the door. From the little glass hole on the door, his eyes saw a surprise in front of the door. He opened the door and smiled his biggest smile.

"Sally . . ."

She was dressed in a cute long sleeved, v-neck, knee-length skirt, greenish-gray color dress and her feet wore her low heeled gray shoes. Her blond hair was in a high curly ponytail. Her right arm carried her small gray hand bag.

"Hi, Danny." She sweetly spoke.

He stepped closer and wrapped his arms around her. Sally slipped her arms around him. They both squeezed each other tightly.

His sad voice said, "I miss you."

The blonde champ let out, "I missed you too."

At the same time, the lovers took a step back and their lips sweetly kissed each other. The kiss ended in a few long moments.

Daniel asked, "What's up?"

Sally answered, "Mommy & Daddy wants us to meet them in the dining room."

Chagrin young Gray wondered, "Am I dressed appropriately?"

Her bluish-gray eyes looked at his apparel.

"Um, could you put on a nicer shirt?" She questioned her fiance.

Danny went inside his room for his roller suitcase. He found his dressy white shirt. His fingers pulled off his green t-shirt and started to button up his shirt.

Sally followed him and caught a sight of his toned and sculpted arms, chest, and abs. She was impressed of Ally's off-ice training.

His brown eyes looked down and figured out what Sally was admiring at. They both blushed and laughed a little.

Miss Hunt tried to calmly say, "Um, Ally's pilate workouts did you wonders."

Young Mr. Gray respond, "Yes-um, they did."

His shaky fingers could not button up his shirt.

Kind Sally walked in front of him and she buttoned his dress shirt. She was having fun dressing up her special dog trainer.

"You didn't have to do that." Grateful Daniel replied.

When she finished, Sally said, "Yes, I did."

She lifted up her sunshine face and explained, "You've been so wonderful to me when I needed to be away from Mommy, I just wanted to treat you nicely."

Danny leaned down and softly kissed the loving girl in front of him. His thoughts were, *I'm sorry that Ally, Rich, and I have to ruin your long program. I can't bear to let you be your mother's ticket to get an Olympic gold medal.*

As he pulled away, Sally told him, "We need to go to the dining room."

She turned away from him and left the room first.

The dog trainer's heart was crushed.

"I Love You too . . ." he mumbled to himself unhappily.

His legs moved from the guest room, down the stairs, and made it to the dining room. He saw Paul Hunt in nice black slacks and a light gray dress shirt and Joy Hunt in cream dress pants and dark green blouse.

All three Hunts were sitting at a medium size dark brown square table with four chairs around it. They were waiting for Daniel to arrive.

He entered the room and made his way toward the Hunt's table.

Joy's green eyes saw Daniel Gray heading over to the table. Her heart did not want him there. She wondered if she could trick him into ruining Ally's quad-quad combo jump.

That would not be a bad idea. She snickered in her head. *Sally will be his if he could 'tamper' Ally's skates to make her not do her special jump combo.*

Then Danny sat in the empty chair between Paul and Sally. He greeted them, "Hi."

"Evening, Daniel." All the Hunts spoke in unison.

They noticed a waiter coming to the table and handed them menus. For a few minutes, the group was discussing what to have for dinner that night.

An hour later, everyone at the small dinner table finished having their delicious meals. They all wanted to turn in for the night.

Before leaving the table, Joy said, "Tomorrow, the Senior Ladies' event will begin mid-afternoon with the Opening Ceremony and then the short program. Lots of cameramen and crew will be there. Daniel, I expect you to be on your best behavior while being around the media and such."

He answered strongly, "Yes, Ma'am."

Paul firmly replied, "And make sure you stay away from Ally-Loop while the cameras are on so the press won't think Sally's fiance is a cheater."

Speak for your wife. His mind thought.

"Yes, Sir." Danny answered.

Joy told her daughter, "Sally, let's get you ready for bed."

The cute blonde spoke, "Okay, Mommy."

Everyone left the table and walked up stairs to the third floor.

After Danny & Sally kissed good-night, Joy asked, "May I have a word with you, Danny?"

Great . . . he sarcastically wondered, *what does she want now?*

He had his full attention to his future mother-in-law in an empty hotel hallway.

She started out, "I know you love Sally and I'm sure you want her to win, don't you?"

Daniel lied, "Yes, I do."

Mrs. Hunt did not buy a word he said.

"I know you're lying to me." Her superior voice spoke. She walked around him. "I know about Ally's quad-quad combo jump. I saw you there. Cheering for her instead of your own fiancee. You-are-a-figure-cheater . . ."

He was not going to give in to Joy's sinister lies or pessimistic words. He stood strong and acted like Allison Rigden & Richard McCarthy together.

"I was only cheering for my Figure Instructor's skating skills, not her as a woman." Danny protested.

"Doesn't matter." Mrs. Hunt stopped walking around and eyed at the young man. "You rather be with that whore figure tamp than my own daughter."

The Pet trainer snarled, "No."

The horrid figure coach snickered, "I knew about her 'almost rape' story. Truth is: she wanted to get on with Big Mike or any other hockey player that came by her way. Why do you think she's always eyeing at PHL players?"

"You don't know Ally's side." Danny hissed. He wanted to tell her the real story, but he knew he had to close his mouth before spilling out her & McCarthy's relationship.

"Think about this, young Gray." Joy offered. "You want to win my daughter without doing figure skating, don't you?"

"It was what I wanted before I tried ice skating." Daniel expressed out. "Now, I really like to figure skate."

The red haired woman huffed, "My husband may have skated for himself, but for someone like you to like this sport is not normal. I have a little tamper job for you."

She pressed on the Pet trainer's button more.

"If you do ruin Allison's skates, I can make your life more worth while than you working at your stinky Pet training job. No more work, no stress over other people's dogs, and you won't have to take of your beagle dog anymore."

Danny figured it was all 'just talk' from Joy Hunt.

He loved his job, showing their owners how to do dog training, and he would never stop loving or be Butch's care taker. More importantly, he did not have the heart to stoop to Joy Hunt's level by betraying his Figure Instructor.

"No, Joy." He firmly replied. "I made a promise to you & your husband and I am going to fulfill them."

Mrs. Hunt snarled, "Have it your way."

She turned her back on him and went to her & Paul's shared hotel room.

Her voice spoke, "Good evening."

Chapter Twenty-Three

Daniel Gray could not sleep.

It was 3:12 in the morning after looking at his cell for the thirtieth time. His heart was making him nervous and scared to face Nationals. He shifted in his hotel bed again.

After thinking on what to do, he got up from the comfy bed for a walk around the hotel building. He was dressed in black sweat pants, light blue t-shirt, and black thin socks. He slipped on his tennis shoes, grabbed his cell, and his room key cards.

Danny stepped out of his guest room to head down the stairway. Slowly and carefully making his way for the main hotel floor, his mind thought of what Joy Hunt was trying to do to Allison.

How can Joy be so selfish and demanding? Why didn't Paul win a gold medal himself and give it to Joy? Maybe I should ask them that question.

When he made it to the first floor, Danny wanted to go to the outdoor patio. It did not take him long to find it. The patio area was not unoccupied.

His brown eyes noticed another person sitting lonely in the dark of night and sitting on a wooden, cushioned chair. He knew who that was.

"Ally?"

The person turned its head and sure enough it was Ally-Loop. Her eyes were full of tears and her cheeks had tear stains on them. She was dressed in jeans, her N+ running shoes, and a Tiger Shark's black team jersey. Her feet were under her legs.

"Hi, Danny." Her sad voice spoke.

She sniffled.

He sat on another wooden chair next to her. He wondered, "What's wrong?"

Ally started to cry again. Warm tears were stinging her eyes and cheeks. The jersey's long black sleeves were whipping away her tears.

Danny knew it must be serious since she & Richard were not together. He hesitantly asked, "Did you & McCarthy have a fight?"

She bawled out louder than she did before and the sleeves covered her face.

Poor, Ally. McCarthy's a total duchebag to ditch Ally-Loop for someone other skanky bitch. His sad heart thought.

A minute later, Ally uncovered her face and answered, "He's, um, happily sleeping now."

She shifted herself to cross her legs.

Her body leaned down to reach for something under her chair. It was a small purple spiral notebook. Hanging on the metal spring was a purple gel pen. She opened the book to write something in it.

"Sleeping without you?" Daniel curiously wondered.

She handed him the book and it read: *Talk in code, Danny, in case Joy or someone from the press is spying on me.*

"Yes, he's resting." Ally said casually.

Danny handed back her book.

Without looking at her figure student, Allison wrote some more and asked, "Why aren't you sleeping?"

The Pet trainer stuttered, "I-uh, I fffeellll neerrrvouuusss fffooorrr my fiunceeee's ppprrooogrrammmm tomorrow."

She stuck out her notebook and he quickly grabbed it.

I know what Joy asked you to do. Thank you for sticking up for us. The notebook read.

"It's okay to feel nervous for all the figures during Nationals." Allison assured him.

He wrote with the purple pen, *How?*

Danny passed her book back and saw his question.

"In fact," she started to write again, "it's natural to be scared to perform in front of millions people out on the ice."

She showed him what she wrote.

George and his staff members promised to keep a close eye and ear when the Hunts are around. It's also good Joy doesn't have a clue about the Figure Pact's plan.

"Good advice to remember, Ally." Danny sacredly spoke. He took the pen to write something for Ally.

Her eyes saw the note he wrote.

Why are you out here?

The Figure Instructor softly answered, "I'm not tired."

Daniel leaned over and whispered, "What about Richard?"

She whispered back, "He understands my situation. He's the same way before a PHL game. I pretend to sleep and pay special attention for him. What gets to me is that no matter how tough a person is, especially for someone like Captain McCarthy, they are afraid to live through a competitive sport, or a war, even if they do say they love the sport and enjoy being out on the ice shooting the puck to win goals. All they do is keep surviving from what they learned and know what to do in certain situations. They do the best they can because they may never know if it is their last or not."

What Ally stated really caught Danny's attention.

In other words, we are human and very few males can be open about their feelings and emotions during his fighting years. During the top of their game and the down falls. Typical fights could be building up a career, being an athlete, a soldier of war, or just working, day and night.

That was why Allison & Richard were made for each other. They both fight on ice, but off ice, they care for each other as lovers and they could make each other stronger than ever before.

Daniel wondered if the Loop & Number 65 knew that reason too. The figure student declared, "I think I'm able to get some sleep now."

He slowly lifted up from the chair he sat in and went back inside the hotel building. His feet climbed up the stairs, walked through the long hallway, and made it back to his hotel room.

Just when he was about to use his key card, his ears heard, "You okay, Danny?"

He knew where that voice came from. His body turned around to see McCarthy in the hallway. The hockey dude was only dressed in dark green sweat pants and was barefoot.

"I couldn't sleep earlier." The Pet trainer admitted. "I can now."

Richard crossed his muscular arms over his buffed chest. He asked, "Talking to Ally?"

Danny confessed, "Yes."

He was afraid the Tiger Shark's Captain was going to beat him down to a pulp by talking to his girl behind his back.

"She's a good person to talk to." Rich sighed and dropped his arms to his side.

Daniel was glad Number 65 did not feel the urge to punch him on the face. He listened more to the puck chaser.

"For my time of need as a pro-athlete, she knows how to help me and the team out. That's all Ally-Loop knows in life. Teamwork and being a fair judge. That was another reason why I was named 'Captain.' What she taught me was learn about the other players' moves and it made me understand how to beat the opposing team."

"She is fair and tough." Danny squirmed.

"Hey, I'm not going to beat you up for talking to Allison." Richard calmly said. "If it was another PHL player or some other bozo tailing her from behind, I literally would act like Number 65 off ice."

The Pet trainer nervously replied, "Wouldn't be the first time I was beaten up by a hockey player."

Rich was confused. "Why do you say that?"

Daniel told him, "Just before Sally & I first met, I was in a brawl against an old bully, Hefty Walter, and Sally and her figure friends came into my rescue."

With a crooked smile on his face, McCarthy spoke, "I knew you weren't hockey material, Gray, and I'm glad to learn Walter's real reason to leave the sport."

The Pet trainer still remembered that night. He closed his eyes and thought over every detail from his seventeenth birthday night. His friends ditching him at the skating rink, facing Walter's punches, meeting the woman of his dreams, and a surprised fuzzy friend remained faithful to him for four long years.

Daniel opened his tired brown eyes.

Richard was leaning against the opposite wall from Danny's hotel room.

"Thanks for being right, McCarthy." Was the last thing the dog trainer told the puck chaser that early morning.

Rich watched Daniel get into his guest room and shut the door behind him. The third floor hallway was quiet until the hockey Captain's ears listened closely to someone's footsteps coming up the stairs.

He walked over to a corner, his eyes looked down the stairs, and his heart smiled when he saw slumping Ally-Loop heading for the third floor.

She raised up her head and saw Rich standing on the top step. Her legs raced to the top step.

Richard opened his arms and caught her.

Their arms wrapped around each other tightly and comfortably. Both their hearts were filled with love.

With her head on his warm smooth chest, Ally asked softly, "Are they all asleep?"

McCarthy strongly stated, "Yes."

He also put in, "Had a good talk with Danny?"

She pulled back and her loving brown eyes told him, "Joy Hunt doesn't know he's a snitch."

"Sweet." He bent forward to kiss Ally's lips.

Number 65 teased, "Good thing none of the other Tiger Sharks aren't here to see you in my favorite jersey."

They both let out soft giggles.

From their laughter, Allison said, "I think I'm ready to get some sleep myself."

"Come on."

Their arms dropped to their sides and strolled toward Ally's guest room hand-in-hand.

After sleeping for seven hours, Danny woke up in his hotel bed knowing today was part one of the exposing plan. His cell phone started to ring and he answered it, "Hello?"

"Rise and shine, Figure Gray."

He chuckled, "Thanks for the wake-up call, Ally."

She replied, "Meet me & Richard at my hotel room in fifteen minutes."

"Will do." The Pet trainer ended the call.

He got up, showered, and put on jeans and a light blue t-shirt. His feet wore his tennis shoes. Both his jeans pockets held his cell, wallet, and his hotel room card keys. He carried his red folder containing the Pact's plan steps.

He casually left his hotel room for Allison's guest room. He turned to his right and his eyes caught something on Sally's door. It was a white piece of paper taped on.

Danny,

Mommy & Daddy, and I want to see you in the dining room at 10:00 a.m.

Love you . . .

He checked on the time from his phone.

It said 9:40 a.m.

There was plenty of time for him to talk to the Pact and meet the Hunts in the dining room without anyone getting suspicious that something illegal was going to happen in Nationals.

Danny found Ally's hotel room and knocked on the door. The door opened by smily Ally-Loop in black sweats and a purple t-shirt.

"Come on in, Daniel." She invited him.

The room was big with a little living area, kitchen bar, and two other door ways for the bathroom and the bedroom. He sat on a cushioned chair in the living area.

Ally went to the bedroom for something.

Daniel's eyes saw the bathroom door open and out came a whistling Richard McCarthy dressed in jeans and a well-fitted black t-shirt. His hands were rubbing his wet brown hair with a small white hand towel.

The hockey dude's hazel eyes saw Daniel in the room. He stopped using the towel and tossed it on bathroom's floor.

"Hey, Danny."

"Morning, McCarthy." The Pet trainer spoke back.

Ally came out of the bedroom with her purple folder in hand. She sat in the sofa by Danny's chair. Rich sat next to Ally on the sofa.

"Well, gentlemen . . ." Ally started out, "It's a big day and we have been waiting for this a long time. Danny, what's the Hunts plan for today?"

Danny replied, "I have to meet them in the dining room ten a.m."

"Oh." Disappointed Allison sighed, "Maybe we need to wait a little longer."

"That's ok." The dog trainer assured his Figure Instructor. "I'm sure this won't take too long."

Rich said, "Ally & I will be in the dining room too."

The hockey Captain got up from the sofa for his hockey bag. He found a turquoise and white color Tiger Shark logo cap and his black shades. He slipped on his hat backwards and the shades over his golden hazel eyes.

"Now Joy would not know who I am." He snickered.

"I think I need to go." Danny hurriedly stated.

The Pet trainer got up from the chair and left Ally's hotel room. He quickly went inside his room. He put his red folder on his bed before leaving for the hotel's dining room.

After going down the stairs, Danny arrived where the Hunts was located at and having breakfast. Joy & Paul were having waffles, coffee, eggs, bacon, and small bowl of fruits. Sally was having toast, three different types of fruits, and milk to drink.

Daniel calmly walked in the room.

Paul saw Danny heading toward the table. He said, "Come on over, Daniel."

Sally was slowly eating a banana.

Joy was looking at a paper booklet for Nationals.

Danny sat next his fiancee.

"What's for breakfast?" He cheerfully wondered.

Right on cue, a waitress handed him a menu and left the table. Daniel asked Sally, "How are you, Sally-babe?"

Her bluish-gray eyes looked at him and answered, "I'm a little nervous, Danny."

His left hand took her right hand and gave her a big squeeze. "I'll be there to cheer for you."

The couple leaned in for a long kiss.

When their kiss ended, Danny's brown eyes looked at breakfast section in the menu. He also noticed Ally walking in the room. A minute later, the disguised Tiger Shark's Captain appeared in the room too.

The Loop sat by a table at one far end of the room and Number 65 at the opposite end with the Hunt's table in center point. Both their eyes spied at the Hunt's table if Joy was going to anything funny during breakfast time.

Joy looked up from the booklet and her green eyes saw Ally-Loop sitting in the dining room all by her lonesome self. She was talking to a waiter for her breakfast meal.

She told Danny, "Daniel, you, Sally, and Paul will meet me at the front door six p.m. today. Try not to get yourself into any mischief."

He agreed, "All right, Joy."

The waitress who gave Danny his menu came back to the table and he ordered his food. *Something healthy would please Joy. Maybe more healthier than Sally's meal.*

He spoke, "Just orange juice and oatmeal for me."

The waitress left the table for the swinging kitchen doors.

Mrs. Hunt was surprised at Daniel's order. She questioned her future son-in-law, "You sure you don't want anything else?"

The Pet trainer explained, "It's going to be a busy day for Sally and something light to eat sounds good to me."

Stunned Joy dropped the subject or an idea to argue against his requested meal.

His brown eyes watched Sally finish her meal and surreptitiously looked at Rich & Ally's tables. They were having light meals too.

All three figures in the Pact did certain hand signals to each other. Rich gently tipped his sunglasses, Ally's fingers played with her hair, and Danny lightly tapping his fingers on the wooden table.

It was ten till eleven when the dog trainer completed his oatmeal and juice and all the Hunts left the table. Danny did not mind that. Sally gave him a kiss before leaving the dining room.

The Loop & Number 65 got up from their tables and went to sit with Danny.

"The meeting is at 6 p.m. in front of hotel's door." He whispered to the group.

McCarthy slightly turned his head. He noticed Joy Hunt leaving the hotel building so soon. He said, "Let's go."

The three left the dining room.

Joy drove in her red SUV from the lot.

Richard closely watched the red SUV going west from the Rink's Hotel building. He and his figure friends went for his truck. He unarmed the truck with his key chain. The black truck's lights flashed orange colors.

Danny opened the passenger door. He saw a box wrapped in dark blue wrapping paper on the seat. His hands lifted the box off the seat and sat down with the box on his lap.

Ally & Rich kissed and the Pet trainer's ears heard them say, "Be careful.", "We'll be okay, Ally-Loop."

McCarthy got in the truck, started it up, and drove out of the lot.

Danny asked, "What's this for?"

"Open it."

Reluctantly, his fingers carefully pulled the wrapping paper off the box. The tan box was taped up too. Danny took the clear tape off the lid's flap and opened it.

What he saw in there was a surprise. He pulled out an ordinary looking black baseball cap. He wondered what he was going to do with that.

As the truck moved south from the hotel building, Rich spoke, "It's a cap with a secret camera inside."

Danny flipped the cap upside down and saw a thin black camera was attached to the upper part of the cap. And when he looked at the front view of the cap, his eyes saw a very tiny camera lenses on the cap's hole.

"Very cool, McCarthy." Then Figure Gray questioned the hockey Captain, "How do you turn it on?"

Number 65 spoke out, "I'll show you when we reach the rink."

Five minutes later, the truck arrived at the rink Richard knew Joy was going to be at. Her red SUV was in the lot. The parking lot looked deserted.

Rich explained, "There's a button on the camera's bottom part to turn on and off. Don't turn it on before going into the rink. Keep yourself hidden and be quick."

"I will." Danny promised.

He carefully held the cap in his left hand and exit the shiny black truck. He slowly walked inside the empty ice rink.

The inside of the building was very cold to him.

Daniel made it inside the rink.

Sure enough, Joy, her 'figure puppet', and the man with the laptop were there getting Sally's 'MMMs'. He turned the cap upside down, pressed the tiny silver button on the camera, and he slipped the black cap on his head.

On his knees, Danny hid himself behind the rink's wall. He carefully listened to Joy's skating instructions.

"From the beginning!" She shouted to her 'puppet'.

Classical music was playing and the figure girl was skating Sally's short program.

When the routine was over, the man with the laptop announced, "That was perfect!"

"Excellent!" Joy declared loudly.

Danny hastily took the cap off and pressed the camera's silver button again. The camera stopped working. He left the rink in a hurry. Joy, the man with the laptop, or the blue eyed figure girl did not see him in the rink.

At the parking lot, Danny ran toward Richard's truck. He got in and breathed out, "Go!"

Rich knew Ally's figure student had done a good job to get the taping evidence. The truck made it the Rink's hotel lot in ten minutes. Both guys got out of the truck and rushed back to Ally's hotel room.

Inside her room, Allison was playing on her black color laptop and sitting on the bed. She could not wait to see what Danny had video tape of Joy and her thieving group.

Her ears heard a bleeping noise coming from her door's lock. *The guys must be back.*

The door opened and who came in were Danny and Rich. They were smiling. Must be good news.

Daniel handed Ally his baseball cap. "Hey, Ally."

"Hi, Danny." She said back.

Richard gave the Loop the camera's special black UBS cord. He & she sat on the bed.

Danny found a wooden chair and sat next to the bed.

Ally connected the cord to the camera and her laptop. It was buffering up a video program from the camera. After doing a few clicks with the computer's built-in mouse pad, the video program showed what Danny had caught at Joy's secret ice rink.

The clipping showed Joy out on the ice with a figure girl with brown hair and a peach color long sleeved and turtleneck shirt. The 'figure puppet' did look familiar to Ally.

Her heart was struck with a little flashback in her mind. She closed her brown eyes and she felt as if she was a little girl. The Figure Instructor opened her eyes. She wondered where she seen that girl before.

All three figures watched the 'puppet' do Sally's short program, Joy yelling at the figure to do a quad-quad combo jump, and the man with the laptop at the stands from Ally's laptop screen.

The Loop was excited to show this to the world.

"You did wonderful, Danny." Ally praised her figure student.

"Thank you."

An important thought came to his mind, "What about Sally's routine?"

Happy Richard respond, "That's my job. I'm going to be in the Zamboni's box since I'll be disguised as the resurfacer for the events today."

"Sounds good, McCarthy." Danny thought that was good cover-up.

The time was close to noon.

Allison told the guys, "I need to get ready."

She turned off her laptop, gave Rich the black baseball cap, and got up from the bed. Her lithe form gathered her skating gear in the closet.

"To play it safe, Rich & I will go to the rink separately." She suggested.

Daniel left the guest room first and went to his room. He laid on the King size bed. He did do a good job for the Loop.

Phase one was done. Rich got Phase two. The twenty-eighth would be Phase three and Danny's turn. The hardest part was Phase four: showing the world what a phony Sally Hunt really was in figure skating.

The dog trainer was all set at ten till six that evening.

He showered, put on nice tan pants, black dress shirt, polished black dress shoes, and was ready to face Nationals with the Hunts. His cell and wallet with the room card keys inside the bill fold were in his pant pockets.

Danny walked out of the guest room, down the stairs, and saw all the Hunts by the front door without Sally's skating gear. He stepped up to the group.

"I'm ready."

Joy was dressed in a professional navy blue suit and her hair was up in a bun. Paul was in a black suit and tie. Sally on the other hand was in jeans and a light pink sweater.

Daniel wondered why his fiancee would wear street clothes instead of something more professional.

They all left the hotel building together.

The hotel manager, George, was standing behind the front counter as he watched the group leave the hotel without Sally's skating bag. He hoped the Figure Pact knew what they were doing.

Paul drove the red SUV to the Tiger Sharks' main arena parking lot. Joy handed all of them their badges.

The huge silver building was very crowded with tens of thousands of skating fans, camera crews, and cars passing through. Mr. Hunt managed to get through the enormous thong of people and parked the SUV at the delivery truck's hub entrance.

Daniel knew Sally needed to get out sooner than he thought. He kissed her and whispered, "I Love You . . ."

"I Love You too, Danny . . ."

Joy got out the passenger side and Sally left the car too. Both girls ran for the back entrance.

Paul drove out of the truck's lot for the building's main lot. The gentlemen left the SUV and walked through the special front entrance with their lanyard badges around their necks. Hundreds of t.v. crews were taping, taking photos, or interviewing people for the figure skating event.

Danny keep close to his future father-in-law. He did not want to get lost in the large crowd of figure skating fans. They made it for the stands.

As they sat in their seat at the front row, Daniel's brown eyes saw the disguised Number 65 resurfacing the rink with the Tiger Shark's special Zamboni truck.

Rich saw Danny at the stands with Paul Hunt and he tugged on the black cap's rim. Danny pulled on his lanyard's red and blue color strap.

When the Zamboni left the rink and McCarthy pushed the extra snow and water off the ice with a long stick squeegee, a male announcer spoke in the mic, "Thank you, Captain McCarthy, of the Tiger Sharks."

The box was closed and locked up.

Paul cursed, "Why would a PHL player do shitty, low-life chore like that?"

Daniel was hurt. He wished he could tell Mr. Hunt about McCarthy's past. But he knew he could not tell out that secret to Paul.

The male announcer talked in the mic again.

"Hello skating fans and welcome to day five of the 2012 USIS National figure skating championship. This evening's event is the short program for Senior Ladies. Let's give around of applause to the ladies this evening!"

Eleven girls were skating out on the ice for the Opening Ceremony. The audience clapped and cheered for the ladies who were competing. After a minute watching the Senior Ladies practice their moves, Daniel did not see Sally out on the ice. He saw Ally dressed in her ruby red skating dress and her hair was pulled back in a low bun. She was not doing quads in her spin jumps.

Danny turned his head and asked Paul, "Where's Sally?"

Happy Paul spoke back, "Probably talking to the press with Joy."

That made the Pet trainer pissed off. He got up from his seat, walked up the stand's stairs, and needed to find Sally.

After walking around for ten minutes, he found Sally and Joy at a photo stand talking to a news crew. *What the hell are they doing? Sally should not be doing this, Joy.*

He noticed Sally was still in her jeans and light pink sweater. Her hair was in a French braid with her headband. She needed to get ready for her program, not be happy, sunshine Sally Hunt in front of the camera before the event was over. Joy looked calm and content to see her daughter babble with news reports. The scene made Danny feel sick.

He noticed the time from his cell. It was quarter after seven. He turned around and went back to the stands.

After Daniel left, Joy and Sally ended the interview to go to the girl's locker room. The room was empty. The Hunt girls went to work.

It was time for the Senior Ladies to do their short program. A lady announcer announced to the audience, "First up is Sally Hunt from Santa Rosa, California."

The audience cheered for the sunshine gold medalist figure skater. Danny noticed the man with the laptop stationed in one of the Tiger Shark's penalty boxes pretending to act like a staff member.

Daniel wondered if Joy paid someone to keep their mouth's shut so the man with the laptop could be there. He was worried Joy would know about the figure's exposing plan before Saturday.

Sally was skating out on the ice in her short program dress and her hair was all fixed up in so little time.

Her fiance figured, *She was wearing the microchips and flexible wires under her jeans and sweater all that time. And what Paul told me earlier with Sally and Joy talking to the press, that was a code term telling him the girls were waiting for the locker room to be empty.*

His brown eyes saw Richard standing in the Zamboni box doing the video taping of Sally's short program. The dog trainer kept cool during the first day for Senior Ladies' Nationals competition.

Paul Hunt was impressed that Danny could last through the sitting of a very big figure skating event. What surprised the former male figure was Daniel Gray was not only watching the figures skate, he was thinking of the moves they were doing.

It was nine p.m. and the Senior Ladies' short program event ended.

Sally Hunt was placed first and Allison Rigden was in second place. But would that be the last time for the scores to say that?

The time was ten-thirty p.m.

Tired Danny walked toward the Rink's Hotel building with the Hunts. Some people of the press followed the group, but four security guards told them to back off from the hotel's property. He & Sally went up the stairs together. Paul & Joy were behind them.

As they reached the third floor and her guest room, Sally told her love, "Thank you for being there for me."

His arms tightly wrapped around the blond's achy body. "I Love You . . ."

"And I Love You too . . ."

Their eyes meet each others and their lips softly touched. Danny was glad Sally was the only thing that made him keep his mouth shut about the figure's exposing plan. His heart knew it had to be done. He hoped Sally would not get hurt. Physically or emotionally.

The lovers part from their loving embrace so Ms. Hunt could get some sleep. Sally used her card key and walked inside her room alone.

Daniel stood in front of her closed door for a few moments. His head slump down and whispered, "Sleep well, Sally-babe."

He turned to his left and went to his room.

The Pet trainer changed out of his evening clothes and into black sweats and a long sleeved white shirt. He called up his folks to check on Butchie-Wutchie. Mrs. Gray told her son, "Butch really misses you, Daniel. He's sleeping on your old bed."

That touched his heart.

"Give him a big hug for me." He requested.

His mother smiled, "I always do."

They ended their phone conversation.

His tired eyes noticed the press was surrounding the parking lot from his window. Camera lights were flashing, lots of reports were chattering in their mic, and in the center of the commotion was a beautiful long stretched limo.

The limo's passenger door was opened from the chauffeur and out came Ally-Loop in jeans and her favorite purple long sleeved shirt. She refused to talk to the press. Two big security guards helped Allison through the large crowd of news reporters and camera crews.

Danny wondered why Richard McCarthy was not there to help her.

Then he remembered Ally's reason: The press and the media would invade them and ask them personal questions. They needed to stay strong during their fighting years.

He left his room and waited in the hallway for Ally to return to the third floor.

A few minutes later, Ally & Rich were heading to her hotel room together with her roller suitcase. The Loop did look tired from doing her routine and passing through the claustrophobic media crowd.

Both their eyes saw Daniel waiting for them.

"Hi, Danny." Allison breathed out.

She walked up to her student and they gave each other a big hug of skating success.

Daniel whispered, "Good job, teach."

Ally cried a little and her eyes were forming of warm tears. She stepped away from her figure friend. Richard used his key card for Ally's room and the three friends went inside.

Inside of the Hunt's couple room, Joy looked through the glass key hole on the door to see Ally and Danny go inside of the Loop's room.

She had a feeling those two figures were up to something suspicious.

What happened inside of Ally's hotel room was Danny and Richard were watching both of the tapings from her black laptop. The figure puppet and Sally's moves were exactly the same.

The tapings were saved on Ally's laptop and all three figures agreed to meet the next night for a late night skating session at the big, big skating rink after Rich finish resurfacing the rink from the Senior Men's short program.

Danny cautiously exit Allison's hotel room. He wanted to make sure Joy was not checking up on Ally or himself. His wary eyes saw no one in the hallway. He quickly found his key card, zipped to his hotel door, unlocked it, and changed his clothes for bed.

"That was close." He whispered.

The next morning, Daniel woke up around eight-thirty and got himself ready to see the Hunts. He wore his nice jeans, long sleeved dark blue shirt, and his tennis shoes. He left his room with his key card and cell phone in his jeans pockets.

His eyes did not see a note on Sally's guest room door. Danny decided to go to the dining room and see if they were there. At the dining room, he saw none of the Hunts there. He went to the parking lot. The red SUV was still there.

Danny thought, *Maybe they're still sleeping from last night's skating event.*

His legs moved out of the lot and into the Rink's Hotel building. He climbed up the stairs, reached the third floor, and he wanted to check on Sally. Just when he passed Joy & Paul's guest room, Danny heard the sound of an intense argument from the other side of the door.

He wondered, *What's going on now?*

The Hunt's couple door opened and angry Paul Hunt stormed out. The door slammed shut behind him and his face was surprised to see Daniel in the hallway.

"Daniel." He asked, "What brings you out here?"

"Waiting for you guys." The dog trainer admitted.

Mr. Hunt demanded, "Did you go into Allison's room last night?"

Ah, crud . . . the young man's mind said. *Joy's spying again.*

He gulped, "Yes."

"Why?" Paul sternly questioned his daughter's fiance.

Danny had to think of a good cover up lie.

"To discuss about my routine and figure terms." He explained.

Paul was stunned with disbelief.

"Look, son, I don't believe that." Figure Hunt said. "What were you doing in Ally's room?"

Before he could answer, Allison spoke, "Danny was helping me with my routine, Paul."

Mr. Hunt turned around to see Ally in the hallway. She was dressed in long stretched black pants and a hot pink tight t-shirt.

"Listen to me, missy, I don't want Sally's heart broken because you and Daniel slept together in bed." He warned the Loop.

"I thought we've gone over this before from Sectionals." Ally annoyingly stated.

"My wife saw you two go inside your room." Paul argued.

Joy came out of her shared hotel room and announced, "Daniel Gray, I know you and Ally-Loop are up to something tomorrow. You cannot go to the rink to see Sally perform her long program. Please hand me your badge, card keys, and cell phone."

Shit, his heart cried out. *Damn, now what?*

He knew Joy Hunt got him good and the Figure Pact's exposing plan could not go on the next day.

Danny opened his guest room's door to disappear for a minute. He stood in the doorway and sadly handed Joy Hunt his key cards, all-access lanyard badge, and cell.

She pressed on, "And to make sure nothing strange happens tomorrow, your room's cord phone has been cut off and two well armed security guards will be at your door for the duration of your stay."

The big male guards were walking in the hallway and both were dressed in black like from a SWAT team with loaded rifles in their hands.

Ally left the hallway for her room.

The two male guards stood at each side of Danny's guest room.

Joy Hunt snickered, "Have a pleasant stay, Mr. Gray."

Chapter Twenty-Four

The guest hotel door was shut.

The room was quiet.

Daniel Gray could not leave his room without a way back in. The guards did not look friendly to him so he gave up from trying to ask them for a favor or two. He sat on his bed and softly cried himself to sleep.

What he did all day in his hotel room was nothing. He just laid or sat on his King Size bed and looked inside his skating bag. His black suede figure boots continued to amaze Danny. He was glad he could figure skate in those beautiful skating boots. It was hard for him to stay calm.

Laying on the bed with the pillows behind his head, he mumbled to himself, "The Hunts win. Sally's going to get the gold, Ally would never get the chance to prove of the Hunt's cheating scheme in figure skating again, and I'll never get my girl out of her mother's claws. Ah, shit, I screwed up. I wish for some help . . ."

In Ally's hotel room, she was feeling depressed for Daniel. Being locked up in his room and without a way to call out for help. She could not believe that Joy would still spy on her and her figure student.

The Loop's heart was happy the devil's bitch did not know about her relationship with Tiger Shark's Number 65 or what she really did off ice.

To keep herself distracted from Danny's troublesome problem, Ally was lying on her stomach on the King Size bed and watching the 'figure puppet's' taping on her laptop. She wanted to watch the brunette with blue eyes skate again. The Figure Instructor was sure she had seen her before. When was the question to the Loop's curiosity.

She closed her eyes to remember her grade school years. Before figure skating came into her life. That was hard to do. Ally could not think of a time when she had not loved figure skating.

Richard McCarthy noticed Allison watch the taping for the tenth time in the past hour. He sat next to her and asked, "Ally?"

She looked up from the computer screen to listen to his question.

"What's wrong?" He wondered and his eyes glanced at the Joy Hunt's 'figure puppet' do her skating moves from Ally's laptop.

The Loop's dazed eyes was strange to Richard. She never seemed so lost or out of focus of anything before. Something was wrong with Allison Rigden.

He questioned Ally, "Do you know that girl?"

Ally chocked. Her mouth opened, but no sound came out. She rose up from the bed and went straight for the walk-in closet. Her left hand got her guarded figure boots. She ran out of the room with the front door slamming behind her.

Sitting on the big empty bed, Captain McCarthy was hurt. He wondered what was up with Allison and how he could make her feel better. His heart demand an answer from the Loop's unusual behavior. He hated the idea of acting like a violent hockey brawler toward her. But if she would not talk to him sensibly, he would have some drastic to get her attention.

After deciding what he should do, Rich slipped his Tiger Shark's logo black cap on his head and black shades over his eyes. He left Allison's hotel room to follow her. He knew where she was going to with her skates. Ally wanted to skate in his team's home rink.

Richard walked five minutes east from the Rink's Hotel building. He was glad no one recognized him or was stopped by crazed Tiger Shark fans. He got inside from the truck delivery's entrance.

The inside was quiet and dark for a few minutes.

As the hockey Captain made it to the Zamboni's box doorway, his ears heard the sound of someone crying and a loud metal ballad song playing from the speakers.

Both his hazel eyes saw Ally skating on the ice all by her lonesome self. Standing in front of the large strong glass walls, Richard admired Allison's figure skills. He also noticed something special on the Loop.

"Awe, Ally . . ."

She was wearing his flamed jersey shirt when he tried out the open draft pick.

Richard was full of emotions after seeing Allison in the old jersey shirt. He knew how she brought the shirt without him knowing it. She stuffed it in one of her figure boots.

McCarthy thought Ally-Loop would make a cute figure in hockey skates. But that would be something the two of them would have to do secretly.

He leaned down and unlocked the truck's gate door.

Ally's ears heard a loud metal click inside the rink. Her eyes saw McCarthy walking out of the Zamboni box. She did not want to talk to him or anyone else.

"Ally!" He yelled out. "Can we talk?"

She choose to ignore his calls. Her strong blades made her glide around the beautiful rink fast. She wanted to be the best against Number 65 that night.

But the PHL Captain figured out a plan to outsmart his Figure Instructor. He raced off the ice in his running shoes for his team's locker room.

Allison's brown eyes glanced at McCarthy leaving the big ice rink.

Good riddance. She thought and continued to skate around the whole rink.

Twenty minutes later, a new song was about to play when the building's speakers made a loud, annoying static noise. Ally stopped gliding on the ice and her hands covered her ears from hearing that horrible screeching sound. The rink got quiet and all the lights were turned off.

Tired Ally got worried.

She hoped there was nothing wrong with the building's power surge. She did not want to be locked inside or face the fact that tomorrow's skating event was canceled due to electrical problems.

Allison's cold hands slowly uncovered her ears and she stood at the center part of the rink. The ice rink was pitch black from her eyes. She stood strong. She felt the cold air blowing around her. Both her hands held together, close to her chest.

"Hello," her scared voice echoed in the cold, dark, empty arena, "What the hell is going on here?"

'Look & Annihilate' started to play from the rink's speakers. Her ears also heard the whirling sound of something mechanical coming down from the ceiling.

Ally's heart was a little relieved that the silver rink's building had not lost power. But she was starting to feel sleepy. Her mind wondered if she should leave the arena building for her hotel room. After all, she needed to be well rested to do her quadruple-quadruple edge jump the next day and she did not want to have another twisted ankle from tired feet again.

Leaving the rink was probably the best thing for her to do. Even if she had to exit the Tiger Shark's domain arena and sleep in her guest room without Richard McCarthy.

Just when Ally wanted to glide toward one of the team's sitting booths for her shoes, someone's voice was heard from the speakers.

"Hello, Tiger Shark fans! Are you ready to swim with PHL's most dangerous night-hunters tonight?"

Then bright turquoise lights were shining on the ice rink and computerized images of swimming sharks appeared on the ice.

Allison sighed unimpressively at that announcement. She knew what was going to happen next. The Loop was not in the mood to watch a show.

What came down from the ceiling was the Tiger Shark's entrance head. It stood in front the gate door for the team's locker room hallway.

Ally looked up at the score board's t.v. screens. It wasn't on to show who was coming out from the team's locker room.

The shark's eyes were glowing red and fog was steaming out of its wide-open, sharp teeth mouth. And who came gliding out of the shark's mouth was none other than Captain Richard McCarthy. He was dressed in his team's home game jersey shirt and skated around the turquoise color rink with his black color hockey stick.

Ally just stood in the center of the rink with a stunned look on her face. She wondered why Rich would do the hockey team's pre-game entrance for her. She watched him skate around the ocean themed patch of ice.

When Number 65 finished his third quick lap around the rink, both his hands held his black wooden stick and he skated up to Allison. He knew this was going to get Ally to talk.

Richard's left hand let go of the hockey stick and his right hand kept it close by his right hip. His tired voice spoke kindly to the Loop, "Now do I have your attention?"

Allison Rigden only nodded her head a few times and began to skate forward around the turquoise color ice rink.

That was not the kind of response Richard McCarthy was expecting. The team's entrance song stopped playing.

Richard threw his gloves and hockey stick on the ice. He glided up behind Ally and slowly grab her in his arms.

"Richard!" She gasped.

He lifted her up and carried her over his left shoulder. He slowly glided on the ice for the shark's head.

Ally's fists punched on McCarthy's back. "Put me down, right now!"

They passed through the shark's mouth and the Tiger Shark's Captain was walking on the carpeted floor.

Even though Allison's punches were not strong enough to hurt him, Richard requested, "Could you stop hitting me?"

Her pounding fists ceased from hitting his turquoise jersey shirt. Then she questioned him, "Where are we going?"

Ally was afraid her hunky player was going to turn into brawler Number 65.

Richard lifted the Loop off his shoulder and lowered her down for the carpet floor. She stood strong in front of the tough puck chaser with her arms across her chest.

He had one reasonable question to ask first. "Why did you come here?"

Ally sighed, "To get away from everyone."

Upset Rich wondered, "Even me?"

Her tearful eyes made her nod her head five times.

McCarthy unstrapped his black color hockey helmet. He took it off his head and threw it on the floor. The angry puck chaser turned away from Allison. He marched on the carpet floor to get his hockey stick and gloves off the ice.

On his way out, he shouted, "Fuck! Nothing I do is ever good enough for you, Ally-Loop!"

Allison was not sure if Richard could understand her grade school years like Daniel Gray. She just figured out when and where she seen Joy's 'puppet' before.

"Donna . . ."

Ally leaned down to pick up Captain McCarthy's helmet and walked on the carpet floor for the rink.

In the long stretch hallway, she saw angry Rich McCarthy with his gloves and hockey stick in hand. His angry voice demanded, "You leaving?"

Her firm voice answered, "Yes."

"Did you want me to stay away from you too?" He rudely offered and his left hand jerked his helmet out of her hands.

Ally's heart shattered. She was going to let out more tears. Her eyes were felt warm and tears rolled down on her cold pink cheeks.

"No."

Richard grunted, "Ally, I don't-"

He lost his grip of his hockey gear and the gear fell on the carpet floor. He growled, "What the fuck is up with you?"

Allison gulped, "I think I know who is Joy's 'figure puppet.'"

Her broken voice confessed, "It's Donna."

"Who's Donna?" McCarthy strongly wondered.

Ally let out some more tears before she answered.

"My best-grade school . . . friend . . ."

She sat on the carpet floor with her legs stuck out in front of her. She cried and cried some more.

Ally felt tired and lightheaded. Her back was against the tan wooden wall to make her be more attentive.

Richard sat on the floor with the Loop.

"What makes you think it's your old school friend?" The Captain spoke.

Allison sniffled, "Because-I would recognize her anywhere. I had a deja vu feeling that I seen her before. I wanted to have a clear mind to see if my hunch is right."

She declared, "I know I'm right."

Rich was surprised.

"You never told you had a friend." He pointed out. "How come you never mention her before?"

Allison lifted up herself from the floor and suggested, "Can we talk about it back at the hotel?"

She yawned and stretched out her arms.

"Okay . . ." The puck chaser strained.

He grabbed his gloves, helmet, and wooden stick and stood up on his blades.

Before they part, Ally asked, "Hey, are we cool?"

With his gloves and black helmet in his left hand and wooden stick in his right hand, Richard McCarthy gave Ally-Loop a tight hug.

"We're good." He happily replied.

"Thank you." She breathed out lovingly.

He only had one thing for her to do.

"Next time you're in your 'I don't feel like talking to anybody mood,' remember this: I am not 'anybody' in your eyes. You can always talk to me about anything." Richard softly explained to her.

She pulled back and her eyes were locked to his beautiful hazel eyes. "I promise to be more open to you, Captain McCarthy."

They sealed their agreement with a long loving kiss.

Richard went to the locker room while Allison skated out on the turquoise colored ice rink for her shoes in one of the hockey team's sitting booths. The rink's turquoise light was turned off and white lights were on. The Tiger Shark's head was lifted up from the ice.

Ally was taking off her right figure boot and putting on her right shoe when she heard a pretty melody song from the rink's speakers. She decided not to take off her left boot and put back on her right boot as quick as she could.

The Figure Instructor was out on the ice. She pulled the black flamed jersey shirt off of her. Her feet made her dance more graceful than ever before. Spinning centered spins, jumping up high in the air, creating her own flowing dance steps, and gliding happily forward and backwards.

As the street clothed hockey dude walked on the light gray carpet, Richard was still a little pissed off from Allison's strange behavior until he watched her figure skate to an unexpected pretty love song.

He could no longer be angry at the Loop. All he did was watch and admire the way controlled herself on the ice with her moves in her white figure boots.

When the song ended, Ally-Loop did a show stop at the center part of the rink and did a beautiful pose with her right arm up and curved and her left arm down her left side. Her face was lit up brightly after doing a whole new skating routine.

Rich stepped out on the ice in his running shoes and walked toward Ally. She turned around to see McCarthy heading for her. She lowered her right arm.

The figure lovers stood face-to-face on the ice and tightly held each other.

From the rink's speakers, their ears heard, "Kiss her, McCarthy!"

They laughed and their lips softly kissed each other.

What else came out from the speakers were the voices of cheering, whooping, and hands clapping.

As Rigden and McCarthy parted from their kiss, she asked the Captain, "Um, who's here, Richard?"

Brawler Number 65 pointed out the lit up announcer's desk on the third floor. There were five of the Tiger Sharks dressed in their turquoise jersey shirts and standing behind the large screen window. They sure had big smiles on their faces.

"I ran into some of the guys in the locker room and they helped me with your surprise." He explained proudly.

One of the guys spoke in the mic, "Kiss her again!"

With a stern look on his face, Rich shook his head for a 'no' answer.

The guys moaned and groaned with disappointment. One of them turned off the box's light.

Ally giggled again and smiled from ear-to-ear. She and the team's Captain stepped of the ice for the booth that contained her running shoes. She quickly took off her boots and her purple and white N+ running shoes were back on her tired, achy feet.

The figure couple left the Tiger Shark's domain rink and walked back to the Rink Hotel.

The time was ten after eleven at night when Allison & Richard made it to her guest room. Their previous clothes were off and into their night clothes. Ally put on dark purple shorts and her hunky player's flamed jersey shirt. Rich was only in navy blue sweat pants.

He requested from the Loop, "Tell me about Donna."

Ally told him, "Donna and I used to be inseparable during third and fourth grade. But after we reached fifth grade, I found a special book about a girl's biography for her love of ice skating and it made me want to skate myself. I got so involved with the book I forgot about my friendship with Donna. I gave up her just so I could figure skate."

She put in, "I wonder when she and Joy got together. I think I know why Donna wants to do figure skating herself and help the devil's bitch. To get back at me."

After hearing that short tale, Richard suggested, "Maybe tomorrow before the event, we should go to the other rink and have you and Donna make up your quarrels. That way Donna won't do Sally's routine."

"That could work." Ally replied. "Then again, it's been ten years since we last seen each other and we always end up fighting or arguing about stupid things."

McCarthy left the closet for the King Size bed.

Allison's mind thought of something sad about Daniel's current situation while she & Rich passed by her figure student's well-guarded hotel door.

Still standing in the walk-in closet, she asked her loving puck chaser, "Rich, what are we going to do about Danny? We can't do the exposing plan without him."

Rich was lying on his back and thinking thoroughly on how to trick the guards into letting him & Ally 'break' Daniel out from his guest room.

The hockey Captain placed his left arm behind his head and sadly spoke, "I'm not sure, Ally."

Upset Allison walked out of the closet box and joined with the hunky player in bed. The left side of her body snuggled next to his warm, hot-looking bod. Her head was on his chest and her right hand curved around the right side of his neck.

Her voice breathed out, "I wish we can help him."

McCarthy's left hand moved from the back of his head and brushed Ally's long soft brown hair. He too wanted to help out Danny, but those guards had guns in their hands and Tiger Shark's Number 65 would not dare to talk to those armed men.

"Me too, honey."

His right arm lifted up to hug Ally-Loop tight. He added, "We'll talk about it tomorrow."

"I feel that's-going to be too late." She yawned.

"Sleep is necessary for now, Allison." His lips kissed her hair. "You have a big, big day for National's tomorrow."

Even though her eyes were very tired, Ally let go of Richard's embrace to sit up in bed. Her legs were crossed and her fingers were constantly combing her hair nervously.

Rich sat up next to her.

"Hey," he cooed.

Their eyes touched each other's hearts. Both leaned in for a sweet kiss.

After their lips part, McCarthy looked down at his first jersey with adoring eyes. "Can't believe you actually kept it."

Her broken voice confessed, "I kept it just like how you asked me to."

"You know, during my first year with the team and after telling the guys that you stole my heart, one of them asked me 'how the hell could you fall in love and have so much patience for a teenage figure skater?' I stated, 'Ally is not just a figure skater and she won't be a teenager forever. I Love her as the woman she is.'" His loving hazel eyes made Ally fall in love with McCarthy all over again. "Do you remember when I gave you the shirt?"

Ally thought back Richard McCarthy's big day to be officially part of the PHL's Tiger Sharks after spending a year in training camp.

17 year old Ally-Loop was driving down to San Jose to see Richard with the other Tiger Sharks in their main rink. She was in her cute silver Horundi car with the top during a really hot August day. She wore a black tang top and short jeans shorts with her purple and black running shoes.

She tiredly mumbled to herself, "Only twenty more minutes of driving."

Two hours of driving was a lot for her to handle on a warm summer afternoon. Good thing she brought three big water bottles before she went on the road and her small rectangular blueberry MP3 player for entertainment.

Ally made it to the Tiger Shark's rink parking lot. She parked her car and turned on her car alarm. Her brown eyes saw McCarthy waiting for her by his bran-new dark blue sports truck.

He was carrying the blue and black hockey bag Jessica gave him when he did the open try-out. He was in jeans, a white t-shirt, and tennis shoes.

"Nice truck!" The Loop announced.

"Thank you!" Richard smug. "Thought I drive in style for now on."

Both of them laughed.

They walked up the stairs, through the lot's front doors, rode on the escalator, and went around the building for the stands. The rink was cold to them, but their eyes gazed at the enormous patch of ice.

Chilly Ally crossed her arms over her chest and she whispered, "It's beautiful . . ."

"What is?" Rich wondered.

"This rink." She gasped and her hands rubbed her arms. "I'm so jealous of you."

McCarthy cheerfully spoke, "Maybe one day you'll skate here."

Allison Rigden mumbled, "One day . . ."

Richard walked down the stand's stairs for the first row. Ally tagged along with her first figure student. They stood at the stands by the team's locker room hallway entrance.

Before he left Allison, Rich expressed out, "I know I said this before, but thank you, Ally-Loop, for being the best skating teacher ever."

His left hand took her right hand and gave her a comforting squeeze. She did not squeeze his hand in return. His heart was not happy that Ally could not show loving affection toward him.

She will someday . . . He thought.

"Ally, will you keep something for me?" Richard requested.

"What is it?" She asked confusingly.

He leaned down to softly say, "My flames jersey?"

The Loop surprised. "Why don't you keep it?"

"Because it's special and I don't want to lose it or see it ruined." He solemnly replied. "And maybe it would help you to open yourself for me."

"Rich," Allison disappointedly stated, "we can't work out a relationship. It's best for us to go on our separate ways. You got what many young athletes would die to have. Hopefully in the near future, you'll have a very lucky girl in your life off ice."

"Allison . . . don't act like I'm Big Mike and his thugs. I care a great deal for you . . ."

Richard McCarthy begged, "Please watch over my flames jersey?"

He had to bring in the big guns. His face gave her an adorable puppy face with the sad, pouty lips.

Ally-Loop was scared to love someone more than figure skating. Ever since she first started skating lessons, she was never close to anyone. She was unsure if she was willing to change her mind on having friends in her life again.

Her mouth opened but could not say anything.

She saw Coach Hartman and the other Tiger Sharks out on the ice. They were in their uniforms and the hockey dudes started to skate around the freshly cut patch of ice.

Just to make McCarthy happy, Allison Rigden let down her guard and promised, "Okay. I'll look after your flames jersey shirt."

Rich excitedly replied, "Thank you, Ally." He leaned down to unzip his hockey bag and handed his Figure Instructor the black jersey shirt. He added, "Who knows. Maybe it'll be worth something in twenty years."

Both skaters laughed at the prediction.

"Maybe." Ally reluctantly agreed and stood by the stair's handrail.

Instead of holding the jersey shirt, she slipped it on her. It was a bit too big for her figure form.

Richard turned to his right. He walked up three steps and tossed his hockey bag on the carpet floor to leap over the stair's steel handrails.

Allison softly giggled at McCarthy's jump.

Good thing he excelled well in figure jumps to jump up that high. Her mind snickered.

Richard walked through the long hallway with his blue and black hockey bag behind his bag. His heart was excited to be part of a PHL team. He knew there would be lots of hard work for him to do on and off ice with the team, but he was determined to do what he needed to do to stay on the team and climb to the top.

His hazel eyes noticed lots of tiny lit light bulbs on the ceiling when he finally reached the team's locker room front wooden double doors. On the left was the team's logo on the tan wooden wall.

McCarthy slowly moved forward for the large double doors. His shaky left hand pulled the door's silver pole handle on his left side. Behind the doors was a huge PHL locker room for the Tiger Sharks. The door he opened was closed shut after he passed through the doorway.

Inside the room were lots of wooden cubby boxes attached to the creamy color cement walls, wooden benches under the boxes, and dark colored, stripped carpet on the floor. The cubby boxes contained the team player's name plate and number and official PHL skating gear. On the wooden benches were each of the team player's bag full of fan freebie gifts.

Richard found his cubby box in the middle left row. It had to be his since it was the only one with a turquoise jersey shirt hanging from a metal hook under the wooden box.

He stood in front of his box. He saw his name plate.

Logo of the team's Tiger Sharks:

McCarthy, Number 65

He made it. He got the dream of being an athlete. And not just an athlete. A Professional Hockey Player.

He placed his old hockey bag on the carpet floor and changed into his new hockey uniform.

When he finished, Number 65 left the locker room for the team's introduction event. He walked on the carpet floor in his old hockey skates for the rink.

Coach Hartman and the rest of the Tiger Sharks were out on the ice and McCarthy glided toward the group. He was instantly part of the PHL team.

Richard looked around for Allison at the stands. She was not there. He frowned a little because his Figure Instructor did not care enough to watch her first student become a somebody from her figure teachings and knowledge.

With her hands in his hands, Captain McCarthy sadly asked Ally-Loop, "Why did you leave early that day?"

Ally confessed to her hunky player, "It was the right thing to do. Didn't want you in trouble for getting involved with a minor. I had to stay away from you so you can be strong in the Professional Hockey League."

Rich spoke, "I understand. I have pestered you a lot throughout my first Pro year. I was surprised when you wanted me to help you with your private rink."

"Well, the other hockey dudes did not want to forget their first passion spark in ice skating and they also wanted some time away from their team, coaches, fans, schedules, traveling times, and especially the media." She sighed tiredly. "Besides, you're the only one I could really trust to run an ice rink for me. I was also jealous of you being around other girls and I wanted to keep you away from them."

Smily Rich chuckled, "I knew it."

Allison blushed brightly. "Again, I am sorry you had to be patient with me. I appreciate it."

"It was worth the fight, Ally-Loop." McCarthy relieved. He let go of her hands and his body laid comfortably in their shared hotel bed.

He smug, "I'm glad I won."

"Rich, you always won my heart." Rigden confessed. "When you got picked, it was the wrong time for us to be together. Now is the perfect time for us to bond on and off ice." The hockey Captain declared, "Let's not ruin it."

His left hand wrapped around the upper part of Ally's right arms, pulled her close him, and kissed her deeply.

"I Love You, puck chaser . . ."

Richard chuckled, "And I Love You too, toe-jumper . . ."

Their eyes were closed and both skaters happily drifted off to sleep.

When Allison Rigden's eyes opened up the next morning, it was ten a.m. and her ears heard the shower head on. She looked at the empty messy King size bed.

She sleepily mumbled to herself, "Richard must be in the shower."

Ally's heart was pounding hard and fast because it was the last day for Sally's skating competitive years, the expose the Hunt's cheating scheme to the world, and it would also be her turn to shine with her edge quadruple-quadruple combo jump.

Her body flipped over on her right side and noticed something on the sliding glass mirrored door for the walk-in closet box. It was a white sheet of paper that was taped on the mirror sliding door.

Lightheaded Ally lifted herself off the bed. She slowly went toward the sliding door and her tired eyes read the note.

Ally,

I figured out a plan to 'break' Daniel out of his hotel room. If you're not up by the time I'm finished with my shower, I'll have to do the plan myself and you get yourself for your long program.

My plan is: at precisely ten after ten, go into Paul & Joy Hunt's room to get Sally's skates, her gear, and Danny's things. When you get those items, return to your room and I'll get Danny out while you prepare yourself for today's competition event.

Keep your mouth shut and be quick & alert, Ally-Loop.

Captain Number 65

Allison thought that a good plan from her hunky player. She also knew what he meant by 'keep your mouth shut.' Do not talk to Richard.

The shower head stopped spraying out water. Her heart raced. She looked at the time on her phone's screen.

10:05 a.m.

Ally pushed the glass mirrored door to her left and hastily took off her purple shorts and McCarthy's old jersey shirt. She slipped on jeans and her maroon shirt. Her running shoes were laced up. She also remembered to get something important out from her skating bag. An extra, small-sized purple skating bag.

She got one of Joy & Paul Hunt's card keys on the small wooden computer desk behind the bedroom. Richard labeled the cards by placing rough cream color tape on them and with a black marker it read 'Hunts' room.'

Ally had her phone in hand.

She quietly stood in front of her room's front door. Her right eye looked through the glass key hole. She saw Paul & Joy Hunt leaving their room along with Sally by their side.

The Loop glanced at the time on her phone. It just changed to 10:10 a.m.

Her left hand pressed down the door's handle, slipped out of her room, and sneaked over to the Hunt's couple room. Her left hand held the key card. She used it on the door and made a beeping noise that the door was unlocked.

She dashed inside. The door was closed and Ally looked inside the dark room. She flipped on the switch. Lights lit up the room. On the sofa was the very thing that she needed to get.

"Sally's skating gear." Allison whispered.

It was Hunt's pink duffle bag.

The Loop went forth for the floral patterned sofa. She sat on the sofa to unzip Sally's skating bag and sure enough, there were Sally's special skating gear. Nude color flexible wires, lots of small circular, sticker-like, gold color microchips, a light material, nude color, body suit, the jeweled headband with wires hanging on one side, and the 'special skates'.

Allison unzipped her purple bag and took out a normal pair of white figure boots with sharpened blades. She stuffed in Sally's gear in the purple bag and the regular figure boots in the pink duffle bag.

Just when she wanted to leave the room, Ally's brown eyes saw Danny's lanyard badge, card keys, and cell phone on the kitchen's bar counter top. She took them in her right hand.

She casually left the Hunt's room with her purple skating bag. Her brown eyes looked quickly at the armed guards by Daniel Gray's door. She hoped they were not going to say a word about what she did.

Her mind ignored them and got back inside her room.

In the room, Ally went to the bedroom, threw the small purple skating bag and Daniel's things on the bed, and hastily unzipped the bag. Her hands took out Sally's skates, the microchips, wires, headband, and bodysuit.

"Hey . . ."

She raised her head up and saw Richard McCarthy all dressed up in jeans and dark blue t-shirt. He stood in the doorway connection for the bathroom and bedroom.

"Good job, babe." He strutted in and sat on the bed with Ally-Loop. His lips kissed hers.

When they part, McCarthy asked, "Where's Danny's card keys?"

Rigden pulled up Danny's card keys, cell phone, and lanyard badge.

She handed them and her pink and black tie-dye colored, her smooth suede material computer sleeve to Rich.

"Good luck."

A new question came in the hunky player's mind after seeing Sally's special skates. "How is Sally going to skate in her long program without her special skates?"

"I put regular figure skates in her duffle bag." Ally snickered. "Can't let sunshine Sally Hunt ice skate without proper figure boots."

"Smart thinking." Rich said.

They kissed again.

Richard let go of the kiss to leave the room with all the gear essentials to show the tapings.

After leaving the room, Ally got herself for National's Senior Ladies' long program.

Walking in the hotel's third floor's hallway, Number 65 was wearing his black Tiger Shark's logo cap and shades covered his eyes. He made it to Danny's room. The guards were still there with rifles in their hands.

Number 65 sternly spoke, "Gentlemen."

Both guards stepped away from the door and turned their back from the PHL Captain.

Rich used one of Danny's card keys. It unlocked and he slowly stepped inside the dark room. He spoke out, "Daniel?"

Number 65 took off his shades and his ears heard, "Richard?"

Daniel's voice sounded weak and tired.

The hockey dude turned on the lights.

Allison's figure student lying on the floor next to the King size bed and not looking so good to Captain McCarthy. His hair was all messed up, his eyes looked very tired and red color, he had not changed his clothes, or had anything to eat.

Richard put the computer sleeve and Danny's personal items on the bed.

"Let's get the hell out of here, Gray." The puck chaser declared.

His nose smelled the Pet trainer's horrible body odor.

"Actually, you need to get clean and look presentable for the Hunts." He helped Daniel to his feet and went for the bathroom instead of the room's front door.

"Rich, Rich, Rich . . ."

McCarthy was confused of Danny's delusional voice. "What up, man?"

He was about to step inside the bathroom when Danny requested, "Dude, I wanna-" gulp "wanna-dii-diiieeeee . . ."

Richard was shocked. He helped the dog trainer in the bathroom.

"Danny, you're not going to die." McCarthy strongly stated.

The Pet trainer was barely conscious and wide awake as Rich let him sit on the white color toilet seat. His body could not sit up straight.

Number 65 quickly took off Danny's stinky clothes off his body. His strong hands lifted the broken hearted figure male off the seat and made it for the showering area.

The faucet had water flowing in the tub.

When the water was warm, naked Danny was standing in the tan color showering area and warm water was spraying from the silver steel shower head.

Richard ordered the dog trainer, "Get clean and hurry up! Joy and her family are in the dining room! We need to leave the hotel as soon as we can!"

"Rich, I don't-I don't want to-" Daniel stuttered.

He sat in the white tub and began to cry.

The pucker chaser knew what was Gray's problem.

Rich left the bathroom for the cord phone next to the bed. The cord phone did not work. He used his cell to call for room service.

He spoke, "I need an order of today's brunch special."

Then he hung up his phone and went for the bathroom.

He saw sobbing Danny sitting the tub with the spray on. The young Pet trainer did not want to get clean or want to help Number 65 or the Loop with their exposing plan.

The tough hockey dude knew what he needed to do.

"Daniel!"

The sorrowful dog trainer did not listen to Richard.

"Get on your fuckin' feet!"

Danny's sad face looked up at the pissed off hockey player. He whined, "Why?"

"Ally & I cannot do the plan without you." He strongly replied. "We're so close to expose Sally Hunt's phony skating routines."

The upset twenty-one year old spoke, "Doesn't matter. The Hunts won."

Twenty-five year old Rich protested, "No, they haven't. We still have a chance if you get back on your blades and fight your hardest against Joy Hunt!"

For Danny's heart, that did not sound like Ally's loving hunky player. That was a strong command from the Tiger Shark's Captain. The Pet trainer got the strength to get on his blades and stood under the shower head to wash his body and clean his hair.

While Daniel showered his tired body, Richard looked through Gray's roller suitcase and picked out jeans and a dark green t-shirt as Danny's wearing apparel. Then the Captain's ears heard knocking at the door.

He stepped toward the front door and looked through the small glass key hole. There was a staff member with a roller cart in front of him. On the cart was a steel lid covering the breakfast plate, clean silverware, and two glasses. One filled with orange juice and the other milk.

Richard unlocked and opened the door.

The male staff member was surprised to McCarthy in Daniel Gray's room.

The hockey Captain said, "Pretend I'm not here and bill it to me, Jesse."

"Yes, sir." Jesse agreed.

The staff employee left the third floor for the elevator.

Rich's hazel eyes noticed the guards by Joy & Paul's room. The plan was still in play. He brought the cart inside of Danny's room.

The bathroom door opened and out came moist Daniel Gray wrapped in a white towel on his waistline. He saw McCarthy with a cart in the room.

"What's this?" He wondered.

"Brunch." Rich presented the dog trainer what was under the steel lid.

Big stack of pancakes, eggs, bacon, sausages, and yummy warm syrup. Looking at the plate full of food did make Sally's fiance feel very hungry. He had not eaten anything in over a day.

Danny saw the clothes McCarthy picked out for him. He immediately put on the clothes, ate his brunch, and drank the juice and milk at the same time.

The Pet trainer questioned the hockey player, "How the hell did you get in here without Joy knowing?"

"Ally broke into Joy & Paul's guest room and got your card keys, cell, and your badge. And those guards Joy called up aren't really guys from a SWAT team. They're two of my teammates in disguise in case the devil's bitch was going to outsmart us." Richard handed Danny his things. "Let's go. You're going to stick with me today."

After that was said, Danny finished his meal. He put on his lanyard badge, stuffed his wallet, cell phone, and card keys in his jeans front right pocket.

"I'm ready." He felt determined to fight against the devil's bitch.

Rich grabbed Ally's computer sleeve. He and Danny left the room for his truck. McCarthy drove off his truck from the hotel's parking lot to Joy's secret skating rink.

Chapter Twenty-Five

Both guys laid low in the shiny black truck and waited in the other ice rink's parking lot for Joy's red SUV to arrive. The time was twelve in the afternoon and the inside of the truck was quiet.

Calmed Richard McCarthy laid back in the driver's seat with his eyes shut. Wary Daniel Gray cautiously looked around the lot.

The Tiger Shark's Captain softly ordered, "It's not a good idea to spy at the lot, Danny."

The dog trainer replied back, "Why? Aren't your window's tinted black?"

"They are." Rich said. "But you need to stay cool while you're doing the video taping."

"Dude, how can you stay so cool around Joy Hunt?" Worried Danny wondered.

With his eyes still closed and his arms behind his head, the puck chaser explained, "Well first off, Joy never actually saw me or know Ally & I are together. Secondly, she does not scare me at all. And third, I have a strong feeling we're going to 'annihilate' her cheating scheme today."

Another thought came to young Gray's hastily mind.

"How do you know when it's time to do the long routine taping?"

The not-so-concerned stick dude told him, "I usually think about past pro games with the team. The timings for each game. Plays the guys and I did. And my ears listen closely to the sound of Joy Hunt's SUV coming in the lot."

Danny thought that was clever way to be sneaky and pass the time. It was a shame he was not a professional hockey player himself. But when he heard the word 'timings', Daniel Gray had an idea.

He closed his eyes to think about Ally and Sally's skating routines. He thought of his own skating routine too.

Then his ears caught a strange sound.

It was the sound of rubber tires rolling on the cement ground. They screeched to a halt. A car door opened and closed. And Danny heard heeled shoes walking on the ground.

When both guys opened their eyes, they saw Joy Hunt walking inside the other skating rink. The front door closed.

Danny grabbed the black baseball on top of the dashboard and hurried out of the truck. He made it inside the skating rink.

The dog trainer activate the thin camera and slipped on the baseball cap.

When the time was two p.m. and Joy had not shown back in the Rink's hotel building, Paul Hunt was worried about his wife. He could not call her since her cell was with him. He had to get Sally ready for her routine himself.

Paul got in Sally's dark room.

"Sally!"

His sleepy blond daughter was waking up from a nap. She slowly sat up in the King size bed.

"What's wrong, Daddy?" Her tired voice asked him.

He sat on the bed to unstrap Sally's orthotic night splints from her feet. "We need to get you ready."

Paul lifted up from the bed and placed the splints next to her hotel bed. He carefully carried Sally in his arms. Sally was placed on a comfy chair by the bed.

Sally stretched out her tighten arched feet. They did hurt her. She could not wait for the season to be over. She was worried about competing in Worlds in a couple of months.

Paul carefully laced up Sally's special tennis shoes on her feet. He also gave her some ibuprofen and acetaminophen to help reduce the inflammation in her feet. She drank some water from a small glass.

Acting like a father for Sally, Paul sat on the floor and his hands massaged the back of her calves and both her feet. He did feel his daughter's uptight muscles. He knew Sally was in no physical condition to compete next year. Least yet, never again in her life.

Her massage was done in fifteen minutes.

"How do you feel, Sally?" Paul asked.

"A little better, Daddy." She said.

He got up from the floor to go to his & his wife's shared hotel room. His eyes found Sally's pink duffle bag on the sofa and slipped the strap over his right shoulder. What he did not know was the weight of the bag had gotten lighter.

Paul looked out the window for the hotel's parking lot. Joy's red SUV had not come back. He felt very chagrin to help Sally bath herself. He knew what to do.

Mr. Hunt left the room and went to Ally's guest room. His left fist pounded on the door. The door opened.

Behind the open door was Ally dressed in jeans and her maroon shirt. "Paul?"

"Hey, Allison." Paul breathed out nervously. "I need some assistance with Sally."

Ally scolded, "Uh, isn't that your wife's job?"

Paul firmly stated, "Joy's not here and I don't want to bath my daughter."

The Loop could not believe on what she just heard.

Joy not here? Ally's concerned mind thought. *That means Danny and Richard are not back here too. I think they're in trouble . . .*

"All right, Paul." Ally replied unhappily. "I'll help you out."

She turned around to get her card key and left her room for Sally's room.

Paul and Allison walked inside the sunshine champ's room. Sally's bluish-gray eyes saw Ally in the room.

"Oh, great." She complained. "What's she doing here? Where's Mommy?"

"Sally, honey, I honestly don't know." Paul sadly spoke.

He put in, "As for Ally being here, she's going to help you with your bath and get you ready for your long program."

"But Daddy-"

"It's either her or me." Paul stated her choices.

Sally thought for a minute. She drank some more water and respond, "Okay, Ally."

Allison stepped in front of Sally, grabbed her hand, and helped her up from the chair she sat in. Both girls walked carefully for the bathroom.

Sally sat on the toilet seat and slowly took off her night clothes.

Ally turned on the tub's water. It got warm quickly. The tub's silver lid covered the drain's hole.

The Loop stepped away from the tub to help unclothed Sally up from the toilet and into the tub. She kindly asked the blonde, "Anything else?"

"I'll be done in twenty minutes." Sally Hunt replied.

She closed her eyes and relaxed in the warm tub.

Ally was disgusted of helping out Sally in her time of need. Then her mind thought, *Well, she's really not my rival. Donna is my figure rival.*

The Loop left the bathroom.

Sitting on the flower patterned sofa, Paul saw Allison exit the bathroom.

"How's Sally?" He wondered.

"She'll be fine for the next twenty minutes." Ally told him. "I'll be back."

The brunette figure exit Sally's room for her room.

Ally did a quick shower, dried herself, put on her nice tan tights, light blue jeans, her purple t-shirt, and lastly not her skating rink's team jacket but Captain McCarthy's favorite black team jersey. She felt proud to wear his Tiger Shark's jersey shirt.

Her legs moved her out of her hotel room for Sally's room. Her left hand knocked on the door.

The door opened and Paul let her in with surprising eyes. "What's with the jersey?"

When the door was closed shut, Ally whispered, "I'm involved with one of the Tiger Sharks. Please don't tell Joy."

Indifferent Paul promised, "Not a word."

She walked toward the bathroom's door. Her right hand turned the silver handle and headed inside. Her brown eyes saw Sally all wet and soap bubbles were in the tub.

"Ready to get out?" Ally offered.

Sally nodded her head.

Allison grabbed some white towels from the little silver rack next to the tub. She spread out one small towel on the tile floor and two big ones on the toilet seat.

She helped up Sally from the bubbled tub.

"Why are you wearing that jersey shirt?" Sally questioned the Loop. She was helped out of the tub and sat on the toweled cover toilet seat.

"It's Richard's." Ally told out and carried another white towel.

Sally snickered, "I won't tell Mommy."

The runner up figure dried up the figure champ.

Ally went out of the bathroom to get Sally's clothes.

Ten minutes later, Sally Hunt was clothed and ready for the event. She walked in her special tennis shoes.

Paul asked Sally, "How are you, Sally?"

Ally left the room.

"I'm fine, Daddy." Sally replied.

"Let's go then."

The remaining Hunts exit the hotel building and walked toward the Tiger Shark's domain arena.

At the other rink, Joy was talking to her 'figure puppet' and the man with the laptop. She kept telling the figure to jump up higher and work more on back spins.

Danny was on his knees and behind the rink's wall. Right above the wall was the baseball cap.

Then the sun was starting to shine through the rink's large glass windows. Joy continued to yell at her 'figure puppet' to keep doing a quad. The figure girl felt very tired from doing two hours of trying to do quads in her spin jumps and always ended up falling down hard on the ice.

Joy Hunt shouted, "Up!"

She pressed on, "Do you want to be paid?"

The brunette figure with blue eyes stepped back on her blades and did her best to feel not so exhausted in front of Joy Hunt. The figure skated around the rink backwards until something bright was shining inside the rink. She banged herself against a corner wall and fell down again.

"Hey!" Joy protested. "What the hell was that?"

The figure argued, "Something flashed at my eyes!"

Joy looked at the man with the laptop. She demanded, "Stop shining light at her eyes!"

The man looked up and yelled out, "It's not from my laptop's camera!"

Mrs. Hunt's green eyes looked at the small camera. There was no sunlight reflecting from the lenses.

Before Danny ducked down and turned off the tiny camera, Joy spotted a shine of light coming from behind the rink's walls.

She questioned loudly, "Who's there?"

The Pet trainer knew it was time for him to leave the rink. He slowly crawled on the floor for the front door.

Joy stepped off the ice to see who was in the rink. She saw someone leaving the rink with a black baseball cap in its hands. She knew who the someone was.

"Daniel Gray, you will regret this!" She loudly declared to her daughter's fiance.

Her hands grabbed her black purse and left the rink.

Disguised Paul and Sally Hunt in hats and sunglasses walked toward the big silver building with Sally Hunt's skating gear. They walked through the huge thong of skating fans. The two Hunt did not wear their badges so they would not cause any attention. It was embarrassing to her and her dad that they had to walk instead of driving to the rink.

Paul's left hand held Sally's right hand tightly.

Sally's left hand carried her pink duffle bag and a special bag for her dresses. The duffle felt lighter to her for some odd reason.

They made it to the back entrance. It looked empty. There were no trucks or anyone around the underground hub.

Paul tried one of the doors. It was locked.

Sally held her pink skating bag and huffed unhappily, "Front entrance?"

Mr. Hunt agreed. "Let's go."

Both father and daughter went for the rink's front entrance. They climbed up the stairs, put on their lanyard badges around their necks, and made it through the V.I.P. line.

The inside was packed with skaters, fans, and the press. Sally and Paul arrived at the girl's locker room without being harassed by media reporters or camera crew. The sunshine Champ had to go in and get herself ready all alone.

Paul went for the stands. He hoped his daughter could fix herself up without any help or getting caught.

What happened in the girl's locker were all the girls, except Ally, were looking at Sally Hunt without her Mommy by her side. Then all the girls were fixing up their hair, make-up, costumes, skates, and their confidence for the ice.

Hunt found an empty area in the room to unzip her pink duffle bag. In the bag, she did not find her microchips, wires, bodysuit, or her special skates. All she found were her skating tights and ordinary pair of figure skates.

Sally was shocked. Her heart was filled with fear. She could not skate without her special suit and senor chip boots. She did not know what to do. She never felt so lonely.

The sunshine champ silently cried.

Ally saw scared Sally Hunt looking in her pink bag for her gear. She thought, *Your Mommy and MMMs will not help you win now. Let's see if you can skate by yourself, cheater.*

The Loop left the locker room. She was ready to practice her figure moves and talk to her coach.

Sally slowly took off her shoes, her clothes, and fixed up her soft blond hair in a bun instead of a French braid. She was having a hard time standing barefoot on the carpet floor. Her arches were not feeling good to her. She wondered if she could take the padding out from her tennis shoes and place them in her figure boots to help her skate.

The blonde gold medalist grabbed her shoes to pull out the special padding. They could not be pulled out. The sunshine figure was stump.

Her ears did hear people clap and cheer for the Senior Ladies out on the ice. She needed to get out there to skate for them. For the judges, her father, and her mommy.

With bravely and determination, Sally Hunt sat on a wooden bench and put on her tights. Then she slipped on her cream color dress and lastly, she carefully laced up the ordinary figure skates. She knew her mommy was not going to like this.

The sunshine Champ's feet were uncomfortable in the boots. She wished for her special skates. But she could not let down her chance to make her mommy proud of her in Nationals. She made it out from the locker.

The press and media reports were there to take her picture or talk to her.

"Sally, are you nervous to do your program?"

"Why did you change your hairstyle?"

"Where's your mother Joy?"

"Do you think you're going to win the gold tonight?"

Sally Hunt did not say a thing.

While she was shined by lots of flashing bright lights, she lowered her head and just pushed aside the press to go to the rink.

Joy Hunt ran outside the other skating rink building.

Daniel Gray rushed inside of Richard McCarthy's black truck.

"Step on it!" He requested.

Richard saw Joy running out of the arena building for his truck. He put the truck in drive and drove off from the parking lot.

The hockey Captain questioned Danny strongly, "What happened?"

The dog trainer held the baseball cap close to him and explained, "The sunlight touched the camera's lenses and the figure's eyes were blinded from the light."

"Damn . . ."

Rich's hazel eyes saw Joy's ruby red SUV racing after his truck.

"Ah, shit."

Danny looked behind the truck.

"Fuck. Joy's following us." He sighed sadly.

Captain McCarthy had an idea.

"Let's give her a wild goose chase." He snickered.

"For how long?" Young Gray wondered.

Rich's eyes looked at the time from the truck's entertainment touch screen.

3:16 p.m.

"Maybe half an hour. Just before Sally's turn to skate."

The Tiger Shark's hockey dude sped up and lead Joy Hunt around the San Jose area.

Standing on the walkway, Sally Hunt saw her father at the stands. He looked worried that Joy was not at the rink to help out their daughter.

The blonde Champ wanted to tell him about her different outlook when all the Senior Ladies left the rink for the locker room to change into their routine costumes.

Sally was very, very nervous to face the rink on her own. *Mommy's not here. Neither is Danny. Where could they be?*

Her plantar fascia pain were bothering feet. She ignored it by thinking of her routine and walking around the carpeted floor hallway. All the moves she had to do from jumps, spins, dance steps, and freestyle pose positions. Except, she was scared to do them by herself. Her microchips helped her be a champ with them. Without them, she was not sure if she could beat Ally-Loop.

The lights dimmed and a female announcer talked to the audience.

In Richard's black truck, he was driving around the San Jose area to get Joy away from the rink before the Senior Ladies' turn to do their practice session for the audience. He had fun playing a trick on Joy. His only concern was: was Ally going to okay on her own?

Danny enjoyed the ride too. He was also worried about Sally and her long skating routine. Maybe it was a bad idea to keep Joy away from her daughter. She would know how to take care of Sally when she would wake up from bed and putting her down for the night.

Joy continued to follow Richard's black truck.

The time was quarter till four.

Danny suggested, "I think we should go to the rink."

The Captain's hazel eyes looked at the time.

"All right." He said. "Let's do this."

The shiny black truck rushed back the Tiger Shark's domain arena.

At the big, big beautiful ice rink, the lady announcer spoke into the mic, "Our first Senior Lady is Santa Rosa's Sally Hunt."

The audience applauded and cheered for Sally.

She took some deep breathes and stepped out on the ice. She sacredly smiled at the fans, judges, and her father by doing some power strokes around the freshly cut ice.

Her feet's heels were bugging her more.

Instead of wincing, Sally smiled and breathed through the pain. Seemed to work for her at first.

Paul Hunt got more scared when he saw Sally skating on the ice without her headband on. He got up from his seat to go to the walkway on the other side of the rink.

At the center part of the rink, Sally posed and soothing classical music was playing. She skated forward fast and gracefully. Her plantar fascia pain was getting more intense. Her muscle bands were really inflamed and the burn was strongly stabbing on the bottom parts of both her feet.

Then it was time to do her first flip jump.

Sally managed to get enough speed, did the flip's set-up, take off, and was able to do the flip with three back spins. She crossed her arms across her chest during the 'in the air' back spins.

The crowd cheered loudly.

Just outside the Tiger Shark's home rink, Richard McCarthy made it to the parking and was about to drop off Daniel Gray at the front doors.

As he drove, Rich instructed Danny, "Take Ally's computer sleeve and wait for me by the escalators."

The Pet trainer did what the hockey dude told him. He got the baseball cap and Ally's colorful sleeve in his arms.

"When I count to three, you dash inside the building." Rich added firmly.

Danny's right hand unlocked his door.

"One . . ."

The Pet trainer took some deep breathes and his right hand was on the door's handle.

"Two . . ."

The truck just reached the front doors.

"Three . . ."

Danny pulled the handle and raced out of Richard's black truck. He ran and ran for the front doors.

Richard drove out of the arena's parking lot.

Joy stopped her car. She lowered her window and yelled out, "Daniel, get back here!"

He made it inside.

Danny lowered his arms so the ticket man could see his 'all-access' badge. He let the Pet trainer through without questioning the items he had in his arms. He rode on the escalator to the second floor. His mind wondered how long was he going to have to wait for Richard. Probably not long.

"Our first Senior Lady is Santa Rosa's Sally Hunt." He heard a lady announcer speak in the mic.

The audience cheered for Sally Hunt.

Danny was upset for not being there to cheer the love of his life. He could not be part of the fans if he wanted Sally out of figure skating forever.

His sad brown eyes saw Richard running in the building and up the moving steps.

The hockey dude shouted, "Danny! This way!"

Both men ran toward an elevator.

They got in and just before the steel sliding doors closed, Dave, the African-American employee the three figures talked during their private ice time, got inside the box too.

"Richard. Daniel." Dave pressed the number 3 button on the wall. "You two are a sight for sore eyes."

"Hey, Dave." Out of breath Rich spoke. "We need your help."

The doors closed and the box moved up.

"Sure. With what?" The rink employee wondered.

McCarthy stepped close to whisper something into Dave's left ear. Dave spoke something quietly back to Richard. The two guys nodded their heads.

All three men stepped out from the box and headed to the security room. Dave unlocked the security room's door. He, Richard and Daniel walked inside the small cube room with lots of desk-top computers and two large t.v. screens with a large button table to control the lightings and security cameras for the whole building.

Four other workers were in there to do their jobs. They paid no attention to the newcomers.

Dave lead Danny and McCarthy to three empty rolling chairs. They all sat in them.

The Pet trainer pulled out Ally's black laptop from her suede material computer sleeve and placed it on the table. He did take out the camera's UBS cable from the sleeve too. His fingers carefully connected the cable cord to the camera and the laptop.

Dave sat next to Danny. His fingers were playing on the keyboards. He told the dog trainer, "Daniel, give me the laptop."

Danny did.

What Dave had in mind was email the video clippings to one of the computers and then transfer the files to the score board screen. It worked like a charm.

Just before the clippings were shown, his eyes saw his fiancee skate on the ice from a t.v. screen. His heart had a feeling something bad was going to happen to Sally.

Sally Hunt felt herself being lowered down on the ice from her triple flip jump. Her right boot was ready to land. The blade touched the ice, but the heel of her right foot's bands snap and the figure blond fell down. The back of her head banged hard against the ice and was laying on her back.

The sunshine figure Champ was yelling out in pain and her legs and feet squirmed. Her plantar fascia got the best of her that night.

Music stopped playing.

Audience and judge officials gasped.

"Sally!" Her ears heard her father calling out for her.

Sally Hunt managed to roll over on her knees.

She softly cried and slowly crawled over toward the open gate door where Paul was waiting for her. Her right foot felt very uncomfortable in her figure boot.

The audience clapped for her bravery after that horrifying fall.

"Good job, honey!" Paul cheerfully shouted. "You're almost there!"

She was five feet away from the open gate door. Her hands and knees were getting very cold and wet from crawling away her fell site. Her voice continued to cry out in pain. She would not be able to stand on her right foot.

At last, she was in front of her caring father.

Paul leaned down to get his daughter's cold hands from the ice and helped her stand up.

When Sally tried to push up from her left foot, the band snapped too and the upper part of her body fell off the ice. She yelled out in pain again.

Mr. Hunt grabbed Sally's weak body to carry her off the ice.

The audience wondered what was wrong with the sunshine figure skater.

Paul had bawling Sally in his arms and placed her in a folded chair. He took off her figure boots as fast as he could.

Sally shouted, "Mommy! I want Mommy!"

The lady announcer questioned Paul Hunt, "Will Sally be able continue her routine?"

Paul held crying Sally in his arms and answered loudly, "No! She's done from doing figure skating!"

Everyone at the stands groaned with disappointment.

The camera crew grouped around Paul and Sally to take pictures and tried to talk to them. Father and daughter ignored them.

"Why?" The lady announcer strictly wondered.

From the rink's security room, Daniel, Richard, Dave and the rest of the employees in the room watched Sally fall down from her triple flip jump.

Danny cried out, "No! No! Sally . . ."

He started to get up from the chair, but Richard's hands stopped him by pinning him back in the roller chair.

"Not yet." Declared the hockey Captain.

Dave gave the Pet trainer a black mic headset. "Put them on and you'll be able to talk to the audience and judges."

Danny put on the skinny plastic headset and adjusted the flexible mic set. His ears heard Sally cry and Paul yelling out for her.

Everyone in the security room watched Sally Hunt fall down in front of the open gate door. The blonde Champ yelled out in pain again.

The Pet trainer heard the lady announcer if Sally was going to continue with her routine. He listened to Paul's response. He was glad Mr. Hunt was really going to stand up against his wife this time.

After the lady announcer said, 'why,' Daniel spoke in his mic, "I can answer that."

Dave opened the email for the clippings and it was ready to be played at the score board's t.v. screens.

A male announcer asked, "Who is this?"

Danny's sad eyes looked to Richard's strong eyes. The stern looking Tiger Shark's Captain nodded his head.

"My name is Daniel Gray. I am Sally Hunt's fiance."

The audience was stunned.

At the stands, everyone was shocked to hear about sunshine Sally Hunt's lover. Paul and Sally were surprised too. They wondered where Daniel was at.

Then another surprise came out of the blue.

Joy Hunt shouted, "Stop! Don't listen to him!"

She, the man with the laptop, and her figure puppet all came walking on the walkway.

"Joy!" Paul argued. He continued to comfort his hurtful daughter in his arms. "Enough of this already! Look at your daughter! She's done competing!"

"Don't tell me what's best for our daughter, Hunt!" Joy protested.

Sally cried out, "Mommy! My bands broke! I can't even walk!"

She announced, "I quit!"

More tears came rolling down from her eyes.

"Skating fans and judge officials, if you thought Sally Hunt was a gold medalist Champion, she never really was." Danny spoke.

The score board's t.v. screens changed from what was at the walkway to Joy's figure puppet's and Sally's short program video clippings.

Figure skating fans, judges, announcers, and other Senior Lady skaters were shocked.

Both girls' skating moves were exactly the same.

It also showed Joy being harsh to her figure puppet and the man with the laptop doing some typing and video taping the puppet.

Joy watched the clippings and heard Sally's cry. Since her cheating scheme was no longer a secret, she reluctantly gave up her dream on having an Olympic gold medal.

Mrs. Hunt did not join her husband's loving embrace to make their child feel better. She walked toward the locker room's hallway, found her cell in her purse, and called up someone for help.

Inside the rink's security room, Daniel explained, "Sally has plantar fascia for six years now. When she was teenager, her mother thought of a plan to use memory muscle microchips, flexible wires, special figure boots, and another figure skater to use her moves so Sally could win the gold."

He added, "I'm sorry for ruining your career, Sally, but it was for the best."

The clippings ended and Danny took the headset off his head. He sighed heavily. His hands rubbed his face.

It was done. The Figure Pact's plan worked.

Richard proudly said, "Good job, Gray."

The guys high-five their success.

McCarthy gathered Ally's computer into her suede computer sleeve. He and Danny got up from the chairs to exit the security room.

In the girl's locker room hallway, Ally was dressed up in her 'Ace's Wings' routine costume when she heard the exposing news. She also heard other figure girls talking about Sally's cheating scheme.

Now it was her 'make up time with Donna.'

Ally-Loop walked out of the hallway and made it for the walkway. She saw Donna and said, "Hey, Donna."

The brunette with blue eyes scolded, "Oh, look who's here. It's 'runner-up' Ally-Loop."

Allison knew she could not be nice to an old friend if she talked to her that way.

"How could you work for Joy?" She protested.

The figure puppet argued back, "Because you stopped being friends with me so you can be a figure skater!"

"I can't let go of this wonderful passion of mine! I had to do something about it!" Ally debated.

"By coming in second place during your competitive years against Sally Hunt?" The Loop's real rival smug.

The Figure Instructor growled, "How the fuckin' hell did you get so good?"

"Paul & Joy Hunt taught me!" Donna bragged. "They taught me more than their own precious daughter! I got so well on ice, I can do better skills than you could from your coach!"

"That's enough, ladies!" A male announcer shouted in his microphone.

He continued on, "Sally, Joy & Paul Hunt, you are exiled from any future USIS figure skating events. So are your friends. Please leave the building now."

Ally teased, "Yeah! Throw out the washed-up, has-beens out of here!"

Six of the rink's security guards forced the Hunts, Donna, and the man with the laptop out the rink's building.

After they were gone, the lady announcer spoke solemnly, "We're very sorry about this, ladies and gentlemen. Let's welcome our next Senior Lady, Allison Ridgen from Santa Rosa, California!"

The audience cheered for the Loop.

Ally and her coach stood by the gates.

Barbra whispered, "Show them passion, Ally-Loop."

The Loop stepped out on the ice and was ready to do her 'Ace's Wings' routine.

Lights were off except for a bright search light on the ice. The song started to play and Ally skated around the ice. Back pivot, dance steps, and toe dances. Especially her long backward split spiral.

At the stands, proud Richard McCarthy gazed at his Figure Instructor skating her heart out. Disappointing Daniel Gray did not stay to watch Allison skate. He silently left the silver building's ice arena for the Rink's hotel.

The Tiger Shark's Captain watched the Loop's figure moves. From jumps, spins, dance steps, freestyle positions, or just gliding around the ice forwards and backwards, Ally was one hard-core figure skater who deserved the gold.

Barbra watched her student move strongly and gracefully in her routine. No mess ups or any flaws happened.

Ally-Loop felt good to have the rink all to herself.

The lady announcer told to the audience, "For those who remembered from Sectionals in Salt Lake City, Ally announced she has a very special combo jump to show us tonight. I believe it's going to happen after doing her final combo spins."

From her last combination spins, Ally sped around the ice counter clockwise backwards. Her heart felt ready to do her special combo jump. She calmly and carefully jumped up extra high for a quad axel and landed quickly for a quad loop.

She landed strongly without any mess ups.

The audience gasped and their hearts were stunned.

The male announcer spoke, "I don't believe my eyes! Allison Rigden, Ally-Loop, the first figure skater to do a quadruple-quadruple edge jump combo! What an event to remember!"

Everyone at the stands stood up and applauded at Ally's beyond incredible figure skating skills.

The Loop did a triple flip to end her routine.

She show stopped and smiled big for the happy skating fans. She was very tired and content.

Ally slowly bowed gracefully twice.

At the stands, Richard yelled, "That's my Ally-Loop!"

He was very surprised that Allison could do a super hard jump combo. Even he, Number 65, could not out skate his Figure Instructor.

At the medal ceremony, Allison Rigden was presented the gold for coming in first place. The audience cheered loudly and clapped their hardest. Camera crews were video taping or taking pictures of the three top Senior Ladies that evening.

The Loop was shaky and crying while her gold and ruby red ribbon was placed around her neck. This was her night to shine as a passionate figure skater who won the gold fairly. Her heart was very excited to be at the top. Her left hand held a large bouquet of red roses and her right hand lifted up her bright gold metal medallion. She kissed the round metal medallion with her lips.

Tired Ally stepped down from the velvet red podium and walked on the red carpet on the ice.

Barbra was very proud of her student's brave figure skill accomplishment. She helped Allison off the ice and they went to the girl's locker room.

Inside the room, Ally slowly changed into her pervious street clothes, placed her skating stuff in her roller suitcase, and slipped on her earned gold medal around her neck. Her right hand carried her roses while her left hand pulled her roller behind her.

When she exit the locker room, it was very crowded with skating fans and news crews. Also, the press wanted to talk to her. She did not want chat with them yet. Her tired legs ran toward Richard McCarthy and they ran off from the Tiger Shark's domain ice rink for the Hotel. The figure lovers made it safely to the Loop's hotel room.

The room's front door was locked up. Most of their clothes were quickly taken off. Richard placed Allison's gold medal around her neck and deeply kissed her. Their loving arms wrapped around each other's warm bodies.

From their kiss, Ally whispered, "I'm the Champ, Rich. It feels so wonderful to be at the top."

"You earned it, Ally-Loop." His lips touched her forehead. "The best female figure skater of the 21st century is in my arms. How the hell did that happen?"

"Because you earned me, Captain McCarthy." Allison confessed. "You believed in me on and off ice and we worked so hard with each other's skating skills, it was meant to be."

Their eyes looked into each other's hearts.

Passion was all they could feel that night.

Both of the figure lovers went to their shared hotel bed and just peacefully closed their eyes for a very long slumber in each other's arms.

Chapter Twenty-Six

What Daniel Gray did after the Figure Pact's exposing plan was he left the Tiger Shark's domain arena for his hotel guest room. He felt bad by embarrassing his fiancee's skating routine, but it was the right thing to do.

Inside his hotel room and waking up from a three hour nap, Danny showered, put on night clothes, called up his parents to know how his cute beagle, Butch, was doing, and he thought over what was going to happen next with him & Sally.

He muttered to himself, "Sally can't skate anymore. I think she's going to the hospital for her feet. I hope Joy & Paul would let me see her again. Crazy as it may seem, but I still Love that girl."

Danny knew there was something he needed to do before going to bed. He grabbed his cell and called up Sally's cell phone. It rang three times.

"Hi, Daniel." Joy answered her daughter's cell.

"Hi, Joy." He respond back.

Annoyed Mrs. Hunt wondered, "Did you want to talk to Sally?"

Danny's heart beat fast. "If that's okay."

Joy honestly replied, "No, Daniel. Not tonight. We're at the hospital now and Sally's going in for surgery this Monday. Paul & I are sorry we left you behind, but Sally needed medical attention and we had to quickly drive to Santa Rosa after being 'exiled' from the USIS."

The Pet trainer said, "I understand and Allison could give me a ride back."

"I have to go now." Joy told him. "You can visit Sally the day after her surgery. It's at the memorial hospital not far from my house. Good night."

"Thank you, Joy."

Both of them hung up their phones.

Danny was able to get some sleep from hearing Joy's good news that he could see Sally.

The next morning, Daniel Gray woke up in his quiet hotel room. He was feeling broken hearted because he could not see Sally until after she had her foot surgery. He slowly sat up in bed and lifted himself up on his feet.

"I need a shower." He mumbled.

Danny had a hot shower and put on jeans, white t-shirt, and his tennis shoes. Then he packed up his things in his skating bag and roller suitcase. He gathered all his belongings and was ready to leave the room.

Standing in the hallway with his rolling suitcase behind him and skating bag strap on his right shoulder, Danny's brown eyes saw Allison Rigden & Richard McCarthy with their skating bags.

The two lovers stopped walking to talk to their friend.

Ally greeted him warmly, "Morning."

Daniel said, "Good morning."

His eyes noticed something really special around her neck. "And congratulations on your first gold medal."

The Loop's eyes were full of tears. "Thank you, Danny."

Taking the Loop's right hand in his left, Richard asked, "How's Sally?"

The dog trainer explained, "She's at the hospital now. Joy told me she's going to have foot surgery on tomorrow and I'll be able to see her on Tuesday."

Confused Ally-Loop wondered, "In San Jose?"

Danny shook his head 'no.' He spoke, "The Hunts immediately left San Jose to go back to Santa Rosa for Sally's feet problem."

"So, in other words, you have no ride back." Rich pointed out.

"Yup." The Pet trainer answered sadly.

Ally thought of a plan.

"I'll drive you back after we have something to eat." She told the guys. "Rich will follow me in his truck."

"Sounds like a good plan." McCarthy agreed.

The Figure Pact went down from the third floor to the first floor. They had a tasty big breakfast and chatted some more.

Ally and Danny handed in their card keys and George gave Ally-Loop a very special gift. It was in a wrapped up square box. In the square box was a beautiful silver chain bracelet with figure charms on it. Boots, blades, and two female figures doing poses.

"Thank you, George." Ally gasped.

Richard helped his girl put on the bracelet on her left wrist. He too thanked the hotel manager for the lovely gift.

All three figures left the hotel building.

McCarthy put his bag on his truck's flat bed and settled himself in the truck.

Ally and Danny put their bags in her cute white Horundi convertible. They got in the two seats and Ally drove off the lot with the hockey Captain behind her.

Two hours later, Danny and Ally made it to the Pet trainer's apartment building without Richard following them. McCarthy drove to his place.

Allison and Daniel stepped out of the white convertible. The trunk was unlocked. Danny lifted up the trunk's hood and pulled out his overnight case and skating bag.

"Thank you, Ally." He breathed out.

Their arms hugged each other.

"Thank you, Danny." She gratefully spoke.

The figures' embrace was let go.

Ally continued, "For helping me in my skating routines and saying it's okay to trust people."

Daniel was confused. "I thought McCarthy did that."

Ally explained, "He is the love of my life, but what I wanted was a friend and you helped me understand how to open my heart outside of the rink. Going to the gym, taking Butchie-Wutchie to the Pet store, and you being so considerate to me without any judgments did make me have a nicer attitude toward others."

Danny felt happy to turn Ally into a fun-loving girl after befriending her for almost four months.

"Well, I better pick up Butch from my parent's home and get ready for work tomorrow." He told his Figure Instructor.

He grabbed his things in his hands.

Just when he wanted to leave, Ally suggested, "Let's not have skating sessions for the next week or so."

Daniel concernedly asked, "Why?"

She sighed tiredly, "Now that I'm the Senior Ladies' gold medalist, the press would be hounding on me and I need a break from the ice."

The Pet trainer nodded his head at her prediction.

"I will call you when I'm ready to face the media music." She cheerfully said. "I hope Sally feels better."

His crushed heart made him reply, "Me too, Ally."

Danny carried his bags to the apartment building and up the stairs for his unit door. He unlocked it, stepped inside his empty home, and slowly put away his things.

He was feeling very lonely without Butch.

The dog trainer decided to go to his folks' home.

Danny went down the stairs for the parking garage and drove to his parent's home.

Two hours later, Daniel and his loving beagle, Butch, were at the beach. They ran on the sandy ground. Played together. Ate some hotdogs together. And both smiled happily to be back together again.

Work the next day was not the human's only concern. His relationship with Sally Hunt worried him the most. He hoped his fiancee would get better from her foot surgery. Their wedding date was coming up. He did not have a tux ready nor know what to do for an ice skating themed wedding.

Now that he thought of it, Danny knew Sally would not be in any condition to get married on the ice. Maybe when he visit Sally at the hospital, he and Hunts could talk about the wedding ceremony.

If there was going to be a wedding after all.

During Danny and Butch's visit to the beach, gold medalist Allison Rigden was with Richard McCarthy that night. He treated her with a really nice dinner and a movie at his home.

It was ten p.m. when they were settling for bed.

Rich was dressed in black sweat pants and laying in his King size bed on his back. Ally headed out of his master bathroom in her navy blue stretch pants and tight hot pink shirt. Her left wrist still wore the silver bracelet George gave her at the Rink's Hotel.

When Richard's hazel eyes saw Allison walking in the bedroom, he gasped, "Oh, my fuckin' God! It's figure champ, Allison Rigden, in my home!"

That made Ally laugh her hardest from his tease.

She got back at him by saying, "Who happens to be madly in love with the Tiger Shark's Captain, Richard McCarthy!"

Rich got up from his black & turquoise themed bed to capture her in his arms. "And don't you ever forget that."

He leaned down and kissed her.

From their kiss, Ally pointed out, "How could I forget the man who helped me through my biggest downfall out on the ice?"

"Have no idea," snickered McCarthy.

Both figure lovers climbed into bed with the covers and blankets over them. Ally laid down first with Rich laying next to her. Arms wrapped each other tightly and comfortably.

Their hearts were filled with love and satisfaction. Their minds only thought of the person they cherish so much on & off ice. Their souls were entwined from the inside out.

With his head on her chest, Richard questioned the Loop, "So, what's next for us?"

She had to tell him what she told Daniel Gray earlier.

"Rich," she spoke calmly, "I've been thinking about taking a little vacation for a week."

"By yourself?" He whispered.

She candid, "Yes."

Sad Richard lifted up his head. "Ah, Ally-honey, why so soon? I want come with you."

Allison soothed him, "Because I need some time for myself. Away from people, pressure, and the ice."

Her right hand softly brushed his left cheek.

She also put in, "And you have your leadership duty for your teammates."

Rich scoffed, "Fuck the team."

He sat up in bed and felt his loving heart be crushed up. He did not want to lose Ally or let the two of them not be together every single day.

"Richard, don't say that about the Tiger Sharks." Allison sternly spoke. She sat up with him and added, "You love them and you love to hit the ice with PHL's most dangerous night-hunters."

"I can't be 'Captain McCarthy' if you're not at the stands." He argued.

"It's not a good idea for me to go to your games shortly after winning the gold." Ally continued. "The media would know about us and we won't have any privacy."

She kneeled behind him.

Her soft hands rubbed his strong smooth back and shoulder blades. She slid her arms around his neck, moved closer to him, and whispered lovingly, "I Love You . . ."

She slowly kissed the back of his neck and her nose gently brushed his warm skin.

Worried Richard confessed, "I'm afraid you won't come back to me safely."

His hands took her hands and held them tight. "I don't want to lose my momentum for the team. Not to forget my passion for the ice. And more importantly, always remembering everything you taught me and see if I apply them during drill and game time."

Allison was very proud of Number 65. She took his hands off of hers to sit in front of her hunky player.

She sweetly answered, "I taught so well, you really don't need me to teach you anything more, Richard. Do you teach them to the coach and teammates?"

"It's how it got me to the top." He replied.

Their eyes touched their hearts.

Allison moved onto his lap with her legs wrapped around his waistline and her arms held his neck. "I Love You . . ."

"I Love You too, Ally-Loop . . ."

Richard slid his arms around her hips.

Both their lips kissed each other smoothly and gently.

When they ended their kiss, Ally wondered, "So, why is wrong of me to have a little me time?"

Rich's left hand stroked her brown hair and respond, "I don't think you can really relax if I wasn't with you."

That hit Ally's heart strong. She slumped her head down and felt weak. She started to cry.

"Ally?" Worried Richard asked. "What's wrong?"

His right hand carefully tilted her head up.

Her loving brown eyes were full of tears. The Loop whimpered, "I think you're right."

"That you cannot relax without me?" He insightfully spoke.

Her sad face nodded.

His head leaned toward for a long kiss. Their lips touched each other in ways that was never possible to happen in life.

After they kissed, Allison wondered, "How the hell do you know that?"

"Ally, you're always stressful when I'm not around you." Rich answered. "Besides, I feel the same way too. It's not right for us to be alone."

"What do you recommend to make us not feel so lonely during our separation times, Richard?" She requested from the hockey Captain.

McCarthy slyly smiled. His hands lifted her arms off him and declared, "I have an idea."

Then his hands unwrapped her legs around him.

Ally moved back from the puck chaser and he got up from his bed. He stepped toward his tall black wooden dresser drawer with silver handles. His left hand opened the top box.

She wondered what Number 65 was up to.

He found what he was looking and closed the drawer quickly. He hid Allison's surprise behind his back, sat on the bed, and gave her a really long kiss.

The next morning, Danny woke up feeling very sad and tired after doing the exposing plan for Nationals. He sat up slowly. His left hand ran through his messy brown hair.

What he heard was the sound of Butchie-Wutchie breaking loudly for his morning walk. The Pet trainer got up from bed to check up on his canine friend. His sleepy brown eyes saw his cute beagle sitting by the front door.

Butch turned his little reddish-brown and white head and saw his tired master up from bed. The little dog's mouth opened with his floppy pink tongue sticking out.

"Hey, buddy . . ."

Danny was leaning against a wall corner.

Butch stood on all fours and wagged his cute little white tail for attention.

The dog spoke, "Arf!"

Daniel chuckled at his sweet friend's response.

"I'll get us some food and then we'll go for our walk." He suggested to Butch.

As the boys ate and went out on their morning walk, Danny was still hurt for his fiancee's well-being. He hoped things would get better for her after the surgery. Mostly, after their Valentine wedding date.

When the guys got back to their unit home, Butch was tired from his walk. He had a long drink of water and immediately went for the couch. He napped there while Daniel showered and dressed himself to go back to the Pet store.

He softly spoke, "Sleep well, Butchie-Wutchie."

The kind human left the apartment building in his car.

At the Pet store, he did his morning chores and the training booth was all set up for the day. His heart felt good to do some work again. But just the time reached ten till eleven, Jack Randell came by the booth.

The owner dressed in his dark green work shirt, black pants, and slip resistant shoes walked up to Danny for a little chat.

"Morning, Daniel." He greeted his Pet trainer.

The young man looked at his boss and said back, "Hi, Jack."

"Are you okay?" The owner wondered.

Danny knew what his boss meant by that question.

"I'm surviving." He candid.

"That's good." Jack replied. "I am sorry to hear about your fiancee."

Daniel told him, "Me too."

"Is she going to be all right?"

"Um, her mother told me she's going in for foot surgery today." The dog trainer explained sadly.

"Do you think she's going to compete again?" Jack curiously asked.

The young employee had to be strong to say, "No, Jack, she's through competing. Besides, I've always loved her more than just a figure skater."

Mr. Randell complimented his overall dog trainer, "You're good man, Daniel Gray. Sally's really lucky to have you."

The two men shook hands.

"Thank you, Sir."

Jack showed a hesitant smile and their ears heard, "Mind if we come into the booth?"

The boss and his hard working employee turned their heads and saw five owners with their dogs wanting to come in the booth.

"Step right in, folks." Jack proudly stated.

Daniel Gray unlocked the booth's door metal latch and the owners, including Bob and his dog, Smokey, came inside the training booth.

Jack Randell left the booth to do rounds around his store. He was glad not to give up on Danny as a dog trainer.

The dog trainer's work shift for Monday and Tuesday went smoothly. He was surprised the press or the media had not tracked him down to ask him about Sally Hunt's feet condition and if she was going to continue her skating career.

After his shift on Tuesday, Daniel wanted to drive to the hospital when he noticed the abandoned building not far from the Pet store was all fixed up and it was opened. The large screen windows showed a little display of flowers on a wooden table.

His heart was ecstatic to learn that the building was a floral store. He mutter, "Maybe Sally could work there."

Instead of getting in his car, Daniel walked toward the flower. He pushed the door in the store, a little bell above him rang, and he went through the door way.

What he saw inside the store was the whole store was spacious and yet full of beautiful, colorful bouquets on tables or in chilled fridges. A touch screen cash register and a card slider built to the computer screen. He could picture Sally working here and creating floral arrangements.

A lady in her mid-fifties with curly light brown hair and dressed in a black pants, pinkish red blouse, and a green apron over her shirt and pants walked through the back door.

"Hello there, young man!" She happily greeted Danny. "Welcome to Maggie's Bouquets. How can I help you today?"

Danny walked toward the register table and told the lady, "You can help me with two things. First, I would like to get a special grouping for my sick fiancee."

The lady softly gasped, "Oh, my. What's the matter with her?"

He replied, "She's in the hospital. Recovering from foot surgery."

"The poor dear." The florist sadly spoke. "I think I know what she would like."

The nice lady stepped away from the front counter to go to the other end of the store. Danny followed her.

What the florist did was she found beautiful Irises and Freesias from one of the fridges. She gently pruned them with some shears and tied them together with green color twine.

"Perfectly fixed up," said the sweet florist.

Danny smiled at the lady and respond, "It's beautiful. She'll love them."

The lady wondered, "And what's the second thing did you need?"

The Pet trainer looked around the empty store.

"Do you have any workers?" He questioned the florist.

The flower lady let out a little laugh.

"Oh, my goodness, no." With the pretty bouquet in her right hand, she left the grouping counter for the register. "Who on earth would want to work here with me?"

Danny walked behind the florist and added, "I know someone who would love to work for you."

At the front counter, the flower questioned the young man, "Were you talking about yourself?"

He shook his head 'no.' "Nope, not me."

"Who then?" The lady's fingers were touching the computer screen to turn on the register. The machine made little bleeping noises.

Daniel gulped and let out, "Um, Sally Hunt."

The lady's gray eyes left the computer screen to look surprised at Danny. "My boy, she has better things to do than to play with flowers all day."

She pointed out, "Anyway, how would you know her?"

The dog trainer smug, "She's my fiancee."

The bleeping stop.

"Really?" The flower lady seriously asked Danny.

He nodded sternly.

"What makes you think she want to work here?" The lady spoke.

Daniel expressed, "Sally loves flowers. She knows the names of all the flowers and creates breath taking groupings. And she can no longer figure skate."

Before ringing up the flowers, the flower employee curiously questioned her customer, "Why not? She was such a graceful figure skater."

No, she never was. Danny's mind thought. *Damn, I can't tell the florist Sally was a fraud. That would break her heart.*

He figured out what to tell the florist, "She suffered from lots of foot pain when she was a teen and it got the best of her during her long program in Nationals. That's why she needed foot surgery."

Danny put in, "And I think her working here would be a wonderful thing to happen her from unfinished skating career. I work at the Pet store across the street and I think it would be nice for her & I to work close by."

The florist was touched.

She requested from her customer, "When do you think she'll come by the store? I would love to meet her."

Danny's mind thought over on when.

"Maybe on the twelfth of February." He replied.

The lady introduced herself, "Well, I am Maggie and I cannot wait to meet your sunshine fiancee. Hope she gets better soon."

"Me too."

The Pet trainer looked down at his slip resistant shoes and then back up at the register desk.

Maggie handed the flowers to Danny.

She stated, "This one is on me."

"Wow, thank you." Figure Gray gently gasped out and held the bouquet in his left hand.

He happily left the store for his car.

Danny walked to the Pet store's parking lot and carried his fiancee's gift. He got inside his car to drive over for the hospital Sally and her parents were at.

Half an hour later, the Pet trainer made it to the hospital and parked his car at the visitor's parking area. His right hand carefully held the bouquets of Irises and Freesias from the passenger seat. He got out his car and walked toward the main hospital's building. He called up Joy from his cell and told her he was ready to see Sally.

Mrs. Hunt explained to Daniel, "Take the elevator to the fourth floor, turn right, and Sally's room is at the end of the hallway."

Their phone conversation ended.

He stepped into an elevator box, pressed the fourth floor button on the steel wall, and the box flew up four stories high quickly.

The elevator's door opened.

Daniel Gray moved out of the box and turned to his right. He went down the long stretched, empty hospital hallway. The walls were white. Some of the patient's doors were open, others were closed. The floor looked and smelled really clean. A few wheelchairs were beside some patient room's doors.

He made to the last door at the hallway. The large light tan wooden door was slightly ajar. His left hand slowly pushed the door in the room.

What his brown eyes saw were a single hospital bed with open curtains around it, small bathroom box, two comfy dark pink cushioned chairs, and a large screened window at the left side of the hospital bed.

On the rolling table by the bed and the comfy chairs were lots of flowers, balloons, get well cards, and gift baskets from fans or famous figure skaters.

Daniel noticed his fiancee sitting in a steel handle wheelchair with her legs sticking out in front of her and looking out the window. It seemed to the Pet trainer that Sally was dressed in a grayish color hospital gown, her once beautiful blond hair was all messed up and not so blond, a large pillow with a light blue pillow case was under her legs, and a cream color throw blanket covered her feet and legs.

He had his right hand behind his back to hide the flowers and he raised his left fist to softly knock on the large tan door.

His ears heard Sally's tired voice. "Who's there?"

The dog trainer replied, "It's Danny."

Struggled Sally sighed heavily. She still felt tired from her surgery the day before.

Daniel walked inside of Sally's patient room.

When he got a better view of his fiancee by standing at her left side, the once sunshine Sally Hunt looked very pale, her eyes were tired with bags under them, and her face color turned a bit gray. She looked as if life was draining out of her. Her heart was very depressed.

She gently moved up her weak head to see Danny.

Drowsy Sally spoke, "Hi."

The Pet trainer showed Sally her floral bouquet.

"Oh, Danny . . ."

He handed them to her and her achy hands held the grouping. She brought the flowers to her nose to smell them.

"Mmmmm . . . ." She moaned, "Freesia and Iris. Good choice."

Acting like a man in love, Daniel knelt down on the smooth floor and told her, "I was not the one who created it. It was from Maggie and her new floral store."

"She must be a wonderful florist." Sally moaned.

She's not the only one who knows her way around flowers. His heart thought.

He cheerfully asked his love, "How are you feeling?"

Sally softly cried a little.

A minute later, she breathed out, "Oooohhhh . . . horrible."

Danny's right hand held Sally's left hand. His fingers felt her diamond ring on her ring finger. It was still beautiful and shiny as the day he bought it and when proposed to her.

The dog trainer's knees moved a little closer to Sally and he carefully kissed her not so smooth lips. His left hand cupped the right side of her neck. Their soft kiss ended.

Sally's flowers were on her blanket covered lap.

The lovers held their hands tightly.

Danny's fiancee tearful bluish-gray eyes made him feel sad for her. He could not wait to have her be out of the hospital and away from her controlling mother.

Sally whispered, "I am sorry I put you through this."

"Sally." He looked into her eyes and answered, "You never put me through anything on purpose."

He assured her, "It was your deceiving mother who forced you to do her cheating scheme."

Danny's brown eyes glanced again at his love's three stoned engagement ring. He reached for it with his right hand and his lips kissed the stones.

The tired blonde started to cry again.

Daniel moved his arms around his bride-to-be and embraced her tightly. He soothed her, "Shhh . . . I Love You."

Sally was filled with glee. "You-you still . . . Love me?"

Daniel Gray pulled away from Sally.

He lovingly questioned her, "How can I not Love You?"

"But I-" sniffle "I cheated in competitive figure skating." She honestly admitted.

"Ah, baby . . ." The Pet trainer sighed, "It's just a sport. Not the end of the world."

His words did gave Sally encouragement.

He went on, "Anyway, Allison Rigden is not just a figure skater. She's an inspirational coach. She gave me some really good advice about life's simple joys. What I feel for you is true love and passion. Your love & my love are only meant for each other, Sally."

Danny's left fingers were brushing Sally's messy hair.

Even though she was still a little drugged up and tired, Sally did her very best to give Daniel a big smile.

He smiled back and teased, "There's my girl."

Sally Hunt was able to blush naturally.

"I Love You, Daniel Gray . . ."

Danny promised, "I could never Love You enough . . ."

Their arms slowly embraced each other.

During the young lover's sweet talks and kisses, Paul Hunt stood by the tan door and admired the love scene that happened in his daughter's hospital room. He was happy for Danny & Sally to be in love.

He only wished his wife could be happy for them.

Truth of the matter was: Joy Hunt was very, very angry at Daniel Gray for ruining her secret weapon to win the gold in competitive figure skating.

Later that night in bed, Danny tried to sleep, but his heart would not let him. It was filled with aches and pains for the love of his life. He hated to see her be so unhappy and in aches and pain from her feet surgery. He did not recognize the girl he saw in the hospital from the one who found him in his time of need from his seventeenth birthday and the one he proposed to.

The hours past by without him wanting to close his eyes and sleep. Butch joined with his loving owner in his bed for company. The human would pet, talk, and hug his cute pooch in his arms.

As the sun rose, the Pet trainer felt very tired and he did not want to go back to the training booth to work. He sat up in his messy twin size bed. His mind thought about what he needed to do make himself feel better.

Danny took a shower, ate some breakfast with Butch in the kitchen area, put on street clothes, and took his leashed sweet beagle friend to his car. He figured he was not in the right mind to do dog training if all he could think and worry about Sally in the hospital.

He drove his car to the Pet store. He knew his boss was not going to be happy to see him not ready for work.

The car arrived in the parking lot.

Danny found his work keys, picked up his soft beagle from the passenger seat, and the two boys went toward the back door of the Pet store.

After closing the backdoor, Daniel placed Butch on the smooth floor. He held on to Butch's short black leash as they headed to Jack Randell's office room.

Standing in front of the store owner's office door, Danny knocked on the door with his left fist. His right hand held Butch's leash.

Daniel noticed Butch doing a wonderful sit by his right foot. The dog trainer smiled at his trained beagle friend.

The office door opened and behind the door was surprised Jack Randell to see Danny this early at the Pet store.

"Daniel, you look awful." His boss stated sadly.

Danny's tired voice answered, "I need to talk to you."

"Come on in." Jack happily obliged.

Arf!

Both men looked down at Butch.

Jack kindly said, "You too, Butch."

The guys chuckled together and headed inside of the manager's office room. Mr. Randell sat in his leather chair.

Young Gray was seated in the right chair in front of Jack and Butch laid down on the carpet floor.

"So, what can I do for you, Danny and Butch?" Jack curiously requested.

Even though was still very drowsy, Daniel knew what to tell his boss, but how to start it off was his main problem. His mind calmly thought of Sally being in the hospital and the Valentine wedding date was coming up.

"Sir, I've been up all night thinking about Sally and my up coming wedding in February." His tired voice creaked. "I can't stop wondering if my love's going to okay, what's next for her, and preparing myself for marriage life."

His eyes looked at his boss strongly then down at Butch's cute furry face for assurance. Butch wagged his white tail and rolled over on his side for a little belly rub.

Danny slowly lifted up his head and clearly told Jack, "I need some time off to think and have a serious talk with the Hunts."

Jack was a little disappointed to have Daniel wanting to have some more time off from the training booth. Customers loved his dog training techniques and wished to participate by training with their dogs.

His mind made him remember what Danny was like for the past two days. He did look very sad and distant during training times and he would let the owners do all the hard work. He would not give out long speeches or give out a smile. His heart was not ready to go back to the booth.

Mr. Randell made his decision.

"Daniel, how long were you thinking of not working?" Jack questioned his dog trainer.

It was the first day of February and Wednesday.

He candid, "Well, I'll do my best to finish this week and hopefully next week I could have a week off. Be back on Monday and have Valentine's Day off for the ceremony."

His head looked down at Butch. The sweet beagle fell asleep and was very quiet.

Jack got out his schedule folder from one of his desk's drawers. He placed it on the desk, opened it, and looked at the calendar for February. At first he wanted to use his black pen to mark off the days Danny wanted. But he stopped himself.

The dog trainer's request was not fair for him.

The Pet store owner replied, "Daniel, you have done a lot during these past few months and really grew up. I don't recognize the man I see before me than the teenager who wanted to come work for me."

His eyes looked down and he started to write in his folder. He added, "Instead of a week, I am granting you the month off with a little paycheck bonus."

What Daniel heard really struck his heart hard.

"Why?"

Jack announced, "Well, believe or not, I found another nice dog trainer who would be happy to help you in the booth. Now would be a good time to let the new trainer be in the booth by itself before you to work together."

Danny smiled big.

"Wow, thank you, Sir." He stuck out his left hand and they shook hands.

Jack snickered, "I thought you could use some time off after you & Sally's big date. I contacted Miss Nancy from the animal shelter and she was delighted to hear the news."

Danny got up from his seat. He leaned down to get sleepy Butchie-Wutchie off the carpet floor and in his arms. Butch was woken up after being lifted off the floor.

Mr. Randell was up from his leather chair.

"Good luck, Mr. Gray." He proudly spoke.

The men walked to the door and Danny and Butch left the Pet store for their unit home.

The next morning, Daniel Gray woke up feeling not tired but sad for Sally Hunt. Butch was sleeping on his pillow and letting out soft snoring noises from his cute little muzzle mouth.

Danny continued to be bugged of what Sally told him on New Year's Day. She really wanted to give up figure skating even though she was only doing it to win her mommy's love.

But how was daughter Sally going to earn mother Joy's affection without being a figure champion?

Now that he and Allison got their wish to have Sally Hunt out of the figure skating world, he did think of his Figure Instructor's wise words: *What would happen when Sally's skating years are over? What is next for Joy Hunt?*

The Pet trainer remembered his answer, *She would have to let go of Sally and the thrill of winning the gold.*

Maybe this was his chance to get Sally out of the horrid mansion and live happily ever after their wedding date.

The broken hearted human sat up in bed and thought about what to do that day. His bare feet touched the hard wood floor. Both his hands pushed himself up from the messy bed and went for his bathroom.

Butch's ears heard his owner waking up and shutting the bathroom door. His eyes opened, stretched his little tri-color fur coat, and stood up from his comfy pillow.

He felt his tiny tummy rumble.

The cute beagle scampered off for the kitchen.

As Danny exit the bathroom, his eyes saw Butch running toward the kitchen area.

"I know, fuzzy-butt." He stated. "Breakfast."

Daniel gave Butch some fresh kibbles to eat and water to drink. The dog trainer fixed himself small bowl of cereal.

When they finished their morning meal and Danny had his shower and put on clean street clothes, it was time for their walk.

Butch was attached to his gray retractable leash, Danny had plastic baggies in his back right jeans pocket, keys and wallet in his front jeans' pockets, and both boys were ready for their morning walk.

After an hour and a half walk around the city's downtown, Danny and Butch drank some water and rested in the living room on the couch together. The human's heart longed to see Sally again. He knew what he should do next.

Daniel got up from the comfy couch for his cell in his bedroom. He picked it up, flipped the cover, and pressed not Sally's cell number, but her mother's, Joy. It rang twice.

"Hello, Daniel." Rude Joy Hunt answered.

"Hi, Joy." He respond. "Um, could I possibly see Sally today?"

Mrs. Hunt said, "Sure. Paul & I do need your help."

Danny was surprised.

"Help with what?" He asked.

"To bring Sally home." Joy requested.

The Pet trainer delightfully said, "Sure! I'll help you guys out. What time?"

"Aren't you supposed to be at work now?" His fiancee's mother wondered.

"I asked Jack for some time off and granted me the month off. He found a second dog trainer to work for him." He explained happily.

"Ah." Joy scolded. "Well, then, Paul will pick you up at your apartment building around eleven a.m."

Danny agreed. "Sounds good to me."

Then he asked, "How's Sall-" Click!

"Damn bitch hung up on me." He mumbled.

The time was a half hour till eleven.

Danny decided to clean up his unit and made sure Butch was happy and content before leaving the unit home.

Five minutes till eleven.

Young Gray exit his apartment unit, walked down the stairs, and headed out the front doors. He did not wait long for the Hunt's ruby red SUV to arrive. He got inside the car and sat in the passenger.

Paul was dressed in jeans and a light tan sweater.

"Hey, Danny." Mr. Hunt greeted him.

"Hi, Paul." Annoyed Danny spoke.

The car started to move.

"What's wrong?" Paul asked the angry young man.

"You wife loves to hang up on me." Danny pointed out. "She would not let me ask about how Sally was."

Paul explained, "Sally's tired, but she improved a lot since her surgery. As for Joy, she's still upset that you somehow pulled off a plan by showing the world her cheating scheme for Sally."

He did tell him gratefully, "I am glad you did. Joy's been torturing Sally left and right in figure skating so much, it killed my heart to see my little girl having so suffer from doing my favorite sport."

"Why do you let her do it?" Danny questioned his future father-in-law.

"My wife's been good at being so secretive and smart on how to explain Sally's training, I didn't bother to ask her about Sally's plantar fascia condition. I never thought she was that harsh behind close doors." Paul sighed.

The Pet trainer asked, "Did you know she was spying on me and Ally before Nationals?"

"Ah, Joy . . ."

Disappointed Paul Hunt was not told about that.

"Daniel, I am so sorry for all the shitty nonsense Joy put you and Ally through." He sadly apologized. "How did you know Joy was doing that?"

Danny told Paul, "Allison & her boyfriend were doing driving around the area to see if Joy really was doing some detective work on Ally for Nationals. They got pictures of Mrs. Hunt driving around in a white SUV and wearing disguises."

"I don't know who she is anymore." Disappointed Mr. Hunt breathed out.

The red SUV made it to the hospital's main entrance.

By the front sliding door were pale Sally in her hospital gown and sitting in a wheelchair and stern-looking Joy dressed in dark gray pants and a light tan colored blouse was standing by her daughter. Sally smiled when she saw the red SUV pulling by the entrance. She knew who was in the car. Her father and Daniel Gray.

The SUV stopped. Out came from the passenger side was a smily Danny. "Hi, Sally."

He helped Sally out of her wheel chair and into the car by carrying her in his arms.

Joy went inside the car and sat in the passenger seat.

All four figures were buckled up and ready to leave the hospital. Paul drove to the mansion.

Forty minutes later, Daniel Gray happily had Sally Hunt in his arms and brought her inside the large beautiful home. Paul unlocked and opened the door for the couple. His wife detested to see her daughter be happy with the Pet trainer.

Danny traveled from the front door to the living room. He gently placed Sally on one of the comfy sofas. They shared a sweet kiss.

When they part, the dog trainer kneeled on the rug by her side. Their hands held together. Squeezing with love and comfort for each other.

"How are you, babe?" Danny lovingly asked his girl.

She tried to put on a brave face even though her eyes were looking droopy to him.

Angry Joy Hunt shouted, "Daniel! Please leave!"

He turned his head and requested, "Why?"

Mrs. Hunt declared, "Sally needs her rest and you're no longer needed here. Go now."

"What if I don't want to leave my fiancee?" Danny decided to fight back. His hands held Sally's hands tighter.

"You may have ruined Sally's skating career, but I know what's best for my daughter." The devil's bitch snarled. "And you are not good for Sally."

Don't do this, Joy. Paul thought in his head while he stood in the entrance for the living room.

Joy wanted to leave the room when Danny spoke up.

"What? You don't think I'm good for Sally?" He stood up on his feet and eyed at the red haired woman. "I have something to say to you, Joy Hunt!"

Drowsy Sally begged, "Danny, don't-"

He curt, "No, Sally. All I want is to love your daughter, not sex her up and use her money! I have been busting my ass at work and on the ice for four months now! I became a better skater than I thought I would! Haven't I proven my worthiness to earn your blessing?"

The horrid figure coach calmly answered, "No."

"Why not?" Danny desperately wondered.

Joy walked in front of the dog trainer and sternly said, "I just don't like you."

Daniel felt his heart be smashed into tiny pieces.

"Even though I did what you asked me to do, it's isn't enough for me to marry Sally?" He sadly asked.

Noble Mrs. Hunt huffed, "Oh, Daniel, I only thought of the agreement so I could punish you for dating and loving my talented daughter."

Figure Gray was more hurt than ever. He wanted to cry but he did his best to hold back the tears. His legs started to walk himself out of the living room.

Daniel stood by the front door and with a defeated tone of voice, he announced loudly, "Good-bye, Sally . . ."

Chapter Twenty-Seven

It had been almost an entire week without talking or seeing Sally Hunt. In quiet and clean apartment unit, Daniel Gray just laid unhappily in his bed with his sweet beagle pooch. Butch was on his master's chest and receiving lots of love and affection from the human's hands.

Now Danny wished not asking his boss for some time off from work. His heart and mind were very bored by doing the same old thing.

Wake-up, have breakfast, walk time, stay in the unit or go out for errands, lunch, afternoon walk, dinner, and then off for bed. What he mostly thought was the anger he had against Joy Hunt after she told him she only thought of the figure stipulation to punish him because he wanted to get involved with her daughter.

His heart on the other hand was painfully without Sally in his life. But he felt no need to be with her if her mother continued to act like a stuck-bitch toward him. His passion for the one he loved was really 'annihilate' from Joy's tricks and convincing words.

Danny did not want to talk about his new problem to anyone. Especially to his parents. He only told it to Butch. The good thing was his sweet beagle would only listen instead of barking back to him. That made the Pet trainer feel a little better.

When Wednesday arrived, Daniel got up from bed. Butch was still sleeping happily on his pillow. The human went for the bathroom. The cute beagle woke up from his blissful slumber. His paws moved toward the kitchen for something to eat.

Danny exit the bathroom and noticed Butch in the kitchen for his breakfast. They ate together and the dog trainer got himself ready for Butch's morning walk. Just when he was putting on his tennis shoes, his cell was ringing an electronic tune.

He turned his focus at his nightstand. His left hand grabbed his phone. The ID screen read Allison's cell number.

Danny flipped open his cell cover and said, "Hi, Ally."

"Hello, Daniel!" She sure sound very happy to his ears. "How are you, Figure Gray?"

Annoying Danny honestly answered, "Bored."

Ally sadly wondered, "Oh, why are you so sad?"

He heavily breathed out, "I don't feel comfortable talking about it over the phone. Can we meet up and talk?"

"Shouldn't you getting ready for work at the Pet store?" She questioned her student.

Daniel replied, "Not for this month."

"Did something bad happen at the booth or something?" Allison curiously asked.

The Pet trainer's heart was stabbing badly.

"I can't concentrate on work while Sally's recovering from her foot surgery, what we went through during Nationals, and-" he could not finish the last part of his sentence.

Danny started to cry a little over the phone.

"I'll come and pick you up at your apartment unit in a half hour and we'll skate and talk." She suggested.

"I like that, Ally."

Their conversation ended quickly.

Danny looked down and sadly told Butch, "Sorry, pal. No walk this morning."

The sweet beagle went to the bathroom for his grass.

Upset Danny put on a gray t-shirt, black thin socks, and black sweat pants. His skating bag was all packed up. He gathered his cell, wallet, and keys.

Both boys had some breakfast in the kitchen.

Then Daniel rushed out of his unit and went down the stairs for the building's front doors. By the front doors, his eyes were looking for Ally's cute white Horundi. The Pet trainer was excited to skate again and have a long chat about his new problem with Joy Hunt.

After five minutes of waiting for his Figure Instructor, a very bran-new shiny silver convertible pulled up. The car was a two seater with black leather seats, round front and back, and it looked like a beautiful, futuristic flying car without wings on the side. It parked in front of his apartment building. The car looked so beautiful and sleek, Daniel was surprised to see it in this part of town.

Who he saw driving in the silver car shocked him most of all. It was smily Ally-Loop.

She got out driver's seat and was dressed in new light blue jeans, a cute long sleeved light purple blouse, and not in her N+ running shoes, but in light purple low heeled shoes.

Daniel opened the right door and gasped out, "Ally, what the fuck is that?"

Allison smug, "It's my new car."

"I never seen a car like this before." He stated.

"That's because it's a present to myself if I won the gold." She added. "It's my new Horundi R8 Serpent."

"Damn shit."

They walked toward the hot-looking silver car.

Ally unlocked the Serpent's trunk with her new key chain. Danny put his skating in the trunk box.

He closed the trunk's cover and asked Ally, "Does Richard know about this car?"

Both figures sat in the black leather seats, buckled themselves, and the Loop turned on her new Horundi Serpent.

"He came with me to get my car early this morning." Ally giggled. "He told me 'The Serpent was made for you.'"

The Serpent started to move and it purred like a growling tiger. Their ride traveled north from Danny's apartment building. He knew where they were going.

Short time later, Ally stopped in front of her abandoned building. This time, she did not park across from the building. The Figure Instructor pressed a button on the steering wheel and the sliding door moved toward the right. Danny was confused.

Allison explained, "Richard arranged some secure modifications for the building. Especially with the sliding door to keep our cars safer."

She stepped on the gas pedal and slowly drove inside the building. The figure friends were not the only ones who were going to skate on her private rink. Daniel saw Richard's black truck in the building too. The building's sliding door automatically moved to the left side and it was closed and locked up.

Allison and her figure student got their skating bags out from the trunk to walk toward a door from the right side of the building. Behind that door was an elevator that would go down the basement without leaving the building for the secret side door. They got in the box and Ally pressed the silver steel B button on the button board.

The box smoothly flew down for the basement floor.

Ally questioned Danny, "How are things with you?"

He answered, "Not so well."

Ding!

The elevator's steel doors slide open and the figures were close by the cold ice rink. They moved from the box with their skating bags.

Both their brown eyes saw Captain Richard McCarthy skating around the patch of ice in his hockey skates. He wore jeans and his away game white jersey shirt.

Allison and Daniel sat on the steel benches to lace up their skates. While they laced, snow sprayed them.

"McCarthy!" Ally teasingly protested.

Rich chuckled loudly and skated away from his close figure friends. He was having an awesome time practicing his hockey stops around the rink with his newly sharpened blades.

The Loop and the Pet trainer got on the ice.

All three figures glided and skated smoothly together.

Half an hour later, Ally and Danny had a long talk while Richard practiced his slap shots with the hockey net for that evening's home game at the Tiger Shark's domain arena.

"So, what's wrong Danny?" Concerned Ally sadly asked him.

Danny started off, "Joy hurt me real bad a week ago."

The Figure Instructor was pissed. "What did she say?"

"'I only thought of the agreement so I could punish you for dating and loving my talented daughter.'" He quoted Joy's pessimistic words.

Ally was heart broken. She softly gasped, "Oh, Daniel . . ."

Her voice spoke, "Do you think you & Sally's wedding will still be on?"

"I don't think so." Disappointed Danny replied.

He and Ally skated backwards. He added, "I told Sally, 'Good-bye . . .'"

Daniel's feet pumped up his speed and started to skate around half of the rink really fast. His heart was still hurt to tell Sally 'good-bye.' He had to if Joy really wanted Danny not be part of the family.

Sad Allison stood at the center part of the rink. She watched both her top figure students skate their own way. Danny with his figure moves and Richard working with his hockey stick and pucks.

Her mind thought on what to tell Daniel Gray. That maybe things would get better in the end, or he & Sally really were not meant to be. The last part stung Ally-Loop's heart. She was glad she got what she want, and Sally had a wonderful man in her life. If only there was a way to show Joy Hunt how much Danny loved Sally. Maybe there was.

Allison questioned her student, "Daniel Gray, what makes you happy no matter what happens in life?"

Danny was caught off guard from that question.

He stopped gliding and stood in front of Ally to answer, "Sally."

"Why does Sally Hunt make you happy?" The Figure Instructor wondered.

He explained, "When I'm with Sally, my heart feels love and comfort. I cannot see myself with or have the wants or needs for another girl. I only see and admire 'Sally the woman,' not 'Figure Champ Sally Hunt.'"

Ally then spoke, "How do you keep your passion for Sally alive?"

Danny thought for a moment.

"By remembering her in everything I do when she & I cannot be together or work hand-in-hand." He quoted strongly from his father's point of view on what a loving marriage should be like.

Ally spoke breathlessly, "Wow. I am impressed."

The two started glide off from the middle for a side wall.

At the wall, the dog trainer wondered, "What's impressive?"

Ally chuckled and leaned against the cold wooden wall, "Not many guys can talk or think decently about girls or women these days. Daniel, don't ever lose that sweet loving passion. I have a feeling you're going to regret it for the rest of you life. Sally is lucky to have someone like you in her life."

Daniel thought about why Allison asked him those questions. *They were the three questions Ally created to understand about one's true passion. And I just gave her my answers. Sally is my answer in life.*

His heart did feel better. A curious question came to his mind for his Figure Instructor's future skating career.

"So, what's next for Ally-Loop?"

The two friends started to skate again.

Scrap, crunch . . .

Whoosh . . .

Crunch, scrap . . .

Allison sighed, "Well . . . now that I'm the Senior Ladies' gold medalist for the USIS, it's off to Nice, France for the 2012 World Figure Skating Competition next month."

"Nervous?" The Pet trainer wondered.

"Nope. I'm ready to conquer Worlds for the gold, and hopefully, by 2014, I'll be part of the Winter Olympics."

Danny encouraged her, "You'll do great."

Both figure skaters turned backwards unison.

"Would Number 65 cheer for you during Worlds?" Danny curiously asked Allison.

Her brown eyes looked at the Tiger Shark's Captain skating with his wooden hockey stick and practicing shooting the puck at the net. She shook her head 'no' to Danny.

"He'll still be doing PHL games." Ally sadly explained. "My coach promise to video tape them from my phone and I'll email them to Rich."

Daniel's heart felt good. "That's a nice thing for your coach to do."

The Figure Instructor had an idea. She suggested, "Would you like one more figure skating lesson this Saturday afternoon?"

Her student replied, "Sure. What time?"

"Rich & I will pick you up around noon." Ally decided. "Besides the Hunts, McCarthy wants to test your figure skills too."

"Sounds good." The Pet trainer started to skate around the rink again and skated and skated as much as he wanted to that day.

Thursday went by smoothly for Danny.

He and Butch had a wonderful day spending time together as a man and his dog in their unit home and at the beach. The human's heart once again felt love for Sally Hunt. He only wish he could see or just talk to her again.

Friday morning arrived.

Daniel woke up from his bed feeling sad and lonely. His heart really longed for Sally again. He wondered if he & she were ever going to get back together again and finally be married to each other. He missed having Sally in his bed with him. His arms protecting her throughout the night and her loving him when things got tough for him.

Danny sat up in his twin size bed and noticed Butch was sitting next to the bed. He 'yelped!'

The human groaned, "Hey, fuzzy-butt."

He got up from his messy bed and off for the bathroom.

After Daniel left the bathroom, he heard his cell phone ringing in his bedroom. He immediately rushed to the nightstand. What he saw on the cover was Joy Hunt's phone number. He thought, *Fuck, what does she want now?*

His hands flipped the cover and answered, "Joy."

Mrs. Hunt spoke, "Morning, Daniel."

"Why are you calling me?" He demanded.

"I called to say, 'I am sorry' and Paul & I wish for you to come over to the mansion this afternoon," she expressed out.

For a moment, Danny could have sworn that Joy sounded remorseful and nice to him. That could not be the 'Joy Hunt' he knew.

"Please come?" The sunshine mother pleaded. "Sally needs you. Ever since you left, she refused to eat, take her medicine, or want to get out of her room."

His eyes closed and his heart hurt his insides from knowing his fiancee did not want to live without him. He made up his mind.

"All right. I'll come over, if you promise not to interfere when I'm around Sally." Danny declared. Then he added, "And I get bring my dog."

Mrs. Hunt hastily promised, "I promise not to bother you & Sally, Daniel. I hope your dog is well-trained. Please hurry. It's been over a week since I seen my daughter."

The dog trainer hastily replied, "I will."

Danny hung up his cell. He took a quick shower, ate breakfast with Butch, changed his clothes, and the two boys left the unit together.

When his car arrived at the mansion, Danny and unleashed Butch got out. They walked around the Hunt's grassy property and the sweet did his potty business. Daniel cleaned up this pooch's mess with a small plastic baggy. He tossed it in one of the trash cans by the back doors. His left hand knocked on the door.

Paul Hunt wearing a dark blue long sleeved shirt and tan pants when noticed he Danny at the back doors instead of the front door. He opened the door and asked, "Daniel, what brings you here?"

He let the young man and his sweet beagle dog inside the mansion's kitchen.

"Um, your wife called me to come here and help Sally out of her room." Danny told Paul his plan.

The dog trainer immediately went to the kitchen sink and washed and dried his hands.

Arf!

Butch sounded determined to help his master too.

Danny and Paul's eyes saw Mrs. Hunt walk into the kitchen.

They were both surprised to see her dressed in jeans and a dark green long sleeved shirt. Danny never saw her in casual clothes before. Paul on the other hand had not seen his wife in comfy clothes for a long time.

"Come on, Daniel." Joy spoke.

"Butch, stay with Paul." The human commanded to his good behaved beagle dog.

Butchie-Wutchie calmly sat on the hardwood floor in front of Paul Hunt.

Mrs. Hunt was impressed with Daniel Gray's dog. She and Danny exit the kitchen, walked through the entrance hallway, and walked up the stairs.

As the two were on the second floor, Joy's right hand knocked on Sally's bedroom door.

"Sally, please come out." She called out.

Nothing happened.

Danny suggested, "Let me try."

Joy did not argue with the Pet trainer's idea. She stepped down the stairs and left Daniel alone.

Standing by his love's bedroom door, Danny softly spoke, "Sally-babe, it's Danny."

He took in a few deep breaths and continued on, "Could you open the door? I wanna talk with you."

His right hand was placed on the wooden door. "I Love You . . ."

Danny's heart cried out for his love. "I miss you and-"

The door suddenly opened and there was sad, tired Sally Hunt in her wheelchair. Her crackled voice replied, "I Love You too . . ."

Danny got down on his knees and held her tight.

When he rose up from the carpet floor, his hands and arms got Sally out of her wheelchair, and he slowly made his way down the staircase.

What Paul & Joy Hunt saw in the front entrance was Daniel carrying Sally in his arms. The sunshine's parents were happy to have their daughter out of her room.

Danny gently placed his fiancee in a comfy chair with her legs sticking out in front of her on an ottoman. He was on the floor and sitting next to her chair.

He kindly asked, "Is there anything you want?"

Sally Hunt smiled and softly exclaimed, "Besides you? Mommy, I am kinda hungry."

Joyous Joy said, "Say no more."

She left the living room for the kitchen and fixed up Sally a yummy breakfast of chocolate waffles, eggs, bacon, and orange juice to drink. She also gave Sally some water and painkiller medicine pills for her feet pain.

Daniel was shocked to see Joy be nice to anyone.

Sally Hunt was starting to feel better after eating something, taking her painkillers, and seeing Daniel again.

"Thank you for bringing me out of my room, Danny." The sunshine girl spoke. "It was starting to get stuffy in there."

Everyone laughed at Sally's tease.

Arf!

Butch respond next to Paul's feet.

"Hi, Butchie-Wutchie!" Sally squealed.

Her bluish-gray eyes looked at her Mommy to say, "Thank you, Mommy."

Her mother told her, "You're welcome, Sally."

Paul smiled at his wife and daughter. He was proud that Joy decided to be nicer to Daniel and accept him as Sally's fiance. Mr. Hunt also knew it was time for Mrs. Hunt to explain Danny her reason to do the cheating scheme for their daughter's skating career.

"Joy," he offered, "is there something that you need to tell Danny?"

Mrs. Hunt got up from the sofa for Paul's office room.

Sally was done with her breakfast.

Paul took his daughter's messy plate, empty glasses, and went to the kitchen. Danny got up from the rug floor to sit on the couch next to Sally. Butch jumped up on the couch with his owner.

Joy came back to the living room with Sally's pink skating duffle bag in her left hand. Paul headed into the living room too.

The married Hunts sat on a sofa and Joy unzipped the bag to show Danny Sally's skating gear. Her hands pulled out the flexible nude color wires, lots of sticker-like, gold and silver colored microchips, a nude color body suit, the jewel headband, and the old special figure skates.

Mrs. Hunt put the skating stuff on the coffee table.

She explained, "Allison & her boyfriend, Richard, brought back Sally's skating things last night. They told me they were sorry for taking the gear and why they had to do it. I was still mad at all of you for doing the exposing and told the two off."

"But this morning, Joy & I had a long talk with Ally & Rich and we all came to an understanding between each other," added Paul.

"Wonderful." Danny stated. "That's good news."

Joy put in, "I guess Allison told you the story about Sally's feet problem."

Daniel looked at his fiancee's tired face and back to her parents to say, "Yes, she did. Ally told me the tale on how she knew about Sally's feet problem and the clues she found that you were doing the cheating scheme. She figured it all out after I told her what I saw from the man's laptop screen."

A new interesting question popped into his head.

"How did you keep the man with the laptop and your puppet figure skater close and yet hidden from the public?" Danny wondered.

Joy explained, "They live in secure homes and both traveled privately while my family and I did public transportation. Sally's skating gear went with them too."

Clever idea, Joy. Daniel thought in his head.

The next thing Mrs. Hunt told her daughter's fiance was a hurtful story for her to tell.

"I suppose you want to know how it all began?"

Danny just nodded his head.

"Well, then," Joy started out, "it all happened after Sally was examined from the doctor in the girl's locker room. I did not want my daughter to stop ice skating and I began a research on how to decrease Sally's plantar fascia problem. Paul & I took her to doctors, Sally even went through special physical therapy for her feet, and we did some in-home treatments for her with no lasting success."

Mrs. Hunt breathed out, "One day at a Children's Hospital, I stumbled upon a room with a little girl and a doctor inside. The little girl's left arm was a little limb. The doctor connected flexible wires and sticker microchips from a computer to her head. The little girl had a prosthetic arm to cover her limb. What the prosthetic arm and fingers did was it moved all on its own when the doctor typed on the computer's keyboard to make it move. The little girl was so happy to have her new arm move, I thought, 'That's what I'll do for Sally. Make a computer do the moves for her.'"

Paul jumped in, "At first I thought that would be a very stupid and illegal idea. But Joy wanted to do it anyway. She called up lots of doctors and computer programers on how to make Sally a champ from a computer. All they told her was 'a computer cannot make someone's muscles move if it doesn't have a special muscle memory program to save all muscle movements from an actual human being.'"

Joy told Danny, "How it worked was my figure puppet wore the silver color memory microchips, does a skating routine, the computer program saved her muscle movements, and Sally wore the gold mimic microchips that would make her do the same moves as the other skater. Both girls wore their own hair color headband because the diamond on top the was a special radio signal senor to activate all the chips."

"And that's when Donna, Ally's old friend, came in." Danny pointed out.

"Yes." Joy replied. "I had to find a skater who was strong enough as Sally to make the MMMs work for her. Lots of girls did not make the cut."

She added. "When Donna came to the rink one day, she was really good from doing five months of figure skating lessons. We talked, got to be friends, and offered her a proposition. She agreed since she wanted to get back at Allison Rigden for some reason. Donna never told anyone, even her parents, what she was really doing in figure skating. I knew then I found my perfect puppet so Sally could win the gold."

In other words, Joy could feel like she won the gold from her own daughter. The Pet trainer thought.

Daniel asked Paul Hunt, "Paul, why didn't you win the gold yourself?"

Mr. Hunt was caught off guard. His answer was, "I didn't want to compete or travel the world while Joy was pregnant with Sally."

He continued, "Joy & I married young and Sally came into my life at 22. I quit my skating career so I would be a father to her."

"Daddy was my first coach." Sally replied softly. "He trained me well and I got good. At age seven, Mommy want to take over my skating training and she overworked me. That was why I had plantar fascia."

Joy was feeling a little better by telling the dog trainer her cheating scheme story. She asked, "Daniel Gray, did you still want to be with Sally?"

His right hand took Sally's left hand and held it tight. He answered, "Only if she'll have me."

His & her eyes touched their hearts and the inside of their bodies were filled with love.

Sally lovingly whispered, "I do want you, Danny."

The dog trainer got up from the couch without letting go of Sally's hand. He leaned over and kissed her lips.

Joy Hunt declared, "Paul & I still want to see your skating routine."

"Joy, he does not have to." Paul softly argued.

"Yes, I do." Danny Gray stood up from the couch and told the Hunts, "I made a promise to the family and I don't want to break it."

Joy got up on her feet and said, "Tomorrow night at the small rink. Eight p.m."

"Yes, Ma'am."

After visiting the Hunts, Daniel and Butch went to their apartment unit home for lunch and then went out for a long walk around the neighborhood. What he wanted to do later that day was ice skate as much as he could. Practice his skating routine before meeting up with Ally & Rich and showing the Hunts his skating skills. He was surprised that even though Joy had spied on him and Ally a lot, she did not compliment his figure skills.

He was ready to go ice skating.

Butch was happily napping on his pillow as his master dressed himself in sweat pants, t-shirt, thin socks, and a sweater to keep him warm. His skating bag was all set.

Danny left his unit, locked the door, and went down the stairway for his car.

He arrived at the arena building a little after seven p.m. Paid for admission, headed for the men's locker room, put on his suede figure boots, his things were stored away in his temp locker, and stepped out of the locker room.

Not many people came to the rink that night.

He did not mind that at all.

The Zamboni truck left the freshly cut ice and the driver scrapped off the extra snow and ice from the smooth rink. The truck's gate door slid down.

Time to skate.

Danny's blades touched the ice. His heart was satisfied to be back on the cold patch of ice. He pushed away from the gate door and glided fast around the glassy ice.

What he did throughout that skating session was worked on the basics and practiced his skating routine. He pretend Joy & Paul Hunt were there to judge his figure moves. His mind remembered all the simple basic tips Ally told him from figure positions, to glide smoothly, and keep on moving around the whole rink. He really wanted to impress his future in-laws all he learned from Ally-Loop.

The Pet trainer was happy to skate once again.

He wondered if he wanted to figure skating for fun after the Hunt's judgments and the wedding date.

Saturday morning arrived.

Daniel Gray's brown eyes opened up.

He sat up nervously in his empty twin size bed when thought, *Tonight's a big one for me. It's what I've been waiting for months. I would be like Allison Rigden. It will be my turn to shine in front of the Hunts.*

Danny spoke, "Butch!"

The cute beagle got up from his pillow and looked at his owner.

The beagle owner declared, "Let's go for a run."

Arf!

Butch left the bedroom in a hurry.

Daniel went for the bathroom and then the kitchen for a light breakfast. The two boys were excited for their run that morning.

When they finished, Danny slipped on his tennis shoes, attached Butch to his short leash, got some baggies, and grabbed his keys. The human lead his sweet dog out of their unit home, locked the door, walked down the stairs for the front doors, and the two pals ran around the neighborhood for a half hour.

Tired and exhausting Daniel and Butch made it back to their unit in good timing. The dog trainer was covered in sweat. Butch was drooling and panting like crazy.

They both a long rest in the living room and a very long drink of cold water.

Danny felt good to run again. Like with Ally, he was not alone when he ran. Butch kept with him or Danny would slow down so his loving dog would keep up the pace.

It was close to eleven-thirty a.m. that morning.

The dog trainer had to shower and prepare for his last skating lesson with gold medalist Ally-Loop & her hunky player, Richard McCarthy.

Twenty minutes later, Danny had his skating bag in hand and told his pooped out pooch, "I'll be back later, Butch."

The human left his unit home and locked the door.

Even though he was still a little tired from his run, Daniel made his way down the stairs for the building's front doors. He waited by the doors for Richard's black truck to arrive. He knew it had to McCarthy's truck if he & Ally were going to pick up Danny. There would not be enough room in Ally's Horundi two seated Serpent.

Sure enough, his brown eyes saw McCarthy's shiny black truck pulling up by the curb.

Danny's heart was beating fast. He breathed in heavily to steady down his heart. His left fist opened the door to his right and left the building. His legs moved down the stairs. He made it for the Captain's truck and got inside.

Both Richard & Allison were sitting up at front with big smiles on their faces.

"Afternoon, Danny." She greeted him.

"Hi, Ally. Hi, Rich." Danny said back while he put his skating bag next him and buckling up his seat belt.

Richard drove his truck from the curb. He made the truck go north from Danny's apartment building.

Daniel's last lesson was going to be taken place in Ally-Loop's private rink.

McCarthy asked, "How are you today?"

Danny candid, "Getting better."

"Oh, yea?" Ally wondered. "Why's that?"

He told the figure couple, "I talked and went to see the Hunts yesterday because Sally was not happy without me in her life. Joy told me the whole cheating scheme story."

Both the Loop & Number 65 were surprised that Joy Hunt would open herself to Daniel Gray.

"So, is the wedding still on?" Richard questioned him.

Danny build up his courage and answered, "Um, Joy & Paul will tell me tonight after I do my routine. Why?"

Allison requested, "Richard & I want to be there for you two. The Tiger Shark's Captain already bought a super nice tux, a wonderful wedding present, and planned a private flight to Santa Rosa from Washington D.C. after game night on the thirteenth."

The Pet trainer did remember he owed his Figure Instructor for helping him with his skating skills and his dog training job. He replied, "I'll make sure that you & McCarthy are V.I.P.s from me & future Mrs. Sally Gray."

Rich smiled, "That's not a bad ring. 'Mrs. Sally Gray.'"

His head quickly looked at Ally with sweet loving eyes.

"Maybe not as bad 'Mrs. Allison McCarthy.' Or is it going to be 'Mrs. Number 65' in the future?" Danny teased.

The dog trainer was the only who laughed at the tease.

Ally & Rich did a short glance at each other.

They both wondered, *Does he know?*

Sooner than Daniel thought, Richard pressed a button on the steering wheel so the abandon building's sliding door could open. The black truck slowly rolled inside the building. The sliding door closed shut when all the figures left the truck with their skating bags.

They went for the elevator and the box rolled down to the basement floor. The figure friends headed toward the steel bleachers to lace up their figure boots.

The Pet trainer was a little confused on why Number 65 did not put on his hockey skates.

Then Danny remembered Ally telling him that Richard wanted to judge Figure Gray's skating skills. That was why McCarthy wished to wear his figure skates instead of hockey skates. To act like a figure pro.

They were all ready to skate.

Richard & Ally stepped on the ice first.

When Daniel got a closer look of Allison's hands, she was wearing light black wool gloves. The figure student hardly ever saw his Figure Instructor wear gloves on her hands.

What changed? He thought.

Danny stood by the open gate door, took off his guards, and his blades touched the ice. His legs and feet pushed him around the ice.

Ally found her remote for her MP3 player's speaker.

Music started to play from the speaker. The tune was not a heavy metal song. To the Pet trainer's surprise, it was a sweet love song. He knew something big was going on between Allison Rigden & Richard McCarthy. He had to know what was up.

Daniel decided to skate gracefully for his Figure Instructor and his 'pretend' Paul & Joy Hunt. His ears and heart listened closely to the song's beats and the musical flowing notes.

Richard watched Daniel skate like a figure male. He was impressed and shocked that Ally's teachings was real instead of a fluke of luck. He did remember that special first year of skating with Allison on and off ice. She really helped him a lot in everything he needed to learn in figure skating and do hockey plays.

The puck chaser gazed at Ally skating toward Daniel. He was not jealous of his girl talking to another guy anymore. He simply ignored the two figures by doing spins, jumps, and dance steps.

Stopping in front of Danny, Allison requested one last time, "What would you like to learn today?"

Daniel thought and thought. He did not think there would be anything else for him to learn in figure skating.

He spoke, "Nothing new. Just work more on my routine. I want to be ready for the Hunts."

"Okay."

Ally pointed her remote to her speaker and pressed three buttons to play Danny's skating routine song. He stood at the gate door and began to do forward strokes for the center part of the rink.

Figure Gray did a dance step around the middle and a really good single flip jump. Next up was another dance step.

While Ally admired her student's skating routine, Richard stood next to her and whispered, "Danny's a pretty good novice."

"Thank you for your honesty, Rich."

They quickly gave each other little kiss on the lips.

Daniel's routine lasted for two and a half minutes. He felt very proud of himself when he did his show stop for the ending.

Both Allison & Richard applauded at Danny's routine.

"Good job, Danny." Ally spoke grandly.

"You're really going to impress the Hunts tonight." Candid Richard.

"Thank you both." Tired Danny glided towards them. "For showing me-that it's okay to-figure skate and be cool about it."

They all laughed at that statement.

From their laughter, Rich skated off the ice, slipped on his guards, and went over to the small gray office room.

Ally told Danny, "We have a surprise for you."

Both their eyes noticed McCarthy carrying a big black rectangular box in his arms. He sat on the steel bleacher's first row.

"Come on." The Loop suggested.

She and her student glided to the open gate door, put on their guards, and stepped toward the bleachers.

Ally sat next to Rich and Danny sat beside the two, facing them.

"Hope you like it." McCarthy smug.

Daniel looked down at the shiny black cardboard box. He was very curious on what was inside the box. His fingers lifted the box's cover and placed the cover on the opposite end from the figure friends. In the bottom part of the box were dark blue tissue paper covering something. He carefully lifted up the tissue paper's ends and his eyes saw a silky white dress shirt and black skating pants.

Danny figured out what the shirt and pants were for.

"Thank you." He looked up at his wonderful friends and spoke gratefully.

Ally wondered, "What time does your routine start tonight?"

"Joy told me eight p.m. at the small rink." He explained.

Richard McCarthy suggested, "Why don't your try on your outfit and then practice your routine in it?"

Danny thought that was a good idea. He picked up the box and got up from sitting on the steel bleacher's row. Ally & Rich got up to lead him to the office room.

Allison unlocked the office door with her hot pink & black key. Danny walked inside while Ally closed the door. He turned on the lights, sat on the padded chair, unlaced his suede boots, and quickly took off his pervious clothes.

First he put on the black pants and then the white blouse shirt. His half naked body sure felt cold in the office room. The shirt and pants fit him wonderfully. He did like his routine outfit. He sat back down on the padded chair and laced up his skates. His heart started to beat fast just by wearing his nice figure clothes. He was nervous. This would be a practice on how tonight would be like.

Daniel slowly opened the door and walked out of the office room. His eyes saw the rink being dark and quiet. Then a white spotlight shined a few inches in front of him. He knew he needed to get on the ice.

Acting like Sally Hunt or Ally before their routine turn, the Pet trainer moved from the office room's door and made it toward the open gate door. His eyes did not see Ally or Rich in plain sight. He wondered where they were.

Daniel stood by the open gate door. He breathed in deeply. His lungs were filled with the cold air. The dog trainer gazed at the empty ice rink and music started to play. He stroked around the smooth patch of ice. He began his routine by thinking on his moves and being a strong, graceful figure male. He smiled and glided to the song's musical tune.

In the dark Zamboni box, Richard & Allison watched their figure friend skate like a performer on ice. Both lovers were proud of Danny's skating routine.

When the routine was done, Daniel did a show stop with both his arms sticking up high in the air. The lights turned on and Number 65 & the Loop clapped and cheered for Danny's flawless short program. He saw them in the Zamboni box and bowed at them.

Ally & Rich left the truck's box.

Tired and happy Danny skated to the open gate door.

Allison said, "That was perfect, Danny."

"You did a wonderful job, Figure Gray." Rich complimented.

The guys shook hands and Ally gave her figure student a short hug. All three skaters got on the ice to skate more.

Fifteen minutes after Daniel did his routine, he and Ally talked at the center while Richard skated backwards around the whole rink. The instructor and her student slowly glided on an invisible circle.

Allison spoke, "Daniel Gray, you are ready to be judged by Paul & Joy Hunt. Just remember what you did earlier and you'll pass with flying colors."

"I'm glad you think so, Ally." He confidently replied. "Thank you for your teachings and passionate wise words."

The Figure Instructor sniffled happily, "You're welcome. I'm glad you learned a lot."

Daniel really knew something was up if Allison was acting all emotional. He looked at Rich gliding off the ice.

"Ally, is there something going on between you & McCarthy?" The dog trainer suspiciously wondered.

She turned to see sleeping Richard on the second row of the steel bleachers. She whispered to her student, "Yes."

Danny leaned in close and asked, "Are you pregnant?"

Ally's eyes were wide open from Danny's curiosity. She inaudibly breathed out, "No, I'm not pregnant."

"Then what's up?" He questioned her.

"Um, Rich, he uh-" She giggled her hardest and did a show stop. Her gloved right hand made a rim on her forehead and her left gloved hand was by her left hip.

Serious Danny stopped beside Ally. He never seen his Figure Instructor act so happy or be so girly before. She was blushing, giggling a lot, and acting like a sweet-loving girl.

He wondered, "What's so funny?"

She dropped her right hand down from her forehead.

"Oh, Number 65 did a special treat for me last night and I'm still overwhelmed from my surprise." Smiley Ally said to her figure novice.

"What did McCarthy do for you?" He pressed on.

Still full of emotions in her heart and mind, the new gold medalist figure champ closed her mouth, looked at Danny, and thought about how to tell him what happened between her & Richard McCarthy. Her heart made her have a flashback of the night before after a PHL Tiger Shark's game against the Sauk Hawks.

Chapter Twenty-Eight

The game's third period began and at the stand's first center row, happy Allison Rigden was dressed in comfy blue jeans and a custom made black fan's jersey shirt with the name 'Rigden' on the back. Complimentary from Number 65 himself.

Ally was cheering for the Tiger Shark's return to the ice. Mostly for Captain Richard McCarthy. She had her picture taken from camera crews and was bothered quite a few times from fans or undercover reporters. They wanted to know why she was at a PHL game or what were her thoughts for Worlds next month.

What she told them was, "Please don't talk to me during game time."

She was left alone. The Loop was glad that people did leave her be.

Then one of the Tiger Shark's assistant coaches located her and he whispered to her, "Captain McCarthy needs you to go to the locker room."

Allison was shocked. She thought the surprise Richard gave her before she went on her week long vacation in Los Angeles was a special team pass to see him practice or go to games whenever she wanted to.

She stood up from her seat and the assistant coach lead her to the team's locker room the back way. People with cameras video taped Ally and the assistant coach leaving the stand. Lots of people from the press were trying to talk to her, but she kept her mouth shut and the Tiger Shark's A.C. pushed them away from them.

They made it for the locker room's back way and walked through a long hallway. Standing in front of the locker room doors, the A.C. opened the door on the left. Ally stepped inside in the room alone.

The room was all lit up. She never been inside the Tiger Shark's locker room before. The first thing she saw was Number 65's cubby box in the left center row. She smiled big and wondered what her hunky player had planned for her.

Allison's brown eyes glanced at something from the far end of the room. It was a mannequin stand with the most beautiful spaghetti strap figure skating dress she had ever seen. It was deep color purple with a velvet material top and the skirt was made of rough silk material. She figured Rich wanted her to put on the dress.

Just when she wanted to walk closer to the dress stand, Ally just realized she did not have her tan tights or figure skates. She could not wear the pretty skating dress. The upset Loop thought Captain McCarthy lost his 'two steps ahead' touch. Her eyes looked below the stand.

"Ohhhh . . ." She blushed after seeing her navy blue roller suitcase on the dark colored stripped carpet floor.

Ally sat on the floor and unzipped her skating bag.

She unlaced her new black and turquoise N+ running shoes to match her Tiger Shark's special jersey shirt. Then her socks were off. Her legs lifted herself off the floor to unzip and take off her jeans.

She took out her nylons and slipped them on. She pulled out her special tan tights that would cover up her white figure boots. Her legs wore the second pair of figure tights with the boot covers pushed up to her knees.

Her heart was beating fast.

Ally imagined all the possibilities Rich wished to do for her with the pretty purple dress and her ice skates. She thought, *Maybe he wants to tell the world we're in love. Ah, McCarthy, that's a bad idea. At an ice rink? During a PHL game? What the hell is wrong with the stick dude?*

She gently got the dress off the mannequin stand, lowered the dress to her feet, her feet poked through the skirt's holes, and pulled the dress up.

It was a perfect fit. The velvet material was a little tight from not being used and the rough silky skirt felt light to her thighs. She loved the dress. She wondered where Richard got it from.

Ally sat on one of one of the long wooden benches to put her figure boots on. Her fingers noticed the boots were recently polished. She checked her blades. They were newly sharpened by looking closely at the platinum blades.

He really thought ahead, didn't he? Her happy heart said to her mind.

Her newly polished and sharpened figure guarded boots were laced up and she pulled down her outer lay of tights to hook the boot covers under her boots.

Her brown eyes glanced inside her bag. There was another small box inside her roller suitcase. It was a hot pink & black color metal box with a handle at the top of the carrier. She had her right hand grab the handle, pull the box out from her bag, and opened the box. It was full of make-up essentials. She figured Richard was planning something big.

Looking at the attached mirror in the make-up box, Ally put on some light purple eye shadow on her eye lids, a little tan color foundation, mascara, and light pink lip gloss on her lips.

Lastly was hair. She decided to do a pretty bun with a purple hair tie.

A minute later, Ally-Loop was walking around the Tiger Shark's locker room feeling nervous and lightheaded. Her heart could not stop beating at a fast pace.

There was knock on the door.

Ally spoke, "Enter."

She thought the teams were done from their game. The game was not over yet.

The Tiger Shark's A.C. came inside the locker room and asked Allison, "All set?"

She hesitantly nodded her head. Both of them left the locker room.

"You look very lovely, Ally-Loop." The assistant coach complimented to the brunette gold medalist figure. "Captain McCarthy is very lucky to have you."

"Thank you." She whispered softly.

The assistant coach left Ally and he walked down carpeted floor the back way hallway. She figured she had to walk toward the ice rink instead of the back way.

Ally's heart beat faster and harder. She did not know if she could face the Tiger Sharks, the Sauk Hawks, camera crews, or hockey fans in a gorgeous figure skating outfit during a Professional Hockey League game.

Her legs made her walk until she was twenty feet away from the closed locker room hallway gate door. She stood by the right dark gray cement wall. Her ears heard people clapping and cheering for the finished game.

Allison watched the black jersey shirt Tiger Sharks shake hands with all the white jersey shirt Sauk Hawks and their coaches. Her eyes did see

Captain Richard McCarthy looking happy and tired from a good game that night.

The Loop stepped closer to the door.

Number 65 saw Allison at the gate door and was dressed in her new purple figure dress. He stopped gliding to look at Ally. His lips smiled and his left hand motioned to her to lift up the door's handle.

She lifted up the strong, cold metal door handle and pushed the door away from the gate way. Her upper body leaned down to take off her light purple guards off her blades.

Richard threw his wooden stick, gloves, and his black helmet on the ice.

A male announcer spoke, "Attention, Tiger Shark fans! Tonight is a very special night for Number 65, Captain Richard McCarthy, & USIS's newest Senior Ladies' gold medalist, Allison Rigden."

Everyone in the building clapped and cheered for the figure skater to come out from the gate door. That shocked Ally even more. She never thought PHL fans or the teams would clap and cheer for an ice skater to skate for their entertainment.

The Tiger Shark's mascot, Chompy the Shark, gathered the Captain's hockey gear off the ice and the mascot sat in the team's sitting booth. Richard was the only one out on the ice.

The rink's lights were turned off and two spotlights shined over Rich & Ally.

Allison smiled and stepped out on the ice.

Pretty classical music started to play. The Loop glided around the whole rink like the figure champ she was. Forward and backwards. She did some spin combinations, jumps, dance steps, and freestyle poses.

As Ally skated, Chompy the Shark handed something to Number 65 to give to the figure champ.

When the song ended, the Loop did her special lunge combination at the center part of the rink. She was tired and smiling proudly at the audience. Especially at Richard.

Everyone at the stands clapped for Ally's little routine.

McCarthy glided up to her, leaned down, and his right hand pulled her up on her sharpened blades. The Captain was wearing a hidden microphone that was attached to his black jersey shirt.

His right hand held both of her hands. His left hand was behind his back and holding something small and velvet. Both of their eyes looked at each other with admiration and sweet, sweet love.

Richard McCarthy started to speak to Ally and the fans, "Allison Rigden, even though you won the gold from the USIS's Nationals event, but you have won my heart long before I was in the PHL's Tiger Sharks' team. Before I could even skate. I never would have made it this far without your love and support on and off ice."

His left knee slowly knelt down on the not-so-freshly-cut-ice with his right leg behind him.

Both their eyes looked deep into the other's eyes.

"I want the world to know how much I Love You. You never were just an amazing figure skater or a hot babe to me. When I first met you, I knew I met the one I was destined for. All the training and fun times we had during my skating lessons were the best times of my life. I don't want to let go of our love and friendship," confessed McCarthy.

His left hand fiddled with something behind his back.

"Ally-Loop, will you make me the happiest PHL player by marrying me?"

Allison's eyes were full of tears and her heart were full of loving emotions. She knew her surprise from McCarthy was going to be really special. Having him proposing to her was a wonderful surprise.

She smiled big and yelled out, "Yes!"

Richard's left hand moved from his back to show Allison a white velvet box with a beautiful white gold diamond engagement ring. His right hand took the ring out from the box and slipped on Ally's left ring finger.

Captain McCarthy got up on his blades, held the Loop in his arms, and kissed her deeply.

The audience and PHL members cheered and applauded at the new engaged skaters.

When the flashback ended, instead of Ally telling Daniel Gray the story, all she said was, "McCarthy asked me the marry him and I accepted."

She grinned happily and pulled off her right glove first then her left glove. Her right hand gripped both of her small black wool gloves. She lifted her left hand to show Danny her new engagement ring. It was a white gold band with a square shape diamond in the center and lots of little stud diamonds crossing on each of the sides.

Danny gasped, "Wow, Ally . . ."

He stepped close and hugged his Figure Instructor.

Ally wrapped her arms around Danny.

From their parted friendship hug, the dog trainer wondered, "So, when's the big day?"

Allison giggled, "June 15, 2012."

"Any particular reason to have your wedding date on that day?" Curious Danny asked.

"It would be exactly six years since Richard & I first met." She sweetly explained. "I thought it would be nice to remember the first day he & I first met."

Figure Gray cheerfully spoke, "Sounds like a wonderful reason to me. Could you give me & Sally an invite?"

Allison smug, "You wouldn't mind coming to an ice themed wedding ceremony?"

Chortled Danny candid, "All right."

"Wonderful."

While Richard McCarthy was pretending to nap on the steel bleachers' second row, the Loop and the dog trainer glided forward and backwards around the rink as much as they wanted to.

At three-thirty p.m., Richard, Allison, and Daniel left the private ice rink to go to Daniel's apartment building. He did not bring his skating outfit to his unit home. He changed into his previous sweats and t-shirt before leaving Ally's rink.

Ally told her student, "I will call you at six p.m. and a special car will come to pick you up in front of your apartment building. Make sure you wear nice, professional clothes."

"I will." Danny promised.

Rich put in, "And leave you skating bag with us."

Daniel was shocked. "Why?"

"Richard made arrangements to have your skates sharpened and polished before your routine," explained Ally.

The Pet trainer thought that was a good idea.

The truck stopped moving and Danny left the truck for his unit home. His tired legs climbed up the stairs before he made it to his floor.

Inside Daniel Gray's unit was Butchie-Wutchie waiting patiently for his owner to come back home. His tiny white and reddish-brown furry body sat by the front door and listened to the sound of Danny's feet.

His canine ears heard a familiar sound. He barked.

Arf!

And the sound of someone's metal keys was slipped inside the door's key hole.

The front door open and who came in was his tired caretaker. Danny's voice spoke, "Hey, Butch."

He closed and locked the door.

Daniel sat on the hardwood floor to touch and pet his good pooch. He did give Butch a big hug. He lifted up himself up with his beagle in his arms. His legs moved him to the bedroom. The dog trainer wanted to have a nap before doing his skating routine for the Hunts.

Danny and Butch got in the twin size bed and took a long nap together.

An hour later, Daniel's brown eyes opened.

He sat up in his empty bed to see where Butch was at. The sweet beagle was not in the bedroom. The human got up from bed, walked out of the bedroom, and saw Butchie-Wutchie sitting on the hardwood in front of the front door.

"Hey, Butch." Danny spoke.

The cute white and reddish-brown dog turned his head to see his owner.

"Walk?"

Arf!

Danny chuckled and put on his tennis shoes. He got his dog's retractable leash, slipped on his navy blue synthetic coat, stuff lots of plastic baggies in his right coat pocket, attached Butch to his leash, and gathered his keys.

Both boys left their unit home for a soothing walk.

Daniel was feeling scared to face the Hunts and show them what he could do on the ice. He knew how to make himself be less scared.

Think like Allison Rigden or Richard McCarthy.

He wanted to win. He wanted to be the best for Sally Hunt. He wanted to love her for life. He thought about his skating routine and all the fun skating lessons he and Ally had on the ice.

Danny's heart was feeling better by remembering what he did for the past four months. Just skate, enjoy doing figure tricks, and dance to the music.

As the boys went back to their apartment unit, the happy human felt determined to face his future in-laws at the ice. His mind was focused on all the basic skills he learned in figure skating.

He showered, dried himself, made sure Butch had a full tummy and was content for the next few hours, and choose the kind of clothes Ally suggested he should wear.

Nice black slacks and light blue dress shirt. Thin socks and black dress shoes. He smelled like spicy mint from a little cologne. Hair was all fixed up, clothes looking good, and his heart was ready to skate his best.

His cell was ringing. Must be six p.m.

He walked toward his phone in his bedroom.

Standing by his wooden nightstand, Danny's left hand picked up his cell and noticed Ally's cell number calling him.

"Hello?"

"Wow, Daniel, you sound happy!" Allison exclaimed.

He laughed and said, "I'm ready to show Paul & Joy Hunt my routine."

The gold medalist brunette replied, "Wonderful! Well, a special car should be coming by the apartment unit in a few minutes and it will take you to the rink."

"I'll be there, Ally-Loop." He gratefully respond.

The figure friends hung up their phones.

Danny checked up on Butch.

The cute beagle was laying on the couch in the living room. He was napping and his owner knew not to disturb him.

The Pet trainer got his wallet, cell, keys, and his black wool coat. He left his unit, walked down the stairs, and headed toward the building's front doors.

Daniel waited a few minutes and what pulled up was a beautiful shiny black long stretched limousine. He walked out of the building to the limo car.

The driver got out and it was a Caucasian male in his late thirties dressed in a professional black driver uniform and hat. He saw Danny walking down the stairs and he asked him, "Are you Daniel Gray?"

"Yes, I am." The Pet trainer stated. "Is this the special car Ally-Loop was talking about?"

The driver walked toward the back left side door and opened it. "Let's get going."

Danny grinned back and got inside the beautiful long stretched car. He sat on the back black leather seats.

The limo's driver made it back to the driver seat. He started up the car and drove to the skating rink.

The ride was smooth and quiet to Danny. He did not mind the silence. He needed to think about his skating routine and what would Joy & Paul's reaction was going to be like when he was done with short program. He was looking forward to surprise Joy Hunt with his move on the chilly ice.

The limo stopped moving and the driver parked it.

Then the limo chauffeur lifted himself up his seat, walked toward the left back door, and opened it.

Daniel exit the car. He was surprised to see lots of people surrounding the limo. They were disappointed to see Danny getting out from the pretty black car. They were excepting someone famous or rich.

The dog trainer walked inside the arena building.

By the front doors was a disguised Richard McCarthy looking like a special agent from the FBI. Overall black suit and his black shades covered his eyes.

"This way, Figure Gray." He whispered to Danny.

Both men walked toward the small ice rink. The place was deserted and cold to the Pet trainer.

Then Allison came out of the girl's bathroom from the small rink. She was dressed in a beautiful long flowing cream color sleeveless, collarless silky dress. Her long brown hair was all curly and loose. She even wore make-up to match the dress's color complexion. Her left hand still had her pretty engagement ring. She looked at Danny and Richard coming towards the small rink.

Ally-Loop happily announced, "There's my figure student! You look very handsome, Daniel Gray."

Richard turned away from Ally and Danny to get Figure Gray's skates from the arena's shop.

The Figure Instructor and figure student hugged each other gently.

The dog trainer stated, "You look like a Figure Princess, Ally-Loop."

She smug, "Thank you."

Both of them let go of their short embrace. Their eyes looked at the small rink.

It was freshly cut, empty, and ready to be used from Daniel. Nervousness or fear did not touch his heart and mind. He continued to think about being on the ice.

Ally saw Richard walking toward them with a small white cardboard box in his hands. When he reached the group, he opened the box to show Danny his newly polished boots and clean and sharpened blades.

"My skates looks better than they did when I first got them, McCarthy," complimented Danny.

"You're welcome." Richard said and took the shades off his eyes. He gave Daniel the box and his double sided red plastic guards.

Ally suggested, "Why don't you change into your skating outfit for another practice?"

"Where's my figure clothes?" Danny wondered.

"The box is waiting for you in the men's room." Richard told him.

Danny saw the door for the men's room and walked through the navy blue color door. Inside the room was three long stalls, two urinal stands and sinks, and three old folded up metal chairs. One of the chairs contained his black box.

The dog trainer changed out of his black coat, black shoes, pants, and his blue dress shirt for his white figure shirt and black pants. His mind concentrated of his routine instead of fearing Joy Hunt. She was just a woman who wished to have something that was not meant for her to own.

Danny slipped on his polished suede figure boots.

Standing in his boot and blades, he was more confident to ice skate in front of the Hunts. He did feel a little unhappy from knowing Sally may not be able to come to the rink and watch him skate. That would made his night.

He left the men's room.

In the small rink's small hallway, Ally & Rich saw and knew Danny was ready to do his routine.

"Let's see you do a practice," declared Allison Rigden.

"I'm ready." He walked toward the small rink's gate door by the men's room. He unlocked it and the door swung open. His body leaned to take the guards off his blades and his sharpened platinum blades were on the ice.

Light music started to play and Daniel glided out on the ice. He did a show stop.

Without thinking, he stood at the center and posed with his right blade in front of left and his left toe-pick pointed in the ice. His arms and head were down.

As the musical notes started to pick up, Daniel lifted his arms and head. His right hip made him do a back pivot and began to do forward strokes. He did smooth dance steps, single flip jump, another dance step, and a camel-sit-scratch spin combination when the song got to the first chorus. He stopped and did a special crossover plead act.

Ally & Rich were impressed of seeing Danny being a whole new male figure. McCarthy's right hand held Rigden's left hand and Ally leaned close to Rich.

Figure Gray danced more, did an outside edge spreading eagle, a salchow jump, forward & backward camel with a back scratch spin, crossover plead, single lutz jump, figure eight, and a beautiful single axel jump.

Off ice, Rich whispered, "Damn, he's really good."

Smily Ally spoke back to her hunky fiance, "That's because he learned from the best."

McCarthy stepped Behind Ally and wrapped his love in his arms tightly. "I Love You . . ."

"And I Love You too, Richard . . ."

For the ending, Danny did a camel-jump-camel, back sit, and scratch spin combo and then a show stop with both his arms above his head. The puck chaser and toe-jumper applauded at Daniel's skating routine.

He glided toward the doors feeling tired.

"How do you feel?" Ally wondered.

From his heavy breathing, Danny candid, "I feel good."

"You did a wonderful job, Gray." Richard stated.

"Thank you for all your support."

Allison's brown eyes noticed a dressed up Joy with her husband and daughter. Mrs. Hunt was in a simple long sleeved black dress. Paul wore a nice black suit & tie and a white shirt and he was pushing Sally in her wheelchair. The sunshine blonde was in a cute light pink cotton dress with a blue throw blanket over her legs. Her blond hair was up in a pony tail.

"Danny, look . . ."

He turned his head and all the Hunts were there.

Joy spoke, "Good evening."

Danny quickly put on his red guards to talk to Sally.

He knelt in front of her and asked the blonde, "How are you, Sally-babe?"

She took his hands. Her strong voice said, "I'm very happy to see you again, Danny."

"You look and sound better." He pointed out.

"I can't wait to see you skate." The emotional sunshine girl exclaimed.

He stood up on his guarded blades and Joy explained to him, "Daniel, Paul & I will judge you by your figure skills and artistic styles. Good luck."

The Pet trainer nodded his head in agreement.

Ally had her speaker's remote.

Danny took off his guards. He gulped softly as he glided to the center to do his routine.

This is for Sally. His heart dedicated to his mind.

The soothing song started to play.

Feeling like Ally-Loop, Danny focused on the song and started his back pivot.

Off ice, the Hunts and the engaged winter athletes watched Daniel Gray skate gracefully around the ice. Paul Hunt thought Allison did a grand job with Danny's figure lessons. Joy Hunt noticed Danny having passion in his routine. More than Sally did in her pasting skating programs. Sally cried a little by watching her fiance be a wonderful figure male.

It's almost over, Gray. Danny thought.

He did his camel-jump-camel combo and his show stop. Done.

All the Hunts and Ally & Rich clapped at Danny's short program.

Now came the hardest part for Figure Daniel Gray.

At the open gate door, Paul announced, "Danny, you did a fantastic routine. Perfect 10."

Sally spoke up next. "Danny, I can't believe you could skate so good and be so lithe on the ice. Perfect 10."

He skated to the open door. His heart pounded with love and a little bit of fear.

Joy thought and thought over Daniel's skating skills.

Her green eyes looked at Allison Rigden & Richard McCarthy first. She solemnly expressed out, "Allison, I am sorry for being a-horrid bitch to you. You really deserve the gold for being a strong, passionate figure lover."

Then her eyes glanced back at Danny. "As for you Daniel Gray . . ."

He had a nervous look on his face.

Joy acted like a judge by saying, "You did one hell of a skating routine in my eyes. You were strong and bold. And yet, graceful and artistic. Jumps were done naturally, spins all centered, and your dance steps were smooth and very pretty to watch. You're a terrific male figure."

That made his heart feel good again.

"A perfect 10 for your flawless short program."

Danny smiled big and a huge piece of weight was lifted off his shoulders. He and Joy shook hands. Then Paul shook his hands too.

Tearfully Ally & Rich clapped their hands.

The Pet trainer got on his knees and held his loving fiancee. He began to cry hard. It was something he longed to have from a very long journey through figure skating in his personal life and being an overall dog trainer for his professional life.

Daniel Gray was very tired and satisfied to be at the top of both. All thanks to his wonderful, passionate Figure Instructor.

It was a beautiful day for Sally Hunt & Daniel Gray Valentine's Day wedding day.

Danny was in a guest room in the Hunt's mansion home. He was dressing himself for the ceremony. Like any man who was about to take on the biggest loving commitment in life, Daniel was scared and nervous. And yet, he also could not wait to say his 'I Do' to the love of his life.

His mind had been buzzing about with lots of feelings and emotions, but only one important thing came to his mind.

It's been fourth months and ten days since I proposed to my sweet girl, Sally Hunt. So much has happened during those long months. Me (chuckled) being a terrific male figure skater to the Hunts, overcoming my fear to show dog owners how to obedient train their dogs, learning about Sally's secret skating unearned skills, and her going through foot surgery. Her doctor had inform her, her parents, and I that Sally cannot do anymore competitive figure skating, do long periods of walking, or do any other strenuous activities. We all agreed to the doctor's recommendations for Sally's well-being.

So instead of an ice themed wedding, Joy & Paul Hunt changed it to have the ceremony and reception in the backyard.

In twenty minutes, Sally & I will be married and be living together in a much more comfortable home not far from the Pet Store and Sally's new job as a florist. Maggie loved the idea on having 'Sally Gray' working for her. That would be easy work for her to do during her wheelchair and physical therapy days. Arranging and taking care of flowers for a living.

(Laughter) Even Joy liked her daughter's career change.

A knock on the door made Daniel Gray lose his train of thoughts. Behind the strong wooden door was Paul Hunt.

He stated, "Time to face the music."

Danny nodded at his soon-to-be father-in-law.

They were both dressed nicely pressed black tuxedos with a red flower on their jacket's left chest side. Young Gray followed Mr. Hunt out of the mansion and went for the backyard.

The yard was set up with wedding decorations.

A small group of cream wooded and white padded chairs that were full of guests, including his Figure Instructor who wore a navy blue silky spaghetti strap dress and her hunky player who was dressed in a nice black tuxedo. The aisle was big enough for Paul Hunt to walk down Sally in her wheelchair, and there was a lit-up leaf arbor set up for him & Sally to say their 'I do's' to the minister.

Daniel Gray walked down the aisle slowly and nervously for his last time as a single man. He stood next to the minister, who was dressed in his formal black robe and his white collar around his neck. The Pet trainer's eyes saw his parents at the front row with their love and support for him & Sally. Butch was with them too.

I'll always remember what Dad told me about marriage. It is a road Sally & I will go on together and we shall think and love our special bond in everything we do.

His brown eyes saw happy Allison & Richard holding hands. He glad the Loop was not unhappy and single anymore.

Soft classical music was playing.

With his hands folded in front of him below his waistline, Danny thought more about his past figure lessons.

I will never forget what Ally-Loop told me when it comes to passion. It really is all about the good loving feel you can only receive from something or someone.

His brown eyes saw Paul and Sally moving down the aisle. She rolled herself in her chair with her father by her side. Paul carried her Iris and Freesia floral bouquet.

Sally's blond hair up in a pretty braid bun with a short length vail not covering her face. She was dressed in a comfy simple white gown. Her face lit-up brightly with her bluish-gray eyes and she smiled lovingly when she saw Danny standing under the leafy arbor.

His thoughts fled on, *That's how I feel for Sally Hunt. Having her in my life is passion for my heart to feel, cherish, and love forever.*

Sally reached where her love stood.

Paul leaned down to kiss his daughter on her right cheek and handed her the flower bouquet before he sat next to Joy in a padded chair. The proud Hunts held hands.

Daniel looked down at Sally in her wheelchair. A special warm feeling came into his heart. He took her left hand and got down on his knees to be his love's height.

The small group of guests smiled at the Pet trainer's sweet gesture for Sally.

The minister began the ceremony with his wedding speech. Danny was not interested in listening to the boring, cliche speech. He did not want to hear about commitments and how love should be taken for granted. Allison taught him that long before he made it to the alter. He continued to focus on his heart and his eyes were looking at Sally.

Even though Sally was still 20 and I was 21, we do not want to let each other go and love someone else. She is my reason to live for the future.

"I do." Sally sweetly answered to the minister's question and looked deeply into Danny's brown eyes.

He heard, "Daniel Gray, do you take this woman to be your lawfully wedded wife?"

He spoke lovingly, "I do too."

The young lovers exchanged bran new white gold bands and Danny moved his grass stained pants forward to kiss Sally Gray for the first time.

All the guests and the minister clapped and cheered for the newly husband & wife Grays.

Twenty minutes later, the photo taking were done and it was time for the reception. Sally was lifted up from her wheelchair by her husband and was seated in a special seat. Daniel sat next to his wife.

Allison & Richard got up from their padded chairs after the Loop checked out her phone. She knew it time for them to leave. Before the figure couple left the Hunt's backyard, hand-in-hand, they went over to talk to Sally & Daniel Gray.

At the big reception table, both of them stood in front of the newly wedded couple's chairs and Richard told the newly weds, "Hey, Danny & Sally. Congratulations and good luck you two."

Sally happily said, "Thank you for coming to our wedding, and congratulations on both of your skating careers."

Allison accepted Hunt-actually, Mrs. Gray, as a friend off ice.

The married couple asked Ally & Rich if they were going to stay for the reception.

Allison disappointedly replied, "Can't. We have a special skate date."

Danny smug, "Oh yeah?"

"Ally & I have a special private ice time at the Tiger Sharks' domain today." Proud McCarthy stated.

The newly wedded Grays understood Number 65 & the Loop's passion for the ice.

Sally & Daniel's passion were for each other's happiness. They watched the passionate skating champions leave the yard for the shiny black truck.

Mr. Gray's last thoughts about his Figure Instructor were, *There goes a wonderful life lesson teacher. I can understand why it took her a while to find or discover love. The Figure Instructor had really meet her match. On and off ice.*

Epilogue

Inside the Tiger Shark's home rink, Allison & Richard were in the team's locker room and changing out of their clothes for something more comfortable to wear on ice instead of a suit and a long flowing dress.

The puck chaser put on jeans, his favorite black jersey shirt, and hockey skates. The toe-jumper slipped on long stretched black pants, a hot pink t-shirt, and her figure boots.

Ally asked, "Okay, McCarthy, why did you want us to come here?"

She knew he had something planned for her.

Honest Number 65 spoke, "It's not a good idea to waste a beautiful patch of ice."

"Uh-huh." She was still unsure if he something special planned for the Loop.

Richard laughed and walked out of the locker room.

Allison followed him.

At the freshly cut ice rink, McCarthy skated out first and a pretty love song was playing from the speakers. Rigden stepped on the ice and skated around by doing forward power strokes and crossovers.

Then she did a right inside mohawk turn to do back crossover edge change. She loved being back on the ice. Even though it was probably the last place on earth for anyone to go for excitement, thrills, and fun.

Ally decided to work on some figure moves.

Double flip jump. Forward & backward camel, back scratch spin combo. Fun dance steps. Long split spiral. And finally, a simple single axel jump.

While the Loop was making up her fun skating routine, Captain Richard McCarthy skated off the ice without his fiancee knowing he left the ice.

After Ally finished her axel jump, she heard, "Like some company?"

She turned and saw Donna out on the ice.

Donna was dressed in long stretch pants and a long sleeved blue shirt with her white figure boots.

Surprised Ally asked, "How'd you know I be here?"

Her once rivalry laughed and teasingly answered, "You can't live an entire day without ice skating, Ally!"

"That's true." She mumbled.

Allison's brown eyes saw smily Rich by the locker room hallway.

I figured you were up to something, McCarthy. Her mind suspiciously thought.

Donna stroke toward Allison and solemnly spoke, "I'm sorry I got jealous of you and your desire for figure skating. I guess I missed having my best friend."

Ally skated around Donna backwards. Her voice loudly replied, "I am sorry I ditched you for this 'chilly' sport!"

The two girls laughed together and made up their quarrels by giving each other a big hug. It had been a while since they did something like that.

They both skated forward to talk more.

Donna asked, "So, Ally-Loop, what's next for you?"

Ally-Loop respond, "Worlds in Nice, France and hopefully conquer the next Winter Olympics."

"You need a close friend?" Donna offered.

"You bet I do." Allison accepted her new figure skating friend.

They continued to skate together like old friends.

Ally admired her friend's artistic skating moves.

Donna was happy the new Senior Ladies' Champion was a good instructor on and off ice. The passion for the girl's friendship was stronger than ever before.

What they did throughout the private ice time was skating as best friends instead of competitive figure rivalries.